The Quran With Tafsir Ibn Kathir
Part 30 of 30:
An Nabaa 001 To An Nas 006

The Quran With Tafsir Ibn Kathir Part 30 of 30: An Nabaa 001 To An Nas 006

With
Arabic Script, Transliteration of Arabic, Meaning in English
and Ibn Kathir's Abridged Tafsir (Explanation)

Muhammad Saed Abdul-Rahman
BSc, DipHE

© Muhammad Saed Abdul-Rahman,2012
ISBN 978-1-86179-915-9

All Rights reserved

British Library Cataloguing in Publication Data. A Catalogue record for this book is available from the British Library

Designed, Typeset and produced by:
MSA Publication Limited, 4 Bello Close, Herne Hill,
London SE24 9BW
United Kingdom

Cover design: Houriyah Abdul-Rahman

TABLE OF CONTENTS

TABLE OF CONTENTS V

PRELUDE XVII

    OPENING SERMAN XVII
    OUR MISSION XVIII
    BIOGRAPHY OF HAFIZ IBN KATHIR (701 H - 774 H) XVIII
        Ibn Kathir's Teachers xviii
        Ibn Kathir's Students xix
        Ibn Kathir's Books xix
        Ibn Kathir's Death xx

PREFACE XXI

    ABOUT THIS BOOK XXI
    PERFORMING PROSTRATION WHILE READING THE QUR'AN XXI

PART 30 FULL ARABIC TEXT 1

CHAPTER (SURAH) 78: AN-NABA (THE TIDINGS, THE ANNOUNCEMENT), VERSES 001- 040.17

    Surah: 78 Ayah: 1, Ayah: 2, Ayah: 3, Ayah: 4, Ayah: 5, Ayah: 6, Ayah: 7, Ayah: 8, Ayah: 9,
    Ayah: 10, Ayah: 11, Ayah: 12, Ayah: 13, Ayah: 14, Ayah: 15 & Ayah: 16 17
        Tafsir Ibn Kathir 19
            Refutation against the Idolators' Denial of the Occurrence of the Day of Judgement 19
            Mentioning Allah's Power, and the Proof of His Ability to resurrect the Dead 19
    Surah: 78 Ayah: 17, Ayah: 18, Ayah: 19, Ayah: 20, Ayah: 22, Ayah: 23, Ayah: 24, Ayah:
    25, Ayah: 26, Ayah: 27, Ayah: 28, Ayah: 29 & Ayah: 30 21
        Tafsir Ibn Kathir 23
            Explaining the Day of Decision and what occurs during it 23
    Surah: 78 Ayah: 31, Ayah: 32, Ayah: 33, Ayah: 34, Ayah: 35 & Ayah: 36 26
        Tafsir Ibn Kathir 26
            The Great Success will be for Those Who have Taqwa 26
    Surah: 78 Ayah: 37, Ayah: 38, Ayah: 39 & Ayah: 40 27
        Tafsir Ibn Kathir 28
            No one will dare to speak before Allah -- not even the Angels - without first receiving
            Permission 28
            The Day of Judgement is Near 29

CHAPTER (SURAH) 79: AN-NAZIAT (THOSE WHO DRAG FORTH, SOUL-SNATCHERS), VERSES 001- 046 30

    Surah: 79 Ayah: 1, Ayah: 2, Ayah: 3, Ayah: 4, Ayah: 5, Ayah: 6, Ayah: 7, Ayah: 8, Ayah: 9,
    Ayah: 10, Ayah: 11, Ayah: 12, Ayah: 13 & Ayah: 14 30
        Tafsir Ibn Kathir 31
            Swearing by Five Characteristics that the Day of Judgement will occur 31
            The Description of the Day of Judgement, the People, and what They will say 32

Surah: 79 Ayah: 15, Ayah: 16, Ayah: 17, Ayah: 18, Ayah: 19, Ayah: 20, Ayah: 21, Ayah: 22, Ayah: 23, Ayah: 24, Ayah: 25 & Ayah: 26 33
    Tafsir Ibn Kathir 35
        Mentioning the Story of Musa and that it is a Lesson for Those Who fear Allah 35
Surah: 79 Ayah: 27, Ayah: 28, Ayah: 29, Ayah: 30, Ayah: 31, Ayah: 32 & Ayah: 33 36
    Tafsir Ibn Kathir 37
        Creating the Heavens and the Earth is more difficult than repeating Creation 37
Surah: 79 Ayah: 34, Ayah: 35, Ayah: 36, Ayah: 37, Ayah: 38, Ayah: 39, Ayah: 40, Ayah: 41, Ayah: 42, Ayah: 43, Ayah: 44, Ayah: 45 & Ayah: 46 38
    Tafsir Ibn Kathir 40
        The Day of Judgement, its Pleasures and Hell, and that its Time is not known 40

CHAPTER (SURAH) 80: ABASA (HE FROWNED), VERSES 001–042 41

Surah: 80 Ayah: 1, Ayah: 2, Ayah: 3, Ayah: 4, Ayah: 5, Ayah: 6, Ayah: 7, Ayah: 8, Ayah: 9, Ayah: 10, Ayah: 11, Ayah: 12, Ayah: 113, Ayah: 14, Ayah: 15 & Ayah: 16 41
    Tafsir Ibn Kathir 43
        The Prophet being reprimanded because He frowned at a Weak Man 43
        The Characteristics of the Qur'an 44
Surah: 80 Ayah: 17, Ayah: 18, Ayah: 19, Ayah: 20, Ayah: 21, Ayah: 22, Ayah: 23, Ayah: 24, Ayah: 25, Ayah: 26, Ayah: 27, Ayah: 8, Ayah: 29, Ayah: 30, Ayah: 31 & Ayah: 32 45
    Tafsir Ibn Kathir 46
        The Refutation against Whoever denies Life after Death 46
        The Growth of the Seed and Other Things is a Proof of Life after Death 48
Surah: 80 Ayah: 33, Ayah: 34, Ayah: 35, Ayah: 36, Ayah: 37, Ayah: 38, Ayah: 39, Ayah: 40, Ayah: 41 & Ayah: 42 49
    Tafsir Ibn Kathir 50
        The Day of Judgement and the fleeing of the People from Their Relatives during it 50
        The Faces of the People of Paradise and the People of the Fire on the Day of Judgement 51

INTRODUCTION TO CHAPTER (SURAH) 81: AT-TAKWIR (THE OVERTHROWING) 52

IBN KATHIR'S INTRODUCTION 52
    What has been narrated about This Surah 52

CHAPTER (SURAH) 81: AT-TAKWIR THE OVERTHROWING, VERSES 001- 029 52

Surah: 81 Ayah: 1, Ayah: 2, Ayah: 3, Ayah: 4, Ayah: 5, Ayah: 6, Ayah: 7, Ayah: 8, Ayah: 9, Ayah: 10, Ayah: 11, Ayah: 12, Ayah: 13 & Ayah: 14 52
    Tafsir Ibn Kathir 54
        What will happen on the Day of Judgement, and that is the rolling up of the Sun 54
        Dispersing the Stars 54
        Moving of the Mountains, abandoning of the Pregnant She-Camels, and the gathering of the Wild Beasts 55
        The Blazing of the Seas 56
        Joining the Souls 56

Table of Contents

Questioning the Female Infant Who was buried Alive 56
The Atonement for burying Infant Girls Alive 57
Removing the Heavens, kindling Hellfire, and Paradise being brought near 58
Everyone will know what He has brought on the Day of Judgement 58

Surah: 81 Ayah: 15, Ayah: 16, Ayah: 17, Ayah: 18, Ayah: 19, Ayah: 20, Ayah: 21, Ayah: 22, Ayah: 23, Ayah: 24, Ayah: 25, Ayah: 26, Ayah: 27, Ayah: 28 & Ayah: 29 58

Tafsir Ibn Kathir 60
The Explanation of the Words Al-Khunnas and Al-Kunnas 60
Jibril descended with the Qur'an and it is not the Result of Insanity 61
The Qur'an is a Reminder for all the Worlds and It is not the Inspiration of Shaytan 62

INTRODUCTION TO CHAPTER (SURAH) 82: AL-INFITAR (THE CLEAVING, BURSTING APART) 63

IBN KATHIR'S INTRODUCTION 63
The Virtues of Surat Al-Infitar 63

CHAPTER (SURAH) 82: AL-INFITAR THE CLEAVING, BURSTING APART, VERSES 001- 019 64

Surah: 82 Ayah: 1, Ayah: 2, Ayah: 3, Ayah: 4, Ayah: 5, Ayah: 6, Ayah: 7, Ayah: 8, Ayah: 9, Ayah: 10, Ayah: 11 & Ayah: 12 64

Tafsir Ibn Kathir 65
What will happen on the Day of Judgement. 65

Surah: 82 Ayah: 13, Ayah: 14, Ayah: 15, Ayah: 16, Ayah: 17, Ayah: 18 & Ayah: 19 67

Tafsir Ibn Kathir 68
The Reward of the Righteous and the Sinners Allah informs of what the righteous will receive of delight. 68

CHAPTER (SURAH) 83: AL-MUTAFFIFIN (DEFRAUDING, THE CHEATS, CHEATING), VERSES 001- 036 69

Surah: 83 Ayah: 1, Ayah: 2, Ayah: 3, Ayah: 4, Ayah: 5 & Ayah: 6 69

Tafsir Ibn Kathir 70
Increasing and decreasing in the Measure and Weight will be a Cause for Regret and Loss 70
Threatening the Mutaffifin with standing before the Lord of all that exists 72

Surah: 83 Ayah: 7, Ayah: 8, Ayah: 9, Ayah: 10, Ayah: 11, Ayah: 12, Ayah: 13, Ayah: 14, Ayah: 15, Ayah: 16 & Ayah: 17 73

Tafsir Ibn Kathir 75
The Record of the Wicked and some of what happens to Them 75

Surah: 83 Ayah: 18, Ayah: 19, Ayah: 20, Ayah: 21, Ayah: 22, Ayah: 23, Ayah: 24, Ayah: 25, Ayah: 26, Ayah: 27 & Ayah: 28 78

Tafsir Ibn Kathir 80
The Record Book of the Righteous and Their Reward 80

Surah: 83 Ayah: 29, Ayah: 30, Ayah: 31, Ayah: 32, Ayah: 33, Ayah: 34, Ayah: 35 & Ayah: 36 81

Tafsir Ibn Kathir 82
The Wicked Behavior of the Criminals and Their mocking of the Believers 82

INTRODUCTION TO CHAPTER (SURAH) 84: AL-INSHIQAQ (THE SUNDERING, SPLITTING OPEN) 83

    IBN KATHIR'S INTRODUCTION 83
        The Prostration of Recitation in Surat Al-Inshiqaq 83

CHAPTER (SURAH) 84: AL-INSHIQAQ (THE SUNDERING, SPLITTING OPEN), VERSES 001- 025 84

    Surah: 84 Ayah: 1, Ayah: 2, Ayah: 3, Ayah: 4, Ayah: 5, Ayah: 6, Ayah: 7, Ayah: 8, Ayah: 9, Ayah: 10, Ayah: 11, Ayah: 12, Ayah: 13, Ayah: 14 & Ayah: 15 84
        Tafsir Ibn Kathir 85
        Splitting the Heavens asunder and stretching the Earth forth on the Day of Resurrection 85
        The Recompense for Deeds is True 86
        The Presentation and the Discussion that will take place during the Reckoning 86
    Surah: 84 Ayah: 16, Ayah: 17, Ayah: 18, Ayah: 19, Ayah: 20, Ayah: 21, Ayah: 22, Ayah: 23, Ayah: 24 & Ayah: 25 87
        Tafsir Ibn Kathir 89
        Swearing by the Various Stages of Man's Journey 89
        The Disapproval of Their Lack of Faith, giving Them Tidings of the Torment, and that the Ultimate Pleasure will be for the Believers 90

CHAPTER (SURAH) 85: AL-BUROOJ (THE MANSIONS OF THE STARS, CONSTELLATIONS), VERSES 001- 022 90

    Surah: 85 Ayah: 1, Ayah: 2, Ayah: 3, Ayah: 4, Ayah: 5, Ayah: 6, Ayah: 7, Ayah: 8, Ayah: 9 & Ayah: 10 90
        Tafsir Ibn Kathir 92
        The Interpretation of the Word Buruj Allah swears by the heaven and its Buruj. 92
        The Explanation of the Promised Day and the Witness and the Witnessed 92
        The Oppression of the People of the Ditch against the Muslims 93
        The Story of the Sorcerer, the Monk, the Boy and Those Who were forced to enter the Ditch 93
        The Punishment of the People of the Ditch 98
    Surah: 85 Ayah: 11, Ayah: 12, Ayah: 13, Ayah: 14, Ayah: 15, Ayah: 16, Ayah: 17, Ayah: 18, Ayah: 19, Ayah: 20, Ayah: 21 & Ayah: 22 99
        Tafsir Ibn Kathir 100
        The Reward of the Righteous, and the Harsh Seizing of the Disbelieving Enemies of Allah 100

INTRODUCTION TO CHAPTER (SURAH) 86: AT-TARIQ (THE MORNING STAR, THE NIGHTCOMER) 102

    IBN KATHIR'S INTRODUCTION 102
        The Virtues of Surat At-Tariq 102

Table of Contents

CHAPTER (SURAH) 86: AT-TARIQ (THE MORNING STAR, THE NIGHTCOMER), VERSES 001- 017 102

Surah: 86 Ayah: 1, Ayah: 2, Ayah: 3, Ayah: 4, Ayah: 5, Ayah: 6, Ayah: 7, Ayah: 8, Ayah: 9, Ayah: 10 102

    Tafsir Ibn Kathir 103

        Swearing by the Existence of Humanity surrounded by the Organized System of Allah . 103

        How Man is created is a Proof of Allah's Ability to Return Him to Him 104

        On the Day of Judgement, Man will have no Power or Assistance 104

Surah: 86 Ayah: 11, Ayah: 12, Ayah: 13, Ayah: 14, Ayah: 15, Ayah: 16 & Ayah: 17 105

    Tafsir Ibn Kathir 106

        Swearing to the Truthfulness of the Qur'an and the Failure of Those Who oppose it 106

INTRODUCTION TO CHAPTER (SURAH) 87: AL-ALA (THE MOST HIGH, GLORY TO YOUR LORD IN THE HIGHEST) 107

  IBN KATHIR'S INTRODUCTION 107

    The Virtues of Surat Al-A`la 107

CHAPTER (SURAH) 87: AL-ALA (THE MOST HIGH, GLORY TO YOUR LORD IN THE HIGHEST), VERSES 001- 019 108

Surah: 87 Ayah: 1, Ayah: 2, Ayah: 3, Ayah: 4, Ayah: 5, Ayah: 6, Ayah: 7, Ayah: 8, Ayah: 9, Ayah: 10, Ayah: 11, Ayah: 12 & Ayah: 13 108

    Tafsir Ibn Kathir 110

        The Command to pronounce Tasbih and its Response 110

        The Creation, the Decree, and the bringing forth of Vegetation 110

        The Prophet does not forget the Revelation 111

        The Command to remind 111

Surah: 87 Ayah: 14, Ayah: 15, Ayah: 16, Ayah: 17, Ayah: 18 & Ayah: 19 113

    Tafsir Ibn Kathir 114

        A Statement concerning the People of Success 114

        This World is Worthless in Comparison to the Hereafter 114

        The Scriptures of Ibrahim and Musa 115

INTRODUCTION TO CHAPTER (SURAH) 88: AL-GHASHIYA (THE OVERWHELMING, THE PALL) 116

  IBN KATHIR'S INTRODUCTION 116

    Reciting Surat Al-A`la and Al-Ghashiyah in the Friday Prayer 116

CHAPTER (SURAH) 88 AL-GHASHIYA THE OVERWHELMING, THE PALL, VERSES 001- 026 .. 116

Surah: 88 Ayah: 1, Ayah: 2, Ayah: 3, Ayah: 4, Ayah: 5, Ayah: 6 & Ayah: 7 116

    Tafsir Ibn Kathir 117

        The Day of Judgement and what will happen to the People of the Fire during it Al-Ghashiyah is one of the names of the Day of Judgement. 117

Surah: 88 Ayah: 8, Ayah: 9, Ayah: 10, Ayah: 11, Ayah: 12, Ayah: 13, Ayah: 14, Ayah: 15 & Ayah: 16 118
    Tafsir Ibn Kathir 119
        The Condition of the People of Paradise on the Day of Judgement 119
Surah: 88 Ayah: 17, Ayah: 18, Ayah: 19, Ayah: 20, Ayah: 21, Ayah: 22, Ayah: 23, Ayah: 24, Ayah: 25 & Ayah: 26 121
    Tafsir Ibn Kathir 122
        The Exhortation to look at the Creation of the Camel, the Heaven, the Mountains and the Earth 122
        The Story of Dimam bin Tha`labah 123
        The Messenger is only charged with delivering the Message 124
        The Threat for Whoever turns away from the Truth 125

INTRODUCTION TO CHAPTER (SURAH) 89: AL-FAJR (THE DAWN, DAYBREAK) 125

IBN KATHIR'S INTRODUCTION 125
    Recitation of Surat Al-Fajr in the Prayer 125

CHAPTER (SURAH) 89: AL-FAJR (THE DAWN, DAYBREAK), VERSES 001-030 126

Surah: 89 Ayah: 1, Ayah: 2, Ayah: 3, Ayah: 4, Ayah: 5, Ayah: 6, Ayah: 7, Ayah: 8, Ayah: 9, Ayah: 10, Ayah: 11, Ayah: 12, Ayah: 13 & Ayah: 14 126
    Tafsir Ibn Kathir 128
        The Explanation of Al-Fajr and what comes after it 128
        Explanation of Night 129
        Mentioning the Destruction of `Ad 129
        A Mention of Fir`awn 131
        The Lord is Ever Watchful 131
Surah: 89 Ayah: 15, Ayah: 16, Ayah: 17, Ayah: 18, Ayah: 19 & Ayah: 20 131
    Tafsir Ibn Kathir 132
        Wealth and Poverty are both a Test and Honor or Disgrace for the Servant 132
        From the Evil that the Servant does regarding Wealth 133
Surah: 89 Ayah: 21, Ayah: 22, Ayah: 23, Ayah: 24, Ayah: 25, Ayah: 26, Ayah: 27, Ayah: 28, Ayah: 29 & Ayah: 30 133
    Tafsir Ibn Kathir 135
        On the Day of Judgement Everyone will be recompensed according to what He did of Good or Evil 135

CHAPTER (SURAH) 90: AL-BALAD (THE CITY, THIS COUNTRYSIDE), VERSES 001- 020 136

Surah: 90 Ayah: 1, Ayah: 2, Ayah: 3, Ayah: 4, Ayah: 5, Ayah: 6, Ayah: 7, Ayah: 8, Ayah: 9 & Ayah: 10 136
    Tafsir Ibn Kathir 138
        Swearing by the Sanctity of Makkah and Other Things that Man was created in Hardship 138
        Man is encompassed by Allah and His Bounties 140
        The Ability to distinguish between Good and Evil is also a Blessing 140

Table of Contents

Surah: 90 Ayah: 11, Ayah: 12, Ayah: 13, Ayah: 14, Ayah: 15, Ayah: 16, Ayah: 17, Ayah: 18, Ayah: 19 & Ayah: 20 140
    Tafsir Ibn Kathir 142
        The Encouragement to traverse upon the Path of Goodness 142
        The Companions of the Left Hand and Their Recompense 145

INTRODUCTION TO CHAPTER (SURAH) 91: ASH-SHAMS (THE SUN) 145

    IBN KATHIR'S INTRODUCTION 145

CHAPTER (SURAH) 91: ASH-SHAMS (THE SUN), VERSES 001- 015 145

Surah: 91 Ayah: 1, Ayah: 2, Ayah: 3, Ayah: 4, Ayah: 5, Ayah: 6, Ayah: 7, Ayah: 8, Ayah: 9 & Ayah: 10 145
    Tafsir Ibn Kathir 147
        Allah swears by His Creation that the Person Who purifies Himself will be Successful and the Person Who corrupts Himself will fail 147
Surah: 91 Ayah: 11, Ayah: 12, Ayah: 13, Ayah: 14 & Ayah: 15 150
    Tafsir Ibn Kathir 151
        The Rejection of Thamud and Allah's Destruction of Them 151
        The Story of Salih's She-Camel 152

INTRODUCTION TO CHAPTER (SURAH) 92: AL-LAIL (THE NIGHT) 152

    IBN KATHIR'S INTRODUCTION 152
        The Recitation of Surat Al-Layl in the 'Isha' Prayer 152

CHAPTER (SURAH) 92: AL-LAIL (THE NIGHT), VERSES 001- 021 153

Surah: 92 Ayah: 1, Ayah: 2, Ayah: 3, Ayah: 4, Ayah: 5, Ayah: 6, Ayah: 7, Ayah: 8, Ayah: 9, Ayah: 10 & Ayah: 11 153
    Tafsir Ibn Kathir 154
        Swearing by the Diversity of Mankind in Their Efforts and informing of the Different Results of that 154
        The Narration of Abu Bakr As-Siddiq 155
        The Narration of 'Ali 156
        The Narration of 'Abdullah bin 'Umar 157
Surah: 92 Ayah: 12, Ayah: 13, Ayah: 14, Ayah: 15, Ayah: 16, Ayah: 17, Ayah: 18, Ayah: 19, Ayah: 20 & Ayah: 21 158
    Tafsir Ibn Kathir 159
        The Matter of Guidance and other than it is in the Hand of Allah, and Allah's Warning about the Hellfire 159
        The Cause of this Revelation and the Virtue of Abu Bakr 161

CHAPTER (SURAH) 93: AD-DHUHA (THE MORNING HOURS, MORNING BRIGHT), VERSES 001- 011 162

Surah: 93 Ayah: 1, Ayah: 2, Ayah: 3, Ayah: 4, Ayah: 5, Ayah: 6, Ayah: 7, Ayah: 8, Ayah: 9, Ayah: 10 & Ayah: 11 162

Tafsir Ibn Kathir 164
  The Reason for the Revelation of Surat Ad-Duha 164
  The Hereafter is Better Than This First Life 165
  The Numerous Bounties of the Hereafter are waiting for the Messenger of Allah 165
  A Mention of some of Allah's Favors upon the Messenger Enumerating His favors upon His Messenger, Muhammad 166
  How should this Bounty be responded to 167

CHAPTER 94: AL-INSHIRAH (SOLACE, CONSOLATION, RELIEF), VERSES 001- 008 168

  Surah: 94 Ayah: 1, Ayah: 2, Ayah: 3, Ayah: 4, Ayah: 5, Ayah: 6, Ayah: 7 & Ayah: 8 168
    Tafsir Ibn Kathir 169
    The Meaning of opening the Breast 169
    A Discussion of Allah's Favor upon His Messenger Concerning Allah's statement, ... 169

INTRODUCTION TO CHAPTER (SURAH) 95: AT-TIN (THE FIG, THE FIGTREE) 170

  IBN KATHIR'S INTRODUCTION 170
    The Recitation of Surat At-Tin in the Prayer while traveling 170

CHAPTER (SURAH) 95: AT-TIN (THE FIG, THE FIGTREE), VERSES 001- 008 170

  Surah: 95 Ayah: 1, Ayah: 2, Ayah: 3, Ayah: 4, Ayah: 5, Ayah: 6, Ayah: 7 & Ayah: 8 170
    Tafsir Ibn Kathir 171
    The Explanation of At-Tin and what comes after it 171
    Man becoming Lowly even though He was created in the Best Form 172

CHAPTER (SURAH) 96: AL-ALAQ (THE CLOT, READ), VERSES 001- 019 173

  Surah: 96 Ayah: 1, Ayah: 2, Ayah: 3, Ayah: 4 & Ayah: 5 173
    Tafsir Ibn Kathir 174
    The Beginning of the Prophethood of Muhammad and the First of the Qur'an revealed 174
    The Honor and Nobility of Man is in His Knowledge 175
  Surah: 96 Ayah: 6, Ayah: 7, Ayah: 8, Ayah: 9, Ayah: 10, Ayah: 11, Ayah: 12, Ayah: 13, Ayah: 14, Ayah: 15, Ayah: 16, Ayah: 17, Ayah: 18 & Ayah: 19 175
    Tafsir Ibn Kathir 177
    The Threat against Man's Transgression for the sake of Wealth 177
    Scolding of Abu Jahl and the Threat of seizing Him 178
    Amusement for the Prophet 179

CHAPTER (SURAH) 97: AL-QADR (POWER, FATE), VERSES 001- 005 180

  Surah: 97 Ayah: 1, Ayah: 2, Ayah: 3, Ayah: 4 & Ayah: 5 180
    Tafsir Ibn Kathir 181
    The Virtues of the Night of Al-Qadr (the Decree) 181
    The Descent of the Angels and the Decree for Every Good during the Night of Al-Qadr 181
    Specifying the Night of Decree and its Signs 182
    Supplication during the Night of Decree 185

Table of Contents **xiii**

INTRODUCTION TO CHAPTER (SURAH) 98: AL-BAYYINA (THE CLEAR PROOF, EVIDENCE) .. 185

IBN KATHIR'S INTRODUCTION 185
    The Messenger of Allah recited this Surah to Ubayy 185

CHAPTER (SURAH) 98: AL-BAYYINA (THE CLEAR PROOF, EVIDENCE), VERSES 001- 008 186

Surah: 98 Ayah: 1, Ayah: 2, Ayah: 3, Ayah: 4 & Ayah: 5 ...... *186*
    Tafsir Ibn Kathir 187
        Mentioning the Situation of the Disbelievers among the People of the Scripture and the Idolators 187
        The Differing only occurred after the Knowledge came 188
        The Command of Allah was merely that They make their Religion solely for Him 188
Surah: 98 Ayah: 6, Ayah: 7 & Ayah: 8 ...... *189*
    Tafsir Ibn Kathir 190
        Mentioning the Worse and Best of Creation and Their Recompense 190

INTRODUCTION TO CHAPTER (SURAH) 99: AZ-ZALZALA (THE EARTHQUAKE) 191

IBN KATHIR'S INTRODUCTION 191
    The Virtues of Surat Az-Zalzalah 191

CHAPTER (SURAH) 99: AZ-ZALZALA (THE EARTHQUAKE), VERSES 001-008 192

Surah: 99 Ayah: 1, Ayah: 2, Ayah: 3, Ayah: 4, Ayah: 5, Ayah: 6, Ayah: 7 & Ayah: 8 ...... *192*
    Tafsir Ibn Kathir 194
        The Day of Judgement, what will take place during it, the Condition of the Earth and the Condition of the People 194
        The Recompense for Every Minute Deed Therefore 195

CHAPTER (SURAH) 100: AL-ADIYAT (THE COURSER, THE CHARGERS), VERSES 001- 0011 .. 198

Surah: 100 Ayah: 1, Ayah: 2, Ayah: 3, Ayah: 4, Ayah: 5, Ayah: 6, Ayah: 7, Ayah: 8, Ayah: 9, Ayah: 10 & Ayah: 11 ...... *198*
    Tafsir Ibn Kathir 199
        Swearing by the Horses of War about the Ungratefulness of Man and His Zeal for Wealth 199
        Concerning Allah's statement, ... 200
        The Threat about the Hereafter 201

CHAPTER (SURAH) 101: AL-QARIA (THE CALAMITY, THE STUNNING BLOW, THE DISASTER), VERSES 001-0011 201

Surah: 101 Ayah: 1, Ayah: 2, Ayah: 3, Ayah: 4, Ayah: 5, Ayah: 6, Ayah: 7, Ayah: 8, Ayah: 9, Ayah: 10 & Ayah: 11 ...... *201*
    Tafsir Ibn Kathir 203
        Al-Qari`ah is one of the names of the Day of Judgement, like Al-Haqqah, At-Tammah, As-Sakhkhah, Al-Ghashiyah and other names. 203
        Two Sahihs that the Messenger of Allah said, ... 204

CHAPTER (SURAH) 102: AT-TAKATHUR (RIVALRY IN WORLD INCREASE, COMPETITION), VERSES 001-008..205

   Surah: 102 Ayah: 1, Ayah: 2, Ayah: 3, Ayah: 4, Ayah: 5, Ayah: 6, Ayah: 7 & Ayah: 8..... 205
      Tafsir Ibn Kathir 206
         The Result of Loving the World and Heedlessness of the Hereafter 206
         The Threat of seeing Hell and being questioned about the Delights............................ 208

INTRODUCTION TO CHAPTER (SURAH) 103: AL-ASR (THE DECLINING DAY, EVENTIDE, THE EPOCH) 210

   IBN KATHIR'S INTRODUCTION... 210
      How `Amr bin Al-`As was aware of the Qur'an's Miracle due to this Surah 210

CHAPTER (SURAH) 103: AL-ASR (THE DECLINING DAY, EVENTIDE, THE EPOCH), VERSES 001-003..211

   Surah: 103 Ayah: 1, Ayah: 2 & Ayah: 3.. 211
      Tafsir Ibn Kathir 212
         Al-`Asr is the time in which the movements of the Children of Adam occur, whether good or evil.. 212

CHAPTER (SURAH) 104: AL-HUMAZA (THE TRADUCER, THE GOSSIPMONGER), VERSES 001-009..212

   Surah: 104 Ayah: 1, Ayah: 2, Ayah: 3, Ayah: 4, Ayah: 5, Ayah: 6, Ayah: 7, Ayah: 8 & Ayah: 9 212
      Tafsir Ibn Kathir 214
         Concerning Allah's statement,... 214

CHAPTER (SURAH) 105: AL-FIL (THE ELEPHANT), VERSES 001-005 215

   Surah: 105 Ayah: 1, Ayah: 2, Ayah: 3, Ayah: 4 & Ayah: 5.. 215
      Tafsir Ibn Kathir 216
         A Summary of the Story of the People of the Elephant.. 216
         Dhu Nafr was captured and taken along with the army of Abrahah. 217
         Concerning Allah's statement,... 220

CHAPTER (SURAH) 106: QURAISH (WINTER, QURAYSH), VERSES 001-004 222

   Surah: 106 Ayah: 1, Ayah: 2, Ayah: 3 & Ayah: 4.. 222
      Tafsir Ibn Kathir 222
         This Surah has been separated from the one that preceded it in the primary Mushaf (the original copy of `Uthman).. 222

CHAPTER (SURAH) 107: AL-MAUN (SMALL KINDNESSES, ALMSGIVING, HAVE YOU SEEN), VERSES 001-007..224

   Surah: 107 Ayah: 1, Ayah: 2, Ayah: 3, Ayah: 4, Ayah: 5, Ayah: 6 & Ayah: 7.................... 224
      Tafsir Ibn Kathir 225

| Allah says, "O Muhammad! Have you seen the one who denies the Din" | 225 |
| This was said by Masruq and Abu Ad-Duha | 225 |

CHAPTER (SURAH) 108: AL-KAUTHER (ABUNDANCE, PLENTY), VERSES 001-003 ... 227

Surah: 108 Ayah: 1, Ayah: 2 & Ayah: 3 ... 227
    Tafsir Ibn Kathir ... 227
    The Enemy of the Prophet is Cut Off ... 230

INTRODUCTION TO CHAPTER (SURAH) 109: AL-KAFIROON (THE DISBELIEVERS, ATHEISTS) ... 231

IBN KATHIR'S INTRODUCTION ... 231
    The Recitation of these Surahs in the Optional Prayers ... 231

CHAPTER (SURAH) 109: AL-KAFIROON THE DISBELIEVERS, ATHEISTS, VERSES 001-006 ... 232

Surah: 109 Ayah: 1, Ayah: 2, Ayah: 3, Ayah: 4, Ayah: 5 & Ayah: 6 ... 232
    Tafsir Ibn Kathir ... 233
    The Declaration of Innocence from Shirk ... 233
    He commanded His Messenger to disavow himself from their religion completely ... 233

INTRODUCTION TO CHAPTER (SURAH) 110: AN-NASR (SUCCOUR, DIVINE SUPPORT) ... 234

IBN KATHIR'S INTRODUCTION ... 234
    The Virtues of Surat An-Nasr ... 234

CHAPTER (SURAH) 110: AN-NASR (SUCCOUR, DIVINE SUPPORT), VERSES 001-003 ... 234

Surah: 110 Ayah: 1, Ayah: 2 & Ayah: 3 ... 234
    Tafsir Ibn Kathir ... 235
    This Surah informs of the Completion of the Life of Allah's Messenger ... 235

CHAPTER (SURAH) 111: AL-MASADD (PALM FIBRE, THE FLAME), VERSES 001-005 ... 237

Surah: 111 Ayah: 1, Ayah: 2, Ayah: 3, Ayah: 4 & Ayah: 5 ... 237
    Tafsir Ibn Kathir ... 238
    The Reason for the Revelation of this Surah and the Arrogance of Abu Lahab toward the Messenger of Allah ... 238
    The Destiny of Umm Jamil, the Wife of Abu Lahab ... 239
    A Story of Abu Lahab's Wife harming the Messenger of Allah ... 240

INTRODUCTION TO CHAPTER (SURAH) 112: AL-IKHLAS (SINCERITY) ... 240

IBN KATHIR'S INTRODUCTION ... 240
    The Reason for the Revelation of this Surah and its Virtues ... 240
    A Hadith on its Virtues ... 241
    A Hadith that mentions this Surah is equivalent to a Third of the Qur'an ... 242
    Another Hadith that its Recitation necessitates Admission into Paradise ... 242
    A Hadith about repeating this Surah ... 243
    Another Hadith about supplicating with it by Allah's Names ... 244
    A Hadith about seeking a Cure by these Surahs ... 244

CHAPTER (SURAH) 112: AL-IKHLAS (SINCERITY), VERSES 001-004 244

Surah: 112 Ayah: 1, Ayah: 2, Ayah: 3 & Ayah: 4 244

Tafsir Ibn Kathir 245

Allah is Above having Children and procreating 245

INTRODUCTION TO CHAPTER (SURAH) 113: AL-FALAQ (THE DAYBREAK, DAWN) 247

IBN KATHIR'S INTRODUCTION 247

The Position of Ibn Mas`ud concerning Al-Mu`awwidhatayn 247

The Virtues of Surahs Al-Falaq and An-Nas 247

Another Narration 247

Another Narration 248

Another Narration 248

Another Hadith 249

CHAPTER (SURAH) 113: AL-FALAQ (THE DAYBREAK, DAWN), VERSES 001-005 249

Surah: 113 Ayah: 1, Ayah: 2, Ayah: 3, Ayah: 4 & Ayah: 5 249

Tafsir Ibn Kathir 250

Discussion of the Bewitchment of the Prophet 252

INTRODUCTION TO CHAPTER (SURAH) 114: AN-NAS (MANKIND) 253

IBN KATHIR'S INTRODUCTION 253

CHAPTER (SURAH) 114: AN-NAS (MANKIND), VERSES 001-006 253

Surah: 114 Ayah: 1, Ayah: 2, Ayah: 3, Ayah: 4, Ayah: 5 & Ayah: 6 253

Tafsir Ibn Kathir 254

PRELUDE

Opening Serman

Indeed, all praise is due to Allah. We praise Him and seek His help and forgiveness. We seek refuge with Allah from our soul's evil and our wrong doings. He whom Allah guides, no one can misguide; and he whom He misguides, no one can guide

I bear witness that there is no (true) god except Allah – alone without a partner, and I bear witness that Muhammad (peace and blessings of Allah be upon him) is His 'abd (servant) and messenger.

يَٰٓأَيُّهَا ٱلَّذِينَ ءَامَنُوا۟ ٱتَّقُوا۟ ٱللَّهَ حَقَّ تُقَاتِهِۦ وَلَا تَمُوتُنَّ إِلَّا وَأَنتُم مُّسْلِمُونَ ۝

O you who believe! Fear Allâh (by doing all that He has ordered and by abstaining from all that He has forbidden) as He should be feared. (Obey Him, be thankful to Him, and remember Him always), and die not except in a state of Islâm (as Muslims (with complete submission to Allâh)).

يَٰٓأَيُّهَا ٱلنَّاسُ ٱتَّقُوا۟ رَبَّكُمُ ٱلَّذِى خَلَقَكُم مِّن نَّفْسٍ وَٰحِدَةٍ وَخَلَقَ مِنْهَا زَوْجَهَا وَبَثَّ مِنْهُمَا رِجَالًا كَثِيرًا وَنِسَآءً وَٱتَّقُوا۟ ٱللَّهَ ٱلَّذِى تَسَآءَلُونَ بِهِۦ وَٱلْأَرْحَامَ إِنَّ ٱللَّهَ كَانَ عَلَيْكُمْ رَقِيبًا ۝

O mankind! Be dutiful to your Lord, Who created you from a single person (Adam), and from him (Adam) He created his wife (Hawwâ (Eve)) and from them both He created many men and women; and fear Allâh through Whom you demand (your mutual rights), and (do not cut the relations of) the wombs (kinship). Surely, Allâh is Ever an All-Watcher over you.

يُصْلِحْ لَكُمْ أَعْمَٰلَكُمْ وَيَغْفِرْ لَكُمْ ذُنُوبَكُمْ وَمَن يُطِعِ ٱللَّهَ وَرَسُولَهُۥ فَقَدْ فَازَ فَوْزًا عَظِيمًا ۝

He will direct you to do righteous good deeds and will forgive you your sins. And whosoever obeys Allâh and His Messenger (peace be upon him), he has indeed achieved a great achievement (i.e. he will be saved from the Hell-fire and will be admitted to Paradise).

Indeed, the best speech is Allah's Book and the best guidance is Muhammad's () guidance. The worst affairs (of religion) are those innovated (by people), for every such innovation is an act of misguidance leading to the Fire

Our Mission

Our mission is to gather in one place, for the English-speaking public, all relevant information needed to make the Qur'an more understandable and easier to study. This book tries to do this by providing the following:

1. The Arabic Text for those who are able to read Arabic
2. Transliteration of the Arabic text for those who are unable to read the Arabic script. This will give them a sample of the sound of the Qur'an, which they could not otherwise comprehend from reading the English meaning.
3. The meaning of the qur'an (translated by Dr. Muhammad Taqi-ud-Din Al-Hilali, Ph.D. and Dr. Muhammad Muhsin Khan)
4. Explanation (abridged Tafsir) by Ibn Kathir (translated by Safi-ur-Rahman al-Mubarakpuri)

We hope that by doing this an ordinary English-speaker will be able to pick up a copy of this book and study and comprehend The Glorious Qur'an in a way that is acceptable to the understanding of the Rightly-guided Muslim Ummah (Community).

Biography of Hafiz Ibn Kathir (701 H - 774 H)

By the Honored Shaykh `Abdul-Qadir Al-Arna'ut, may Allah protect him.

He is the respected Imam, Abu Al-Fida', `Imad Ad-Din Isma il bin 'Umar bin Kathir Al-Qurashi Al-Busrawi - Busraian in origin; Dimashqi in training, learning and residence.

Ibn Kathir was born in the city of Busra in 701 H. His father was the Friday speaker of the village, but he died while Ibn Kathir was only four years old. Ibn Kathir's brother, Shaykh Abdul-Wahhab, reared him and taught him until he moved to Damascus in 706 H., when he was five years old.

Ibn Kathir's Teachers

Ibn Kathir studied Fiqh - Islamic jurisprudence - with Burhan Ad-Din, Ibrahim bin `Abdur-Rahman Al-Fizari, known as Ibn Al-Firkah (who died in 729 H). Ibn Kathir heard Hadiths from `Isa bin Al-Mutim, Ahmad bin Abi Talib, (Ibn Ash-Shahnah) (who died in 730 H), Ibn Al-Hajjar, (who died in 730 H), and the Hadith narrator of Ash-Sham (modern day Syria and surrounding areas); Baha Ad-Din Al-Qasim bin Muzaffar bin `Asakir (who died in 723 H), and Ibn Ash-Shirdzi, Ishaq bin Yahya Al-Ammuddi, also known as `Afif Ad-Din, the Zahiriyyah Shaykh who died in 725 H, and Muhammad bin Zarrad. He remained with Jamal Ad-Din, Yusuf bin Az-Zaki AlMizzi who died in 724 H, he benefited from his knowledge and also married his daughter. He also read with Shaykh Al-Islam, Taqi Ad-Din Ahmad bin `Abdul-Halim bin `Abdus-Salam bin Taymiyyah who died in 728 H. He also read with the Imam Hafiz and historian Shams Ad-Din, Muhammad bin Ahmad bin Uthman bin Qaymaz Adh-Dhahabi, who died in 748 H. Also, Abu Musa Al-Qarafai, Abu Al-Fath Ad-Dabbusi and

'Ali bin `Umar As-Suwani and others who gave him permission to transmit the knowledge he learned with them in Egypt.

In his book, Al-Mu jam Al-Mukhtas, Al-Hafiz Adh-Dhaliabi wrote that Ibn Kathir was, "The Imam, scholar of jurisprudence, skillful scholar of Hadith, renowned Faqih and scholar of Tafsir who wrote several beneficial books."

Further, in Ad-Durar Al-Kdminah, Al-Hafiz Ibn Hajar AlAsqalani said, "Ibn Kathir worked on the subject of the Hadith in the areas of texts and chains of narrators. He had a good memory, his books became popular during his lifetime, and people benefited from them after his death."

Also, the renowned historian Abu Al-Mahasin, Jamal Ad-Din Yusuf bin Sayf Ad-Din (Ibn Taghri Bardi), said in his book, AlManhal As-Safi, "He is the Shaykh, the Imam, the great scholar `Imad Ad-Din Abu Al-Fida'. He learned extensively and was very active in collecting knowledge and writing. He was excellent in the areas of Fiqh, Tafsfr and Hadith. He collected knowledge, authored (books), taught, narrated Hadith and wrote. He had immense knowledge in the fields of Hadith, Tafsir, Fiqh, the Arabic language, and so forth. He gave Fatawa (religious verdicts) and taught until he died, may Allah grant him mercy. He was known for his precision and vast knowledge, and as a scholar of history, Hadith and Tafsir."

Ibn Kathir's Students

Ibn Hajji was one of Ibn Kathir's students, and he described Ibn Kathir: "He had the best memory of the Hadith texts. He also had the most knowledge concerning the narrators and authenticity, his contemporaries and teachers admitted to these qualities. Every time I met him I gained some benefit from him."

Also, Ibn Al-`Imad Al-Hanbali said in his book, Shadhardt Adh-Dhahab, "He is the renowned Hafiz `Imad Ad-Din, whose memory was excellent, whose forgetfulness was miniscule, whose understanding was adequate, and who had good knowledge in the Arabic language." Also, Ibn Habib said about Ibn Kathir, "He heard knowledge and collected it and wrote various books. He brought comfort to the ears with his Fatwas and narrated Hadith and brought benefit to other people. The papers that contained his Fatwas were transmitted to the various (Islamic) provinces. Further, he was known for his precision and encompassing knowledge."

Ibn Kathir's Books

1 - One of the greatest books that Ibn Kathir wrote was his Tafsir of the Noble Qur'an, which is one of the best Tafsir that rely on narrations [of Ahadith, the Tafsir of the Companions, etc.]. The Tafsir by Ibn Kathir was printed many times and several scholars have summarized it.

2- The History Collection known as Al-Biddyah, which was printed in 14 volumes under the name Al-Bidayah wanNihdyah, and contained the stories of the Prophets and previous nations, the Prophet's Seerah (life story) and Islamic history until his time. He also added a book Al-Fitan, about the Signs of the Last Hour.

3- At-Takmil ft Ma`rifat Ath-Thiqat wa Ad-Du'afa wal Majdhil which Ibn Kathir collected from the books of his two Shaykhs Al-Mizzi and Adh-Dhahabi; Al-Kdmal and Mizan Al-Ftiddl. He added several benefits regarding the subject of Al-Jarh and AtT'adil.

4- Al-Hadi was-Sunan ft Ahadith Al-Masdnfd was-Sunan which is also known by, Jami` Al-Masdnfd. In this book, Ibn Kathir collected the narrations of Imams Ahmad bin Hanbal, Al-Bazzar, Abu Ya`la Al-Mawsili, Ibn Abi Shaybah and from the six collections of Hadith: the Two Sahihs [Al-Bukhari and Muslim] and the Four Sunan [Abu Dawud, At-Tirmidhi, AnNasa and Ibn Majah]. Ibn Kathir divided this book according to areas of Fiqh.

5-Tabaqat Ash-Shaf iyah which also contains the virtues of Imam Ash-Shafi.

6- Ibn Kathir wrote references for the Ahadith of Adillat AtTanbfh, from the Shafi school of Fiqh.

7- Ibn Kathir began an explanation of Sahih Al-Bukhari, but he did not finish it.

8- He started writing a large volume on the Ahkam (Laws), but finished only up to the Hajj rituals.

9- He summarized Al-Bayhaqi's 'Al-Madkhal. Many of these books were not printed.

10- He summarized `Ulum Al-Hadith, by Abu `Amr bin AsSalah and called it Mukhtasar `Ulum Al-Hadith. Shaykh Ahmad Shakir, the Egyptian Muhaddith, printed this book along with his commentary on it and called it Al-Ba'th Al-Hathfth fi Sharh Mukhtasar `Ulum Al-Hadith.

11- As-Sfrah An-Nabawiyyah, which is contained in his book Al-Biddyah, and both of these books are in print.

12- A research on Jihad called Al-Ijtihad ft Talabi Al-Jihad, which was printed several times.

Ibn Kathir's Death

Al-Hafiz Ibn Hajar Al-Asgalani said, "Ibn Kathir lost his sight just before his life ended. He died in Damascus in 774 H." May Allah grant mercy upon Ibn Kathir and make him among the residents of His Paradise.

PREFACE

In the name of Allah, Most Gracious, Most Merciful.

About this book

The previous publication of this book included some background information to the chapters of the Qur'an by an Islamic scholar known as Abul Ala Maududi. This information was used to shed more light on the chapters by giving a summery of why each chapter was given its name, It's period of revelation and the circumstances surrounding its revelatiom. However, some Muslims objected to the inclusion of the contributions of Maududi.

In this new publication of Tafsir Ibn Kathir, we have removed all traces of the contribution of Abul Ala Maududi. Personally, I do not know the reasons for the objections to Maududi, but this work concerns only the tafsir of Ibn Kathir, so we have not included anything from Maududi in it. We have also corrected all the typing and formatting errors found in the previous publication. We have not alter the structure of the book. The reader is still able to read the full Arabic Text of the thirty Parts of the Qur'an and follow its meanings in the English language. The transliteration of the Arabic text should also give the reader a taste of the sound of the original Arabic.

May Almighty Allah accept this effort from us, and make it a source of blessings for us in this world and in the next. I bear witness that there is none worthy of worship but Allah and I bear witness that Muhammad (may the peace and blessings of Allah be upon him) is the slave and messenger of Allah.

Performing Prostration While Reading the Qur'an

Question:

Could you please give a list of the Qur'anic verses when a prostration is recommended? What happens if we read these verses and not perform a prostration?

A. Jalil

Answer:

There are 15 verses in the Qur'an that mention prostration before God Almighty as a good action by God-fearing believers. Therefore, it is strongly recommended to perform such a prostration when we read or listen to any of these verses, whether during prayer or in any situation.

Some scholars are of the view that even if one has not performed ablution, one should prostrate oneself. These verses are given here, starting with the Arabic title of the surah which is followed by two numbers, the first indicating the surah, and the second indicating the verse,: Al-Araf 7: 206; Al-Raad 13: 15; Al-Nahl 16: 50; Al-Isra 17: 109; Maryam 19: 58; Al-Hajj 22: 18 & 22: 77; Al-Furqan 25: 60; Al-Naml 27: 26;

Al-Sajdah 32: 15; Saad 38: 25; Fussilat 41: 38; Al-Najm 53: 62; Al-Inshiqaq 84: 21 and Al-Alaq 96: 19.

If you do not perform a prostration when you read or listen to any of these verses, you have done badly because you miss out on the reward of performing a prostration for God. You incur no sin and violate no divine order.

Reference:
http://archive.arabnews.com/?page=5&section=0&article=97811&d=1&m=7&y=2007

The Glorious Qur'an Juz' 30 (Part 30): Chapter (Surah) 78: An-Nabaa (The Tidings, The Announcement) 001 To Chapter (Surah) 114: An-Nas (Mankind) 6

PART 30 FULL ARABIC TEXT

Chapter (Surah) 78: An-Nabaa 001-040

بِسْمِ ٱللَّهِ ٱلرَّحْمَٰنِ ٱلرَّحِيمِ

﴿ عَمَّ يَتَسَآءَلُونَ ۝ عَنِ ٱلنَّبَإِ ٱلْعَظِيمِ ۝ ٱلَّذِى هُمْ فِيهِ مُخْتَلِفُونَ ۝ كَلَّا سَيَعْلَمُونَ ۝ ثُمَّ كَلَّا سَيَعْلَمُونَ ۝ أَلَمْ نَجْعَلِ ٱلْأَرْضَ مِهَٰدًا ۝ وَٱلْجِبَالَ أَوْتَادًا ۝ وَخَلَقْنَٰكُمْ أَزْوَٰجًا ۝ وَجَعَلْنَا نَوْمَكُمْ سُبَاتًا ۝ وَجَعَلْنَا ٱلَّيْلَ لِبَاسًا ۝ وَجَعَلْنَا ٱلنَّهَارَ مَعَاشًا ۝ وَبَنَيْنَا فَوْقَكُمْ سَبْعًا شِدَادًا ۝ وَجَعَلْنَا سِرَاجًا وَهَّاجًا ۝ وَأَنزَلْنَا مِنَ ٱلْمُعْصِرَٰتِ مَآءً ثَجَّاجًا ۝ لِنُخْرِجَ بِهِۦ حَبًّا وَنَبَاتًا ۝ وَجَنَّٰتٍ أَلْفَافًا ۝ إِنَّ يَوْمَ ٱلْفَصْلِ كَانَ مِيقَٰتًا ۝ يَوْمَ يُنفَخُ فِى ٱلصُّورِ فَتَأْتُونَ أَفْوَاجًا ۝ وَفُتِحَتِ ٱلسَّمَآءُ فَكَانَتْ أَبْوَٰبًا ۝ وَسُيِّرَتِ ٱلْجِبَالُ فَكَانَتْ سَرَابًا ۝ إِنَّ جَهَنَّمَ كَانَتْ مِرْصَادًا ۝ لِّلطَّٰغِينَ مَـَٔابًا ۝ لَّٰبِثِينَ فِيهَآ أَحْقَابًا ۝ لَّا يَذُوقُونَ فِيهَا بَرْدًا وَلَا شَرَابًا ۝ إِلَّا حَمِيمًا وَغَسَّاقًا ۝ جَزَآءً وِفَاقًا ۝ إِنَّهُمْ كَانُوا۟ لَا يَرْجُونَ حِسَابًا ۝ وَكَذَّبُوا۟ بِـَٔايَٰتِنَا كِذَّابًا ۝ وَكُلَّ شَىْءٍ أَحْصَيْنَٰهُ كِتَٰبًا ۝ فَذُوقُوا۟ فَلَن نَّزِيدَكُمْ إِلَّا عَذَابًا ۝ إِنَّ لِلْمُتَّقِينَ مَفَازًا ۝ حَدَآئِقَ وَأَعْنَٰبًا ۝ وَكَوَاعِبَ أَتْرَابًا ۝ وَكَأْسًا دِهَاقًا ۝ لَّا يَسْمَعُونَ فِيهَا لَغْوًا وَلَا كِذَّٰبًا ۝ جَزَآءً مِّن رَّبِّكَ عَطَآءً حِسَابًا ۝ رَّبِّ ٱلسَّمَٰوَٰتِ وَٱلْأَرْضِ وَمَا بَيْنَهُمَا ٱلرَّحْمَٰنِ لَا يَمْلِكُونَ مِنْهُ خِطَابًا ۝ يَوْمَ يَقُومُ ٱلرُّوحُ وَٱلْمَلَٰٓئِكَةُ صَفًّا لَّا يَتَكَلَّمُونَ إِلَّا مَنْ

أَذِنَ لَهُ ٱلرَّحْمَٰنُ وَقَالَ صَوَابًا ۝ ذَٰلِكَ ٱلْيَوْمُ ٱلْحَقُّ ۖ فَمَن شَآءَ ٱتَّخَذَ إِلَىٰ رَبِّهِۦ مَـَٔابًا ۝ إِنَّآ أَنذَرْنَٰكُمْ عَذَابًا قَرِيبًا يَوْمَ يَنظُرُ ٱلْمَرْءُ مَا قَدَّمَتْ يَدَاهُ وَيَقُولُ ٱلْكَافِرُ يَٰلَيْتَنِى كُنتُ تُرَٰبًۢا ۝

(An-Nabaa 001-040)

Chapter (Surah) 79: An-Nazi'at 001-046

بِسْمِ ٱللَّهِ ٱلرَّحْمَٰنِ ٱلرَّحِيمِ

وَٱلنَّٰزِعَٰتِ غَرْقًا ۝ وَٱلنَّٰشِطَٰتِ نَشْطًا ۝ وَٱلسَّٰبِحَٰتِ سَبْحًا ۝ فَٱلسَّٰبِقَٰتِ سَبْقًا ۝ فَٱلْمُدَبِّرَٰتِ أَمْرًا ۝ يَوْمَ تَرْجُفُ ٱلرَّاجِفَةُ ۝ تَتْبَعُهَا ٱلرَّادِفَةُ ۝ قُلُوبٌ يَوْمَئِذٍ وَاجِفَةٌ ۝ أَبْصَٰرُهَا خَٰشِعَةٌ ۝ يَقُولُونَ أَءِنَّا لَمَرْدُودُونَ فِى ٱلْحَافِرَةِ ۝ أَءِذَا كُنَّا عِظَٰمًا نَّخِرَةً ۝ قَالُوا۟ تِلْكَ إِذًا كَرَّةٌ خَاسِرَةٌ ۝ فَإِنَّمَا هِىَ زَجْرَةٌ وَٰحِدَةٌ ۝ فَإِذَا هُم بِٱلسَّاهِرَةِ ۝ هَلْ أَتَىٰكَ حَدِيثُ مُوسَىٰٓ ۝ إِذْ نَادَىٰهُ رَبُّهُۥ بِٱلْوَادِ ٱلْمُقَدَّسِ طُوًى ۝ ٱذْهَبْ إِلَىٰ فِرْعَوْنَ إِنَّهُۥ طَغَىٰ ۝ فَقُلْ هَل لَّكَ إِلَىٰٓ أَن تَزَكَّىٰ ۝ وَأَهْدِيَكَ إِلَىٰ رَبِّكَ فَتَخْشَىٰ ۝ فَأَرَىٰهُ ٱلْءَايَةَ ٱلْكُبْرَىٰ ۝ فَكَذَّبَ وَعَصَىٰ ۝ ثُمَّ أَدْبَرَ يَسْعَىٰ ۝ فَحَشَرَ فَنَادَىٰ ۝ فَقَالَ أَنَا۠ رَبُّكُمُ ٱلْأَعْلَىٰ ۝ فَأَخَذَهُ ٱللَّهُ نَكَالَ ٱلْءَاخِرَةِ وَٱلْأُولَىٰٓ ۝ إِنَّ فِى ذَٰلِكَ لَعِبْرَةً لِّمَن يَخْشَىٰٓ ۝ ءَأَنتُمْ أَشَدُّ خَلْقًا أَمِ ٱلسَّمَآءُ ۚ بَنَىٰهَا ۝ رَفَعَ سَمْكَهَا فَسَوَّىٰهَا ۝ وَأَغْطَشَ لَيْلَهَا وَأَخْرَجَ ضُحَىٰهَا ۝ وَٱلْأَرْضَ بَعْدَ ذَٰلِكَ دَحَىٰهَآ ۝ أَخْرَجَ مِنْهَا مَآءَهَا وَمَرْعَىٰهَا ۝ وَٱلْجِبَالَ أَرْسَىٰهَا ۝ مَتَٰعًا لَّكُمْ وَلِأَنْعَٰمِكُمْ ۝ فَإِذَا جَآءَتِ ٱلطَّآمَّةُ ٱلْكُبْرَىٰ ۝ يَوْمَ يَتَذَكَّرُ ٱلْإِنسَٰنُ مَا سَعَىٰ ۝ وَبُرِّزَتِ ٱلْجَحِيمُ لِمَن يَرَىٰ ۝ فَأَمَّا مَن طَغَىٰ ۝ وَءَاثَرَ ٱلْحَيَوٰةَ ٱلدُّنْيَا ۝ فَإِنَّ ٱلْجَحِيمَ هِىَ ٱلْمَأْوَىٰ ۝ وَأَمَّا مَنْ خَافَ مَقَامَ رَبِّهِۦ وَنَهَى ٱلنَّفْسَ عَنِ ٱلْهَوَىٰ ۝ فَإِنَّ ٱلْجَنَّةَ هِىَ ٱلْمَأْوَىٰ ۝ يَسْـَٔلُونَكَ عَنِ ٱلسَّاعَةِ أَيَّانَ

مُرْسَىٰهَا ۝ فِيمَ أَنتَ مِن ذِكْرَىٰهَا ۝ إِلَىٰ رَبِّكَ مُنتَهَىٰهَآ ۝ إِنَّمَآ أَنتَ مُنذِرُ مَن يَخْشَىٰهَا ۝ كَأَنَّهُمْ يَوْمَ يَرَوْنَهَا لَمْ يَلْبَثُوٓا۟ إِلَّا عَشِيَّةً أَوْ ضُحَىٰهَا ۝

(An-Nazi'at 001-046)

Chapter (Surah) 80: 'Abasa 001-042

بِسْمِ ٱللَّهِ ٱلرَّحْمَٰنِ ٱلرَّحِيمِ

عَبَسَ وَتَوَلَّىٰٓ ۝ أَن جَآءَهُ ٱلْأَعْمَىٰ ۝ وَمَا يُدْرِيكَ لَعَلَّهُۥ يَزَّكَّىٰٓ ۝ أَوْ يَذَّكَّرُ فَتَنفَعَهُ ٱلذِّكْرَىٰٓ ۝ أَمَّا مَنِ ٱسْتَغْنَىٰ ۝ فَأَنتَ لَهُۥ تَصَدَّىٰ ۝ وَمَا عَلَيْكَ أَلَّا يَزَّكَّىٰ ۝ وَأَمَّا مَن جَآءَكَ يَسْعَىٰ ۝ وَهُوَ يَخْشَىٰ ۝ فَأَنتَ عَنْهُ تَلَهَّىٰ ۝ كَلَّآ إِنَّهَا تَذْكِرَةٌ ۝ فَمَن شَآءَ ذَكَرَهُۥ ۝ فِى صُحُفٍ مُّكَرَّمَةٍ ۝ مَّرْفُوعَةٍ مُّطَهَّرَةٍ ۝ بِأَيْدِى سَفَرَةٍ ۝ كِرَامٍۭ بَرَرَةٍ ۝ قُتِلَ ٱلْإِنسَٰنُ مَآ أَكْفَرَهُۥ ۝ مِنْ أَىِّ شَىْءٍ خَلَقَهُۥ ۝ مِن نُّطْفَةٍ خَلَقَهُۥ فَقَدَّرَهُۥ ۝ ثُمَّ ٱلسَّبِيلَ يَسَّرَهُۥ ۝ ثُمَّ أَمَاتَهُۥ فَأَقْبَرَهُۥ ۝ ثُمَّ إِذَا شَآءَ أَنشَرَهُۥ ۝ كَلَّا لَمَّا يَقْضِ مَآ أَمَرَهُۥ ۝ فَلْيَنظُرِ ٱلْإِنسَٰنُ إِلَىٰ طَعَامِهِۦٓ ۝ أَنَّا صَبَبْنَا ٱلْمَآءَ صَبًّا ۝ ثُمَّ شَقَقْنَا ٱلْأَرْضَ شَقًّا ۝ فَأَنۢبَتْنَا فِيهَا حَبًّا ۝ وَعِنَبًا وَقَضْبًا ۝ وَزَيْتُونًا وَنَخْلًا ۝ وَحَدَآئِقَ غُلْبًا ۝ وَفَٰكِهَةً وَأَبًّا ۝ مَّتَٰعًا لَّكُمْ وَلِأَنْعَٰمِكُمْ ۝ فَإِذَا جَآءَتِ ٱلصَّآخَّةُ ۝ يَوْمَ يَفِرُّ ٱلْمَرْءُ مِنْ أَخِيهِ ۝ وَأُمِّهِۦ وَأَبِيهِ ۝ وَصَٰحِبَتِهِۦ وَبَنِيهِ ۝ لِكُلِّ ٱمْرِئٍ مِّنْهُمْ يَوْمَئِذٍ شَأْنٌ يُغْنِيهِ ۝ وُجُوهٌ يَوْمَئِذٍ مُّسْفِرَةٌ ۝ ضَاحِكَةٌ مُّسْتَبْشِرَةٌ ۝ وَوُجُوهٌ يَوْمَئِذٍ عَلَيْهَا غَبَرَةٌ ۝ تَرْهَقُهَا قَتَرَةٌ ۝ أُو۟لَٰٓئِكَ هُمُ ٱلْكَفَرَةُ ٱلْفَجَرَةُ ۝

('Abasa 001-042)

Chapter (Surah) 81: At-Takwir 001-029

بِسْمِ ٱللَّهِ ٱلرَّحْمَٰنِ ٱلرَّحِيمِ

﴿ إِذَا ٱلشَّمْسُ كُوِّرَتْ ۝ وَإِذَا ٱلنُّجُومُ ٱنكَدَرَتْ ۝ وَإِذَا ٱلْجِبَالُ سُيِّرَتْ ۝ وَإِذَا ٱلْعِشَارُ عُطِّلَتْ ۝ وَإِذَا ٱلْوُحُوشُ حُشِرَتْ ۝ وَإِذَا ٱلْبِحَارُ سُجِّرَتْ ۝ وَإِذَا ٱلنُّفُوسُ زُوِّجَتْ ۝ وَإِذَا ٱلْمَوْءُۥدَةُ سُئِلَتْ ۝ بِأَىِّ ذَنۢبٍ قُتِلَتْ ۝ وَإِذَا ٱلصُّحُفُ نُشِرَتْ ۝ وَإِذَا ٱلسَّمَآءُ كُشِطَتْ ۝ وَإِذَا ٱلْجَحِيمُ سُعِّرَتْ ۝ وَإِذَا ٱلْجَنَّةُ أُزْلِفَتْ ۝ عَلِمَتْ نَفْسٌ مَّآ أَحْضَرَتْ ۝ فَلَآ أُقْسِمُ بِٱلْخُنَّسِ ۝ ٱلْجَوَارِ ٱلْكُنَّسِ ۝ وَٱلَّيْلِ إِذَا عَسْعَسَ ۝ وَٱلصُّبْحِ إِذَا تَنَفَّسَ ۝ إِنَّهُۥ لَقَوْلُ رَسُولٍ كَرِيمٍ ۝ ذِى قُوَّةٍ عِندَ ذِى ٱلْعَرْشِ مَكِينٍ ۝ مُّطَاعٍ ثَمَّ أَمِينٍ ۝ وَمَا صَاحِبُكُم بِمَجْنُونٍ ۝ وَلَقَدْ رَءَاهُ بِٱلْأُفُقِ ٱلْمُبِينِ ۝ وَمَا هُوَ عَلَى ٱلْغَيْبِ بِضَنِينٍ ۝ وَمَا هُوَ بِقَوْلِ شَيْطَٰنٍ رَّجِيمٍ ۝ فَأَيْنَ تَذْهَبُونَ ۝ إِنْ هُوَ إِلَّا ذِكْرٌ لِّلْعَٰلَمِينَ ۝ لِمَن شَآءَ مِنكُمْ أَن يَسْتَقِيمَ ۝ وَمَا تَشَآءُونَ إِلَّآ أَن يَشَآءَ ٱللَّهُ رَبُّ ٱلْعَٰلَمِينَ ۝ ﴾

(At-Takwir 001-029)

Chapter (Surah) 82: Al-Infitar 001-019

بِسْمِ ٱللَّهِ ٱلرَّحْمَٰنِ ٱلرَّحِيمِ

﴿ إِذَا ٱلسَّمَآءُ ٱنفَطَرَتْ ۝ وَإِذَا ٱلْكَوَاكِبُ ٱنتَثَرَتْ ۝ وَإِذَا ٱلْبِحَارُ فُجِّرَتْ ۝ وَإِذَا ٱلْقُبُورُ بُعْثِرَتْ ۝ عَلِمَتْ نَفْسٌ مَّا قَدَّمَتْ وَأَخَّرَتْ ۝ يَٰٓأَيُّهَا ٱلْإِنسَٰنُ مَا غَرَّكَ بِرَبِّكَ ٱلْكَرِيمِ ۝ ٱلَّذِى خَلَقَكَ فَسَوَّىٰكَ فَعَدَلَكَ ۝ فِىٓ أَىِّ صُورَةٍ مَّا شَآءَ رَكَّبَكَ ۝ كَلَّا بَلْ تُكَذِّبُونَ بِٱلدِّينِ ۝ وَإِنَّ عَلَيْكُمْ لَحَٰفِظِينَ ۝ كِرَامًا كَٰتِبِينَ ۝ يَعْلَمُونَ مَا تَفْعَلُونَ ۝ إِنَّ ٱلْأَبْرَارَ لَفِى نَعِيمٍ ۝ وَإِنَّ ٱلْفُجَّارَ لَفِى جَحِيمٍ ۝ يَصْلَوْنَهَا يَوْمَ ٱلدِّينِ ۝ وَمَا هُمْ عَنْهَا بِغَآئِبِينَ ۝ وَمَآ أَدْرَىٰكَ مَا يَوْمُ ٱلدِّينِ ۝ ثُمَّ مَآ أَدْرَىٰكَ مَا يَوْمُ ٱلدِّينِ ۝ يَوْمَ لَا تَمْلِكُ نَفْسٌ لِّنَفْسٍ شَيْـًٔا

وَٱلْأَمْرُ يَوْمَئِذٍ لِّلَّهِ ۩

(Al-Infitar 001-019)

Chapter (Surah) 83: Al-Mutaffifeen
001-036

بِسْمِ ٱللَّهِ ٱلرَّحْمَٰنِ ٱلرَّحِيمِ

﴿ وَيْلٌ لِّلْمُطَفِّفِينَ ۝ ٱلَّذِينَ إِذَا ٱكْتَالُوا۟ عَلَى ٱلنَّاسِ يَسْتَوْفُونَ ۝ وَإِذَا كَالُوهُمْ أَو وَّزَنُوهُمْ يُخْسِرُونَ ۝ أَلَا يَظُنُّ أُو۟لَٰٓئِكَ أَنَّهُم مَّبْعُوثُونَ ۝ لِيَوْمٍ عَظِيمٍ ۝ يَوْمَ يَقُومُ ٱلنَّاسُ لِرَبِّ ٱلْعَٰلَمِينَ ۝ كَلَّآ إِنَّ كِتَٰبَ ٱلْفُجَّارِ لَفِى سِجِّينٍ ۝ وَمَآ أَدْرَىٰكَ مَا سِجِّينٌ ۝ كِتَٰبٌ مَّرْقُومٌ ۝ وَيْلٌ يَوْمَئِذٍ لِّلْمُكَذِّبِينَ ۝ ٱلَّذِينَ يُكَذِّبُونَ بِيَوْمِ ٱلدِّينِ ۝ وَمَا يُكَذِّبُ بِهِۦٓ إِلَّا كُلُّ مُعْتَدٍ أَثِيمٍ ۝ إِذَا تُتْلَىٰ عَلَيْهِ ءَايَٰتُنَا قَالَ أَسَٰطِيرُ ٱلْأَوَّلِينَ ۝ كَلَّا ۖ بَلْ ۜ رَانَ عَلَىٰ قُلُوبِهِم مَّا كَانُوا۟ يَكْسِبُونَ ۝ كَلَّآ إِنَّهُمْ عَن رَّبِّهِمْ يَوْمَئِذٍ لَّمَحْجُوبُونَ ۝ ثُمَّ إِنَّهُمْ لَصَالُوا۟ ٱلْجَحِيمِ ۝ ثُمَّ يُقَالُ هَٰذَا ٱلَّذِى كُنتُم بِهِۦ تُكَذِّبُونَ ۝ كَلَّآ إِنَّ كِتَٰبَ ٱلْأَبْرَارِ لَفِى عِلِّيِّينَ ۝ وَمَآ أَدْرَىٰكَ مَا عِلِّيُّونَ ۝ كِتَٰبٌ مَّرْقُومٌ ۝ يَشْهَدُهُ ٱلْمُقَرَّبُونَ ۝ إِنَّ ٱلْأَبْرَارَ لَفِى نَعِيمٍ ۝ عَلَى ٱلْأَرَآئِكِ يَنظُرُونَ ۝ تَعْرِفُ فِى وُجُوهِهِمْ نَضْرَةَ ٱلنَّعِيمِ ۝ يُسْقَوْنَ مِن رَّحِيقٍ مَّخْتُومٍ ۝ خِتَٰمُهُۥ مِسْكٌ ۚ وَفِى ذَٰلِكَ فَلْيَتَنَافَسِ ٱلْمُتَنَٰفِسُونَ ۝ وَمِزَاجُهُۥ مِن تَسْنِيمٍ ۝ عَيْنًا يَشْرَبُ بِهَا ٱلْمُقَرَّبُونَ ۝ إِنَّ ٱلَّذِينَ أَجْرَمُوا۟ كَانُوا۟ مِنَ ٱلَّذِينَ ءَامَنُوا۟ يَضْحَكُونَ ۝ وَإِذَا مَرُّوا۟ بِهِمْ يَتَغَامَزُونَ ۝ وَإِذَا ٱنقَلَبُوٓا۟ إِلَىٰٓ أَهْلِهِمُ ٱنقَلَبُوا۟ فَكِهِينَ ۝ وَإِذَا رَأَوْهُمْ قَالُوٓا۟ إِنَّ هَٰٓؤُلَآءِ لَضَآلُّونَ ۝ وَمَآ أُرْسِلُوا۟ عَلَيْهِمْ حَٰفِظِينَ ۝ فَٱلْيَوْمَ ٱلَّذِينَ ءَامَنُوا۟ مِنَ ٱلْكُفَّارِ يَضْحَكُونَ ۝ عَلَى ٱلْأَرَآئِكِ يَنظُرُونَ ۝ هَلْ ثُوِّبَ ٱلْكُفَّارُ مَا كَانُوا۟ يَفْعَلُونَ ۝ ﴾

(Al-Mutaffifeen 001-036)

Chapter (Surah) 84: Al-Inshiqaq 001-025

بِسْمِ ٱللَّهِ ٱلرَّحْمَٰنِ ٱلرَّحِيمِ

﴿ إِذَا ٱلسَّمَآءُ ٱنشَقَّتْ ۝ وَأَذِنَتْ لِرَبِّهَا وَحُقَّتْ ۝ وَإِذَا ٱلْأَرْضُ مُدَّتْ ۝ وَأَلْقَتْ مَا فِيهَا وَتَخَلَّتْ ۝ وَأَذِنَتْ لِرَبِّهَا وَحُقَّتْ ۝ يَٰٓأَيُّهَا ٱلْإِنسَٰنُ إِنَّكَ كَادِحٌ إِلَىٰ رَبِّكَ كَدْحًا فَمُلَٰقِيهِ ۝ فَأَمَّا مَنْ أُوتِىَ كِتَٰبَهُۥ بِيَمِينِهِۦ ۝ فَسَوْفَ يُحَاسَبُ حِسَابًا يَسِيرًا ۝ وَيَنقَلِبُ إِلَىٰٓ أَهْلِهِۦ مَسْرُورًا ۝ وَأَمَّا مَنْ أُوتِىَ كِتَٰبَهُۥ وَرَآءَ ظَهْرِهِۦ ۝ فَسَوْفَ يَدْعُواْ ثُبُورًا ۝ وَيَصْلَىٰ سَعِيرًا ۝ إِنَّهُۥ كَانَ فِىٓ أَهْلِهِۦ مَسْرُورًا ۝ إِنَّهُۥ ظَنَّ أَن لَّن يَحُورَ ۝ بَلَىٰٓ إِنَّ رَبَّهُۥ كَانَ بِهِۦ بَصِيرًا ۝ فَلَآ أُقْسِمُ بِٱلشَّفَقِ ۝ وَٱلَّيْلِ وَمَا وَسَقَ ۝ وَٱلْقَمَرِ إِذَا ٱتَّسَقَ ۝ لَتَرْكَبُنَّ طَبَقًا عَن طَبَقٍ ۝ فَمَا لَهُمْ لَا يُؤْمِنُونَ ۝ وَإِذَا قُرِئَ عَلَيْهِمُ ٱلْقُرْءَانُ لَا يَسْجُدُونَ ۩ ۝ بَلِ ٱلَّذِينَ كَفَرُواْ يُكَذِّبُونَ ۝ وَٱللَّهُ أَعْلَمُ بِمَا يُوعُونَ ۝ فَبَشِّرْهُم بِعَذَابٍ أَلِيمٍ ۝ إِلَّا ٱلَّذِينَ ءَامَنُواْ وَعَمِلُواْ ٱلصَّٰلِحَٰتِ لَهُمْ أَجْرٌ غَيْرُ مَمْنُونٍ ۝ ﴾

(Al-Inshiqaq 001-025)

Chapter (Surah) 85: Al-Buruj 001-022

بِسْمِ ٱللَّهِ ٱلرَّحْمَٰنِ ٱلرَّحِيمِ

﴿ وَٱلسَّمَآءِ ذَاتِ ٱلْبُرُوجِ ۝ وَٱلْيَوْمِ ٱلْمَوْعُودِ ۝ وَشَاهِدٍ وَمَشْهُودٍ ۝ قُتِلَ أَصْحَٰبُ ٱلْأُخْدُودِ ۝ ٱلنَّارِ ذَاتِ ٱلْوَقُودِ ۝ إِذْ هُمْ عَلَيْهَا قُعُودٌ ۝ وَهُمْ عَلَىٰ مَا يَفْعَلُونَ بِٱلْمُؤْمِنِينَ شُهُودٌ ۝ وَمَا نَقَمُواْ مِنْهُمْ إِلَّآ أَن يُؤْمِنُواْ بِٱللَّهِ ٱلْعَزِيزِ ٱلْحَمِيدِ ۝ ٱلَّذِى لَهُۥ مُلْكُ ٱلسَّمَٰوَٰتِ وَٱلْأَرْضِ وَٱللَّهُ عَلَىٰ كُلِّ شَىْءٍ شَهِيدٌ

Juz' 30 (Part 30): An Nabaa (The Tidings) 1 - An Nas (Mankind) 6   7

﴿ إِنَّ ٱلَّذِينَ فَتَنُوا۟ ٱلْمُؤْمِنِينَ وَٱلْمُؤْمِنَـٰتِ ثُمَّ لَمْ يَتُوبُوا۟ فَلَهُمْ عَذَابُ جَهَنَّمَ وَلَهُمْ عَذَابُ ٱلْحَرِيقِ ۝ إِنَّ ٱلَّذِينَ ءَامَنُوا۟ وَعَمِلُوا۟ ٱلصَّـٰلِحَـٰتِ لَهُمْ جَنَّـٰتٌ تَجْرِى مِن تَحْتِهَا ٱلْأَنْهَـٰرُ ذَٰلِكَ ٱلْفَوْزُ ٱلْكَبِيرُ ۝ إِنَّ بَطْشَ رَبِّكَ لَشَدِيدٌ ۝ إِنَّهُۥ هُوَ يُبْدِئُ وَيُعِيدُ ۝ وَهُوَ ٱلْغَفُورُ ٱلْوَدُودُ ۝ ذُو ٱلْعَرْشِ ٱلْمَجِيدُ ۝ فَعَّالٌ لِّمَا يُرِيدُ ۝ هَلْ أَتَىٰكَ حَدِيثُ ٱلْجُنُودِ ۝ فِرْعَوْنَ وَثَمُودَ ۝ بَلِ ٱلَّذِينَ كَفَرُوا۟ فِى تَكْذِيبٍ ۝ وَٱللَّهُ مِن وَرَآئِهِم مُّحِيطٌۢ ۝ بَلْ هُوَ قُرْءَانٌ مَّجِيدٌ ۝ فِى لَوْحٍ مَّحْفُوظٍۭ ۝ ﴾

(Al-Buruj 001-022)

Chapter (Surah) 86: At-Tariq 001-017

﴿ وَٱلسَّمَآءِ وَٱلطَّارِقِ ۝ وَمَآ أَدْرَىٰكَ مَا ٱلطَّارِقُ ۝ ٱلنَّجْمُ ٱلثَّاقِبُ ۝ إِن كُلُّ نَفْسٍ لَّمَّا عَلَيْهَا حَافِظٌ ۝ فَلْيَنظُرِ ٱلْإِنسَـٰنُ مِمَّ خُلِقَ ۝ خُلِقَ مِن مَّآءٍ دَافِقٍ ۝ يَخْرُجُ مِنۢ بَيْنِ ٱلصُّلْبِ وَٱلتَّرَآئِبِ ۝ إِنَّهُۥ عَلَىٰ رَجْعِهِۦ لَقَادِرٌ ۝ يَوْمَ تُبْلَى ٱلسَّرَآئِرُ ۝ فَمَا لَهُۥ مِن قُوَّةٍ وَلَا نَاصِرٍ ۝ وَٱلسَّمَآءِ ذَاتِ ٱلرَّجْعِ ۝ وَٱلْأَرْضِ ذَاتِ ٱلصَّدْعِ ۝ إِنَّهُۥ لَقَوْلٌ فَصْلٌ ۝ وَمَا هُوَ بِٱلْهَزْلِ ۝ إِنَّهُمْ يَكِيدُونَ كَيْدًا ۝ وَأَكِيدُ كَيْدًا ۝ فَمَهِّلِ ٱلْكَـٰفِرِينَ أَمْهِلْهُمْ رُوَيْدًۢا ۝ ﴾

(At-Tariq 001-017)

Chapter (Surah) 87: Al-A'la 001-019

﴿ سَبِّحِ ٱسْمَ رَبِّكَ ٱلْأَعْلَى ۝ ٱلَّذِى خَلَقَ فَسَوَّىٰ ۝ وَٱلَّذِى قَدَّرَ فَهَدَىٰ ۝

وَٱلَّذِىٓ أَخْرَجَ ٱلْمَرْعَىٰ ۝ فَجَعَلَهُۥ غُثَآءً أَحْوَىٰ ۝ سَنُقْرِئُكَ فَلَا تَنسَىٰٓ ۝ إِلَّا مَا شَآءَ ٱللَّهُ ۚ إِنَّهُۥ يَعْلَمُ ٱلْجَهْرَ وَمَا يَخْفَىٰ ۝ وَنُيَسِّرُكَ لِلْيُسْرَىٰ ۝ فَذَكِّرْ إِن نَّفَعَتِ ٱلذِّكْرَىٰ ۝ سَيَذَّكَّرُ مَن يَخْشَىٰ ۝ وَيَتَجَنَّبُهَا ٱلْأَشْقَى ۝ ٱلَّذِى يَصْلَى ٱلنَّارَ ٱلْكُبْرَىٰ ۝ ثُمَّ لَا يَمُوتُ فِيهَا وَلَا يَحْيَىٰ ۝ قَدْ أَفْلَحَ مَن تَزَكَّىٰ ۝ وَذَكَرَ ٱسْمَ رَبِّهِۦ فَصَلَّىٰ ۝ بَلْ تُؤْثِرُونَ ٱلْحَيَوٰةَ ٱلدُّنْيَا ۝ وَٱلْآخِرَةُ خَيْرٌ وَأَبْقَىٰٓ ۝ إِنَّ هَٰذَا لَفِى ٱلصُّحُفِ ٱلْأُولَىٰ ۝ صُحُفِ إِبْرَٰهِيمَ وَمُوسَىٰ ۝

(Al-A'la 001-019)

Chapter (Surah) 88: Al-Gashiya 001-026

بِسْمِ ٱللَّهِ ٱلرَّحْمَٰنِ ٱلرَّحِيمِ

هَلْ أَتَىٰكَ حَدِيثُ ٱلْغَٰشِيَةِ ۝ وُجُوهٌ يَوْمَئِذٍ خَٰشِعَةٌ ۝ عَامِلَةٌ نَّاصِبَةٌ ۝ تَصْلَىٰ نَارًا حَامِيَةً ۝ تُسْقَىٰ مِنْ عَيْنٍ ءَانِيَةٍ ۝ لَّيْسَ لَهُمْ طَعَامٌ إِلَّا مِن ضَرِيعٍ ۝ لَّا يُسْمِنُ وَلَا يُغْنِى مِن جُوعٍ ۝ وُجُوهٌ يَوْمَئِذٍ نَّاعِمَةٌ ۝ لِّسَعْيِهَا رَاضِيَةٌ ۝ فِى جَنَّةٍ عَالِيَةٍ ۝ لَّا تَسْمَعُ فِيهَا لَٰغِيَةً ۝ فِيهَا عَيْنٌ جَارِيَةٌ ۝ فِيهَا سُرُرٌ مَّرْفُوعَةٌ ۝ وَأَكْوَابٌ مَّوْضُوعَةٌ ۝ وَنَمَارِقُ مَصْفُوفَةٌ ۝ وَزَرَابِىُّ مَبْثُوثَةٌ ۝ أَفَلَا يَنظُرُونَ إِلَى ٱلْإِبِلِ كَيْفَ خُلِقَتْ ۝ وَإِلَى ٱلسَّمَآءِ كَيْفَ رُفِعَتْ ۝ وَإِلَى ٱلْجِبَالِ كَيْفَ نُصِبَتْ ۝ وَإِلَى ٱلْأَرْضِ كَيْفَ سُطِحَتْ ۝ فَذَكِّرْ إِنَّمَآ أَنتَ مُذَكِّرٌ ۝ لَّسْتَ عَلَيْهِم بِمُصَيْطِرٍ ۝ إِلَّا مَن تَوَلَّىٰ وَكَفَرَ ۝ فَيُعَذِّبُهُ ٱللَّهُ ٱلْعَذَابَ ٱلْأَكْبَرَ ۝ إِنَّ إِلَيْنَآ إِيَابَهُمْ ۝ ثُمَّ إِنَّ عَلَيْنَا حِسَابَهُم ۝

(Al-Gashiya 001-026)

Chapter (Surah) 89: Al-Fajr 001-030

بِسْمِ ٱللَّهِ ٱلرَّحْمَٰنِ ٱلرَّحِيمِ

وَٱلْفَجْرِ ۝ وَلَيَالٍ عَشْرٍ ۝ وَٱلشَّفْعِ وَٱلْوَتْرِ ۝ وَٱلَّيْلِ إِذَا يَسْرِ ۝ هَلْ فِى

ذَٰلِكَ قَسَمٌ لِّذِى حِجْرٍ ۝ أَلَمْ تَرَ كَيْفَ فَعَلَ رَبُّكَ بِعَادٍ ۝ إِرَمَ ذَاتِ ٱلْعِمَادِ ۝ ٱلَّتِى لَمْ يُخْلَقْ مِثْلُهَا فِى ٱلْبِلَٰدِ ۝ وَثَمُودَ ٱلَّذِينَ جَابُوا۟ ٱلصَّخْرَ بِٱلْوَادِ ۝ وَفِرْعَوْنَ ذِى ٱلْأَوْتَادِ ۝ ٱلَّذِينَ طَغَوْا۟ فِى ٱلْبِلَٰدِ ۝ فَأَكْثَرُوا۟ فِيهَا ٱلْفَسَادَ ۝ فَصَبَّ عَلَيْهِمْ رَبُّكَ سَوْطَ عَذَابٍ ۝ إِنَّ رَبَّكَ لَبِٱلْمِرْصَادِ ۝ فَأَمَّا ٱلْإِنسَٰنُ إِذَا مَا ٱبْتَلَىٰهُ رَبُّهُ فَأَكْرَمَهُ وَنَعَّمَهُ فَيَقُولُ رَبِّى أَكْرَمَنِ ۝ وَأَمَّآ إِذَا مَا ٱبْتَلَىٰهُ فَقَدَرَ عَلَيْهِ رِزْقَهُ فَيَقُولُ رَبِّى أَهَٰنَنِ ۝ كَلَّا ۖ بَل لَّا تُكْرِمُونَ ٱلْيَتِيمَ ۝ وَلَا تَحَٰٓضُّونَ عَلَىٰ طَعَامِ ٱلْمِسْكِينِ ۝ وَتَأْكُلُونَ ٱلتُّرَاثَ أَكْلًا لَّمًّا ۝ وَتُحِبُّونَ ٱلْمَالَ حُبًّا جَمًّا ۝ كَلَّآ إِذَا دُكَّتِ ٱلْأَرْضُ دَكًّا دَكًّا ۝ وَجَآءَ رَبُّكَ وَٱلْمَلَكُ صَفًّا صَفًّا ۝ وَجِا۟ىٓءَ يَوْمَئِذٍۭ بِجَهَنَّمَ ۚ يَوْمَئِذٍ يَتَذَكَّرُ ٱلْإِنسَٰنُ وَأَنَّىٰ لَهُ ٱلذِّكْرَىٰ ۝ يَقُولُ يَٰلَيْتَنِى قَدَّمْتُ لِحَيَاتِى ۝ فَيَوْمَئِذٍ لَّا يُعَذِّبُ عَذَابَهُۥٓ أَحَدٌ ۝ وَلَا يُوثِقُ وَثَاقَهُۥٓ أَحَدٌ ۝ يَٰٓأَيَّتُهَا ٱلنَّفْسُ ٱلْمُطْمَئِنَّةُ ۝ ٱرْجِعِىٓ إِلَىٰ رَبِّكِ رَاضِيَةً مَّرْضِيَّةً ۝ فَٱدْخُلِى فِى عِبَٰدِى ۝ وَٱدْخُلِى جَنَّتِى ۝

(Al-Fajr 001-030)

Chapter (Surah) 90: Al-Balad 001-020

بِسْمِ ٱللَّهِ ٱلرَّحْمَٰنِ ٱلرَّحِيمِ

﴿ لَآ أُقْسِمُ بِهَٰذَا ٱلْبَلَدِ ۝ وَأَنتَ حِلٌّۢ بِهَٰذَا ٱلْبَلَدِ ۝ وَوَالِدٍ وَمَا وَلَدَ ۝ لَقَدْ خَلَقْنَا ٱلْإِنسَٰنَ فِى كَبَدٍ ۝ أَيَحْسَبُ أَن لَّن يَقْدِرَ عَلَيْهِ أَحَدٌ ۝ يَقُولُ أَهْلَكْتُ مَالًا لُّبَدًا ۝ أَيَحْسَبُ أَن لَّمْ يَرَهُۥٓ أَحَدٌ ۝ أَلَمْ نَجْعَل لَّهُۥ عَيْنَيْنِ ۝ وَلِسَانًا وَشَفَتَيْنِ ۝ وَهَدَيْنَٰهُ ٱلنَّجْدَيْنِ ۝ فَلَا ٱقْتَحَمَ ٱلْعَقَبَةَ ۝ وَمَآ أَدْرَىٰكَ مَا ٱلْعَقَبَةُ ۝ فَكُّ رَقَبَةٍ ۝ أَوْ إِطْعَٰمٌ فِى يَوْمٍ ذِى مَسْغَبَةٍ ۝ يَتِيمًا ذَا مَقْرَبَةٍ

﴿ أَوْ مِسْكِينًا ذَا مَتْرَبَةٍ ۝ ثُمَّ كَانَ مِنَ ٱلَّذِينَ ءَامَنُوا۟ وَتَوَاصَوْا۟ بِٱلصَّبْرِ وَتَوَاصَوْا۟ بِٱلْمَرْحَمَةِ ۝ أُو۟لَٰٓئِكَ أَصْحَٰبُ ٱلْمَيْمَنَةِ ۝ وَٱلَّذِينَ كَفَرُوا۟ بِـَٔايَٰتِنَا هُمْ أَصْحَٰبُ ٱلْمَشْـَٔمَةِ ۝ عَلَيْهِمْ نَارٌ مُّؤْصَدَةٌۢ ۝ ﴾

(Al-Balad 001-020)

Chapter (Surah) 91: Ash-Shams 001-015

بِسْمِ ٱللَّهِ ٱلرَّحْمَٰنِ ٱلرَّحِيمِ

﴿ وَٱلشَّمْسِ وَضُحَىٰهَا ۝ وَٱلْقَمَرِ إِذَا تَلَىٰهَا ۝ وَٱلنَّهَارِ إِذَا جَلَّىٰهَا ۝ وَٱلَّيْلِ إِذَا يَغْشَىٰهَا ۝ وَٱلسَّمَآءِ وَمَا بَنَىٰهَا ۝ وَٱلْأَرْضِ وَمَا طَحَىٰهَا ۝ وَنَفْسٍ وَمَا سَوَّىٰهَا ۝ فَأَلْهَمَهَا فُجُورَهَا وَتَقْوَىٰهَا ۝ قَدْ أَفْلَحَ مَن زَكَّىٰهَا ۝ وَقَدْ خَابَ مَن دَسَّىٰهَا ۝ كَذَّبَتْ ثَمُودُ بِطَغْوَىٰهَآ ۝ إِذِ ٱنۢبَعَثَ أَشْقَىٰهَا ۝ فَقَالَ لَهُمْ رَسُولُ ٱللَّهِ نَاقَةَ ٱللَّهِ وَسُقْيَٰهَا ۝ فَكَذَّبُوهُ فَعَقَرُوهَا فَدَمْدَمَ عَلَيْهِمْ رَبُّهُم بِذَنۢبِهِمْ فَسَوَّىٰهَا ۝ وَلَا يَخَافُ عُقْبَٰهَا ۝ ﴾

(Ash-Shams 001-015)

Chapter (Surah) 92: Al-Lail 001-021

بِسْمِ ٱللَّهِ ٱلرَّحْمَٰنِ ٱلرَّحِيمِ

﴿ وَٱلَّيْلِ إِذَا يَغْشَىٰ ۝ وَٱلنَّهَارِ إِذَا تَجَلَّىٰ ۝ وَمَا خَلَقَ ٱلذَّكَرَ وَٱلْأُنثَىٰٓ ۝ إِنَّ سَعْيَكُمْ لَشَتَّىٰ ۝ فَأَمَّا مَنْ أَعْطَىٰ وَٱتَّقَىٰ ۝ وَصَدَّقَ بِٱلْحُسْنَىٰ ۝ فَسَنُيَسِّرُهُۥ لِلْيُسْرَىٰ ۝ وَأَمَّا مَنۢ بَخِلَ وَٱسْتَغْنَىٰ ۝ وَكَذَّبَ بِٱلْحُسْنَىٰ ۝ فَسَنُيَسِّرُهُۥ لِلْعُسْرَىٰ ۝ وَمَا يُغْنِى عَنْهُ مَالُهُۥٓ إِذَا تَرَدَّىٰٓ ۝ إِنَّ عَلَيْنَا لَلْهُدَىٰ ۝ وَإِنَّ لَنَا لَلْـَٔاخِرَةَ وَٱلْأُولَىٰ ۝ فَأَنذَرْتُكُمْ نَارًا تَلَظَّىٰ ۝ لَا يَصْلَىٰهَآ إِلَّا ٱلْأَشْقَى ۝ ٱلَّذِى كَذَّبَ وَتَوَلَّىٰ ۝ وَسَيُجَنَّبُهَا ٱلْأَتْقَى ۝ ٱلَّذِى يُؤْتِى مَالَهُۥ يَتَزَكَّىٰ ۝ وَمَا

لِأَحَدٍ عِندَهُۥ مِن نِّعْمَةٍ تُجْزَىٰٓ ۝ إِلَّا ٱبْتِغَآءَ وَجْهِ رَبِّهِ ٱلْأَعْلَىٰ ۝ وَلَسَوْفَ يَرْضَىٰ ۝

(Al-Lail 001-021)

Chapter (Surah) 93: Ad-Dhuha 001-011

بِسْمِ ٱللَّهِ ٱلرَّحْمَٰنِ ٱلرَّحِيمِ

﴿ وَٱلضُّحَىٰ ۝ وَٱلَّيْلِ إِذَا سَجَىٰ ۝ مَا وَدَّعَكَ رَبُّكَ وَمَا قَلَىٰ ۝ وَلَلْءَاخِرَةُ خَيْرٌ لَّكَ مِنَ ٱلْأُولَىٰ ۝ وَلَسَوْفَ يُعْطِيكَ رَبُّكَ فَتَرْضَىٰٓ ۝ أَلَمْ يَجِدْكَ يَتِيمًا فَـَٔاوَىٰ ۝ وَوَجَدَكَ ضَآلًّا فَهَدَىٰ ۝ وَوَجَدَكَ عَآئِلًا فَأَغْنَىٰ ۝ فَأَمَّا ٱلْيَتِيمَ فَلَا تَقْهَرْ ۝ وَأَمَّا ٱلسَّآئِلَ فَلَا تَنْهَرْ ۝ وَأَمَّا بِنِعْمَةِ رَبِّكَ فَحَدِّثْ ۝ ﴾

(Adh-Dhuha 001-011)

Chapter (Surah) 94: Al-Sharh 001-008

بِسْمِ ٱللَّهِ ٱلرَّحْمَٰنِ ٱلرَّحِيمِ

﴿ أَلَمْ نَشْرَحْ لَكَ صَدْرَكَ ۝ وَوَضَعْنَا عَنكَ وِزْرَكَ ۝ ٱلَّذِىٓ أَنقَضَ ظَهْرَكَ ۝ وَرَفَعْنَا لَكَ ذِكْرَكَ ۝ فَإِنَّ مَعَ ٱلْعُسْرِ يُسْرًا ۝ إِنَّ مَعَ ٱلْعُسْرِ يُسْرًا ۝ فَإِذَا فَرَغْتَ فَٱنصَبْ ۝ وَإِلَىٰ رَبِّكَ فَٱرْغَب ۝ ﴾

(Al-Sharh 001-008)

Chapter (Surah) 95: At-Tin 001-008

بِسْمِ ٱللَّهِ ٱلرَّحْمَٰنِ ٱلرَّحِيمِ

﴿ وَٱلتِّينِ وَٱلزَّيْتُونِ ۝ وَطُورِ سِينِينَ ۝ وَهَٰذَا ٱلْبَلَدِ ٱلْأَمِينِ ۝ لَقَدْ خَلَقْنَا ٱلْإِنسَٰنَ فِىٓ أَحْسَنِ تَقْوِيمٍ ۝ ثُمَّ رَدَدْنَٰهُ أَسْفَلَ سَٰفِلِينَ ۝ إِلَّا ٱلَّذِينَ ءَامَنُوا۟ وَعَمِلُوا۟ ٱلصَّٰلِحَٰتِ فَلَهُمْ أَجْرٌ غَيْرُ مَمْنُونٍ ۝ فَمَا يُكَذِّبُكَ بَعْدُ بِٱلدِّينِ

﴿ أَلَيْسَ ٱللَّهُ بِأَحْكَمِ ٱلْحَٰكِمِينَ ۝ ﴾

(At-Tin 001-008)

Chapter (Surah) 96: Al-'Alaq 001-019

بِسْمِ ٱللَّهِ ٱلرَّحْمَٰنِ ٱلرَّحِيمِ

﴿ ٱقْرَأْ بِٱسْمِ رَبِّكَ ٱلَّذِى خَلَقَ ۝ خَلَقَ ٱلْإِنسَٰنَ مِنْ عَلَقٍ ۝ ٱقْرَأْ وَرَبُّكَ ٱلْأَكْرَمُ ۝ ٱلَّذِى عَلَّمَ بِٱلْقَلَمِ ۝ عَلَّمَ ٱلْإِنسَٰنَ مَا لَمْ يَعْلَمْ ۝ كَلَّآ إِنَّ ٱلْإِنسَٰنَ لَيَطْغَىٰٓ ۝ أَن رَّءَاهُ ٱسْتَغْنَىٰٓ ۝ إِنَّ إِلَىٰ رَبِّكَ ٱلرُّجْعَىٰٓ ۝ أَرَءَيْتَ ٱلَّذِى يَنْهَىٰ ۝ عَبْدًا إِذَا صَلَّىٰٓ ۝ أَرَءَيْتَ إِن كَانَ عَلَى ٱلْهُدَىٰٓ ۝ أَوْ أَمَرَ بِٱلتَّقْوَىٰٓ ۝ أَرَءَيْتَ إِن كَذَّبَ وَتَوَلَّىٰٓ ۝ أَلَمْ يَعْلَم بِأَنَّ ٱللَّهَ يَرَىٰ ۝ كَلَّا لَئِن لَّمْ يَنتَهِ لَنَسْفَعًۢا بِٱلنَّاصِيَةِ ۝ نَاصِيَةٍ كَٰذِبَةٍ خَاطِئَةٍ ۝ فَلْيَدْعُ نَادِيَهُۥ ۝ سَنَدْعُ ٱلزَّبَانِيَةَ ۝ كَلَّا لَا تُطِعْهُ وَٱسْجُدْ وَٱقْتَرِب ۩ ۝ ﴾

(Al-'Alaq 001-019)

Chapter (Surah) 97: Al-Qadr 001-05

بِسْمِ ٱللَّهِ ٱلرَّحْمَٰنِ ٱلرَّحِيمِ

﴿ إِنَّآ أَنزَلْنَٰهُ فِى لَيْلَةِ ٱلْقَدْرِ ۝ وَمَآ أَدْرَىٰكَ مَا لَيْلَةُ ٱلْقَدْرِ ۝ لَيْلَةُ ٱلْقَدْرِ خَيْرٌ مِّنْ أَلْفِ شَهْرٍ ۝ تَنَزَّلُ ٱلْمَلَٰٓئِكَةُ وَٱلرُّوحُ فِيهَا بِإِذْنِ رَبِّهِم مِّن كُلِّ أَمْرٍ ۝ سَلَٰمٌ هِىَ حَتَّىٰ مَطْلَعِ ٱلْفَجْرِ ۝ ﴾

(Al-Qadr 001-005)

Chapter (Surah) 98: Al-Baiyina 001-08

بِسْمِ ٱللَّهِ ٱلرَّحْمَٰنِ ٱلرَّحِيمِ

﴿ لَمْ يَكُنِ ٱلَّذِينَ كَفَرُوا۟ مِنْ أَهْلِ ٱلْكِتَٰبِ وَٱلْمُشْرِكِينَ مُنفَكِّينَ حَتَّىٰ تَأْتِيَهُمُ

۩ ٱلۡبَيِّنَةُ ۞ رَسُولٞ مِّنَ ٱللَّهِ يَتۡلُواْ صُحُفٗا مُّطَهَّرَةٗ ۞ فِيهَا كُتُبٞ قَيِّمَةٞ ۞ وَمَا تَفَرَّقَ ٱلَّذِينَ أُوتُواْ ٱلۡكِتَٰبَ إِلَّا مِنۢ بَعۡدِ مَا جَآءَتۡهُمُ ٱلۡبَيِّنَةُ ۞ وَمَآ أُمِرُوٓاْ إِلَّا لِيَعۡبُدُواْ ٱللَّهَ مُخۡلِصِينَ لَهُ ٱلدِّينَ حُنَفَآءَ وَيُقِيمُواْ ٱلصَّلَوٰةَ وَيُؤۡتُواْ ٱلزَّكَوٰةَۚ وَذَٰلِكَ دِينُ ٱلۡقَيِّمَةِ ۞ إِنَّ ٱلَّذِينَ كَفَرُواْ مِنۡ أَهۡلِ ٱلۡكِتَٰبِ وَٱلۡمُشۡرِكِينَ فِي نَارِ جَهَنَّمَ خَٰلِدِينَ فِيهَآۚ أُوْلَٰٓئِكَ هُمۡ شَرُّ ٱلۡبَرِيَّةِ ۞ إِنَّ ٱلَّذِينَ ءَامَنُواْ وَعَمِلُواْ ٱلصَّٰلِحَٰتِ أُوْلَٰٓئِكَ هُمۡ خَيۡرُ ٱلۡبَرِيَّةِ ۞ جَزَآؤُهُمۡ عِندَ رَبِّهِمۡ جَنَّٰتُ عَدۡنٖ تَجۡرِي مِن تَحۡتِهَا ٱلۡأَنۡهَٰرُ خَٰلِدِينَ فِيهَآ أَبَدٗاۖ رَّضِيَ ٱللَّهُ عَنۡهُمۡ وَرَضُواْ عَنۡهُۚ ذَٰلِكَ لِمَنۡ خَشِيَ رَبَّهُۥ ۞

(Al-Baiyina 001-008)

Chapter (Surah) 99: Al-Zalzalah 001-008

بِسۡمِ ٱللَّهِ ٱلرَّحۡمَٰنِ ٱلرَّحِيمِ

۩ إِذَا زُلۡزِلَتِ ٱلۡأَرۡضُ زِلۡزَالَهَا ۞ وَأَخۡرَجَتِ ٱلۡأَرۡضُ أَثۡقَالَهَا ۞ وَقَالَ ٱلۡإِنسَٰنُ مَا لَهَا ۞ يَوۡمَئِذٖ تُحَدِّثُ أَخۡبَارَهَا ۞ بِأَنَّ رَبَّكَ أَوۡحَىٰ لَهَا ۞ يَوۡمَئِذٖ يَصۡدُرُ ٱلنَّاسُ أَشۡتَاتٗا لِّيُرَوۡاْ أَعۡمَٰلَهُمۡ ۞ فَمَن يَعۡمَلۡ مِثۡقَالَ ذَرَّةٍ خَيۡرٗا يَرَهُۥ ۞ وَمَن يَعۡمَلۡ مِثۡقَالَ ذَرَّةٖ شَرّٗا يَرَهُۥ ۞

(Al-Zalzalah 001-008)

Chapter (Surah) 100: Al-'Adiyat 001-011

بِسۡمِ ٱللَّهِ ٱلرَّحۡمَٰنِ ٱلرَّحِيمِ

۩ وَٱلۡعَٰدِيَٰتِ ضَبۡحٗا ۞ فَٱلۡمُورِيَٰتِ قَدۡحٗا ۞ فَٱلۡمُغِيرَٰتِ صُبۡحٗا ۞ فَأَثَرۡنَ بِهِۦ نَقۡعٗا ۞ فَوَسَطۡنَ بِهِۦ جَمۡعًا ۞ إِنَّ ٱلۡإِنسَٰنَ لِرَبِّهِۦ لَكَنُودٞ ۞ وَإِنَّهُۥ عَلَىٰ ذَٰلِكَ لَشَهِيدٞ ۞ وَإِنَّهُۥ لِحُبِّ ٱلۡخَيۡرِ لَشَدِيدٌ ۞ أَفَلَا يَعۡلَمُ إِذَا بُعۡثِرَ مَا فِي ٱلۡقُبُورِ ۞ وَحُصِّلَ مَا فِي ٱلصُّدُورِ ۞ إِنَّ رَبَّهُم بِهِمۡ يَوۡمَئِذٖ لَّخَبِيرُۢ ۞

(Al-'Adiyat 001-011)

Chapter (Surah) 101: Al-Qari'a 001-011

بِسْمِ اللَّهِ الرَّحْمَنِ الرَّحِيمِ

﴿ ٱلْقَارِعَةُ ۝ مَا ٱلْقَارِعَةُ ۝ وَمَآ أَدْرَىٰكَ مَا ٱلْقَارِعَةُ ۝ يَوْمَ يَكُونُ ٱلنَّاسُ كَٱلْفَرَاشِ ٱلْمَبْثُوثِ ۝ وَتَكُونُ ٱلْجِبَالُ كَٱلْعِهْنِ ٱلْمَنفُوشِ ۝ فَأَمَّا مَن ثَقُلَتْ مَوَٰزِينُهُ ۝ فَهُوَ فِى عِيشَةٍ رَّاضِيَةٍ ۝ وَأَمَّا مَنْ خَفَّتْ مَوَٰزِينُهُ ۝ فَأُمُّهُ هَاوِيَةٌ ۝ وَمَآ أَدْرَىٰكَ مَا هِيَهْ ۝ نَارٌ حَامِيَةٌ ۝ ﴾

(Al-Qari'a 001-011)

Chapter (Surah) 102: At-Takathur 001-008

بِسْمِ اللَّهِ الرَّحْمَنِ الرَّحِيمِ

﴿ أَلْهَىٰكُمُ ٱلتَّكَاثُرُ ۝ حَتَّىٰ زُرْتُمُ ٱلْمَقَابِرَ ۝ كَلَّا سَوْفَ تَعْلَمُونَ ۝ ثُمَّ كَلَّا سَوْفَ تَعْلَمُونَ ۝ كَلَّا لَوْ تَعْلَمُونَ عِلْمَ ٱلْيَقِينِ ۝ لَتَرَوُنَّ ٱلْجَحِيمَ ۝ ثُمَّ لَتَرَوُنَّهَا عَيْنَ ٱلْيَقِينِ ۝ ثُمَّ لَتُسْـَٔلُنَّ يَوْمَئِذٍ عَنِ ٱلنَّعِيمِ ۝ ﴾

(At-Takathur 001-008)

Chapter (Surah) 103: Al-'Asr 001-003

بِسْمِ اللَّهِ الرَّحْمَنِ الرَّحِيمِ

﴿ وَٱلْعَصْرِ ۝ إِنَّ ٱلْإِنسَـٰنَ لَفِى خُسْرٍ ۝ إِلَّا ٱلَّذِينَ ءَامَنُوا۟ وَعَمِلُوا۟ ٱلصَّـٰلِحَـٰتِ وَتَوَاصَوْا۟ بِٱلْحَقِّ وَتَوَاصَوْا۟ بِٱلصَّبْرِ ۝ ﴾

(Al-'Asr 001-003)

Chapter (Surah) 104: Al-Humaza 001-009

بِسْمِ اللَّهِ الرَّحْمَنِ الرَّحِيمِ

﴿ وَيْلٌ لِّكُلِّ هُمَزَةٍ لُّمَزَةٍ ۝ ٱلَّذِى جَمَعَ مَالًا وَعَدَّدَهُ ۝ يَحْسَبُ أَنَّ مَالَهُ أَخْلَدَهُ ۝ كَلَّا لَيُنۢبَذَنَّ فِى ٱلْحُطَمَةِ ۝ وَمَآ أَدْرَىٰكَ مَا ٱلْحُطَمَةُ ۝ نَارُ ٱللَّهِ

ٱلْمُوقَدَةُ ۝ ٱلَّتِى تَطَّلِعُ عَلَى ٱلْأَفْـِٔدَةِ ۝ إِنَّهَا عَلَيْهِم مُّؤْصَدَةٌ ۝ فِى عَمَدٍ مُّمَدَّدَةٍۭ ۝

(Al-Humaza 001-009)

Chapter (Surah) 105: Al-Fil 001-005

بِسْمِ ٱللَّهِ ٱلرَّحْمَٰنِ ٱلرَّحِيمِ

أَلَمْ تَرَ كَيْفَ فَعَلَ رَبُّكَ بِأَصْحَٰبِ ٱلْفِيلِ ۝ أَلَمْ يَجْعَلْ كَيْدَهُمْ فِى تَضْلِيلٍ ۝ وَأَرْسَلَ عَلَيْهِمْ طَيْرًا أَبَابِيلَ ۝ تَرْمِيهِم بِحِجَارَةٍ مِّن سِجِّيلٍ ۝ فَجَعَلَهُمْ كَعَصْفٍ مَّأْكُولٍۭ ۝

(Al-Fil 001-005)

Chapter (Surah) 106: Quraish 001-004

بِسْمِ ٱللَّهِ ٱلرَّحْمَٰنِ ٱلرَّحِيمِ

لِإِيلَٰفِ قُرَيْشٍ ۝ إِۦلَٰفِهِمْ رِحْلَةَ ٱلشِّتَآءِ وَٱلصَّيْفِ ۝ فَلْيَعْبُدُوا۟ رَبَّ هَٰذَا ٱلْبَيْتِ ۝ ٱلَّذِىٓ أَطْعَمَهُم مِّن جُوعٍ وَءَامَنَهُم مِّنْ خَوْفٍۭ ۝

(Quraish 001-004)

Chapter (Surah) 107: Al-Ma'un 001-007

بِسْمِ ٱللَّهِ ٱلرَّحْمَٰنِ ٱلرَّحِيمِ

أَرَءَيْتَ ٱلَّذِى يُكَذِّبُ بِٱلدِّينِ ۝ فَذَٰلِكَ ٱلَّذِى يَدُعُّ ٱلْيَتِيمَ ۝ وَلَا يَحُضُّ عَلَىٰ طَعَامِ ٱلْمِسْكِينِ ۝ فَوَيْلٌ لِّلْمُصَلِّينَ ۝ ٱلَّذِينَ هُمْ عَن صَلَاتِهِمْ سَاهُونَ ۝ ٱلَّذِينَ هُمْ يُرَآءُونَ ۝ وَيَمْنَعُونَ ٱلْمَاعُونَ ۝

(Al-Ma'un 001-007)

Chapter (Surah) 108: Al-Kauthar 001-003

بِسْمِ ٱللَّهِ ٱلرَّحْمَٰنِ ٱلرَّحِيمِ

إِنَّآ أَعْطَيْنَٰكَ ٱلْكَوْثَرَ ۝ فَصَلِّ لِرَبِّكَ وَٱنْحَرْ ۝ إِنَّ شَانِئَكَ هُوَ ٱلْأَبْتَرُ ۝

(Al-Kauthar 001-003)

Chapter (Surah) 109: Al-Kafirun 001-006

بِسْمِ اللَّهِ الرَّحْمَٰنِ الرَّحِيمِ

﴿ قُلْ يَٰٓأَيُّهَا ٱلْكَٰفِرُونَ ۝ لَآ أَعْبُدُ مَا تَعْبُدُونَ ۝ وَلَآ أَنتُمْ عَٰبِدُونَ مَآ أَعْبُدُ ۝ وَلَآ أَنَا۠ عَابِدٌ مَّا عَبَدتُّمْ ۝ وَلَآ أَنتُمْ عَٰبِدُونَ مَآ أَعْبُدُ ۝ لَكُمْ دِينُكُمْ وَلِىَ دِينِ ۝ ﴾

(Al-Kafirun 001-006)

Chapter (Surah) 110: An-Nasr 001-003

بِسْمِ اللَّهِ الرَّحْمَٰنِ الرَّحِيمِ

﴿ إِذَا جَآءَ نَصْرُ ٱللَّهِ وَٱلْفَتْحُ ۝ وَرَأَيْتَ ٱلنَّاسَ يَدْخُلُونَ فِى دِينِ ٱللَّهِ أَفْوَاجًا ۝ فَسَبِّحْ بِحَمْدِ رَبِّكَ وَٱسْتَغْفِرْهُ إِنَّهُۥ كَانَ تَوَّابًۢا ۝ ﴾

(An-Nasr 001-003)

Chapter (Surah) 111: Al-Masad 001-005

بِسْمِ اللَّهِ الرَّحْمَٰنِ الرَّحِيمِ

﴿ تَبَّتْ يَدَآ أَبِى لَهَبٍ وَتَبَّ ۝ مَآ أَغْنَىٰ عَنْهُ مَالُهُۥ وَمَا كَسَبَ ۝ سَيَصْلَىٰ نَارًا ذَاتَ لَهَبٍ ۝ وَٱمْرَأَتُهُۥ حَمَّالَةَ ٱلْحَطَبِ ۝ فِى جِيدِهَا حَبْلٌ مِّن مَّسَدٍۭ ۝ ﴾

(Al-Masad 001-005)

Chapter (Surah) 112: Al-Ikhlas 001-004

بِسْمِ اللَّهِ الرَّحْمَٰنِ الرَّحِيمِ

﴿ قُلْ هُوَ ٱللَّهُ أَحَدٌ ۝ ٱللَّهُ ٱلصَّمَدُ ۝ لَمْ يَلِدْ وَلَمْ يُولَدْ ۝ وَلَمْ يَكُن لَّهُۥ كُفُوًا أَحَدٌۢ ۝ ﴾

(Al-Ikhlas 001-004)

Chapter (Surah) 113: Al-Falaq 001-005

بِسْمِ اللَّهِ الرَّحْمَٰنِ الرَّحِيمِ

﴿ قُلْ أَعُوذُ بِرَبِّ ٱلْفَلَقِ ۝ مِن شَرِّ مَا خَلَقَ ۝ وَمِن شَرِّ غَاسِقٍ إِذَا وَقَبَ ۝ وَمِن شَرِّ ٱلنَّفَّٰثَٰتِ فِى ٱلْعُقَدِ ۝ وَمِن شَرِّ حَاسِدٍ إِذَا حَسَدَ ۝ ﴾

(Al-Falaq 001-005)

Chapter (Surah) 114: An-Nas 001-006

بِسْمِ اللَّهِ الرَّحْمَٰنِ الرَّحِيمِ

﴿ قُلْ أَعُوذُ بِرَبِّ ٱلنَّاسِ ۝ مَلِكِ ٱلنَّاسِ ۝ إِلَٰهِ ٱلنَّاسِ ۝ مِن شَرِّ ٱلْوَسْوَاسِ ٱلْخَنَّاسِ ۝ ٱلَّذِى يُوَسْوِسُ فِى صُدُورِ ٱلنَّاسِ ۝ مِنَ ٱلْجِنَّةِ وَٱلنَّاسِ ۝ ﴾

(An-Nas 001-006)

CHAPTER (SURAH) 78: AN-NABA (THE TIDINGS, THE ANNOUNCEMENT), VERSES 001- 040

Surah: 78 Ayah: 1, Ayah: 2, Ayah: 3, Ayah: 4, Ayah: 5, Ayah: 6, Ayah: 7, Ayah: 8, Ayah: 9, Ayah: 10, Ayah: 11, Ayah: 12, Ayah: 13, Ayah: 14, Ayah: 15 & Ayah: 16

(بِسْمِ اللَّهِ الرَّحْمَٰنِ الرَّحِيمِ)

In the Name of Allah, the Most Gracious, the Most Merciful.

﴿ عَمَّ يَتَسَآءَلُونَ ۝ ﴾

1. What are they asking (one another) about?

﴿ عَنِ ٱلنَّبَإِ ٱلْعَظِيمِ ۝ ﴾

2. About the great news, (i.e. Islâmic Monotheism, the Qur'ân, which Prophet Muhammad (peace be upon him) brought and the Day of Resurrection)

﴿ ٱلَّذِى هُمْ فِيهِ مُخْتَلِفُونَ ۝ ﴾

3. About which they are in disagreement.

﴿ كَلَّا سَيَعْلَمُونَ ۝ ﴾

4. Nay, they will come to know!

﴿ ثُمَّ كَلَّا سَيَعْلَمُونَ ۝ ﴾

5. Nay, again, they will come to know!

﴿ أَلَمْ نَجْعَلِ الْأَرْضَ مِهَادًا ۝ ﴾

6. Have We not made the earth as a bed,

﴿ وَالْجِبَالَ أَوْتَادًا ۝ ﴾

7. And the mountains as pegs?

﴿ وَخَلَقْنَاكُمْ أَزْوَاجًا ۝ ﴾

8. And We have created you in pairs (male and female, tall and short, good and bad, etc.).

﴿ وَجَعَلْنَا نَوْمَكُمْ سُبَاتًا ۝ ﴾

9. And We have made your sleep as a thing for rest.

﴿ وَجَعَلْنَا اللَّيْلَ لِبَاسًا ۝ ﴾

10. And have made the night as a covering (through its darkness),

﴿ وَجَعَلْنَا النَّهَارَ مَعَاشًا ۝ ﴾

11. And We have made the day for livelihood.

﴿ وَبَنَيْنَا فَوْقَكُمْ سَبْعًا شِدَادًا ۝ ﴾

12. And We have built above you seven strong (heavens),

﴿ وَجَعَلْنَا سِرَاجًا وَهَّاجًا ۝ ﴾

13. And We have made (therein) a shinning lamp (sun).

﴿ وَأَنزَلْنَا مِنَ الْمُعْصِرَاتِ مَاءً ثَجَّاجًا ۝ ﴾

14. And We have sent down from the rainy clouds abundant water.

﴿ لِنُخْرِجَ بِهِ حَبًّا وَنَبَاتًا ۝ ﴾

15. That We may produce therewith corn and vegetations,

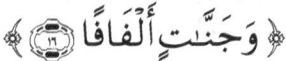

16. And gardens of thick growth.

Transliteration

1. AAamma yatasaaloona 2. AAani alnnaba-i alAAatheemi 3. Allathee hum feehi mukhtalifoona 4. Kalla sayaAAlamoona 5. Thumma kalla sayaAAlamoona 6. Alam najAAali al-arda mihadan 7. Waaljibala awtadan 8. Wakhalaqnakum azwajan 9. WajaAAalna nawmakum subatan 10. WajaAAalna allayla libasan 11. WajaAAalna alnnahara maAAashan 12. Wabanayna fawqakum sabAAan shidadan 13. WajaAAalna sirajan wahhajan 14. Waanzalna mina almuAAsirati maan thajjajan 15. Linukhrija bihi habban wanabatan 16. Wajannatin alfafan

Tafsir Ibn Kathir

Refutation against the Idolators' Denial of the Occurrence of the Day of Judgement

In rejection of the idolators' questioning about the Day of Judgement, due to their denial of its occurrence, Allah says,

(What are they asking about About the great news,) meaning, what are they asking about They are asking about the matter of the Day of Judgement, and it is the great news. Meaning the dreadful, horrifying, overwhelming information.

(About which they are in disagreement.) meaning, the people are divided into two ideas about it. There are those who believe in it and those who disbelieve in it. Then Allah threatens those who deny the Day of Judgement by saying,

(Nay, they will come to know! Nay, again, they will come to know!) This is a severe threat and a direct warning.

Mentioning Allah's Power, and the Proof of His Ability to resurrect the Dead

Then, Allah begins to explain His great ability to create strange things and amazing matters. He brings this as a proof of His ability to do whatever He wishes concerning the matter of the Hereafter and other matters as well. He says,

(Have We not made the earth as a bed,) meaning, an established, firm and peaceful resting place that is subservient to them.

(And the mountains as pegs) meaning, He made them as pegs for the earth to hold it in place, make it stable and firm. This is so that it may be suitable for dwelling and not quake with those who are in it. Then Allah says,

(And We have created you in pairs.) meaning, male and female, both of them enjoying each other, and by this means procreation is achieved. This is similar to Allah's statement,

(And among His signs is this that He created for you wives from among yourselves, that you may find repose in them, and He has put between you affection and mercy.) (30:21)

(And We have made your sleep as a thing for rest.) meaning, a cessation of movement in order to attain rest from the frequent repetition and going about in search of livelihood during the day. A similar Ayah has been mentioned previously in Surat Al-Furqan.

(And We have made the night as a covering,) meaning, its shade and darkness covers the people. This is as Allah says,

(By the night as it conceals it.) (91:4) Qatadah commented;

(And We have made the night as a covering,) meaning, a tranquil residence. Concerning Allah's statement,

(And We have made the day for livelihood.) meaning, `We made it radiant, luminous, and shining so that the people would be able to move about in it.' By it they are able to come and go for their livelihood, earning, business dealings and other than that as well. In reference to Allah's statement,

(And We have built above you seven strong,) meaning, the seven heavens in their vastness, loftiness, perfection, precision, and adornment with both stable and moving stars. Thus, Allah says,

(And We have made (therein) a shining lamp.) meaning, the radiant sun that gives light to all of the world. Its light glows for all of the people of the earth. Allah then says,

(And We have sent down from the Mu`sirat water Thajjaj.) `Ali bin Abi Talhah reported from Ibn `Abbas that he said, "From the Mu`sirat means from the clouds." This was also stated by `Ikrimah, Abu Al-`Aliyah, Ad-Dahhak, Al-Hasan, Ar-Rabi` bin Anas, Ath-Thawri, and it is preferred by Ibn Jarir. Al-Farra' said, "They are the clouds that are filled with rain, but they do not bring rain. This is like the woman being called Mu`sir when (the time of) her menstrual cycle approaches, yet she does not menstruate." This is as Allah says,

(Allah is He Who sends the winds, so that they raise clouds, and spread them along the sky as He wills, and then break them into fragments, until you see rain drops come forth from their midst!) (30:48) meaning, from its midst. Concerning Allah's statement,

(water Thajjaj) Mujahid, Qatadah, and Ar-Rabi` bin Anas all said, "Thajjaj means poured out." At-Thawri said, "Continuous." Ibn Zayd said, "Abundant." In the Hadith of the woman with prolonged menstrual bleeding, when the Messenger of Allah said to her,

《أَنْعَتُ لَكِ الْكُرْسُفَ》

(I suggest you to make an absorbent cloth for yourself.)" Meaning, `dress the area with cotton.' The woman replied, "O Messenger of Allah! It (the bleeding) is too much for that. Verily, it flows in profusely (Thajja)." This contains an evidence for using the word Thajj to mean abundant, continuous and flowing. And Allah knows best. Allah said,

(That We may produce therewith corn and vegetation, and gardens that are Alfaf.) meaning, `so that We may bring out great abundance, goodness, benefit, and blessing through this water.'

(grains) This refers to that which is preserved for (the usage) of humans and cattle.

(and vegetations) meaning, vegetables that are eaten fresh.

(And gardens) meaning, gardens of various fruits, differing colors, and a wide variety of tastes and fragrances, even if it is ingathered at one location of the earth. This is why Allah says

(And gardens that are Alfaf.) Ibn `Abbas and other said, "Alfaf means gathered." This is similar to Allah's statement,

(And in the earth are neighboring tracts, and gardens of vines, and green crops, and date palms, growing into two or three from a single stem root, or otherwise, watered with the same water; yet some of them We make more excellent than others to eat. Verily, in these things there are Ayat for the people who understand.) (13:4)

Surah: 78 Ayah: 17, Ayah: 18, Ayah: 19, Ayah: 20, Ayah: 22, Ayah: 23, Ayah: 24, Ayah: 25, Ayah: 26, Ayah: 27, Ayah: 28, Ayah: 29 & Ayah: 30

﴿إِنَّ يَوْمَ ٱلْفَصْلِ كَانَ مِيقَٰتًا ۝﴾

17. Verily, the Day of Decision is a fixed time,

﴿يَوْمَ يُنفَخُ فِى ٱلصُّورِ فَتَأْتُونَ أَفْوَاجًا ۝﴾

18. The Day when the Trumpet will be blown, and you shall come forth in crowds (groups after groups). (Tafsir At-Tabari)

﴿وَفُتِحَتِ ٱلسَّمَآءُ فَكَانَتْ أَبْوَٰبًا ۝﴾

19. And the heaven shall be opened, and it will become as gates,

﴿وَسُيِّرَتِ ٱلْجِبَالُ فَكَانَتْ سَرَابًا ۝﴾

20. And the mountains shall be moved away from their places and they will be as if they were a mirage.

﴿ إِنَّ جَهَنَّمَ كَانَتْ مِرْصَادًا ﴾

21. Truly, Hell is a place of ambush -

﴿ لِّلطَّٰغِينَ مَـَٔابًا ﴾

22. A dwelling place for the Tâghûn (those who transgress the boundary limits set by Allâh like polytheists, disbelievers in the Oneness of Allâh, hypocrites, sinners, criminals),

﴿ لَّٰبِثِينَ فِيهَآ أَحْقَابًا ﴾

23. They will abide therein for ages,

﴿ لَّا يَذُوقُونَ فِيهَا بَرْدًا وَلَا شَرَابًا ﴾

24. Nothing cool shall they taste therein, nor any drink.

﴿ إِلَّا حَمِيمًا وَغَسَّاقًا ﴾

25. Except boiling water, and dirty wound discharges -

﴿ جَزَآءً وِفَاقًا ﴾

26. An exact recompense (according to their evil crimes).

﴿ إِنَّهُمْ كَانُوا۟ لَا يَرْجُونَ حِسَابًا ﴾

27. For verily, they used not to look for a reckoning.

﴿ وَكَذَّبُوا۟ بِـَٔايَٰتِنَا كِذَّابًا ﴾

28. But they belied Our Ayât (proofs, evidences, verses, lessons, signs, revelations, and that which Our Prophet (peace be upon him) brought) completely.

﴿ وَكُلَّ شَىْءٍ أَحْصَيْنَٰهُ كِتَٰبًا ﴾

29. And all things We have recorded in a Book.

﴿ فَذُوقُوا۟ فَلَن نَّزِيدَكُمْ إِلَّا عَذَابًا ﴾

30. So taste you (the results of your evil actions). No increase shall We give you, except in torment.

Transliteration

17. Inna yawma alfasli kana meeqatan 18. Yawma yunfakhu fee alssoori fata/toona afwajan 19. Wafutihati alssamao fakanat abwaban 20. Wasuyyirati aljibalu fakanat saraban 21. Inna jahannama kanat mirsadan 22. Lilttagheena maaban 23. Labitheena feeha ahqaban 24. La yathooqoona feeha bardan wala sharaban 25. Illa hameeman waghassaqan 26. Jazaan wifaqan 27. Innahum kanoo la yarjoona hisaban 28. Wakaththaboo bi-ayatina kiththaban 29. Wakulla shay-in ahsaynahu kitaban 30. Fathooqoo falan nazeedakum illa AAathaban

Tafsir Ibn Kathir

Explaining the Day of Decision and what occurs during it

Allah says about the Day of Decision -- and it is the Day of Judgement -- that it is at a fixed time, with a set appointment. Its time cannot be added to or decreased. No one knows its exact time except Allah. This is as Allah says,

(And We delay it only for a term fixed.) (11:104)

(The Day when the Trumpet will be blown, and you shall come forth in crowds.) Mujahid said, "Groups after groups." Ibn Jarir said, "This means that each nation will come with its Messenger. It is similar to Allah's statement,

(The Day when We shall call together all human beings with their Imam.) (17:71)" Al-Bukhari reported concerning the explanation of Allah's statement,

(The Day when the Trumpet will be blown, and you shall come forth in crowds.) Abu Hurayrah said that the Messenger of Allah said,

«مَا بَيْنَ النَّفْخَتَيْنِ أَرْبَعُون»

(That which is between the two blowings is forty.) Someone asked, "Is it forty days, O Abu Hurayrah" But he (Abu Hurayrah) refused to reply, saying "no comment." They then asked, "Is it forty months" But he (Abu Hurayrah) refused to reply, saying "no comment." They asked again, "Is it forty years" But he (Abu Hurayrah) refused to reply, saying "no comment." (Abu Hurayrah added:) "Then the Prophet went on to say,

«ثُمَّ يُنْزِلُ اللهُ مِنَ السَّمَاءِ مَاءً فَيَنْبُتُونَ كَمَا يَنْبُتُ الْبَقْلُ، لَيْسَ مِنَ الْإِنْسَانِ شَيْءٌ إِلَّا يَبْلَى، إِلَّا عَظْمًا وَاحِدًا، وَهُوَ عَجْبُ الذَّنَبِ، وَمِنْهُ يُرَكَّبُ الْخَلْقُ يَوْمَ الْقِيَامَة»

(Then Allah will send down a rain from the sky and the dead body will sprout just as a green plant sprouts. Every part of the last person will deteriorate except for one bone, and it is the coccyx bone (tailbone). From it the creation will be assembled on the Day of Judgement.)"

(And the heaven shall be opened, and it will become as gates.) meaning, paths, and routes for the descending of the angels.

(And the mountains shall be moved away from their places and they will be as if they were a mirage.) This is similar to Allah's statement,

(And you will see the mountains and think them solid, but they shall pass away as the passing away of the clouds.) (27:88) He also says,

(And the mountain will be like carded wool.) (101:5) And Allah says here,

(As if they were a mirage.) meaning, they appear to the one who looks at them as if they are something, but they are actually nothing. After this they will be completely removed. Nothing will be seen of them, and there will be neither base nor trace of them. This is as Allah says,

(And they ask you concerning the mountains, say: "My Lord will blast them and scatter them as particles of dust. Then He shall leave them as a level smooth plain. You will see therein nothing crooked or curved.") (20:105-107) And He says,

(And the Day We shall cause the mountains to pass away, and you will see the earth as a leveled plain.) (18:47) Allah then says,

(Truly, Hell is a place of ambush) meaning, it is waiting in preparation.

(for the Taghun) These are the disobedient rejectors who oppose the Messengers.

(A dwelling place) meaning, a place of return, final destination, final outcome, and residence. Allah said,

(They will abide therein Ahqab.) meaning, they will remain in it for Ahqab, which is the plural of Huqb. Huqb means a period of time. Khalid bin Ma`dan said, "This Ayah, and the Ayah,

except your Lord wills.)11:107(both refer to the people of TawhJ0d. Ibn Jar0r recorded this statement. Ibn Jar0r also recorded from Sa0lim that he heard Al-HJasan being asked about Allah s statement,

(They will abide therein Ahqab) "In reference to Ahqab, it has no specific amount of time other than its general meaning of eternity in the Hellfire. However, they have mentioned that the Huqb is seventy years, and every day of it is like one thousand years according to your reckoning (in this life)." Sa`id reported from Qatadah that he said, "Allah says,

(They will abide therein Ahqab.) (78:23) And it is that which has no end to it. Whenever one era comes to an end, a new era follows it. It has been mentioned to us that the Huqb is eighty years." Ar-Rabi` bin Anas said,

Chapter 78: An-Naba (The Tidings, The Announcement), Verses 001-040

(They will abide therein Ahqab) "No one knows how much time this Ahqab is, except for Allah, the Mighty and Sublime. It has been mentioned to us that one Huqb is eighty years, and the year is three hundred and sixty days, and each day is equivalent to one thousand years according to your reckoning (in this life)." Ibn Jarir has recorded both of these statements. Allah's statement:

(Nothing cool shall they taste therein, nor any drink.) meaning, they will not find any coolness in Hell for their hearts, nor any good drink for them to partake of. Thus, Allah says,

(Except Hamim, and Ghassaq) Abu Al-`Aliyah said, "The Hamim has been made an exception to the coolness, and Ghassaq is the exception to the drink." This has also been said by Ar-Rabi` bin Anas. In reference to the Hamim, it is the heat that has reached its maximum temperature and point of boiling. The Ghassaq is gathered from the pus, sweat, tears, and wounds of the people of Hellfire. It is unbearably cold with an intolerable stench. May Allah save us from that by His beneficence and grace. Then He continues,

(An exact recompense.) meaning, that which will happen to them of this punishment is in accordance with their wicked deeds, which they were doing in this life. Mujahid, Qatadah, and others have said this. Then Allah said,

(For verily, they used not to look for a reckoning.) (78:27) meaning, they did not believe that there would be an abode in which they would be taken to account.

(But they denied Our Ayat Kidhdhaba.) meaning, they used to deny the evidences of Allah and His proofs for His creation, which He revealed to His Messengers. So they met these proofs with rejection and obstinance. His statement,

(Kidhdhaba) it means rejection, and it is considered a verbal noun that does not come from a verb. Allah said;

(And all things We have recorded in a Book.) meaning, `surely We know the deeds of all of the creatures, and We have written these deeds for them. We will reward them based upon this.' If their deeds were good then their reward will be good, and if their deeds were evil their reward will be evil. Allah then says,

(So taste you. No increase shall We give you, except in torment.) This means that it will be said to the people of the Hellfire, "Taste that which you were in. We will never increase you in anything except torment according to its type (of sin), and something else similar to it." Qatadah reported from Abu Ayyub Al-Azdi, who reported from `Abdullah bin `Amr that he said, "Allah did not reveal any Ayah against the people of the Hellfire worse than this Ayah,

(So taste you. No increase shall We give you, except in torment.)" Then he said, "They will continue increasing in torment forever."

Surah: 78 Ayah: 31, Ayah: 32, Ayah: 33, Ayah: 34, Ayah: 35 & Ayah: 36

﴿ إِنَّ لِلْمُتَّقِينَ مَفَازًا ﴾

31. Verily, for the Muttaqûn, there will be a success (Paradise);

﴿ حَدَآئِقَ وَأَعْنَـٰبًا ﴾

32. Gardens and vineyards,

﴿ وَكَوَاعِبَ أَتْرَابًا ﴾

33. And young full-breasted (mature) maidens of equal age,

﴿ وَكَأْسًا دِهَاقًا ﴾

34. And a full cup (of wine).

﴿ لَّا يَسْمَعُونَ فِيهَا لَغْوًا وَلَا كِذَّٰبًا ﴾

35. No Laghw (dirty, false, evil talk) shall they hear therein, nor lying;

﴿ جَزَآءً مِّن رَّبِّكَ عَطَآءً حِسَابًا ﴾

36. A reward from your Lord, an ample calculated gift (according to the best of their good deeds).

Transliteration

31. Inna lilmuttaqeena mafazan 32. Hada-iqa waaAAnaban 33. WakawaAAiba atraban 34. Waka/san dihaqan 35. La yasmaAAoona feeha laghwan wala kiththaban 36. Jazaan min rabbika AAataan hisaban

Tafsir Ibn Kathir

The Great Success will be for Those Who have Taqwa

Allah informs about the happy people and what He has prepared for them of esteem, and eternal pleasure. Allah says,

(Verily, for those who have Taqwa, there will be a success;) Ibn `Abbas and Ad-Dahhak both said, "A place of enjoyable recreation." Mujahid and Qatadah both said, "They are successful and thus, they are saved from the Hellfire." The most obvious meaning here is the statement of Ibn `Abbas, because Allah says after this,

(Hada'iq) And Hada'iq are gardens of palm trees and other things.

(And vineyards, and Kawa`ib Atrab,) meaning, wide-eyed maidens with fully developed breasts. Ibn `Abbas, Mujahid and others have said,

(Kawa`ib) "This means round breasts. They meant by this that the breasts of these girls will be fully rounded and not sagging, because they will be virgins, equal in age. This means that they will only have one age." The explanation of this has already been mentioned in Surat Al-Waqi`ah. Concerning Allah's statement,

(And a cup Dihaq.) Ibn `Abbas said, "Continuously filled." `Ikrimah said, "Pure." Mujahid, Al-Hasan, Qatadah, and Ibn Zayd all said,

(Dihaq) "This means completely filled." Then Allah says,

(No Laghw shall they hear therein, nor lying;) This is similar to Allah's statement,

(Free from any Laghw, and free from sin.) (52:23) meaning, there will not be any vain, worthless speech therein, nor any sinful lying. Rather, it will be the abode of peace, and everything that is in it will be free of any shortcomings. Allah then says,

(Rewarded from your Lord with a sufficient gift.) meaning, `this that We have mentioned to you is what Allah will reward them with, and they will be given it by His favor and from Him. It will be a kindness, mercy, gift, and recompense from Him. It will be sufficient, suitable, comprehensive and abundant.' The Arabs say, "He gave me and he sufficed me." This means that he sufficiently provided for me." From this comes the saying, "Allah is sufficient for me."

Surah: 78 Ayah: 37, Ayah: 38, Ayah: 39 & Ayah: 40

﴿ رَّبِّ ٱلسَّمَـٰوَٰتِ وَٱلْأَرْضِ وَمَا بَيْنَهُمَا ٱلرَّحْمَـٰنِ لَا يَمْلِكُونَ مِنْهُ خِطَابًا ۝ ﴾

37. (From) the Lord of the heavens and the earth, and whatsoever is in between them, the Most Gracious, with Whom they cannot dare to speak (on the Day of Resurrection except by His Leave).

﴿ يَوْمَ يَقُومُ ٱلرُّوحُ وَٱلْمَلَـٰٓئِكَةُ صَفًّا ۖ لَّا يَتَكَلَّمُونَ إِلَّا مَنْ أَذِنَ لَهُ ٱلرَّحْمَـٰنُ وَقَالَ صَوَابًا ۝ ﴾

38. The Day that Ar-Rûh (Jibrîl (Gabriel) or another angel) and the angels will stand forth in rows, they will not speak except him whom the Most Gracious (Allâh) allows, and he will speak what is right.

﴿ ذَٰلِكَ ٱلْيَوْمُ ٱلْحَقُّ ۖ فَمَن شَآءَ ٱتَّخَذَ إِلَىٰ رَبِّهِۦ مَـَٔابًا ۝ ﴾

39. That is without doubt the True Day. So, whosoever wills, let him seek a place with (or a way to) His Lord (by obeying Him in this worldly life)!

﴿ إِنَّآ أَنذَرْنَـٰكُمْ عَذَابًا قَرِيبًا يَوْمَ يَنظُرُ ٱلْمَرْءُ مَا قَدَّمَتْ يَدَاهُ وَيَقُولُ ٱلْكَافِرُ

﴿يَـٰلَيْتَنِى كُنتُ تُرَٰبَا ۝﴾

40. Verily, We have warned you of a near torment - the Day when man will see that (the deeds) which his hands have sent forth, and the disbeliever will say: "Woe to me! Would that I were dust!"

Transliteration

37. Rabbi alssamawati waal-ardi wama baynahuma alrrahmani la yamlikoona minhu khitaban 38. Yawma yaqoomu alrroohu waalmala-ikatu saffan la yatakallamoona illa man athina lahu alrrahmanu waqala sawaban 39. Thalika alyawmu alhaqqu faman shaa ittakhatha ila rabbihi maaban 40. Inna antharnakum AAathaban qareeban yawma yanthuru almaro ma qaddamat yadahu wayaqoolu alkafiru ya laytanee kuntu turaban

Tafsir Ibn Kathir

No one will dare to speak before Allah -- not even the Angels - without first receiving Permission

Allah informs of His magnificence and His majesty, and that He is the Lord of the heavens and the earth, and whatever is in them and between them. He explains that He is the Most Gracious, Whose mercy covers all things. Then He says,

(With Whom they cannot dare to speak.) meaning, no one is able to begin addressing Him except by His permission. This is as Allah says,

(Who is he that can intercede with Him except with His permission) (2:255) It is also similar to His statement,

(On the Day when it comes, no person shall speak except by His leave.) (11:105)

(The Day that Ar-Ruh and the angels will stand forth in rows, they will not speak) (78:38) The word Ruh here is referring to the angel Jibril. This has been said by Ash-Sha`bi, Sa`id bin Jubayr and Ad-Dahhak. This is as Allah says,

(Which the trustworthy Ruh has brought down. Upon your heart that you may be of the warners.) (26:193-194) Muqatil bin Hayyan said, "The Ruh is the noblest of the angels, the closest of them to the Lord, and the one who delivers the revelation." Allah said;

(except him whom Ar-Rahman allows,) This is similar to Allah's statement,

(On the Day when it comes, no person shall speak except by His leave.) (11:105) This is similar to what has been confirmed in the Sahih, that the Prophet said,

«وَلَا يَتَكَلَّمُ يَوْمَئِذٍ إِلَّا الرُّسُلُ»

(And none will speak on that Day except the Messengers.)" Allah said, (and he will speak what is right.) meaning, the truth. And from the truth is the fact that there is no god worthy of worship except Allah. This is as Abu Salih and `Ikrimah both said. In reference to Allah's statement,

(That is the True Day.) meaning, it will come to pass and there is no avoiding it.

(So, whosoever wills, let him seek a place with His Lord!) meaning, a place of return, a path that leads to Him, and a way that he may pass by to get to Him.

The Day of Judgement is Near

Allah said, (Verily, We have warned you of a near torment) meaning, the Day of Judgement. It is mentioned here to emphasize the fact that its occurrence has become close, because everything that is coming will certainly come to pass.

(the Day when man will see that which his hands have sent forth,) meaning, all of his deeds will be presented to him -- the good and bad, and the old and new. This is similar to Allah's statement, (And they will find all that they did, placed before them.) (18:49) t It is also similar to His statement,

(On that Day man will be informed of what he sent forward, and what he left behind.) (75:13) Then Allah says,

(and the disbeliever will say: "Woe to me! Would that I were dust!") meaning, the disbeliever on that Day will wish that he had only been dust in the worldly life.

He will wish that he had not been created and that he had never come into existence. This will be when he sees the torment of Allah and he looks at his wicked deeds that will be written down against him by the noble righteous scribes among angels. It has been said that he will only wish for that when Allah passes judgement between all of the animals that were in the worldly life. He will rectify matters between them with His just wisdom that does not wrong anyone. Even the hornless sheep will be allowed to avenge itself against the sheep with horns.

Then, when the judgement between them is finished, He (Allah) will say to them (the animals), "Be dust." So they will all become dust. Upon witnessing this the disbeliever will say,

(Would that I were dust!) meaning, `I wish I was an animal so that I would be returned to dust.' Something of similar meaning to this has been reported in the well-known Hadith about the Sur. There are also narrations recorded from Abu Hurayrah, `Abdullah bin `Amr, and others concerning this. This is the end of the Tafsir of Surat An-Naba'. And all praise and thanks are due to Allah. He is the Giver of success and protection from error.

CHAPTER (SURAH) 79: AN-NAZIAT (THOSE WHO DRAG FORTH, SOUL-SNATCHERS), VERSES 001- 046

Surah: 79 Ayah: 1, Ayah: 2, Ayah: 3, Ayah: 4, Ayah: 5, Ayah: 6, Ayah: 7, Ayah: 8, Ayah: 9, Ayah: 10, Ayah: 11, Ayah: 12, Ayah: 13 & Ayah: 14

(بِسْمِ اللَّهِ الرَّحْمَـٰنِ الرَّحِيمِ)

In the Name of Allah, the Most Gracious, the Most Merciful.

﴿ وَٱلنَّـٰزِعَـٰتِ غَرْقًا ۝ ﴾

1. By those (angels) who pull out (the souls of the disbelievers and the wicked) with great violence.

﴿ وَٱلنَّـٰشِطَـٰتِ نَشْطًا ۝ ﴾

2. By those (angels) who gently take out (the souls of the believers).

﴿ وَٱلسَّـٰبِحَـٰتِ سَبْحًا ۝ ﴾

3. And by those that swim along (i.e. angels or planets in their orbits).

﴿ فَٱلسَّـٰبِقَـٰتِ سَبْقًا ۝ ﴾

4. And by those that press forward as in a race (i.e. the angels or stars or the horses).

﴿ فَٱلْمُدَبِّرَٰتِ أَمْرًا ۝ ﴾

5. And by those angels who arrange to do the Commands of their Lord, (so verily, you disbelievers will be called to account).

﴿ يَوْمَ تَرْجُفُ ٱلرَّاجِفَةُ ۝ ﴾

6. On the Day (when the first blowing of the Trumpet is blown), the earth and the mountains will shake violently (and everybody will die).

﴿ تَتْبَعُهَا ٱلرَّادِفَةُ ۝ ﴾

7. The second blowing of the Trumpet follows it (and everybody will be resurrected).

﴿ قُلُوبٌ يَوْمَئِذٍ وَاجِفَةٌ ۝ ﴾

8. (Some) hearts that Day will shake with fear and anxiety.

﴿ أَبْصَٰرُهَا خَٰشِعَةٌ ۝ ﴾

9. Their eyes will be downcast.

﴿ يَقُولُونَ أَءِنَّا لَمَرْدُودُونَ فِى ٱلْحَافِرَةِ ۝ ﴾

10. They say: "Shall we indeed be returned to (our) former state of life?

﴿ أَءِذَا كُنَّا عِظَٰمًا نَّخِرَةً ۝ ﴾

11. "Even after we are crumbled bones?"

﴿ قَالُوا۟ تِلْكَ إِذًا كَرَّةٌ خَاسِرَةٌ ۝ ﴾

12. They say: "It would in that case, be a return with loss!"

﴿ فَإِنَّمَا هِىَ زَجْرَةٌ وَٰحِدَةٌ ۝ ﴾

13. But it will be only a single Zajrah (shout (i.e., the second blowing of the Trumpet)) (See Verse 37:19).

﴿ فَإِذَا هُم بِٱلسَّاهِرَةِ ۝ ﴾

14. When behold, they find themselves on the surface of the earth alive after their death,

Transliteration

1. WaalnnaziAAati gharqan 2. Waalnnashitati nashtan 3. Waalssabihati sabhan 4. Faalssabiqati sabqan 5. Faalmudabbirati amran 6. Yawma tarjufu alrrajifatu 7. TatbaAAuha alrradifatu 8. Quloobun yawma-ithin wajifatun 9. Absaruha khashiAAatun 10. Yaqooloona a-inna lamardoodoona fee alhafirati 11. A-itha kunna AAithaman nakhiratan 12. Qaloo tilka ithan karratun khasiratun 13. Fa-innama hiya zajratun wahidatun 14. Fa-itha hum bialssahirati

Tafsir Ibn Kathir

Swearing by Five Characteristics that the Day of Judgement will occur

Ibn Mas`ud, Ibn `Abbas, Masruq, Sa`id bin Jubayr, Abu Salih, Abu Ad-Duha and As-Suddi all said,

(By those who pull out, drowning.) "These are the angels who remove the souls from the Children of Adam." Among them are those whose souls are removed by the angels with difficulty, as if he is being drowned during its removal. There are those people whose souls the angels remove with ease, as if they were unraveling him (i.e., his soul from him) due to their briskness. This is the meaning of Allah's statement,

(By those who free briskly.) This has been mentioned by Ibn `Abbas. In reference to Allah's statement,

(And by the swimmers, swimming.) Ibn Mas`ud said, "They are the angels." Similar statements have been reported from `Ali, Mujahid, Sa`id bin Jubayr, and Abu Salih. Concerning Allah's statement,

(And by the racers, racing.) It has been narrated from `Ali, Masruq, Mujahid, Abu Salih, and Al-Hasan Al-Basri that this means the angels. Then Allah says,

(And by those who arrange affairs.) `Ali, Mujahid, `Ata', Abu Salih, Al-Hasan, Qatadah, Ar-Rabi` bin Anas, and As-Suddi all said, "They are the angels." Al-Hasan added, "They control the affairs from the heaven to the earth, meaning by the command of their Lord, the Mighty and Majestic."

The Description of the Day of Judgement, the People, and what They will say

Then Allah says,

(On the Day the Rajifah shakes, followed by the Radifah.) Ibn `Abbas said, "These are the two blasts (of the Trumpet) -- the first and the second." Mujahid, Al-Hasan, Qatadah, Ad-Dahhak and others have made similar statements. It has been reported from Mujahid that he said, "In reference to the first, it is the statement of Allah,

(On the Day the Rajifah shakes,) This is similar to Allah's statement,

(On the Day the earth and the mountains shake.) (73:14) The second is Ar-Radifah, and it is like the Allah's statement,

(And the earth and mountains shall be removed from their places, and crushed with a single crushing.) (69:14)" Concerning Allah's statement,

(Hearts that Day will tremble.) Ibn `Abbas said, "This means afraid." Mujahid and Qatadah also said this.

(Their vision humiliated.) meaning, the eyes of the people. It means that the eyes will be lowly and disgraced from what they will witness of terrors. Allah then says,

(They say: "Shall we indeed be brought back from Al-Hafirah") meaning, the idolators of the Quraysh and whoever rejects the Hereafter as they did. They consider the occurrence of the resurrection after being placed in Al-Hafirah -- which are the graves -- as something farfetched. This has been said by Mujahid. They feel that this is something impossible after the destruction of their physical bodies and the disintegration of their bones and their decaying. Thus, Allah says,

(Even after we are bones Nakhirah) It has also been recited: (نَاخِرَةً) (Nakhirah) Ibn `Abbas, Mujahid and Qatadah, all said, "This means decayed." Ibn `Abbas said, "It is the bone when it has decayed and air enters into it." Concerning their saying,

(It would in that case be a return with loss.) (79:12) Muhammad bin Ka`b said that the Quraysh said, "If Allah brings us back to life after we die, then surely we will be losers." Allah then says,

(But it will be only a single Zajrah. When behold, they are at As-Sahirah.) meaning, this is a matter that is from Allah that will not occur twice, nor will there be any opportunity to affirm it or verify it. The people will be standing and looking. This will be when Allah commands the angel Israfil to blow into the Sur, which will be the blowing of the resurrection. At that time the first people and the last people will all be standing before their Lord looking. This is as Allah says,

(On the Day when He will call you, and you will answer with His praise and obedience, and you will think that you have stayed but a little while!) (17:52) Allah has also said,

(And our commandment is but one as the twinkling of an eye.) (54:50) Allah also says,

(And the matter of the Hour is not but as a twinkling of the eye, or even nearer.) (16:77) Allah then says,

(When behold, they are at As-Sahirah.) Ibn `Abbas said, "As-Sahirah means the entire earth." Sa`id bin Jubayr, Qatadah and Abu Salih have all said this as well. `Ikrimah, Al-Hasan, Ad-Dahhak, and Ibn Zayd have all said, "As-Sahirah means the face of the earth." Mujahid said, "They will be at its (the earth's) lowest part, and they will be brought out to highest part." Then he said, "As-Sahirah is a level place." Ar-Rabi` bin Anas said,

(When behold, they are at As-Sahirah.) "Allah says,

(On the Day when the earth will be changed to another earth and so will be the heavens, and they will appear before Allah, the One, the Irresistible.) (14:48) and He says,

(And they ask you concerning the mountains: say, "My Lord will blast them and scatter them as particles of dust. Then He shall leave them as a level smooth plain.You will see therein nothing crooked or curved.) (20:105-107) and Allah says,

(And the Day We shall cause the mountains to pass away, and you will see the earth as a leveled plain.) (18:47) and the earth will be brought forth which will have mountains upon it, and it will not be considered from this earth (of this life). It will be an earth that no sin will be performed on it, nor will any blood be shed upon it."

Surah: 79 Ayah: 15, Ayah: 16, Ayah: 17, Ayah: 18, Ayah: 19, Ayah: 20, Ayah: 21, Ayah: 22, Ayah: 23, Ayah: 24, Ayah: 25 & Ayah: 26

﴿ هَلْ أَتَىٰكَ حَدِيثُ مُوسَىٰٓ ۝ ﴾

15. Has there come to you the story of Mûsa (Moses)?

﴿ إِذْ نَادَاهُ رَبُّهُۥ بِٱلْوَادِ ٱلْمُقَدَّسِ طُوًى ﴾

16. When his Lord called him in the sacred valley of Tûwa,

﴿ ٱذْهَبْ إِلَىٰ فِرْعَوْنَ إِنَّهُۥ طَغَىٰ ﴾

17. Go to Fir'aun (Pharaoh); verily, he has transgressed all bounds (in crimes, sins, polytheism, disbelief).

﴿ فَقُلْ هَل لَّكَ إِلَىٰٓ أَن تَزَكَّىٰ ﴾

18. And say to him: "Would you purify yourself (from the sin of disbelief by becoming a believer)?"

﴿ وَأَهْدِيَكَ إِلَىٰ رَبِّكَ فَتَخْشَىٰ ﴾

19. And that I guide you to your Lord, so you should fear Him?

﴿ فَأَرَىٰهُ ٱلْءَايَةَ ٱلْكُبْرَىٰ ﴾

20. Then (Mûsa (Moses)) showed him the great sign (miracles).

﴿ فَكَذَّبَ وَعَصَىٰ ﴾

21. But (Fir'aun (Pharaoh)) belied and disobeyed.

﴿ ثُمَّ أَدْبَرَ يَسْعَىٰ ﴾

22. Then he turned his back, striving (against Allâh).

﴿ فَحَشَرَ فَنَادَىٰ ﴾

23. Then he gathered (his people) and cried aloud,

﴿ فَقَالَ أَنَا۠ رَبُّكُمُ ٱلْأَعْلَىٰ ﴾

24. Saying: "I am your lord, most high."

﴿ فَأَخَذَهُ ٱللَّهُ نَكَالَ ٱلْءَاخِرَةِ وَٱلْأُولَىٰٓ ﴾

25. So Allâh, seized him with punishment for his last and first transgression. (Tafsir At-Tabari)

﴿ ءَأَنتُمْ أَشَدُّ خَلْقًا أَمِ ٱلسَّمَآءُ بَنَىٰهَا ﴾

26. Are you more difficult to create or is the heaven that He constructed?

Transliteration

15. Hal ataka hadeethu moosa 16. Ith nadahu rabbuhu bialwadi almuqaddasi tuwan 17. Ithhab ila firAAawna innahu tagha 18. Faqul hal laka ila an tazakka 19. Waahdiyaka ila rabbika fatakhsha 20. Faarahu al-ayata alkubra 21. Fakaththaba waAAasa 22. Thumma adbara yasAAa 23. Fahashara fanada 24. Faqala ana rabbukumu al-aAAla 25. Faakhathahu Allahu nakala al-akhirati waal-oola 26. Inna fee thalika laAAibratan liman yakhsha

Tafsir Ibn Kathir

Mentioning the Story of Musa and that it is a Lesson for Those Who fear Allah

Allah informs His Messenger Muhammad about His Messenger Musa. He mentions that he sent Musa to Fir`awn and He aided him with miracles. Yet, even after this, Fir`awn continued in his disbelief and transgression until Allah seized him with a mighty and powerful punishment. Thus is the punishment of whoever opposes you (Muhammad) and rejects that which you have been sent with. This is why Allah says at the end of the story,

(In this is a Lesson for whoever fears.) Allah begins by saying,

(Has there come to you the story of Musa) meaning, have you heard of his story

(When his Lord called him) meaning, He called out speaking to him.

(in the holy valley) meaning purified

(Tuwa) According to what is correct, it is the name of a valley, as preceded in Surah Ta Ha. So, He said to him:

(Go to Fir`awn; verily, he has transgressed all bounds.) meaning, he has become haughty, rebellious and arrogant.

(And say to him: "Would you purify yourself") meaning, say to him, "Will you respond to the path and way that will purify you" This means, `will you submit (accept Islam) and be obedient'

(And that I guide to your Lord,) meaning, `I will guide you to the worship of your Lord.'

(so that you fear) meaning, `so that your heart will become humble, obedient, and submissive to Him after it was hard, evil, and far away from goodness.'

(Then he showed him the great sign.) This means that Musa showed him -- along with this truthful call -- a strong evidence and a clear proof of the truthfulness of what he had come up with from Allah.

(But he denied and disobeyed.) meaning, he (Fir`awn) rejected the truth and opposed what Musa commanded him with of obedience. So what happened with him was that his heart disbelieved, and Musa (i.e., his call) could not internally or externally affect it. Along with this, his knowledge that what Musa had come to him with was the truth, did not necessitate his being a believer in it. This is because recognition is the knowledge of the heart, and faith is its action. And it (faith) is to comply with the truth and submit to it. Concerning Allah's statement,

(Then he turned back, striving.) meaning, in responding to the truth with falsehood. This was by his gathering the group of magicians in order to confront that which Musa had come up with of spectacular miracles.

(So he gathered (his people) and called out) meaning, among his people.

(Saying; I am your lord, most high.") Ibn `Abbas and Mujahid both said, "This is the word which Fir`awn said after he said,

(`I have not known of any other god for you all other than me) for the past forty years.'" Allah then says,

(So Allah seized him with a punishing example for the Hereafter and the first (life).) meaning, Allah avenged Himself against him with a severe vengeance, and He made an example and admonition of him for those rebellious people in the world who are like him.

(And on the Day of Resurrection, evil indeed is the gift gifted (i.e., the curse (in this world) pursued by another curse (in this world) pursued by another curse (in the Hereafter)).) (11:99) This is as Allah says,

(And We made them leaders inviting to the Fire: and on the Day of Resurrection, they will not be helped.) (28:41) Allah said;

(In this is a lesson for whoever fears.)

Surah: 79 Ayah: 27, Ayah: 28, Ayah: 29, Ayah: 30, Ayah: 31, Ayah: 32 & Ayah: 33

﴿ ءَأَنتُمْ أَشَدُّ خَلْقًا أَمِ ٱلسَّمَآءُ بَنَىٰهَا ۝ ﴾

27. Are you more difficult to create or is the heaven that He constructed?

﴿ رَفَعَ سَمْكَهَا فَسَوَّىٰهَا ۝ ﴾

28. He raised its height, and He has perfected it.

﴿ وَأَغْطَشَ لَيْلَهَا وَأَخْرَجَ ضُحَىٰهَا ۝ ﴾

29. Its night He covers with darkness and its forenoon He brings out (with light).

﴿ وَٱلْأَرْضَ بَعْدَ ذَٰلِكَ دَحَىٰهَآ ۝ ﴾

30. And after that He spread the earth,

$$﴿ أَخْرَجَ مِنْهَا مَآءَهَا وَمَرْعَاهَا ۝ ﴾$$

31. And brought forth therefrom its water and its pasture.

$$﴿ وَالْجِبَالَ أَرْسَاهَا ۝ ﴾$$

32. And the mountains He has fixed firmly,

$$﴿ مَتَاعًا لَّكُمْ وَلِأَنْعَامِكُمْ ۝ ﴾$$

33. (To be) a provision and benefit for you and your cattle.

Transliteration

27. Aantum ashaddu khalqan ami alssamao banaha 28. RafaAAa samkaha fasawwaha 29. Waaghtasha laylaha waakhraja duhaha 30. Waal-arda baAAda thalika dahaha 31. Akhraja minha maaha wamarAAaha 32. Waaljibala arsaha 33. MataAAan lakum wali-anAAamikum

Tafsir Ibn Kathir

Creating the Heavens and the Earth is more difficult than repeating Creation

in refutation of the claim rejecting resurrection due to the renewal of creation after its original state, Allah says;

(Are you) `O people'

(more difficult to create or is the heaven...) meaning, `rather the heaven is more difficult to create than you.' As Allah said;

(the creation of the heavens and the earth is greater than the creation of mankind;) (40:57) And His saying;

(Is not the One Who created the heavens and the earth, capable of creating the similar to them. Yes, indeed! He is the Supreme Creator, the All-Knowing.) (36:81) Then Allah says,

(He constructed) He explains this by His statement,

(He raised its height, and has perfected it.) meaning, He made it a lofty structure, vast in its space, with equal sides, and adorned with stars at night and in the darkness. Then Allah says,

(Its night He covers and He brings out its forenoon.) meaning, He made its night dark and extremely black, and its day bright, luminous, shining and clear. Ibn `Abbas said,

"He did Aghtasha of its night means that He made it dark." Mujahid, `Ikrimah, Sa`id bin Jubayr and a large group have said this as well. In reference to Allah's statement,

(And He brings out its forenoon.) meaning, He illuminated its day. Then Allah says,

(And after that He spread the earth,) He explains this statement by the statement that follows it,

(And brought forth therefrom its water and its pasture.) It already has been mentioned previously in Surat Ha Mim As-Sajdah that the earth was created before the heaven was created, but it was only spread out after the creation of the heaven. This means that He brought out what was in it with a forceful action. This is the meaning of what was said by Ibn `Abbas and others, and it was the explanation preferred by Ibn Jarir. In reference to the statement of Allah,

(And the mountains He has fixed firmly,) meaning, He settled them, made them firm, and established them in their places. And He is the Most Wise, the All-Knowing. He is Most Kind to His creation, Most Merciful. Allah then says,

(As provision and benefit for you and your cattle.) meaning, He spread out the earth, caused its springs to gush forth, brought forth its hidden benefits, caused its rivers to flow, and caused its vegetation, trees, and fruits to grow. He also made its mountains firm so that it (the earth) would be calmly settled with its dwellers, and He stabilized its dwelling places. All of this is a means of beneficial enjoyment for His creatures (mankind) providing them of what cattle they need, which they eat and ride upon. He has granted them these beneficial things for the period that they need them, in this worldly abode, until the end of time and the expiration of this life.

Surah: 79 Ayah: 34, Ayah: 35, Ayah: 36, Ayah: 37, Ayah: 38, Ayah: 39, Ayah: 40, Ayah: 41, Ayah: 42, Ayah: 43, Ayah: 44, Ayah: 45 & Ayah: 46

﴿ فَإِذَا جَآءَتِ ٱلطَّآمَّةُ ٱلْكُبْرَىٰ ۝ ﴾

34. But when there comes the greatest catastrophe (i.e. the Day of Recompense) -

﴿ يَوْمَ يَتَذَكَّرُ ٱلْإِنسَٰنُ مَا سَعَىٰ ۝ ﴾

35. The Day when man shall remember what he strove for.

﴿ وَبُرِّزَتِ ٱلْجَحِيمُ لِمَن يَرَىٰ ۝ ﴾

36. And Hell-fire shall be made apparent in full view for (every) one who sees.

﴿ فَأَمَّا مَن طَغَىٰ ۝ ﴾

37. Then for him who transgressed all bounds, (in disbelief, oppression and evil deeds of disobedience to Allâh).

Chapter 79: An-Naziat (Those Who Drag Forth, Soul-Snatchers), Verses 001-046

﴿ وَءَاثَرَ ٱلْحَيَوٰةَ ٱلدُّنْيَا ۝ ﴾

38. And preferred the life of this world (by following his evil desires and lusts),

﴿ فَإِنَّ ٱلْجَحِيمَ هِيَ ٱلْمَأْوَىٰ ۝ ﴾

39. Verily, his abode will be Hell-fire;

﴿ وَأَمَّا مَنْ خَافَ مَقَامَ رَبِّهِۦ وَنَهَى ٱلنَّفْسَ عَنِ ٱلْهَوَىٰ ۝ ﴾

40. But as for him who feared standing before his Lord, and restrained himself from impure evil desires and lusts.

﴿ فَإِنَّ ٱلْجَنَّةَ هِيَ ٱلْمَأْوَىٰ ۝ ﴾

41. Verily, Paradise will be his abode.

﴿ يَسْـَٔلُونَكَ عَنِ ٱلسَّاعَةِ أَيَّانَ مُرْسَىٰهَا ۝ ﴾

42. They ask you (O Muhammad (peace be upon him) about the Hour - when will be its appointed time?

﴿ فِيمَ أَنتَ مِن ذِكْرَىٰهَآ ۝ ﴾

43. You have no knowledge to say anything about it.

﴿ إِلَىٰ رَبِّكَ مُنتَهَىٰهَآ ۝ ﴾

44. To your Lord belongs (the knowledge of) the term thereof?

﴿ إِنَّمَآ أَنتَ مُنذِرُ مَن يَخْشَىٰهَا ۝ ﴾

45. You (O Muhammad (Peace be upon him)) are only a warner for those who fear it,

﴿ كَأَنَّهُمْ يَوْمَ يَرَوْنَهَا لَمْ يَلْبَثُوٓا۟ إِلَّا عَشِيَّةً أَوْ ضُحَىٰهَا ۝ ﴾

46. The Day they see it, (it will be) as if they had not tarried (in this world) except an afternoon or a morning.

Transliteration

34. Fa-itha jaati alttammatu alkubra 35. Yawma yatathakkaru al-insanu ma saAAa
36. Waburrizati aljaheemu liman yara 37. Faamma man tagha 38. Waathara alhayata addunya 39. Fa-inna aljaheema hiya alma/wa 40. Waama man khafa maqama rabbihi wanaha alnnafsa AAani alhawa 41. Fa-inna aljannata hiya alma/wa

42. Yas-aloonaka AAani alssaAAati ayyana mursaha 43. Feema anta min thikraha 44. Ila rabbika muntahaha 45. Innama anta munthiru man yakhshaha 46. Kaannahum yawma yarawnaha lam yalbathoo illa AAashiyyatan aw duhaha

Tafsir Ibn Kathir

The Day of Judgement, its Pleasures and Hell, and that its Time is not known

Allah says,

(But when there comes the Great Catastrophe) This refers to the Day of Judgement. This has been said by Ibn `Abbas. It has been called this because it will overcome every matter. It will be frightful and horrifying. As Allah says,

(And the Hour will be more grievous and more bitter.) (54:46) Then Allah says,

(The Day when man shall remember what he strove for.) meaning, at that time the Son of Adam will reflect upon all of his deeds, both the good and the evil. This is as Allah says,

(On the Day will man remember, but how will that remembrance avail him) (89:23) Then Allah says,

(And Hell shall be made apparent for whoever sees.) meaning, it will become apparent for the onlookers, so the people will see it with their own eyes.

(Then for him who transgressed) meaning, who rebels and behaves arrogantly.

(And preferred the life of this world,) meaning, he gives it precedence over the matters of his religion and his Hereafter.

(Verily his abode will be the Hell;) meaning, his final destination will be Hell, his food will be from the tree of Zaqqum, and his drink will be from Hamim.

(But as for him who feared standing before his Lord and forbade himself from desire.) meaning, he fears the standing before Allah, he fears Allah's judgement of him, he prevents his soul from following its desires, and he compels it to obey its Master.

(Verily Paradise will be his abode.) meaning, his final abode, his destination, and his place of return will be the spacious Paradise. Then Allah says,

(They ask you about the Hour -- when will be its appointed time What do you have to mention of it. To your Lord it is limited.) meaning, its knowledge is not with you, nor with any creature. Rather the knowledge of it is with Allah. He is the One Who knows the exact time of its occurrence.

(Heavy is its burden through the heavens and the earth. It shall not come upon you except all of a sudden. They ask you as if you have a good knowledge of it. Say: "The knowledge thereof is with Allah.") (7:187) Allah says here,

(To your Lord it is limited.) Thus, when Jibril asked the Messenger of Allah about the time of the last Hour he said,

«مَا الْمَسْؤُولُ عَنْهَا بِأَعْلَمَ مِنَ السَّائِلِ»

(The one questioned about it knows no more than the questioner.) Allah said,

(You are only a warner for those who fear it,) meaning, `I sent you to warn mankind and caution them to beware of the torment and punishment of Allah. So whoever fears Allah, fears standing before Him, and His threat, then he will follow you, and thus be successful and victorious. However, whoever denies you and opposes you, then he will only suffer loss and failure.' Allah then says,

(The Day they see it (it will be) as if they had not tarried (in this world) except an (`Ashiyyah) afternoon or its (Duha) morning.) meaning, when they stand up from their graves to go to the place of Gathering, they will feel that the period of the worldy life was short, it will seem to them that it was only the afternoon of one day. Juwaybir reported from Ad-Dahhak from Ibn `Abbas:

(The Day they see it (it will be) as if they had not tarried (in this world) except an (`Ashiyyah) afternoon or its (Duha) morning.) "As for `Ashiyyah, it is the time between noon until the setting of the sun.

(Or its (Duha) morning) what is between sunrise and midday (noon)." Qatadah said, "This refers to the time period of the worldly life in the eyes of the people when they see the Hereafter." This is the end of the Tafsir of Surat An-Nazi`at. And to Allah belongs all praise and thanks.

CHAPTER (SURAH) 80: ABASA (HE FROWNED), VERSES 001–042

Surah: 80 Ayah: 1, Ayah: 2, Ayah: 3, Ayah: 4, Ayah: 5, Ayah: 6, Ayah: 7, Ayah: 8, Ayah: 9, Ayah: 10, Ayah: 11, Ayah: 12, Ayah: 113, Ayah: 14, Ayah: 15 & Ayah: 16

(بِسْمِ اللَّهِ الرَّحْمَـنِ الرَّحِيمِ)

In the Name of Allah, the Most Gracious, the Most Merciful.

﴿عَبَسَ وَتَوَلَّىٰ ۝﴾

1. (The Prophet (Peace be upon him)) frowned and turned away.

﴿أَن جَاءَهُ الْأَعْمَىٰ ۝﴾

2. Because there came to him the blind man (i.e. 'Abdullâh bin Umm-Maktûm, who came to the Prophet (peace be upon him) while he was preaching to one or some of the Quraish chiefs).

﴿ وَمَا يُدْرِيكَ لَعَلَّهُۥ يَزَّكَّىٰٓ ۝ ﴾

3. And how can you know that he might become pure (from sins)?

﴿ أَوْ يَذَّكَّرُ فَتَنفَعَهُ ٱلذِّكْرَىٰٓ ۝ ﴾

4. Or he might receive admonition, and the admonition might profit him?

﴿ أَمَّا مَنِ ٱسْتَغْنَىٰ ۝ ﴾

5. As for him who thinks himself self-sufficient,

﴿ فَأَنتَ لَهُۥ تَصَدَّىٰ ۝ ﴾

6. To him you attend;

﴿ وَمَا عَلَيْكَ أَلَّا يَزَّكَّىٰ ۝ ﴾

7. What does it matter to you if he will not become pure (from disbelief: you are only a Messenger, your duty is to convey the Message of Allâh).

﴿ وَأَمَّا مَن جَآءَكَ يَسْعَىٰ ۝ ﴾

8. But as to him who came to you running,

﴿ وَهُوَ يَخْشَىٰ ۝ ﴾

9. And is afraid (of Allâh and His punishment).

﴿ فَأَنتَ عَنْهُ تَلَهَّىٰ ۝ ﴾

10. Of him you are neglectful and divert your attention to another,

﴿ كَلَّآ إِنَّهَا تَذْكِرَةٌ ۝ ﴾

11. Nay, (do not do like this); indeed it (this Qur'ân) are an admonition.

﴿ فَمَن شَآءَ ذَكَرَهُۥ ۝ ﴾

12. So whoever wills, let him pay attention to it.

﴿ فِى صُحُفٍ مُّكَرَّمَةٍ ۝ ﴾

13. (It is) in Records held (greatly) in honor (Al-Lauh Al-Mahfûz).

Chapter 80:. Abasa (He Frowned), Verses 001-042

﴿ مَّرْفُوعَةٍ مُّطَهَّرَةٍ ۝ ﴾

14. Exalted (in dignity), purified,

﴿ بِأَيْدِى سَفَرَةٍ ۝ ﴾

15. In the hands of scribes (angels).

﴿ كِرَامٍ بَرَرَةٍ ۝ ﴾

16. Honorable and obedient.

Transliteration

1. AAabasa watawalla 2. An jaahu al-aAAma 3. Wama yudreeka laAAallahu yazzakka 4. Aw yaththakkaru fatanfaAAahu alththikra 5. Amma mani istaghna 6. Faanta lahu tasadda 7. Wama AAalayka alla yazzakka 8. Waamma man jaaka yasAAa 9. Wahuwa yakhsha 10. Faanta AAanhu talahha 11. Kalla innaha tathkiratun 12. Faman shaa thakarahu 13. Fee suhufin mukarramatin 14. MarfooAAatin mutahharatin 15. Bi-aydee safaratin 16. Kiramin bararatin

Tafsir Ibn Kathir

The Prophet being reprimanded because He frowned at a Weak Man

More than one of the scholars of Tafsir mentioned that one day the Messenger of Allah was addressing one of the great leaders of the Quraysh while hoping that he would accept Islam. While he was speaking in direct conversation with him, Ibn Umm Maktum came to him, and he was of those who had accepted Islam in its earliest days. He (Ibn Umm Maktum) then began asking the Messenger of Allah about something, urgently beseeching him. The Prophet hoped that the man would be guided, so he asked Ibn Umm Maktum to wait for a moment so he could complete his conversation. He frowned in the face of Ibn Umm Maktum and turned away from him in order to face the other man. Thus, Allah revealed,

(He frowned and turned away. Because there came to him the blind man. And how can you know that he might become pure) meaning, he may attain purification and cleanliness in his soul.

(Or he might receive admonition, and the admonition might profit him) meaning, he may receive admonition and abstain from the forbidden.

(As for him who thinks himself self-sufficient. To him you attend;) meaning, `you face the rich person so that perhaps he may be guided.'

(What does it matter to you if he will not become pure) meaning, `you are not responsible for him if he does not attain purification.'

(But as for him who came to you running. And is afraid.) meaning, `he is seeking you and he comes to you so that he may be guided by what you say to him.'

(Of him you are neglectful and divert your attention to another.) meaning, `you are too busy.' Here Allah commands His Messenger to not single anyone out with the warning. Rather, he should equal warn the noble and the weak, the poor and the rich, the master and the slave, the men and the women, the young and the old. Then Allah will guide whomever He chooses to a path that is straight. He has the profound wisdom and the decisive proof. Abu Ya`la and Ibn Jarir both recorded from `A'ishah that she said about,

(He frowned and turned away.) was revealed." At-Tirmirdhi recorded this Hadith but he did not mention that it was narrated by `A'ishah. I say it is reported like this in Al-Muwatta' as well.

The Characteristics of the Qur'an

Allah says,

(Nay; indeed it is an admonition.) meaning, this Surah, or this advice in conveying knowledge equally among people, whether they are of noble or low class. Qatadah and As-Suddi both said,

(Nay; indeed it is an admonition.) "This means the Qur'an."

(So, whoever wills, let him pay attention to Him (it).) meaning, so whoever wills, he remembers Allah in all of his affairs. The pronoun could also be understood to be referring to the revelation since the conversation is alluding to it. Allah said:

(In Records held in honor, exalted, purified.) meaning, this Surah or this admonition. Both meanings are connected to each other. Actually, all of the Qur'an is in honored pages, meaning respected and revered.

(exalted) meaning, elevated in status.

(purified) meaning, from impurity, additions and deficiency. Concerning Allah's statement,

(In the hands of ambassadors (Safarah),) Ibn `Abbas, Mujahid, Ad-Dahhak, and Ibn Zayd, all said, "These are the angels." Al-Bukhari said, "Safarah (ambassadors) refers to the angels. They travel around rectifying matters between themselves. The angels when they descend with the revelation of Allah, bringing it like the ambassador who rectifies matters between people." Allah said,

(Honorable and obedient.) meaning, they are noble, handsome, and honorable in their creation. Their character and their deeds are righteous, pure and perfect. Here it should be noted that it is necessary for one who carries the Qur'an (i.e., the angel) to be following righteousness and guidance. Imam Ahmad recorded from `A'ishah that the Messenger of Allah said,

«الَّذِي يَقْرَأُ الْقُرْآنَ وَهُوَ مَاهِرٌ بِهِ، مَعَ السَّفَرَةِ الْكِرَامِ الْبَرَرَةِ، وَالَّذِي يَقْرَؤُهُ وَهُوَ

Chapter 80:. Abasa (He Frowned), Verses 001-042

عَلَيْهِ شَاقٌّ، لَهُ أَجْرَانِ»

(He who recites the Qur'an proficiently, will be with the noble, righteous, ambassador angels, and the one who recites it with difficulty will receive two rewards.) This Hadith was reported by the group.

Surah: 80 Ayah: 17, Ayah: 18, Ayah: 19, Ayah: 20, Ayah: 21, Ayah: 22, Ayah: 23, Ayah: 24, Ayah: 25, Ayah: 26, Ayah: 27, Ayah: 8, Ayah: 29, Ayah: 30, Ayah: 31 & Ayah: 32

﴿ قُتِلَ ٱلْإِنسَٰنُ مَآ أَكْفَرَهُۥ ﴾

17. Be cursed (the disbelieving) man! How ungrateful he is!

﴿ مِنْ أَىِّ شَىْءٍ خَلَقَهُۥ ﴾

18. From what thing did He create him?

﴿ مِن نُّطْفَةٍ خَلَقَهُۥ فَقَدَّرَهُۥ ﴾

19. From Nutfah (male and female semen drops) He created him and then set him in due proportion.

﴿ ثُمَّ ٱلسَّبِيلَ يَسَّرَهُۥ ﴾

20. Then He makes the Path easy for him.

﴿ ثُمَّ أَمَاتَهُۥ فَأَقْبَرَهُۥ ﴾

21. Then He causes him to die and puts him in his grave.

﴿ ثُمَّ إِذَا شَآءَ أَنشَرَهُۥ ﴾

22. Then when it is His Will, He will resurrect him (again).

﴿ كَلَّا لَمَّا يَقْضِ مَآ أَمَرَهُۥ ﴾

23. Nay, but (man) has not done what He commanded him.

﴿ فَلْيَنظُرِ ٱلْإِنسَٰنُ إِلَىٰ طَعَامِهِۦٓ ﴾

24. Then let man look at his food:

﴿ أَنَّا صَبَبْنَا ٱلْمَآءَ صَبًّا ﴾

25. We pour forth water in abundance.

﴿ ثُمَّ شَقَقْنَا ٱلْأَرْضَ شَقًّا ﴾

26. And We split the earth in clefts.

﴿ فَأَنبَتْنَا فِيهَا حَبًّا ﴾

27. And We cause therein the grain to grow,

﴿ وَعِنَبًا وَقَضْبًا ﴾

28. And grapes and clover plants (i.e. green fodder for the cattle),

﴿ وَزَيْتُونًا وَنَخْلًا ﴾

29. And olives and date-palms,

﴿ وَحَدَآئِقَ غُلْبًا ﴾

30. And gardens dense with many trees,

﴿ وَفَـٰكِهَةً وَأَبًّا ﴾

31. And fruits and herbage

﴿ مَّتَـٰعًا لَّكُمْ وَلِأَنْعَـٰمِكُمْ ﴾

32. (To be) a provision and benefit for you and your cattle.

Transliteration

17. Qutila al-insanu ma akfarahu 18. Min ayyi shay-in khalaqahu 19. Min nutfatin khalaqahu faqaddarahu 20. Thumma alssabeela yassarahu 21. Thumma amatahu faaqbarahu 22. Thumma itha shaa ansharahu 23. Kalla lamma yaqdi ma amarahu 24. Falyanthuri al-insanu ila taAAamihi 25. Anna sababna almaa sabban 26. Thumma shaqaqna al-arda shaqqan 27. Faanbatna feeha habban 28. WaAAinaban waqadban 29. Wazaytoonan wanakhlan 30. Wahada-iqa ghulban 31. Wafakihatan waabban 32. MataAAan lakum wali-anAAamikum

Tafsir Ibn Kathir

The Refutation against Whoever denies Life after Death

Allah rebukes those who deny the Resurrection and the Final Gathering.

(Qutila mankind!) Ad-Dahhak reported from Ibn `Abbas that he said,

(Qutila mankind!) "May man be cursed." Abu Malik also made a similar statement. He said, "This refers to the rejecting type of man, due to his abundant denial without any supporting argument. Rather he denies simply because he thinks it is farfetched and because he lacks knowledge of it." Ibn Jurayj said,

(How ungrateful he is!) "This means none is worse in disbelief than he is." Qatadah said,

(How ungrateful he is!) "This means none is more cursed than he is." Then Allah explains how He created him from something despised and that He is able to bring him back to life just as He created him initially. Allah says,

(From what thing did He create him From a Nutfah He created him, and then set him in due proportion.) meaning, He decreed his life span, his sustenance, his deeds, and whether he would be miserable or happy.

(Then He made the path easy for him.) Al-`Awfi reported from Ibn `Abbas, "Then He made his coming out of his mother's belly easy for him." This was also said by `Ikrimah, Ad-Dahhak, Abu Salih, Qatadah, As-Suddi, and it was the explanation preferred by Ibn Jarir. Mujahid said, "This is similar to Allah's statement,

(Verily, We guided him on the path, he is either grateful or ungrateful.) (76:3) meaning, We explained it to him, clarified it, and made it easy for him to act upon." Al-Hasan and Ibn Zayd both said the same. This is the most correct view and Allah knows best. Concerning Allah's statement,

(Then He causes him to die and puts him in his grave.) After creating man, Allah causes him to die and makes him the inhabitant of a grave. Allah said;

(Then when it is His will, He will resurrect him.) meaning, He resurrects him after his death and this is called Al-Ba`th (resurrection) and An-Nushur (resuscitation).

(And among His signs is this that He created you from dust, and then behold, you are human beings scattered.) (30:20)

(And look at the bones, how We bring them together and clothe them with flesh.) (2:259) In the Two Sahihs it is narrated by way of Al-A`mash from Abu Salih, from Abu Hurayrah that the Prophet said,

«كُلُّ ابْنِ آدَمَ يَبْلَى إِلَّا عَجْبَ الذَّنَبِ، مِنْهُ خُلِقَ، وَفِيهِ يُرَكَّبُ»

(All of the Sons of Adam (men) will decay except for the bone of coccyx (tailbone). From it he (man) was created and by it he will be reconstructed.)" Concerning Allah's statement,

(Nay, but has not done what He commanded him.) Ibn Jarir said, "Allah is saying, `Nay, the matter is not as this disbelieving man says. He claims that he has fulfilled Allah's right upon him regarding himself and his wealth.

(But he has not done what He commanded him.) Allah is saying that man has not fulfilled for his Lord the obligations that were imposed upon him." What seems apparent to me of its actual meaning -- and Allah knows best -- is that the Ayah

(Then when it is His will, He will resurrect him.) means, He will resurrect him.

(Nay! But he has not done what He commanded him.) means, He has not done it (resurrected them) as of yet, until the time period has expired and the extent of the earthly life of humanity is complete, according to the lives of all whom Allah has written it to exist from the time they are brought into existence into the world. Verily, Allah has decreed the existence of mankind, and its duration, therefore, when that is finished with Allah, He resurrects the creatures and repeats their creation just as He initially created them.

The Growth of the Seed and Other Things is a Proof of Life after Death

(Then let man look at his food) This is a call to reflect upon Allah's favor. It also contains an evidence in the vegetation's coming to life from the lifeless earth, that the bodies can be brought to life after being decayed bones and scattered dust.

(We pour forth water in abundance.) meaning, `We sent it down from the sky to the earth.'

(And We split the earth in clefts.) meaning, `We cause it (the water) to settle in it (the earth), and it enters into its boundaries, and mingles with the parts of the seeds that are left in the earth. From this the seeds grow, rise up and appear on the surface of the earth (in the form of vegetation).'

(And We cause therein Habb to grow. And grapes and Qadb,) Al-Habb refers to all types of seeds (or grains). Grapes are well-known. Al-Qadb are the moist (green) herbal plants that animals graze on. It is also called Al-Qat. Ibn `Abbas, Qatadah, Ad-Dahhak and As-Suddi, all said this. Al-Hasan Al-Basri said, "Al-Qadb is fodder."

(And olives) It is well-known, and it is a food just as its juice is a food. It is eaten for breakfast and used as an oil.

(And date palms,) It (i.e., its fruit) is eaten as Balah, Busr, Rutab and Tamr, Niya' and Matbukh, all of which are varieties of dates that range from unripe, ripe and dried in their textures. Its juice is also extracted to make pulpy fruit drinks and vinegar.

(And Ghulb Hada'iq,) meaning, gardens. Al-Hasan and Qatadah both said, "Ghulb are gardens of date palms that are thick and handsome." Ibn `Abbas and Mujahid both said, "It means everything that is gathered and collected." Allah said,

(And fruits (Fakihah) and herbage (Abb).) Fakihah includes every type of fruit. Ibn `Abbas said, "Al-Fakihah is everything that is eaten ripe, and Al-Abb is what the earth grows that is eaten by grazing animals and not people." In one narration reported from him he said, "It is the grass for the livestock animals." Abu `Ubayd Al-Qasim bin Sallam reported from Ibrahim At-Taymi that he said, "Abu Bakr As-Siddiq was asked about Allah's statement,

Chapter 80:. Abasa (He Frowned), Verses 001-042

(And fruits (Fakihah) and herbage (Abb).) and he said, `What sky would shade me and what earth would carry me if I said about the Book of Allah that which I did not have knowledge of.' " hIn reference to what Ibn Jarir recorded from Anas, that he said, "Umar bin Al-Khattab recited

(He frowned and turned away.) then when he reached this Ayah

(And fruits (Fakihah) and herbage (Abb).) he said, `We already know what Al-Fakihah is, but what is Al-Abb' Then he said, `By your life, O Ibn Al-Khattab, this is something over burdensome (i.e., unnecessary to ask about).'" This report has an authentic chain of narration. More than one person has narrated it from Anas. The meaning of the narration is that `Umar wanted to know how it looks, its type and its exact description, because he (`Umar) and everyone who reads this Ayah knows that it is one of the plants that grows from the earth. This is clear due to the Allah's saying,

(And We cause therein the Habb to grow. And grapes and Qadb, and olives and date palms. And Ghulb Hada'iq. And fruits (Fakihah) and herbage (Abb).) And then He says,

(A provision and benefit for you and your cattle.) meaning, a means of livelihood for you all and your cattle in this life until the (coming of) the Day of Judgement.

Surah: 80 Ayah: 33, Ayah: 34, Ayah: 35, Ayah: 36, Ayah: 37, Ayah: 38, Ayah: 39, Ayah: 40, Ayah: 41 & Ayah: 42

﴿ فَإِذَا جَاءَتِ ٱلصَّآخَّةُ ﴾

33. Then when there comes As-Sâkhkhah (the second blowing of Trumpet on the Day of Resurrection)

﴿ يَوْمَ يَفِرُّ ٱلْمَرْءُ مِنْ أَخِيهِ ﴾

34. That Day shall a man flee from his brother,

﴿ وَأُمِّهِ وَأَبِيهِ ﴾

35. And from his mother and his father,

﴿ وَصَٰحِبَتِهِ وَبَنِيهِ ﴾

36. And from his wife and his children.

﴿ لِكُلِّ ٱمْرِئٍ مِّنْهُمْ يَوْمَئِذٍ شَأْنٌ يُغْنِيهِ ﴾

37. Everyman that Day will have enough to make him careless of others.

﴿ وُجُوهٌ يَوْمَئِذٍ مُّسْفِرَةٌ ﴾

38. Some faces that Day will be bright (true believers of Islâmic Monotheism),

﴿ ضَاحِكَةٌ مُّسْتَبْشِرَةٌ ﴾

39. Laughing, rejoicing at good news (of Paradise).

﴿ وَوُجُوهٌ يَوْمَئِذٍ عَلَيْهَا غَبَرَةٌ ﴾

40. And other faces, that Day, will be dust-stained.

﴿ تَرْهَقُهَا قَتَرَةٌ ﴾

41. Darkness will cover them.

﴿ أُوْلَـئِكَ هُمُ ٱلْكَفَرَةُ ٱلْفَجَرَةُ ﴾

42. Such will be the Kafarah (disbelievers in Allâh, in His Oneness, and in His Messenger Muhammad (Peace be upon him), etc.), the Fajarah (wicked evil doers).

Transliteration

33. Fa-itha jaati alssakhkhatu 34. Yawma yafirru almaro min akheehi 35. Waommihi waabeehi 36. Wasahibatihi wabaneehi 37. Likulli imri-in minhum yawma-ithin sha/nun yughneehi 38. Wujoohun yawma-ithin musfiratun 39. Dahikatun mustabshiratun 40. Wawujoohun yawma-ithin AAalayha ghabaratun 41. Tarhaquha qataratun 42. Ola-ika humu alkafaratu alfajaratu

Tafsir Ibn Kathir

The Day of Judgement and the fleeing of the People from Their Relatives during it

Ibn `Abbas said, "As-Sakhkhah is one of the names of the Day of Judgement that Allah has magnified and warned His servants of." Ibn Jarir said, "Perhaps it is a name for the blowing into Trumpet." Al-Baghawi said, "As-Sakhkhah means the thunderous shout of the Day of Judgement. It has been called this because it will deafen the ears. This means that it pierces the hearing to such an extent that it almost deafens the ears."

(That Day shall a man flee from his brother. And from his mother and his father. And from his wife and his children.) meaning, he will see them and then flee from them, and seek to get away from them because horror will be so great and the matter will be so weighty. There is an authentic Hadith related concerning the intercession that states that every one of the great Messengers of firm resolve will be requested to intercede with Allah on behalf of the creation, but each of them will say, "O myself! O myself! Today I will not ask You (O Allah) concerning anyone but myself." Even `Isa bin Maryam will say, "I will not ask Him (Allah) concerning anyone but myself today. I will not even ask Maryam, the woman who gave birth to me." Thus, Allah says,

Chapter 80:. Abasa (He Frowned), Verses 001-042

(That Day shall a man flee from his brother, and from his mother and his father, and from his wife and his children.) Qatadah said, "The most beloved and then the next most beloved, and the closest of kin and then the next closest of kin -- due to the terror of that Day." Allah said,

(Every man that Day will have enough to make him careless of others.) meaning, he will be preoccupied in his business and distracted from the affairs of others. Ibn Abi Hatim recorded from Ibn `Abbas that the Messenger of Allah said,

«تُحْشَرُونَ حُفَاةً عُرَاةً مُشَاةً غُرْلًا»

(You will all be gathered barefoot, naked, walking and uncircumcised.) So his wife said, "O Messenger of Allah! Will we look at or see each other's nakedness" The Prophet replied,

«لِكُلِّ امْرِىءٍ مِنْهُمْ يَوْمَئِذٍ شَأْنٌ يُغْنِيهِ أو قال: مَا أَشْغَلَهُ عَنِ النَّظَرِ»

(Every man among them on that Day will have enough (worries) to make him careless of others) -- or he said: (he will be too busy to look.) Ibn `Abbas narrated that the Prophet said,

«تُحْشَرُونَ حُفَاةً عُرَاةً غُرْلًا»

(You will all be gathered barefoot, naked and uncircumcised.) So a woman said, "Will we see or look at each others nakedness" He replied,

«يَا فُلَانَةُ، لِكُلِّ امْرِىءٍ مِنْهُمْ يَوْمَئِذٍ شَأْنٌ يُغْنِيهِ»

(O so-and-so woman! Every man among them on that Day will have enough (worries) to make him careless of others.) At-Tirmidhi said, "This Hadith is Hasan Sahih."

The Faces of the People of Paradise and the People of the Fire on the Day of Judgement

Allah says;

(Some faces that Day will be bright (Musfirah), laughing, rejoicing at good news.) meaning, the people will be divided into two parties. There will be faces that are Musfirah, which means bright.

(Laughing, rejoicing at good news.) meaning, happy and pleased due to the joy that will be in their hearts. The good news will be apparent on their faces. These will be the people of Paradise.

(And other faces that Day will be dust-stained. Darkness (Qatarah) will cover them.) meaning, they will be overcome and covered with Qatarah, which is darkness. Ibn `Abbas said,

(Darkness (Qatarah) will cover them.) "This means that they (the faces) will be overcome with darkness." Allah said,

(Such will be the disbelieving, the wicked evildoers.) meaning, they are disbelievers in their hearts, evildoers in their actions. This is as Allah says,

(And they will beget none but wicked disbelievers.) (71:27) This is the end of the Tafsir of Surat `Abasa, and to Allah all praise and thanks are due.

INTRODUCTION TO CHAPTER (SURAH) 81: AT-TAKWIR (THE OVERTHROWING)

Ibn Kathir's Introduction

What has been narrated about This Surah

Imam Ahmad recorded from Ibn `Umar that the Messenger of Allah said,

«مَنْ سَرَّهُ أَنْ يَنْظُرَ إِلَى يَوْمِ الْقِيَامَةِ كَأَنَّهُ رَأْيُ عَيْنٍ فَلْيَقْرَأْ:

(إِذَا الشَّمْسُ كُوِّرَتْ) و (إِذَا السَّمَاءُ انفَطَرَتْ) و (إِذَا السَّمَاءُ انشَقَّتْ)»

(Whoever wishes to look at the Day of Judgement as if he is seeing it with his own eyes, then let him read, (When the sun is wound round.) (81:1) (and; (When the heaven is cleft asunder.) (82:1) (and; (When the heaven is split asunder.) (84:1)) Likewise, At-Tirmidhi has also recorded this Hadith.

CHAPTER (SURAH) 81: AT-TAKWIR THE OVERTHROWING, VERSES 001- 029

> Surah: 81 Ayah: 1, Ayah: 2, Ayah: 3, Ayah: 4, Ayah: 5, Ayah: 6, Ayah: 7, Ayah: 8, Ayah: 9, Ayah: 10, Ayah: 11, Ayah: 12, Ayah: 13 & Ayah: 14

(بِسْمِ اللَّهِ الرَّحْمَنِ الرَّحِيمِ)

In the Name of Allah, the Most Gracious, the Most Merciful.

﴿إِذَا الشَّمْسُ كُوِّرَتْ ۝﴾

Chapter 81: At-Takwir (The Overthrowing), Verses 001-029

1. When the sun is wound round and its light is lost and is overthrown.

﴿ وَإِذَا ٱلنُّجُومُ ٱنكَدَرَتْ ۝ ﴾

2. And when the stars shall fall.

﴿ وَإِذَا ٱلْجِبَالُ سُيِّرَتْ ۝ ﴾

3. And when the mountains are made to pass away;

﴿ وَإِذَا ٱلْعِشَارُ عُطِّلَتْ ۝ ﴾

4. And when the pregnant she-camels are neglected;

﴿ وَإِذَا ٱلْوُحُوشُ حُشِرَتْ ۝ ﴾

5. And when the wild beasts are gathered together.

﴿ وَإِذَا ٱلْبِحَارُ سُجِّرَتْ ۝ ﴾

6. And when the seas shall become as blazing Fire or overflow.

﴿ وَإِذَا ٱلنُّفُوسُ زُوِّجَتْ ۝ ﴾

7. And when the souls shall be joined with their bodies, (the good with the good and the bad with the bad).

﴿ وَإِذَا ٱلْمَوْءُۥدَةُ سُئِلَتْ ۝ ﴾

8. And when the female (infant) buried alive (as the pagan Arabs used to do) is questioned:

﴿ بِأَيِّ ذَنۢبٍ قُتِلَتْ ۝ ﴾

9. For what sin, was she killed?

﴿ وَإِذَا ٱلصُّحُفُ نُشِرَتْ ۝ ﴾

10. And when the (written) pages (of deeds (good and bad) of every person) shall be laid open.

﴿ وَإِذَا ٱلسَّمَآءُ كُشِطَتْ ۝ ﴾

11. And when the heaven is stripped off and taken away from its place;

﴿ وَإِذَا ٱلْجَحِيمُ سُعِّرَتْ ۝ ﴾

12. And when Hell-fire is set ablaze.

﴿ وَإِذَا ٱلْجَنَّةُ أُزْلِفَتْ ۝ ﴾

13. And when Paradise is brought near.

﴿ عَلِمَتْ نَفْسٌ مَّآ أَحْضَرَتْ ۝ ﴾

14. (Then) every person will know what he has brought (of good and evil).

Transliteration

1. Itha alshshamsu kuwwirat 2. Wa-itha alnnujoomu inkadarat 3. Wa-itha aljibalu suyyirat 4. Wa-itha alAAisharu AAuttilat 5. Wa-itha alwuhooshu hushirat 6. Wa-itha albiharu sujjirat 7. Wa-itha alnnufoosu zuwwijat 8. Wa-itha almawoodatu su-ilat 9. Bi-ayyi thanbin qutilat 10. Wa-itha alssuhufu nushirat 11. Wa-itha alssamao kushitat 12. Wa-itha aljaheemu suAAAAirat 13. Wa-itha aljannatu ozlifat 14. AAalimat nafsun ma ahdarat

Tafsir Ibn Kathir

What will happen on the Day of Judgement, and that is the rolling up of the Sun

`Ali bin Abi Talhah reported from Ibn `Abbas:

(When the sun is Kuwwirat.) "This means it will be darkened." Al-`Awfi reported from Ibn `Abbas; "It will go away." Qatadah said, "Its light will go away." Sa`id bin Jubayr said, "Kuwwirat means it will sink in." Abu Salih said, "Kuwwirat means it will be thrown down." At-Takwir means to gather one part of something with another part of it (i.e., folding). From it comes the folding of the turban (`Imamah) and the folding of clothes together. Thus, the meaning of Allah's statement,

(Kuwwirat) is that part of it will be folded up into another part of it. Then it will be rolled up and thrown away. When this is done to it, its light will go away. Al-Bukhari recorded from Abu Hurayrah that the Prophet said,

«الشَّمْسُ وَالْقَمَرُ يُكَوَّرَانِ يَوْمَ الْقِيَامَة»

(The sun and the moon will be rolled up on the Day of Judgement.) Al-Bukhari was alone in recording this Hadith and this is his wording of it.

Dispersing the Stars

(And when the stars Inkadarat.) meaning, when they are scattered. This is as Allah says,

(And when the stars have fallen and scattered.) (82:2) The basis of the word Inkidar is Insibab, which means to be poured out. Ar-Rabi` bin Anas reported from Abu Al-`Aliyah, who reported from Ubayy bin Ka`b that he said, "Six signs will take place before the Day of Judgement. The people will be in their marketplaces when the sun's light will go away. When they are in that situation, the stars will be scattered. When they are in that situation, the mountains will fall down upon the face of the earth, and the earth will move, quake and be in a state of mixed up confusion. So the Jinns will then flee in fright to the humans and the humans will flee to the Jinns. The domestic beasts, birds and wild animals will mix together, and they will surge together in a wave (of chaos).

(And when the wild beasts are gathered together.) This means they will be mixed.

(And when the pregnant she camels are neglected;) This means their owners will neglect them.

(And when the seas become as blazing fire)" Then he (Ubayy) went on to say, "The Jinns will say, `We come to you with news.' So they will all go to the sea, and it will be a blazing fire. While they are in that state, the earth will be split with one huge crack that will extend from the lowest, seventh earth to the highest, seventh heaven. So while they are in that state, a wind will come that will kill all of them." Ibn Jarir recorded this narration with this wording.

Moving of the Mountains, abandoning of the Pregnant She-Camels, and the gathering of the Wild Beasts

Concerning Allah's statement,

(And when the mountains are made to pass away;) meaning, they will not remain in their places and they will be destroyed. Then the earth will be left as a flat, level plain. Then Allah says,

(And when the pregnant she-camels (`Ishar) are neglected (`Uttilat);) `Ikrimah and Mujahid said, "`Ishar are (pregnant she-) camels." Mujahid said, "`Uttilat means abandoned and left." Ubayy bin Ka`b and Ad-Dahhak both said, "Their owners will neglect them." Ar-Rabi` bin Khuthaym said, "They will not be milked or tied up. Their masters will leave them abandoned." Ad-Dahhak said, "They will be left with no one to tend to them." And the meaning of all of these statements is similar. What is intended is that the `Ishar is a type of camel. It is actually the best type of camel, and particularly the pregnant females of them when they have reached the tenth month of their pregnancies. One of them is singularly referred to as `Ushara', and she keeps that name until she gives birth. So the people will be too busy to tend to her, take care of her or benefit from her, after she used to be the most important thing to them. This will be due to what will suddenly overtake them of the great, terrifying and horrible situation. This is the matter of the Day of Judgement, the coming together of its causes, and the occurrence of those things that will happen before it.

(And when the wild beasts are gathered together.) meaning, gathered. This is as Allah says,

(There is not a moving creature on earth, nor a bird that flies with its two wings, but are communities like you. We have neglected nothing in the Book, then unto their Lord they shall be gathered.) (6:38) Ibn `Abbas said, "Everything will be gathered, even the flies." This statement was recorded by Ibn Abi Hatim. Allah also says,

(And (so did) the birds assembled.) (38:19) meaning, gathered.

The Blazing of the Seas

Allah says,

(And when the seas become as blazing fire.) Ibn Jarir recorded from Sa`id bin Al-Musayyib that `Ali said to a Jewish man, "Where is the Hell" The man said, "The sea." `Ali then said, "I think he is truthful, as Allah says

(And by the seas kindled (Masjur).) (52:6) and;

(And when the seas become as blazing fire.)" This has already been discussed previously with the explanation of Allah's statement,

(And by the seas kindled (Masjur).) (52:6)

Joining the Souls

Concerning Allah's statement,

(And when the souls are joined with their mates.) meaning, every type (of soul) will be gathered with its peer (or mate). This is as Allah says,

(It will be said to the angels): "Assemble those who did wrong, together with their companions (from the devils).) (37:22) Ibn Abi Hatim recorded from An-Nu`man bin Bashir that the Messenger of Allah said,

((And When the souls are joined with their mates.)(Those who are alike. Every man will be with every group of people who performed the same deeds that he did. (This is because Allah says, (And you (all) will be in three groups. So those on the Right Hand - how (fortunate) will be those on Right Hand! And those on the Left Hand - how (unfortunate) will be those on the Left Hand!) (56: 7-10) (They are those who are alike.)

Questioning the Female Infant Who was buried Alive

Allah says,

(And when the female infant (Al-Maw'udah) buried alive is questioned: For what sin was she killed) The majority have recited it as Su'ilat (she is questioned), as it is here. Al-Maw'udah is the female infant that the people of the pre-Islamic time of ignorance would bury in the dirt due to their hatred of girls. Therefore, on the Day of Judgement, the female infant will be asked what sin she committed that caused here to be murdered. This will be a means of frightening her murderer. For verily, if the one who was wronged is questioned, what does the wrongdoer (the one who is guilty of the oppression) think then `Ali bin Abi Talhah reported that Ibn `Abbas said,

(And when the female infant (Al-Maw'udah) buried alive Su'ilat:) "This means that she will ask." Abu Ad-Duha made a similar statement when he said, "She will ask, meaning she will demand restitution for her blood." The same has been reported from

As-Suddi and Qatadah. Hadiths have been reported concerning the Maw'udah. Imam Ahmad recorded from `A'ishah, who reported from Judamah bint Wahb, the sister of `Ukkashah, that she said, "I was in the presence of the Messenger of Allah when he was with some people, and he said,

«لَقَدْ هَمَمْتُ أَنْ أَنْهَى عَنِ الْغِيلَةِ فَنَظَرْتُ فِي الرُّومِ وَفَارِسَ، فَإِذَا هُمْ يُغِيلُونَ أَوْلَادَهُمْ، وَلَا يَضُرُّ أَوْلَادَهُمْ ذَلِكَ شَيْئًا»

(I was about to prohibit sexual relations with breast feeding women, but then I saw that the Romans and the Persians have sexual relations with their women who breast feed their children and it does not harm the children at all.) Then they asked him about interruption of sexual intercourse to prevent the male discharge from entering the womb of the woman, and he said,

«ذَلِكَ الْوَأْدُ الْخَفِيُّ، وَهُوَ الْمَوْءُودَةُ سُئِلَت»

(That is the minor infanticide and it is the female infant buried alive (Maw'udah) that will be questioned.)" Muslim, Ibn Majah, Abu Dawud, At-Tirmidhi and An-Nasa'i, all recorded this Hadith as well.

The Atonement for burying Infant Girls Alive

`Abdur-Razzaq said that Isra'il informed them from Simak bin Harb, from An-Nu`man bin Bashir, who reported from `Umar bin Al-Khattab that he said concerning Allah's statement,

(And when the female infant buried alive is questioned.) "Qays bin `Asim came to the Messenger of Allah and said, `O Messenger of Allah! Verily, I buried some daughters of mine alive in the period of pre-Islamic ignorance.' The Messenger of Allah said,

«أَعْتِقْ عَنْ كُلِّ وَاحِدَةٍ مِنْهُنَّ رَقَبَة»

(Free a slave for each one of them.) Then Qays said, `O Messenger of Allah! Verily, I am an owner of camels.' The Prophet said,

«فَانْحَرْ عَنْ كُلِّ وَاحِدَةٍ مِنْهُنَّ بَدَنَة»

(Then sacrifice a camel for each one of them.)"

The Distribution of the Pages

Allah says,

(And when the pages are laid open.) Ad-Dahhak said, "Every person will be given his paper in his right hand or in his left hand." Qatadah said, "O Son of Adam ! It (your paper) is written in, then it is rolled up, then it will be distributed to you on the Day of Judgement. So let each man look at what he himself dictated to be written in his paper."

Removing the Heavens, kindling Hellfire, and Paradise being brought near

Allah says,

(And when the heaven is Kushitat;) Mujahid said, "It drawns away." As-Suddi said, "Stripped off." Concerning Allah's statement,

(And when Hell is Su`irat.) As-Suddi said, "It is heated." In reference to Allah's statement,

(And when Paradise is brought near.) Ad-Dahhak, Abu Malik, Qatadah, and Ar-Rabi` bin Khuthaym, all said, "This means it will be brought near to its inhabitants."

Everyone will know what He has brought on the Day of Judgement

Concerning Allah's statement,

(Every person will know what he has brought.) This is the conclusive response of the previous statements, meaning at the time these matters occur, every soul will know what it has done, and that will be brought forth for it, as Allah says,

(On the Day when every person will be confronted with all the good he has done, and all the evil he has done, he will wish that there were a great distance between him and his evil.) (3:30) Allah also says,

(On that Day man will be informed of what he sent forward, and what he left behind.) (75:13)

Surah: 81 Ayah: 15, Ayah: 16, Ayah: 17, Ayah: 18, Ayah: 19, Ayah: 20, Ayah: 21, Ayah: 22, Ayah: 23, Ayah: 24, Ayah: 25, Ayah: 26, Ayah: 27, Ayah: 28 & Ayah: 29

﴿ فَلَآ أُقْسِمُ بِٱلْخُنَّسِ ﴾

15. So verily, I swear by the planets that recede (i.e. disappear during the day and appear during the night).

﴿ ٱلْجَوَارِ ٱلْكُنَّسِ ﴾

16. And by the planets that move swiftly and hide themselves.

﴿ وَٱلَّيْلِ إِذَا عَسْعَسَ ﴾

17. And by the night as it departs.

﴿ وَٱلصُّبْحِ إِذَا تَنَفَّسَ ۝ ﴾

18. And by the dawn as it brightens.

﴿ إِنَّهُ لَقَوْلُ رَسُولٍ كَرِيمٍ ۝ ﴾

19. Verily, this is the Word (this Qur'ân brought by) a most honorable messenger (Jibrîl (Gabriel), from Allâh to the Prophet Muhammad (peace be upon him))

﴿ ذِى قُوَّةٍ عِندَ ذِى ٱلْعَرْشِ مَكِينٍ ۝ ﴾

20. Owner of power, (and high rank) with (Allâh) the Lord of the Throne,

﴿ مُّطَاعٍ ثَمَّ أَمِينٍ ۝ ﴾

21. Obeyed (by the angels in the heavens), and trustworthy.

﴿ وَمَا صَاحِبُكُم بِمَجْنُونٍ ۝ ﴾

22. And (O people) your companion (Muhammad (peace be upon him)) is not a madman.

﴿ وَلَقَدْ رَءَاهُ بِٱلْأُفُقِ ٱلْمُبِينِ ۝ ﴾

23. And indeed he (Muhammad (peace be upon him)) saw him (Jibrîl (Gabriel)) in the clear horizon (towards the east).

﴿ وَمَا هُوَ عَلَى ٱلْغَيْبِ بِضَنِينٍ ۝ ﴾

24. And he (Muhammad (peace be upon him)) withholds not a knowledge of the Unseen.

﴿ وَمَا هُوَ بِقَوْلِ شَيْطَانٍ رَّجِيمٍ ۝ ﴾

25. And it (the Qur'ân) is not the word of the outcast Shaitân (Satan).

﴿ فَأَيْنَ تَذْهَبُونَ ۝ ﴾

26. Then where are you going?

﴿ إِنْ هُوَ إِلَّا ذِكْرٌ لِّلْعَالَمِينَ ۝ ﴾

27. Verily, this (the Qur'ân) is no less than a Reminder to (all) the 'Âlamîn (mankind and jinn)

﴿ لِمَن شَآءَ مِنكُمْ أَن يَسْتَقِيمَ ۝ ﴾

28. To whomsoever among you who wills to walk straight.

﴿ وَمَا تَشَآءُونَ إِلَّآ أَن يَشَآءَ ٱللَّهُ رَبُّ ٱلۡعَٰلَمِينَ ۝ ﴾

29. And you cannot will unless (it be) that Allâh wills - the Lord of the 'Âlamîn (mankind, jinn and all that exists).

Transliteration

15. Fala oqsimu bialkhunnasi 16. Aljawari alkunnasi 17. Waallayli itha AAasAAasa 18. Waalssubhi itha tanaffasa 19. Innahu laqawlu rasoolin kareemin 20. Thee quwwatin AAinda thee alAAarshi makeenin 21. MutaAAin thamma ameenin 22. Wama sahibukum bimajnoonin 23. Walaqad raahu bialofuqi almubeeni 24. Wama huwa AAala alghaybi bidaneenin 25. Wama huwa biqawli shaytanin rajeemin 26. Faayna tathhaboona 27. In huwa illa thikrun lilAAalameena 28. Liman shaa minkum an yastaqeema 29. Wama tashaoona illa an yashaa Allahu rabbu alAAalameena

Tafsir Ibn Kathir

The Explanation of the Words Al-Khunnas and Al-Kunnas

Muslim recorded in his Sahih, and An-Nasa'i in his Book of Tafsir, in explaining this Ayah, from `Amr bin Hurayth that he said, "I prayed the Morning prayer behind the Prophet , and I heard him reciting,

(But nay! I swear by Al-Khunnas, Al-Jawar Al-Kunnas, and by the night when it `As`as, and by the day when it Tanaffas.)" Ibn Jarir recorded from Khalid bin `Ar`arah that he heard `Ali being asked about the Ayah; (Nay! I swear by Al-Khunnas, Al-Jawar Al-Kunnas.) and he said, "These are the stars that withdraw (disappear) during the day and sweep across the sky (appear) at night." Concerning Allah's statement,

(And by the night when it `As`as.) There are two opinions about this statement. One of them is that this refers to its advancing with its darkness. Mujahid said, "It means its darkening." Sa`id bin Jubayr said, "When it begins." Al-Hasan Al-Basri said, "When it covers the people." This was also said by `Atiyah Al-`Awfi. `Ali bin Abi Talhah and Al-`Awfi both reported from Ibn `Abbas:

(when it `As`as) "This means when it goes away." Mujahid, Qatadah and Ad-Dahhak, all said the same. Zayd bin Aslam and his son `Abdur-Rahman also made a similar statement, when they said,

(when it `As`as) "This means when it leaves, and thus it turns away." I believe that the intent in Allah's saying,

(when it `As`as) is when it approaches, even though it is correct to use this word for departing also. However, approachment is a more suitable usage here. It is as if Allah is swearing by the night and its darkness when it approaches, and by the morning and its light when it shines from the east. This is as Allah says,

Chapter 81: At-Takwir (The Overthrowing), Verses 001-029

(By the night as it envelops. By the day as it appears in brightness) (92:1-2) and He also says,

(By the forenoon. By the night when it darkens.) (93:1-2) Allah also says,

(Cleaver of the daybreak. He has appointed night for resting.) (6:96) And there are other similar Ayat that mention this. Many of the scholars of the fundamentals of language have said that the word `As`as is used to mean advancing and retreating, with both meanings sharing the same word. Therefore, it is correct that the intent could be both of them, and Allah knows best. Concerning Allah's statement,

(And by the day when it Tanaffas.) Ad-Dahhak said, "When it rises." Qatadah said, "When it brightens and advances."

Jibril descended with the Qur'an and it is not the Result of Insanity

Concerning Allah's statement,

(Verily, this is the Word of a most honorable messenger.) meaning, indeed this Qur'an is being conveyed by a noble messenger, which is referring to an honorable angel, who has good character and a radiant appearance, and he is Jibril. Ibn `Abbas, Ash-Sha`bi, Maymun bin Mihran, Al-Hasan, Qatadah, Ar-Rabi` bin Anas, Ad-Dahhak and others have said this.

(Dhi Quwwah) This is similar to Allah's statement,

(He has been taught by one mighty in power, Dhu Mirrah.) (53:5-6) meaning, mighty in creation, mighty in strength and mighty in actions.

(with the Lord of the Throne Makin,) meaning, he has high status and lofty rank with Allah.

(Obeyed there,) meaning, he has prestige, his word is listened to, and he is obeyed among the most high gathering (of angels). Qatadah said,

(Obeyed there) "This means in the heavens. He is not one of the lower ranking (ordinary) angels. Rather he is from the high ranking, prestigious angels. He is respected and has been chosen for (the delivery of) this magnificent Message." Allah then says,

(trustworthy.) This is a description of Jibril as being trustworthy. This is something very great, that the Almighty Lord has commended His servant and angelic Messenger, Jibril, just as He has commended His servant and human Messenger, Muhammad by His statement,

(And your companion is not a madman.) Ash-Sha`bi, Maymun bin Mihran, Abu Salih and others who have been previously mentioned, all said, "This refers to Muhammad ." Allah said,

(And indeed he saw him in the clear horizon.) meaning, indeed Muhammad saw Jibril, who brought him the Message from Allah, in the form that Allah created him in (i.e., his true form), and he had six hundred wings.

(in the clear horizon.) meaning, clear. This refers to the first sighting which occurred at Al-Batha' (Makkah). This incident is mentioned in Allah's statement,

(He has been taught by one mighty in power (Jibril). Dhu Mirrah, then he rose. While he was in the highest part of the horizon. Then he approached and came closer. And was at a distance of two bows' length or less. So (Allah) revealed to His servant what He revealed.) (53:5-10) The explanation of this and its confirmation has already preceded, as well as the evidence that proves that it is referring to Jibril. It seems apparent -- and Allah knows best -- that this Surah (At-Takwir) was revealed before the Night Journey (Al-Isra'), because nothing has been mentioned in it except this sighting (of Jibril), and it is the first sighting. The second sighting has been mentioned in Allah's statement,

(And indeed he saw him (Jibril) at a second descent. Near Sidrah Al-Muntaha. Near it is the Paradise of Abode. When that covered the lote tree which did cover it !) (53:13-16) And these Ayat have only been mentioned in Surat An-Najm, which was revealed after Surat Al-Isra' (The Night Journey). The Prophet is not Stingy in conveying the Revelation (He is not Zanin over the Unseen) meaning Muhammad is not following false conjecture about what Allah revealed. Others have recited this Ayah with the `Dad' in the word Danin, which means that he is not stingy, but rather he conveys it to everyone. Sufyan bin `Uyaynah said, "Zanin and Danin both have the same meaning. They mean that he is not a liar, nor is he a wicked, sinful person. The Zanin is one who follows false supposition, and the Danin is one who is stingy." Qatadah said, "The Qur'an was unseen and Allah revealed it to Muhammad , and he did not withhold it from the people. Rather he announced it, conveyed it, and offered it to everyone who wanted it." `Ikrimah, Ibn Zayd and others have made similar statements. Ibn Jarir preferred the recitation Danin. I say that both of recitations have been confirmed by numerous routes of transmission, and its meaning is correct either way, as we have mentioned earlier.

The Qur'an is a Reminder for all the Worlds and It is not the Inspiration of Shaytan

Allah says,

(And it is not the word of the outcast Shaytan.) meaning, this Qur'an is not the statement of an outcast Shaytan. This means that he is not able to produce it, nor is it befitting of him to do so. This is as Allah says,

(And it is not the Shayatin who have brought it down. Neither would it suit them nor they can. Verily, they have been removed far from hearing it.) (26:210-212) Then Allah says,

(Then where are you going) meaning, where has your reason gone, in rejecting this Qur'an, while it is manifest, clear, and evident that it is the truth from Allah. This is as

Abu Bakr As-Siddiq said to the delegation of Bani Hanifah when they came to him as Muslims and he commanded them to recite (something from the Qur'an). So they recited something to him from the so called Qur'an of Musaylimah the Liar, that was total gibberish and terribly poor in style. Thus, Abu Bakr said, "Woe unto you! Where have your senses gone By Allah, this speech did not come from a god." Qatadah said, (Then where are you going) meaning, from the Book of Allah and His obedience. Then Allah says, (Verily, this is no less than a Reminder to the creatures.) meaning, this Qur'an is a reminder for all of mankind. They are reminded by it and receive admonition from it.

(To whomsoever among you who wills to walk straight.) meaning, whoever seeks guidance, then he must adhere to this Qur'an, for verily it is his salvation and guidance. There is no guidance in other than it.

(And you cannot will unless (it be) that Allah wills -- the Lord of all that exists.) This means that the will is not left to you all, so that whoever wishes to be guided, then he is guided, and whoever wishes to be astray, then he goes astray, rather, all of this is according to the will of Allah the Exalted, and He is the Lord of all that exists. It is reported from Sulayman bin Musa that when this Ayah was revealed, (To whomsoever among you who wills to walk straight.) Abu Jahl said, "The matter is up to us. If we wish, we will stand straight, and we do not wish, we will not stand straight." So Allah revealed, (And you cannot will unless (it be) that Allah wills the Lord of the all that exists.) This is the end of the Tafsir of Surat At-Takwir, and all praise and thanks are due to Allah.

INTRODUCTION TO CHAPTER (SURAH) 82: AL-INFITAR (THE CLEAVING, BURSTING APART)

Ibn Kathir's Introduction

The Virtues of Surat Al-Infitar

An-Nasa'i recorded from Jabir that Mu`adh stood and lead the people in the Night prayer, and he made the recitation of his prayer long. So the Prophet said,

«أَفَتَّانٌ أَنْتَ يَا مُعَاذُ؟ أَيْنَ كُنْتَ عَنْ (سَبِّحِ اسْمَ رَبِّكَ الْأَعْلَى) (وَالضُّحَى)

وَ (إِذَا السَّمَاءُ انْفَطَرَتْ)»

(Are you putting the people to trial O Mu`adh Why don't you recite (Glorify the Name of your Lord the Most High) (87), (By the forenoon) (93), and (When the heaven is cleft asunder) (82))" The basis of this Hadith is found in the Two Sahihs, however the mentioning of (When the heaven is cleft asunder.) has only been mentioned by An-Nasa'i. It has been previously mentioned in a narration from `Abdullah bin `Umar that the Prophet said,

«مَنْ سَرَّهُ أَنْ يَنْظُرَ إِلَى الْقِيَامَةِ رَأْيَ عَيْنٍ فَلْيَقْرَأْ: (إِذَا الشَّمْسُ كُوِّرَتْ) و (إِذَا السَّمَاءُ انفَطَرَتْ) و (إِذَا السَّمَاءُ انشَقَّتْ)»

(Whoever would be pleased to look at the Day of Resurrection with his own eyes, then let him recite, (When the sun is Kuwwirat.) (81) and; (When the heaven is cleft asunder) (82) and; (When the heaven is split asunder) (84).)

CHAPTER (SURAH) 82: AL-INFITAR THE CLEAVING, BURSTING APART, VERSES 001- 019

Surah: 82 Ayah: 1, Ayah: 2, Ayah: 3, Ayah: 4, Ayah: 5, Ayah: 6, Ayah: 7, Ayah: 8, Ayah: 9, Ayah: 10, Ayah: 11 & Ayah: 12

(بِسْمِ اللَّهِ الرَّحْمَـنِ الرَّحِيمِ)

In the Name of Allah, the Most Gracious, the Most Merciful.

﴿ إِذَا ٱلسَّمَآءُ ٱنفَطَرَتْ ۝ ﴾

1. When the heaven is cleft asunder.

﴿ وَإِذَا ٱلْكَوَاكِبُ ٱنتَثَرَتْ ۝ ﴾

2. And when the stars have fallen and scattered.

﴿ وَإِذَا ٱلْبِحَارُ فُجِّرَتْ ۝ ﴾

3. And when the seas are burst forth.

﴿ وَإِذَا ٱلْقُبُورُ بُعْثِرَتْ ۝ ﴾

4. And when the graves are turned upside down (and bring out their contents)

﴿ عَلِمَتْ نَفْسٌ مَّا قَدَّمَتْ وَأَخَّرَتْ ۝ ﴾

5. (Then) a person will know what he has sent forward and (what he has) left behind (of good or bad deeds).

﴿ يَـٰٓأَيُّهَا ٱلْإِنسَـٰنُ مَا غَرَّكَ بِرَبِّكَ ٱلْكَرِيمِ ۝ ﴾

6. O man! What has made you careless about your Lord, the Most Generous?

﴿ ٱلَّذِى خَلَقَكَ فَسَوَّىٰكَ فَعَدَلَكَ ۝ ﴾

Chapter 82: Al-Infitar (The Cleaving, Bursting Apart), Verses 001-019

7. Who created you, fashioned you perfectly, and gave you due proportion.

﴿ فِىٓ أَىِّ صُورَةٍ مَّا شَآءَ رَكَّبَكَ ۝ ﴾

8. In whatever form He willed, He put you together.

﴿ كَلَّا بَلْ تُكَذِّبُونَ بِٱلدِّينِ ۝ ﴾

9. Nay! But you deny Ad-Dîn (i.e. the Day of Recompense).

﴿ وَإِنَّ عَلَيْكُمْ لَحَفِظِينَ ۝ ﴾

10. But verily, over you (are appointed angels in charge of mankind) to watch you,

﴿ كِرَامًا كَتِبِينَ ۝ ﴾

11. Kirâman (honorable) Kâtibîn writing down (your deeds),

﴿ يَعْلَمُونَ مَا تَفْعَلُونَ ۝ ﴾

12. They know all that you do.

Transliteration

1. Itha alssamao infatarat 2. Wa-itha alkawakibu intatharat 3. Wa-itha albiharu fujjirat 4. Wa-itha alqubooru buAAthirat 5. AAalimat nafsun ma qaddamat waakhkharat 6. Ya ayyuha al-insanu ma gharraka birabbika alkareemi 7. Allathee khalaqaka fasawwaka faAAadalaka 8. Fee ayyi sooratin ma shaa rakkabaka 9. Kalla bal tukaththiboona bialddeeni 10. Wa-inna AAalaykum lahafitheena 11. Kiraman katibeena 12. YaAAlamoona ma tafAAaloona

Tafsir Ibn Kathir

What will happen on the Day of Judgement.

Allah says,

(When the heaven is cleft asunder (Infatarat).) meaning, it splits. This is as Allah says,

(Whereon the heaven will be cleft asunder (Munfatir)) (73:18) Then Allah says,

(And when the stars Intatharat.) meaning, fallen.

(And when the seas Fujjirat.) `Ali bin Abi Talhah reported from Ibn `Abbas that he said, "Allah will cause some of it to burst forth over other parts of it." Al-Hasan said, "Allah will cause some parts of it to burst forth over other parts of it, and its water will go away." Qatadah said, "Its fresh water will mix with its salt water."

(And when the graves Bu`thirat.) Ibn `Abbas said, "searched." As-Suddi said, "Tub`athiru means that they will be moved and those who are in them will come out."

(A person will know what he has sent forward and left behind.) meaning, when this happens then this will occur. Mankind should not forget about Allah Allah says,

(O man! What has made you careless about your Lord, the Most Generous) This is a threat. It is not an attempt to get a reply as some people mistakenly think. They consider it as if the Most Generous is asking them so that they will say, "His honor deceived him (or made him careless of his Lord)." rather the meaning of this Ayah is, "O Son of Adam! What has deceived you from your Lord, the Most Generous -- meaning the Most Great -- so that you went forth disobeying Him, and you met Him with that which was unbefitting." This is similar to what has been reported in the Hadith,

«يَقُولُ اللهُ تَعَالَى يَوْمَ الْقِيَامَةِ: يَا ابْنَ آدَمَ مَا غَرَّكَ بِي؟ يَا ابْنَ آدَمَ مَاذَا أَجَبْتَ الْمُرْسَلِينَ؟»

(Allah will say on the Day of Judgement: "O Son of Adam! What has deceived you concerning Me O Son of Adam What was your response to the Messengers'") Al-Baghawi mentioned that Al-Kalbi and Muqatil said, "This Ayah was revealed about Al-Aswad bin Shariq who struck the Prophet and he was not punished in retaliation. So Allah revealed,

(What has made you careless about your Lord, the Most Generous)" Then Allah said,

(Who created you, fashioned you perfectly, and gave you due proportion.) meaning, `what has deceived you concerning the Most Generous Lord' (Who created you, fashioned you perfectly, and gave you due proportion.) meaning, `He made you complete, straight, and perfectly balanced and proportioned in stature. He fashioned you in the best of forms and shapes.' Imam Ahmad recorded from Busr bin Jahhash Al-Qurashi that one day the Messenger of Allah spat in his palm and placed his finger on it. Then he said,

«قَالَ اللهُ عَزَّ وَجَلَّ: يَا ابْنَ آدَمَ أَنَّى تُعْجِزُنِي وَقَدْ خَلَقْتُكَ مِنْ مِثْلِ هذِهِ؟ حَتَّى إِذَا سَوَّيْتُكَ وَعَدَلْتُكَ مَشَيْتَ بَيْنَ بُرْدَيْنِ، وَلِلْأَرْضِ مِنْكَ وَئِيدٌ، فَجَمَعْتَ وَمَنَعْتَ حَتَّى إِذَا بَلَغَتِ التَّرَاقِيَ قُلْتَ: أَتَصَدَّقُ وَأَنَّى أَوَانُ الصَّدَقَةِ؟»

(Allah the Mighty and Sublime says: "O Son of Adam! How can you escape Me when I created you from something similar to this (spit) Then I fashioned you and made your creation balanced so that you walked between the two outer garments. And the earth has a burial place for you. So you gathered (wealth) and withheld it until your soul

Chapter 82: Al-Infitar (The Cleaving, Bursting Apart), Verses 001-019

reached your collarbone (i.e., death comes). Then, at that time you say, `I will give charity now.' But how will there be time for charity") This Hadith has also been recorded by Ibn Majah. Concerning Allah's statement, (In whatever form He willed, He put you together.) Mujahid said, "In which resemblance: the father, the mother, the paternal uncle, or the maternal uncle." In the Two Sahihs it is recorded from Abu Hurayrah that a man said, "O Messenger of Allah! Verily, my wife has given birth to a black boy." The Prophet said,

«هَلْ لَكَ مِنْ إِبِلٍ؟»

(Do you have any camels) The man said, "Yes." The Prophet then said,

«فَمَا أَلْوَانُهَا»

(What color are they) The man said, "Red." The Prophet said,

«فَهَلْ فِيهَا مِنْ أَوْرَقَ»

(Do any of them have patches of gray) The man said, "Yes." The Prophet asked him,

«فَأَنَّى أَتَاهَا ذَلِكَ»

(How did this happen to them) The man replied, "It is probably an inherited genetical strain." The Prophet then said,

«وَهَذَا عَسَى أَنْ يَكُونَ نَزَعَهُ عِرْقٌ»

(Likewise, this (with your son) is probably an inherited genetical strain.) The Cause of Deception and alerting to the Fact that Angels record the Deeds of the Children of Adam Concerning Allah's statement, (Nay! But you deny (the Day of) Ad-Din.) meaning, `you are only compelled to oppose the Most Generous and meet Him with disobedience, by your rejection in your hearts of the Hereafter, the recompense and the reckoning.' Concerning Allah's statement, (But verily, over you to watch you (are) Kiraman Katibin, they know all that you do.) (82:10-12) meaning, `indeed there are noble guardian angels over you, so do not meet them with evil deeds, because they write down all that you do.'

Surah: 82 Ayah: 13, Ayah: 14, Ayah: 15, Ayah: 16, Ayah: 17, Ayah: 18 & Ayah: 19

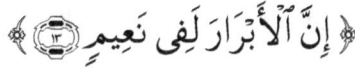

13. Verily, the Abrâr (the pious and righteous) will be in Delight (Paradise);

﴿ وَإِنَّ ٱلْفُجَّارَ لَفِى جَحِيمٍ ﴾

14. And verily, the Fujjâr (the wicked, disbelievers, sinners and evil-doers) will be in the blazing Fire (Hell),

﴿ يَصْلَوْنَهَا يَوْمَ ٱلدِّينِ ﴾

15. Therein they will enter, and taste its burning flame on the Day of Recompense,

﴿ وَمَا هُمْ عَنْهَا بِغَآئِبِينَ ﴾

16. And they (Al-Fujjâr) will not be absent therefrom.

﴿ وَمَآ أَدْرَىٰكَ مَا يَوْمُ ٱلدِّينِ ﴾

17. And what will make you know what the Day of Recompense is?

﴿ ثُمَّ مَآ أَدْرَىٰكَ مَا يَوْمُ ٱلدِّينِ ﴾

18. Again, what will make you know what the Day of Recompense is?

﴿ يَوْمَ لَا تَمْلِكُ نَفْسٌ لِنَفْسٍ شَيْئًا وَٱلْأَمْرُ يَوْمَئِذٍ لِلَّهِ ﴾

19. (It will be) the Day when no person shall have power (to do) anything for another, and the Decision, that Day, will be (wholly) with Allâh.

Transliteration

13. Inna al-abrara lafee naAAeemin 14. Wa-inna alfujjara lafee jaheemin 15. Yaslawnaha yawma alddeeni 16. Wama hum AAanha bigha-ibeena 17. Wama adraka ma yawmu alddeeni 18. Thumma ma adraka ma yawmu alddeeni 19. Yawma la tamliku nafsun linafsin shay-an waal-amru yawma-ithin lillahi

Tafsir Ibn Kathir

The Reward of the Righteous and the Sinners Allah informs of what the righteous will receive of delight.

They are those who obeyed Allah and did not meet Him with disobedience (sins). Then He mentions that the evildoers will be in Hell and eternal torment. Due to this He says,

(Therein they will enter, and taste its burning flame on the Day of Recompense,) meaning, the Day of Reckoning, Recompense, and Judgement.

Chapter 82: Al-Infitar (The Cleaving, Bursting Apart), Verses 001-019   69

(And they will not be absent therefrom.) meaning, they will not be absent for even one hour from the torment. The torment will not be lightened from them, nor will they be granted the death that they will be requesting, or any rest -- not even for a single day.

Allah then says,

(And what will make you know what the Day of Recompense is) This is a magnification of the affair of the Day of Judgement. Then Allah affirms it by saying, (Again, what will make you know what the Day of Recompense is) Then He explains this by saying, ((It will be) the Day when no person shall have power for another,) meaning, no one will be able to benefit anyone else, or help him out of that which he will be in, unless Allah gives permission to whomever He wishes and is pleased with.

We will mention here a Hadith (where the Prophet said),

«يَا بَنِي هَاشِمٍ، أَنْقِذُوا أَنْفُسَكُمْ مِنَ النَّارِ لَا أَمْلِكُ لَكُمْ مِنَ اللهِ شَيْئًا»

(O children of Hashim! Save yourselves from the Fire, for I have no power to cause you any benefit from Allah.) This has been mentioned previously at the end of the Tafsir of Surat Ash-Shu`ara' (see 26:214). Thus, Allah says, (and the Decision, that Day, will be with Allah.) "By Allah, the Decision is for Allah today (now), but on that Day no one will try to dispute with Him about it." This is the end of the Tafsir of Surat Al-Infitar. All praise and blessings are due to Allah, and He is the Giver of success and freedom from error.

CHAPTER (SURAH) 83: AL-MUTAFFIFIN (DEFRAUDING, THE CHEATS, CHEATING), VERSES 001- 036

Surah: 83 Ayah: 1, Ayah: 2, Ayah: 3, Ayah: 4, Ayah: 5 & Ayah: 6

(بِسْمِ اللَّهِ الرَّحْمَـنِ الرَّحِيمِ)

In the Name of Allah, the Most Gracious, the Most Merciful.

﴿ وَيْلٌ لِّلْمُطَفِّفِينَ ۝ ﴾

1. Woe to Al-Mutaffifin (those who give less in measure and weight).

﴿ ٱلَّذِينَ إِذَا ٱكْتَالُواْ عَلَى ٱلنَّاسِ يَسْتَوْفُونَ ۝ ﴾

2. Those who, when they have to receive by measure from men, demand full measure,

﴿ وَإِذَا كَالُوهُمْ أَو وَّزَنُوهُمْ يُخْسِرُونَ ۝ ﴾

3. And when they have to give by measure or weight to (other) men, give less than due.

﴿ أَلَا يَظُنُّ أُولَئِكَ أَنَّهُم مَّبْعُوثُونَ ﴾

4. Do they not think that they will be resurrected (for reckoning),

﴿ لِيَوْمٍ عَظِيمٍ ﴾

5. On a Great Day?

﴿ يَوْمَ يَقُومُ ٱلنَّاسُ لِرَبِّ ٱلْعَالَمِينَ ﴾

6. The Day when (all) mankind will stand before the Lord of the 'Âlamîn (mankind, jinn and all that exists)?

Transliteration

1. Waylun lilmutaffifeena

2. Allatheena itha iktaloo AAala alnnasi yastawfoona

3. Wa-itha kaloohum aw wazanoohum yukhsiroona

4. Ala yathunnu ola-ika annahum mabAAoothoona

5. Liyawmin AAatheemin

6. Yawma yaqoomu alnnasu lirabbi alAAalameena

Tafsir Ibn Kathir

Increasing and decreasing in the Measure and Weight will be a Cause for Regret and Loss

An-Nasa'i and Ibn Majah both recorded from Ibn `Abbas that he said, "When the Prophet came to Al-Madinah, the people of Al-Madinah were the most terrible people in giving measurement (i.e., they used to cheat). Thus, Allah revealed,

(Woe to Al-Mutaffifin.) After this, they began to give good measure." The meaning of the word Tatfif here is to be stingy with measurement and weight, either by increasing it if it is due from the others, or decreasing it if it is a debt. Thus, Allah explains that the Mutaffifin those whom He has promised loss and destruction, whom are meant by "Woe" are

(Those who, when they have to receive by measure from men,) meaning, from among the people.

(demand full measure,) meaning, they take their right by demanding full measure and extra as well.

(And when they have to give by measure or weight to (other) men, give less than due.) meaning, they decrease. Verily, Allah commanded that the measure and weight should be given in full. He says in another Ayah,

(And give full measure when you measure, and weigh with a balance that is straight. That is good and better in the end.) (17:35) Allah also says,

(And give full measure and full weight with justice. We burden not any person, but with that which he can bear.) (6:152) and He says,

(And observe the weight with equity and do not make the balance deficient.) (55:9) Allah destroyed the people of Shu`ayb and wiped them out because of their cheating in weights and measurements. ning, they take their right by demanding full measure and extra as well.

(And when they have to give by measure or weight to (other) men, give less than due.) meaning, they decrease. Verily, Allah commanded that the measure and weight should be given in full.

He says in another Ayah,

(And give full measure when you measure, and weigh with a balance that is straight. That is good and better in the end.) (17:35) Allah also says,

(And give full measure and full weight with justice. We burden not any person, but with that which he can bear.) (6:152) and He says,

(And observe the weight with equity and do not make the balance deficient.) (55:9) Allah destroyed the people of Shu`ayb and wiped them out because of their cheating in weights and measurements. be able to bare. Imam Malik reported from Nafi` who reported from Ibn `Umar that the Prophet said,

《يَوْمَ يَقُومُ النَّاسُ لِرَبِّ الْعَالَمِينَ، حَتَّى يَغِيبَ أَحَدُهُمْ فِي رَشْحِهِ إِلَى أَنْصَافِ أُذُنَيْهِ》

(This will be the Day that mankind will stand before the Lord of all that exists, until one of them will sink up to the middle of his ears in sweat.) Al-Bukhari recorded this Hadith from Malik and `Abdullah bin `Awn, both of whom reported it from Nafi`. Muslim also recorded it from two routes. Another Hadith: Hadith;uA ? give less than due.) meaning, they decrease. Verily, Allah commanded that the measure and weight should be given in full. He says in another Ayah,

(And give full measure when you measure, and weigh with a balance that is straight. That is good and better in the end.) (17:35) Allah also says,

(And give full measure and full weight with justice. We burden not any person, but with that which he can bear.) (6:152) and He says,

(And observe the weight with equity and do not make the balance deficient.) (55:9) Allah destroyed the people of Shu`ayb and wiped them out because of their cheating in weights and measurements.

Threatening the Mutaffifin with standing before the Lord of all that exists

Then Allah says as a threat to them,

(Do they not think that they will be resurrected, on a Great Day) meaning, do these people not fear the resurrection and standing before He Who knows the hidden matters and the innermost secrets, on a Day that contains great horror and tremendous fright Whoever loses on this Day will be made to enter into a blazing fire. Then Allah says,

(The Day when (all) mankind will stand before the Lord of all that exists) meaning, they will stand barefooted, naked and uncircumcised at a station that will be difficult, hard, and distressful for the criminals. They will be covered by the command from Allah, and it will be that, which the strength and the senses will not be able to bare. Imam Malik reported from Nafi` who reported from Ibn `Umar that the Prophet said,

«يَوْمَ يَقُومُ النَّاسُ لِرَبِّ الْعَالَمِينَ، حَتَّى يَغِيبَ أَحَدُهُمْ فِي رَشْحِهِ إِلَى أَنْصَافِ أُذُنَيْهِ»

(This will be the Day that mankind will stand before the Lord of all that exists, until one of them will sink up to the middle of his ears in sweat.) Al-Bukhari recorded this Hadith from Malik and `Abdullah bin `Awn, both of whom reported it from Nafi`. Muslim also recorded it from two routes. Another Hadith: Hadit u ?? ? u A ? Threatening the Mutaffifin with standing before the Lord of all that exists Then Allah says as a threat to them,

(Do they not think that they will be resurrected, on a Great Day) meaning, do these people not fear the resurrection and standing before He Who knows the hidden matters and the innermost secrets, on a Day that contains great horror and tremendous fright Whoever loses on this Day will be made to enter into a blazing fire. Then Allah says,

(The Day when (all) mankind will stand before the Lord of all that exists) meaning, they will stand barefooted, naked and uncircumcised at a station that will be difficult, hard, and distressful for the criminals. They will be covered by the command from Allah, and it will be that, which the strength and the senses will not be able to bare. Imam Malik reported from Nafi` who reported from Ibn `Umar that the Prophet said,

«يَوْمَ يَقُومُ النَّاسُ لِرَبِّ الْعَالَمِينَ، حَتَّى يَغِيبَ أَحَدُهُمْ فِي رَشْحِهِ إِلَى أَنْصَافِ أُذُنَيْهِ»

(This will be the Day that mankind will stand before the Lord of all that exists, until one of them will sink up to the middle of his ears in sweat.) Al-Bukhari recorded this Hadith from Malik and `Abdullah bin `Awn, both of whom reported it from Nafi`.

Muslim also recorded it from two routes. Another Hadith: Imam Ahmad recorded from Al-Miqdad, who was Ibn Al-Aswad Al-Kindi, that he heard the Messenger of Allah saying,

»إِذَا كَانَ يَوْمُ الْقِيَامَةِ أُدْنِيَتِ الشَّمْسُ مِنَ الْعِبَادِ حَتَّى تَكُونَ قَدْرَ مِيلٍ أَوْ مِيلَيْنِ قال فَتَصْهَرُهُمُ الشَّمْسُ فَيَكُونُونَ فِي الْعَرَقِ كَقَدْرِ أَعْمَالِهِمْ، مِنْهُمْ مَنْ يَأْخُذُهُ إِلَى عَقِبَيْهِ، وَمِنْهُمْ مَنْ يَأْخُذُهُ إِلَى رُكْبَتَيْهِ، وَمِنْهُمْ مَنْ يَأْخُذُهُ إِلَى حَقْوَيْهِ، وَمِنْهُمْ مَنْ يُلْجِمُهُ إِلْجَامًا«

(On the Day of Judgement, the sun will draw near the servants until it is a mile or two away from them. Then the sun will burn them, and they will be submersed in sweat based upon the amount of their deeds. From among them there will be those whose sweat will come up to their two heels. From among them there will be those whose sweat will come up to their two knees. From among them there will be those whose sweat will come up to their groins. From among them there will be those who will be bridled in sweat (up to their necks).) This Hadith was recorded by Muslim and At-Tirmidhi. In Sunan Abu Dawud it is recorded that the Messenger of Allah used to seek refuge with Allah from the hardship of standing on the Day of Judgement. It has been reported from Ibn Mas`ud that they will be standing for forty years with their heads raised toward the sky. No one will speak to them, and the righteous and wicked among them will all be bridled in sweat. It has been reported from Ibn `Umar that they will be standing for one hundred years. Both of these statements have been recorded by Ibn Jarir. In the Sunans of Abu Dawud, An-Nasa'i, and Ibn Majah, it is recorded from `A'ishah that the Messenger of Allah used to begin his late night prayer by declaring Allah's greatness ten times, praising Allah ten times, glorifying Allah ten times, and seeking Allah's forgiveness ten times. Then he would say,

»اللَّهُمَّ اغْفِرْ لِي وَاهْدِنِي وَارْزُقْنِي وَعَافِنِي«

(O Allah! Forgive me, guide me, provide for me, and protect me.) Then he would seek refuge from the hardship of the standing on the Day of Judgement.

Surah: 83 Ayah: 7, Ayah: 8, Ayah: 9, Ayah: 10, Ayah: 11, Ayah: 12, Ayah: 13, Ayah: 14, Ayah: 15, Ayah: 16 & Ayah: 17

﴿ كَلَّا إِنَّ كِتَٰبَ ٱلْفُجَّارِ لَفِى سِجِّينٍ ۝ ﴾

7. Nay! Truly, the Record (writing of the deeds) of the Fujjâr (disbelievers, sinners, evil-doers and the wicked) is (preserved) in Sijjîn.

﴿ وَمَآ أَدْرَىٰكَ مَا سِجِّينٌ ۝ ﴾

8. And what will make you know what Sijjîn is?

﴿ كِتَـٰبٌ مَّرْقُومٌ ۝ ﴾

9. A Register inscribed.

﴿ وَيْلٌ يَوْمَئِذٍ لِّلْمُكَذِّبِينَ ۝ ﴾

10. Woe, that Day, to those who deny.

﴿ ٱلَّذِينَ يُكَذِّبُونَ بِيَوْمِ ٱلدِّينِ ۝ ﴾

11. Those who deny the Day of Recompense.

﴿ وَمَا يُكَذِّبُ بِهِۦٓ إِلَّا كُلُّ مُعْتَدٍ أَثِيمٍ ۝ ﴾

12. And none can deny it except every transgressor beyond bounds, (in disbelief, oppression and disobedience of Allâh) the sinner!)

﴿ إِذَا تُتْلَىٰ عَلَيْهِ ءَايَـٰتُنَا قَالَ أَسَـٰطِيرُ ٱلْأَوَّلِينَ ۝ ﴾

13. When Our Verses (of the Qur'ân) are recited to him he says: "Tales of the ancients!"

﴿ كَلَّا بَلْ رَانَ عَلَىٰ قُلُوبِهِم مَّا كَانُوا يَكْسِبُونَ ۝ ﴾

14. Nay! But on their hearts is the Rân (covering of sins and evil deeds) which they used to earn.

﴿ كَلَّآ إِنَّهُمْ عَن رَّبِّهِمْ يَوْمَئِذٍ لَّمَحْجُوبُونَ ۝ ﴾

15. Nay! Surely, they (evil-doers) will be veiled from seeing their Lord that Day.

﴿ ثُمَّ إِنَّهُمْ لَصَالُوا ٱلْجَحِيمِ ۝ ﴾

16. Then, verily they will indeed enter (and taste) the burning flame of Hell.

﴿ ثُمَّ يُقَالُ هَـٰذَا ٱلَّذِى كُنتُم بِهِۦ تُكَذِّبُونَ ۝ ﴾

17. Then, it will be said to them: "This is what you used to deny!"

Transliteration

7. Kalla inna kitaba alfujjari lafee sijjeenin 8. Wama adraka ma sijjeenun 9. Kitabun marqoomun   10. Waylun yawma-ithin lilmukaththibeena   11. Allatheena yukaththiboona biyawmi aldeeni 12. Wama yukaththibu bihi illa kullu muAAtadin

atheemin 13. Itha tutla AAalayhi ayatuna qala asateeru al-awwaleena 14. Kalla bal rana AAala quloobihim ma kanoo yaksiboona 15. Kalla innahum AAan rabbihim yawma-ithin lamahjooboona 16. Thumma innahum lasaloo aljaheemi 17. Thumma yuqalu hatha allathee kuntum bihi tukaththiboona

Tafsir Ibn Kathir

The Record of the Wicked and some of what happens to Them

Allah says truly,

(Nay! Truly, the Record of the wicked is in Sijjin.) meaning, that their final destination and their abode will be in Sijjin, which is derived from the word prison (Sijn), and here it means straitened circumstances. Thus, Allah expresses the greatness of this matter, saying;

(And what will make you know what Sijjin is) meaning, it is a great matter, an eternal prison, and a painful torment. Some have said that it is beneath the seventh earth. It has been mentioned previously in the lengthy Hadith of Al-Bara' bin `Azib that the Prophet said,

«يَقُولُ اللهُ عَزَّ وَجَلَّ فِي رُوحِ الْكَافِرِ اكْتُبُوا كِتَابَهُ فِي سِجِّينٍ. وَسِجِّينٌ هِيَ تَحْتُ الْأَرْضِ السَّابِعَةِ»

(Allah says concerning the soul of the disbeliever, `Record his book in Sijjin.' And Sijjin is beneath the seventh earth.)" it is known that the destination of the wicked people will be Hell, and it is the lowest of the low. For Allah says,

(Then We reduced him to the lowest of the low. Save those who believe and do righteous deeds.) (95:5-6) Here Allah says,

(Nay! Truly, the Record of the wicked is in Sijjin. And what will make you know what Sijjin is) and it is full of hardship and misery. Allah says,

(And when they shall be thrown into a narrow place thereof, chained together, they will exclaim therein for destruction.) (25:13) Then Allah says,

(A Register inscribed.) This is not an explanation of His statement,

(And what will make you know what Sijjin is) It is only an explanation of the destination that will be recorded for them, which is Sijjin. Meaning, it is inscribed, written, and completed. No one can add to it and no one can remove anything from it. This was said by Muhammad bin Ka`b Al-Qurazi. Then Allah said,

(Woe, that Day, to those who deny.) meaning, when they come to the imprisonment, Allah threatened them with, on the Day of Judgement, and the disgraceful torment. The statement, "Woe," has already been discussed previously and there is no need to repeat it here. Basically, it means destruction and devastation. This is like what is said, "Woe to so-and-so." This is similar to what has been recorded in the Musnad and the Sunan collections on the authority of Bahz bin Hakim bin Mu`awiyah bin Haydah,

(Nay! Truly, ! TrulrsA ? the Record of the wicked is in Sijjin. And what will make you know what Sijjin is) and it is full of hardship and misery. Allah says,

(And when they shall be thrown into a narrow place thereof, chained together, they will exclaim therein for destruction.) (25:13) Then Allah says,

(A Register inscribed.) This is not an explanation of His statement,

(And what will make you know what Sijjin is) It is only an explanation of the destination that will be recorded for them, which is Sijjin. Meaning, it is inscribed, written, and completed. No one can add to it and no one can remove anything from it. This was said by Muhammad bin Ka`b Al-Qurazi. Then Allah said,

(Woe, that Day, to those who deny.) meaning, when they come to the imprisonment, Allah threatened them with, on the Day of Judgement, and the disgraceful torment. The statement, "Woe," has already been discussed previously and there is no need to repeat it here. Basically, it means destruction and devastation. This is like what is said, "Woe to so-and-so." This is similar to what has been recorded in the Musnad and the Sunan collections on the authority of Bahz bin Hakim bin Mu`awiyah bin Haydah, who reported from his father, who reported from his grandfather that the Messenger of Allah said,

«وَيْلٌ لِلَّذِي يُحَدِّثُ فَيَكْذِبُ لِيُضْحِكَ النَّاسَ، وَيْلٌ لَهُ وَيْلٌ لَهُ»

(Woe unto whoever speaks, and lies in order to make the people laugh. Woe unto him, woe unto him.) Then Allah says, in explaining who are the wicked, disbelieving deniers,

(Those who deny the Day of Recompense.) meaning, they do not believe it will happen, and they do not believe in its existence. Thus, they consider it a matter that is farfetched. Allah then says,

(And none can deny it except every transgressor, sinner.) meaning, transgressive in his actions by doing that which is forbidden and exceeding the limits when acquiring the permissible. He is a sinner in his statements, because he lies whenever he speaks, he breaks his promises whenever he makes them, and he behaves in an abusive and wicked manner whenever he argues. Concerning Allah's statement,

(When Our Ayat are recited to him, he says: "Tales of the ancients!") meaning, whenever he hears the Words of Allah from the Messenger , he denies it and has ill thoughts about it. Thus, he believes that it is a collection gathered from the books of the ancients. This is as Allah says,

(And when it is said to them: "What is it that your Lord has sent down" They say: "Tales of the men of old!") (16:24) Similarly Allah says,

(And they say: "Tales of the ancients, which he has written down: and they are dictated to him morning and afternoon.") (25:5) Then Allah continues saying,

(Nay! But on their hearts is the Ran (covering) which they used to earn.) meaning, the matter is not as they claim, nor as they say: "Verily, this Qur'an is tales of the ancients." Rather, it is the Word of Allah, His inspiration and His revelation to His Messenger. The only thing that blocked their hearts from believing in it is the dark covering cast over it from the many sins and wrong they committed that has covered up their hearts. Thus, Allah says,

(Nay! But on their hearts is the Ran (covering) which they used to earn.) This dark covering known as Rayn overcomes the hearts of the disbelievers, the covering of Ghaym is for the righteous, and the covering of Ghayn is for those who are near to Allah. Ibn Jarir, At-Tirmidhi, An-Nisa'i, and Ibn Majah all recorded from Abu Hurayrah that the Prophet said,

(...! But on their hearts is the Ran (covering) which they used to earn.) meaning, the matter is not as they claim, nor as they say: "Verily, this Qur'an is tales of the ancients." Rather, it is the Word of Allah, His inspiration and His revelation to His Messenger. The only thing that blocked their hearts from believing in it is the dark covering cast over it from the many sins and wrong they committed that has covered up their hearts. Thus, Allah says, uuA ? "What is it that your Lord has sent down" They say: "Tales of the men of old!") (16:24) Similarly Allah says,

(And they say: "Tales of the ancients, which he has written down: and they are dictated to him morning and afternoon.") (25:5) Then Allah continues saying,

(Nay! But on their hearts is the Ran (covering) which they used to earn.) meaning, the matter is not as they claim, nor as they say: "Verily, this Qur'an is tales of the ancients." Rather, it is the Word of Allah, His inspiration and His revelation to His Messenger. The only thing that blocked their hearts from believing in it is the dark covering cast over it from the many sins and wrong they committed that has covered up their hearts. Thus, Allah says,

(Nay! But on their hearts is the Ran (covering) which they used to earn.) This dark covering known as Rayn overcomes the hearts of the disbelievers, the covering of Ghaym is for the righteous, and the covering of Ghayn is for those who are near to Allah. Ibn Jarir, At-Tirmidhi, An-Nisa'i, and Ibn Majah all recorded from Abu Hurayrah that the Prophet said,

»إِنَّ الْعَبْدَ إِذَا أَذْنَبَ ذَنْبًا كَانَتْ نُكْتَةٌ سَوْدَاءُ فِي قَلْبِهِ، فَإِنْ تَابَ مِنْهَا صُقِلَ قَلْبُهُ، وَإِنْ زَادَ زَادَتْ، فَذلِكَ قَوْلُ اللهِ تَعَالَى:

(كَلاَّ بَلْ رَانَ عَلَى قُلُوبِهِم مَّا كَانُواْ يَكْسِبُونَ)«

(Verily, when the servant commits a sin, a black spot appears in his heart. If he repents from it, his heart is polished clean. However, if he increases (in the sin), the spot will continue to increase. That is the statement of Allah: ((Nay! But on their hearts is the Ran (covering) which they used to earn.)) At-Tirmidhi said, "Hasan Sahih." The wording of An-Nasa'i says,

«إِنَّ الْعَبْدَ إِذَا أَخْطَأَ خَطِيئَةً نُكِتَ فِي قَلْبِهِ نُكْتَةٌ سَوْدَاءُ، فَإِنْ هُوَ نَزَعَ وَاسْتَغْفَرَ وَتَابَ صُقِلَ قَلْبُهُ، فَإِنْ عَادَ زِيدَ فِيهَا حَتَّى تَعْلُوَ قَلْبَهُ فَهُوَ الرَّانُ الَّذِي قَالَ اللهُ تَعَالَى:

(كَلاَّ بَلْ رَانَ عَلَى قُلُوبِهِم مَّا كَانُواْ يَكْسِبُونَ)»

(Whenever the servant commits a wrong, a black spot is put in his heart. So, if he refrains from it, seeks forgiveness and repents, his heart is polished clean. But if he returns to the sin, the spot will increase until it overcomes his (entire) heart, and this is the Ran that Allah mentions when He says: (Nay, but on their hearts is the Ran (covering) which they used to earn.)) Concerning Allah's statement,

(Nay! Surely, they will be veiled from seeing their Lord that Day.) meaning, they will have a place on the Day of Judgement, and lodging in Sijjin. Along with this they will be veiled from seeing their Lord and Creator on the Day of Judgement. Imam Abu `Abdullah Ash-Shafi`i said, "In this Ayah is a proof that the believers will see Him (Allah), the Mighty and Sublime, on that Day." Concerning Allah's statement,

(Then verily, they will indeed enter the burning flame of Hell.) meaning, along with this being prevented from seeing the Most Gracious, they will also be among the people of the Fire.

(Then, it will be said to them: "This is what you used to deny!") (83:17) meaning, this will be said to them by way of scolding, rebuking, belittling, and humi- liation.

Surah: 83 Ayah: 18, Ayah: 19, Ayah: 20, Ayah: 21, Ayah: 22, Ayah: 23, Ayah: 24, Ayah: 25, Ayah: 26, Ayah: 27 & Ayah: 28

﴿ كَلَّا إِنَّ كِتَبَ ٱلْأَبْرَارِ لَفِى عِلِّيِّينَ ۝ ﴾

18. Nay! Verily, the Record (writing of the deeds) of Al-Abrâr (the pious and righteous), is (preserved) in 'Illiyyûn.

﴿ وَمَآ أَدْرَىٰكَ مَا عِلِّيُّونَ ۝ ﴾

19. And what will make you know what 'Illiyyûn is?

Chapter 83: Al-Mutaffifin (Defrauding, The Cheats, Cheating), Verses 001-036

﴿ كِتَٰبٌ مَّرْقُومٌ ۝ ﴾

20. A Register inscribed,

﴿ يَشْهَدُهُ ٱلْمُقَرَّبُونَ ۝ ﴾

21. To which bear witness those nearest (to Allâh, i.e. the angels).

﴿ إِنَّ ٱلْأَبْرَارَ لَفِى نَعِيمٍ ۝ ﴾

22. Verily, Al-Abrâr (the pious and righteous) will be in Delight (Paradise).

﴿ عَلَى ٱلْأَرَآئِكِ يَنظُرُونَ ۝ ﴾

23. On thrones, looking (at all things).

﴿ تَعْرِفُ فِى وُجُوهِهِمْ نَضْرَةَ ٱلنَّعِيمِ ۝ ﴾

24. You will recognize in their faces the brightness of delight.

﴿ يُسْقَوْنَ مِن رَّحِيقٍ مَّخْتُومٍ ۝ ﴾

25. They will be given to drink of pure sealed wine.

﴿ خِتَٰمُهُۥ مِسْكٌ ۚ وَفِى ذَٰلِكَ فَلْيَتَنَافَسِ ٱلْمُتَنَٰفِسُونَ ۝ ﴾

26. The last thereof (that wine) will be the smell of Musk, and for this let (all) those strive who want to strive (i.e. hasten earnestly to the obedience of Allâh).

﴿ وَمِزَاجُهُۥ مِن تَسْنِيمٍ ۝ ﴾

27. It (that wine) will be mixed with Tasnîm:

﴿ عَيْنًا يَشْرَبُ بِهَا ٱلْمُقَرَّبُونَ ۝ ﴾

28. A spring whereof drink those nearest to Allâh.

Transliteration

18. Kalla inna kitaba al-abrari lafee AAilliyyeena 19. Wama adraka ma AAilliyyoona 20. Kitabun marqoomun 21. Yashhaduhu almuqarraboona 22. Inna al-abrara lafee naAAeemin 23. AAala al-ara-iki yanthuroona 24. TaAArifu fee wujoohihim nadrata alnnaAAeemi 25. Yusqawna min raheeqin makhtoomin 26. Khitamuhu miskun wafee thalika falyatanafasi almutanafisoona 27. Wamizajuhu min tasneemin 28. AAaynan yashrabu biha almuqarraboona

Tafsir Ibn Kathir

The Record Book of the Righteous and Their Reward

Allah says that truly,

(Verily, the Record of Al-Abrar (the righteous believers)) These people are in a situation that is the opposite of the wicked people.

(is in `Illiyyin.) meaning, their final destination is `Illiyyin, which is the opposite of Sijjin. It has been reported from Hilal bin Yasaf that Ibn `Abbas asked Ka`b about Sijjin while he was present, and Ka`b said, "It is the seventh earth and in it are the souls of the disbelievers." Then Ibn `Abbas asked him about `Illiyyin, so he said, "It is the seventh heaven and it contains the souls of the believers." This statement -- that it is the seventh heaven -- has been said by others as well. `Ali bin Abi Talhah reported that Ibn `Abbas said concerning Allah's statement,

(Nay! Verily, the Record of Al-Abrar (the righteous believers) is in `Illiyyin.) "This means Paradise." Others besides him have said, "`Iliyyin is located at Sidrat Al-Muntaha." The obvious meaning is that the word `Illiyyin is taken from the word `Uluw, which means highness. The more something ascends and rises, the more it becomes greater and increases. Thus, Allah magnifies its affair and extols its matter by saying,

(And what will make you know what `Illiyyin is) Then He says by way of affirming what will be written for them,

(A Register inscribed. To which bear witness those nearest.) They are the angels. This was stated by Qatadah. Al-`Awfi reported from Ibn `Abbas that he said, "Those nearest to Allah in each heaven will witness it." Then Allah says,

(Verily, Al-Abrar (the righteuos believers) will be in Delight.) meaning, on the Day of Judgement they will be in eternal pleasure and gardens that contain comprehensive bounties.

(On thrones,) These are thrones beneath canopies from which they will be gazing. It has been said, "This means that they will be gazing at their kingdom and what Allah has given them of good and bounties that will not end or perish. It has also been said,

(On thrones, looking.) "This means that they will be looking at Allah, the Mighty and Sublime." This is the opposite of what those wicked people have been described with,

(Nay! Surely, they (evildoers) will be veiled from seeing their Lord that Day.) (83:15) Thus, it has been mentioned that these (righteous people) will be allowed to look at Allah while they are upon their thrones and elevated couches. Concerning Allah's statement,

(You will recognize in their faces the brightness of delight.) meaning, `you will notice a glow of delight in their faces when you look at them.' This is a description of opulence, decorum, happiness, composure, and authority that they will be experiencing from this great delight. Concerning Allah's statement,

(They will be given to drink of pure sealed Rahiq.) meaning, they will be given drink from the wine of Paradise. Ar-Rahiq is one of the names of the wine (in Paradise). Ibn Mas`ud, Ibn `Abbas, Mujahid, Al-Hasan, Qatadah and Ibn Zayd all said this. Ibn Mas`ud said concerning Allah's statement,

(Sealed with musk,) "This means it will be mixed with musk." Al-`Awfi reported from Ibn `Abbas that he said, "Allah will make the wine have a pleasant aroma for them, so the last thing that He will place in it will be musk. Thus, it will be sealed with musk." Qatadah and Ad-Dahhak both said the same. Then Allah says,

(and for this let (all) those strive who want to strive.) meaning, for a situation like this, let the boasters boast, compete, and strive to gain more. Let the competitors compete and race toward the likes of this. This is similar to Allah's statement,

(For the like of this let the workers work.) (37:61) Allah then says,

(It will be mixed with Tasnim.) meaning, this wine that is being described is mixed with Tasnim. This refers to a drink called Tasnim, and it is the most excellent and exalted drink of the people of Paradise. This was said by Abu Salih and Ad-Dahhak. Thus, Allah says,

(A spring whereof drink those nearest to Allah.) (83:28) meaning, those who are near to Allah, will drink from it as they wish, and the companions of the right hand will be given a drink that is mixed with it. This has been said by Ibn Mas`ud, Ibn `Abbas, Masruq, Qatadah and others.

Surah: 83 Ayah: 29, Ayah: 30, Ayah: 31, Ayah: 32, Ayah: 33, Ayah: 34, Ayah: 35 & Ayah: 36

﴿ إِنَّ ٱلَّذِينَ أَجْرَمُوا۟ كَانُوا۟ مِنَ ٱلَّذِينَ ءَامَنُوا۟ يَضْحَكُونَ ۝ ﴾

29. Verily! (During the worldly life) those who committed crimes used to laugh at those who believed.

﴿ وَإِذَا مَرُّوا۟ بِهِمْ يَتَغَامَزُونَ ۝ ﴾

30. And, whenever they passed by them, used to wink one to another (in mockery).

﴿ وَإِذَا ٱنقَلَبُوٓا۟ إِلَىٰٓ أَهْلِهِمُ ٱنقَلَبُوا۟ فَكِهِينَ ۝ ﴾

31. And when they returned to their own people, they would return jesting;

﴿ وَإِذَا رَأَوْهُمْ قَالُوٓا۟ إِنَّ هَـٰٓؤُلَآءِ لَضَآلُّونَ ۝ ﴾

32. And when they saw them, they said: "Verily! These have indeed gone astray!"

$$\left\{ \vphantom{\int} \text{وَمَا أُرْسِلُوا عَلَيْهِمْ حَافِظِينَ} \; ﴿٣٣﴾ \right\}$$

33. But they (disbelievers, sinners) had not been sent as watchers over them (the believers).

$$\left\{ \vphantom{\int} \text{فَالْيَوْمَ الَّذِينَ ءَامَنُوا مِنَ الْكُفَّارِ يَضْحَكُونَ} \; ﴿٣٤﴾ \right\}$$

34. But this Day (the Day of Resurrection) those who believe will laugh at the disbelievers

$$\left\{ \vphantom{\int} \text{عَلَى الْأَرَائِكِ يَنظُرُونَ} \; ﴿٣٥﴾ \right\}$$

35. On (high) thrones, looking (at all things).

$$\left\{ \vphantom{\int} \text{هَلْ ثُوِّبَ الْكُفَّارُ مَا كَانُوا يَفْعَلُونَ} \; ﴿٣٦﴾ \right\}$$

36. Are not the disbelievers paid (fully) for what they used to do?

Transliteration

29. Inna allatheena ajramoo kanoo mina allatheena amanoo yadhakoona 30. Wa-itha marroo bihim yataghamazoona 31. Wa-itha inqalaboo ila ahlihimu inqalaboo fakiheena 32. Wa-itha raawhum qaloo inna haola-i ladalloona 33. Wama orsiloo AAalayhim hafitheena 34. Faalyawma allatheena amanoo mina alkuffari yadhakoona 35. AAala al-ara-iki yanthuroona 36. Hal thuwwiba alkuffaru ma kanoo yafAAaloona

Tafsir Ibn Kathir

The Wicked Behavior of the Criminals and Their mocking of the Believers

Allah informs that the criminals used to laugh at the believers in the worldly life. In other words, they would mock them and despise them. Whenever they would pass by the believers, they would wink at each other about them, meaning in contempt of them. (And when they returned to their own people, they would return jesting.) meaning, when these criminals turn back, or return to their homes, they go back pleased. This means that whatever they request, they find it. Yet, with this, they still are not grateful for Allah's favor upon them. Rather they busy themselves with despising and envying the believers.

(And when they saw them, they said: "Verily, these have indeed gone astray!") meaning, `because they are upon a religion other than their own religion.' Allah then says, (But they were not sent as watchers over them.) meaning, these criminals have not been sent as guardians over the deeds and statements of these believers. These wrongdoers have not been made responsible for them. So, why are they so concerned with them, and why have they made them the focus of their attention This is as Allah says,

(He (Allah) will say: "Remain you in it with ignominy! And speak you not to Me!" Verily there was a party of My servants, who used to say: "Our Lord! We believe, so forgive us, and have mercy on us, for You are the Best of all who show mercy!" But you took them for a laughing stock, so much so that they made you forget My remembrance while you used to laugh at them! Verily, I have rewarded them this Day for their patience: they are indeed the ones that are successful.) (23:108-111) Thus, Allah says here,

(But this Day) meaning, the Day of Judgement.

(those who believe will laugh at the disbelievers) meaning, as retribution for how those people laughed at them.

(On thrones, looking.) meaning, looking at Allah as reward for bearing the false claims against them that they were misguided. They were not misguided at all. Rather they were the close Awliya' of Allah, who will be looking at their Lord in the place of His honor. Concerning Allah's statement,

(Are not the disbelievers paid for what they used to do) meaning, `will the disbelievers be recompensed for their mockery and belittlement against the believers, or not' This means that they surely will be paid in full, completely and perfectly (for their behavior). This is the end of the Tafsir of Surat Al-Mutaffifin, and all praise and thanks are due to Allah.

INTRODUCTION TO CHAPTER (SURAH) 84: AL-INSHIQAQ (THE SUNDERING, SPLITTING OPEN)

Ibn Kathir's Introduction

The Prostration of Recitation in Surat Al-Inshiqaq

It is reported from Abu Salamah that while leading them in prayer, Abu Hurayrah recited,

(When the heaven is split asunder.) and he prostrated during its recitation. Then when he completed the prayer, he informed them that the Messenger of Allah prostrated during its recitation. This was recorded by Muslim and An-Nasa'i on the authority of Malik. Al-Bukhari recorded from Abu Rafi` that he prayed the Night prayer with Abu Hurayrah) recited,

(When the heaven is split asunder.) then he prostrated. So Abu Rafi` said something to him about it (questioning it). Abu Hurayrah replied, "I prostrated behind Abul-Qasim (the Prophet), and I will never cease prostrating during its recitation until I meet him."

CHAPTER (SURAH) 84: AL-INSHIQAQ (THE SUNDERING, SPLITTING OPEN), VERSES 001- 025

Surah: 84 Ayah: 1, Ayah: 2, Ayah: 3, Ayah: 4, Ayah: 5, Ayah: 6, Ayah: 7, Ayah: 8, Ayah: 9, Ayah: 10, Ayah: 11, Ayah: 12, Ayah: 13, Ayah: 14 & Ayah: 15

(بِسْمِ اللَّهِ الرَّحْمَـنِ الرَّحِيمِ)

In the Name of Allah, the Most Gracious, the Most Merciful.

﴿ إِذَا السَّمَآءُ انشَقَّتْ ۝ ﴾

1. When the heaven is split asunder,

﴿ وَأَذِنَتْ لِرَبِّهَا وَحُقَّتْ ۝ ﴾

2. And listens and obeys its Lord - and it must do so.

﴿ وَإِذَا الْأَرْضُ مُدَّتْ ۝ ﴾

3. And when the earth is stretched forth,

﴿ وَأَلْقَتْ مَا فِيهَا وَتَخَلَّتْ ۝ ﴾

4. And has cast out all that was in it and became empty.

﴿ وَأَذِنَتْ لِرَبِّهَا وَحُقَّتْ ۝ ﴾

5. And listens and obeys its Lord - and it must do so.

﴿ يَأَيُّهَا الْإِنسَـنُ إِنَّكَ كَادِحٌ إِلَى رَبِّكَ كَدْحًا فَمُلَـقِيهِ ۝ ﴾

6. O man! Verily, you are returning towards your Lord with your deeds and actions (good or bad), a sure returning, so you will meet (the results of your deeds which you did).

﴿ فَأَمَّا مَنْ أُوتِىَ كِتَـبَهُ بِيَمِينِهِ ۝ ﴾

7. Then as for him who will be given his Record in his right hand,

﴿ فَسَوْفَ يُحَاسَبُ حِسَابًا يَسِيرًا ۝ ﴾

8. He surely will receive an easy reckoning,

Chapter 84: Al-Inshiqaq (The Sundering, Splitting Open), Verses 001-025

﴿ وَيَنقَلِبُ إِلَىٰ أَهْلِهِ مَسْرُورًا ۝ ﴾

9. And will return to his family in joy!

﴿ وَأَمَّا مَنْ أُوتِيَ كِتَٰبَهُۥ وَرَآءَ ظَهْرِهِۦ ۝ ﴾

10. But whosoever is given his Record behind his back,

﴿ فَسَوْفَ يَدْعُواْ ثُبُورًا ۝ ﴾

11. He will invoke (his) destruction,

﴿ وَيَصْلَىٰ سَعِيرًا ۝ ﴾

12. And shall enter a blazing Fire, and be made to taste its burning.

﴿ إِنَّهُۥ كَانَ فِىٓ أَهْلِهِۦ مَسْرُورًا ۝ ﴾

13. Verily, he was among his people in joy!

﴿ إِنَّهُۥ ظَنَّ أَن لَّن يَحُورَ ۝ ﴾

14. Verily, he thought that he would never come back (to Us)!

﴿ بَلَىٰٓ إِنَّ رَبَّهُۥ كَانَ بِهِۦ بَصِيرًا ۝ ﴾

15. Yes! Verily, his Lord has been ever beholding him!

Transliteration

1. Itha alssamao inshaqqat 2. Waathinat lirabbiha wahuqqat 3. Wa-itha al-ardu muddat 4. Waalqat ma feeha watakhallat 5. Waathinat lirabbiha wahuqqat 6. Ya ayyuha al-insanu innaka kadihun ila rabbika kadhan famulaqeehi 7. Faama man ootiya kitabahu biyameenihi 8. Fasawfa yuhasabu hisaban yaseeran 9. Wayanqalibu ila ahlihi masrooran 10. Waamma man ootiya kitabahu waraa thahrihi 11. Fasawfa yadAAoo thubooran 12. Wayasla saAAeeran 13. Innahu kana fee ahlihi masrooran 14. Innahu thanna an lan yahoora 15. Bala inna rabbahu kana bihi baseeran

Tafsir Ibn Kathir

Splitting the Heavens asunder and stretching the Earth forth on the Day of Resurrection

Allah says,

(When the heaven is split asunder,) This refers to the Day of Judgement.

(And listens to and obeys its Lord) meaning, it listens to its Lord and obeys His command to split apart. This will occur on the Day of Judgement.

(and it must do so.) meaning, it is right for it to obey the command of its Lord, because it is great and cannot be rejected, nor overcome. Rather it overpowers everything and everything is submissive to it. Then Allah says,

(And when the earth is stretched forth,) meaning, when the earth is expanded, spread out and extended. Then He says,

(And has cast out all that was in it and became empty.) meaning, it throws out the dead inside of it, and it empties itself of them. This was said by Mujahid, Sa`id, and Qatadah.

(And listens to and obeys its Lord, and it must do so.) The explanation of this is the same as what has preceded.

The Recompense for Deeds is True

Allah says,

(O man! Verily, you are returning towards your Lord with your deeds and actions, a sure returning,) meaning, `verily you are hastening to your Lord and working deeds.'

(and you will meet.) `Then you will meet that which you did of good or evil.' A proof for this is what Abu Dawud At-Tayalisi recorded from Jabir, that the Messenger of Allah said,

«قَالَ جِبْرِيلُ: يَا مُحَمَّدُ، عِشْ مَا شِئْتَ فَإِنَّكَ مَيِّتٌ، وَأَحْبِبْ (مَنْ) شِئْتَ فَإِنَّكَ مُفَارِقُهُ، وَاعْمَلْ مَا شِئْتَ فَإِنَّكَ مُلَاقِيهِ»

(Jibril said, "O Muhammad! Live how you wish, for verily you will die; love what you wish, for verily you will part with it; and do what you wish, for verily you will meet it (your deed).) There are some people who refer the pronoun back to the statement "your Lord." Thus, they hold the Ayah to mean, "and you will meet your Lord." This means that He will reward you for your work, and pay you for your efforts. Therefore, both of these two views are connected. Al-`Awfi recorded from Ibn `Abbas that he said explaining,

(O man! Verily, you are returning towards your Lord with your deeds and actions, a sure returning,) "Whatever deed you do, you will meet Allah with it, whether it is good or bad."

The Presentation and the Discussion that will take place during the Reckoning

Then Allah says,

(Then as for him who will be given his Record in his right hand, he surely, will receive an easy reckoning,) (84:7-8) meaning, easy without any difficulty. This means that he will not be investigated for all the minute details of his deeds. For verily, whoever is

Chapter 84: Al-Inshiqaq (The Sundering, Splitting Open), Verses 001-025   87

reckoned like that, he will certainly be destroyed. Imam Ahmad recorded from `A'ishah that the Messenger of Allah said,

«مَنْ نُوقِشَ الْحِسَابَ عُذِّبَ»

(Whoever is interrogated during the reckoning, then he will be punished.) `A'ishah then said, "But didn't Allah say,

(He surely will receive an easy reckoning,)" The Prophet replied,

«لَيْسَ ذَاكِ بِالْحِسَابِ، وَلَكِنْ ذَلِكِ الْعَرْضُ، مَنْ نُوقِشَ الْحِسَابَ يَوْمَ الْقِيَامَةِ عُذِّبَ»

(That is not during to the Reckoning, rather it is referring to the presentation. Whoever is interrogated during the Reckoning on the Day of Judgement, then he will be punished.) This Hadith has also been recorded by Al-Bukhari, Muslim, At-Tirmidhi, An-Nasa'i and Ibn Jarir. In reference to Allah's statement,

(And will return to his family Masrur!) This means that he will return to his family in Paradise. This was said by Qatadah and Ad-Dahhak. They also said, "Masrur means happy and delighted by what Allah has given him." Allah said;

(But whosoever is given his Record behind his back,) meaning, he will be given his Book in his left hand, behind his back, while his hand is bent behind him.

(He will invoke destruction,) meaning, loss and destruction.

(And he shall enter a blazing Fire, and made to taste its burning. Verily, he was among his people in joy!) meaning, happy. He did not think about the consequences, nor feared what (future) was in front of him. His light happiness will be followed by long grief.

(Verily, he thought that he would never return!) meaning, he used to believe that he would not return to Allah, nor would Allah bring him back (to life) after his death. This was said by Ibn `Abbas, Qatadah and others. Allah then says,

(Yes! Verily, his Lord has been ever beholding him!) meaning, certainly Allah will repeat his creation just as he began his creation, and He will reward him based upon his deeds, whether they were good or bad. He was ever watchful of him,

Surah: 84 Ayah: 16, Ayah: 17, Ayah: 18, Ayah: 19, Ayah: 20, Ayah: 21, Ayah: 22, Ayah: 23, Ayah: 24 & Ayah: 25

﴿ فَلَا أُقْسِمُ بِالشَّفَقِ ۝ ﴾

16. So I swear by the afterglow of sunset;

﴿ وَٱلَّيْلِ وَمَا وَسَقَ ﴾

17. And by the night and whatever it gathers in its darkness,

﴿ وَٱلْقَمَرِ إِذَا ٱتَّسَقَ ﴾

18. And by the moon when it is at the full.

﴿ لَتَرْكَبُنَّ طَبَقًا عَن طَبَقٍ ﴾

19. You shall certainly travel from stage to stage (in this life and in the Hereafter).

﴿ فَمَا لَهُمْ لَا يُؤْمِنُونَ ﴾

20. What is the matter with them, that they believe not?

﴿ وَإِذَا قُرِئَ عَلَيْهِمُ ٱلْقُرْءَانُ لَا يَسْجُدُونَ ﴾

21. And when the Qur'ân is recited to them, they fall not prostrate.

﴿ بَلِ ٱلَّذِينَ كَفَرُواْ يُكَذِّبُونَ ﴾

22. Nay, those who disbelieve belie (Prophet Muhammad (peace be upon him) and whatever he brought, i.e. this Qur'ân and Islâmic Monotheism, etc.).

﴿ وَٱللَّهُ أَعْلَمُ بِمَا يُوعُونَ ﴾

23. And Allâh knows best what they gather (of good and bad deeds),

﴿ فَبَشِّرْهُم بِعَذَابٍ أَلِيمٍ ﴾

24. So announce to them a painful torment.

﴿ إِلَّا ٱلَّذِينَ ءَامَنُواْ وَعَمِلُواْ ٱلصَّـٰلِحَـٰتِ لَهُمْ أَجْرٌ غَيْرُ مَمْنُونٍ ﴾

25. Save those who believe and do righteous good deeds, for them is a reward that will never come to an end (i.e. Paradise).

Transliteration

16. Fala oqsimu bialshshafaqi 17. Waallayli wama wasaqa 18. Waalqamari itha ittasaqa 19. Latarkabunna tabaqan AAan tabaqin 20. Fama lahum la yu/minoona 21. Wa-itha quri-a AAalayhimu alqur-anu la yasjudoona 22. Bali allatheena kafaroo yukaththiboona 23. WaAllahu aAAlamu bima yooAAoona 24. Fabashshirhum biAAathabin aleemin 25. Illa allatheena amanoo waAAamiloo alssalihati lahum ajrun ghayru mamnoonin

Chapter 84: Al-Inshiqaq (The Sundering, Splitting Open), Verses 001-025

Tafsir Ibn Kathir

Swearing by the Various Stages of Man's Journey

It has been reported from `Ali, Ibn `Abbas, `Ubadah bin As-Samit, Abu Hurayrah, Shaddad bin Aws, Ibn `Umar, Muhammad bin `Ali bin Al-Husayn, Makhul, Bakr bin `Abdullah Al-Muzani, Bukayr bin Al-Ashaj, Malik, Ibn Abi Dhi'b, and `Abdul-`Aziz bin Abi Salamah Al-Majishun, they all said, "Ash-Shafaq is the redness (in the sky).`Abdur-Razzaq recorded from Abu Hurayrah that he said, "Ash-Shafaq is the whiteness." So Ash-Shafaq is the redness of the horizon, either before sunset, as Mujahid said or after sunset, as is well known with the scholars of the Arabic Language. Al-Khalil bin Ahmad said, "Ash-Shafaq is the redness that appears from the setting of sun until the time of the last `Isha' (when it is completely dark). When that redness goes away, it is said, `Ash-Shafaq has disappeared.'" Al-Jawhari said, "Ash-Shafaq is the remaining light of the sun and its redness at the beginning of the night until it is close to actual nighttime (darkness)." `Ikrimah made a similar statement when he said, "Ash-Shafaq is that what is between Al-Maghrib and Al-`Isha'." In the Sahih of Muslim, it is recorded from `Abdullah bin `Amr that the Messenger of Allah said,

《وَقْتُ الْمَغْرِبِ مَا لَمْ يَغِبِ الشَّفَقِ》

(The time of Al-Maghrib is as long as Ash-Shafaq has not disappeared.)" In all of this, there is a proof that Ash-Shafaq is as Al-Jawhari and Al-Khalil have said. Ibn `Abbas, Mujahid, Al-Hasan and Qatadah, all said that,

(and what it Wasaqa) means "What it gathers." Qatadah said, "The stars and animals it gathers." `Ikrimah said,

(And by the night and what it Wasaqa,) "What it drives into due to its darkness, because when it is nighttime everything goes to its home." Concerning Allah's statement,

(And by the moon when it Ittasaqa.) Ibn `Abbas said, "When it comes together and becomes complete." Al-Hasan said, "When it comes together and becomes full." Qatadah said, "When it completes its cycle." These statements refer to its light when it is completed and becomes full, as the idea was initiated with "The night and what it gathers." Allah said,

(You shall certainly travel from stage to stage.) Al-Bukhari recorded from Mujahid that Ibn `Abbas said,

(You shall certainly travel from stage to stage.) "Stage after stage. Your Prophet has said this." Al-Bukhari recorded this statement with this wording. `Ikrimah said,

(From stage to stage.) "Stage after stage. Weaned after he was breast feeding, and an old man after he was a young man." Al-Hasan Al-Basri said,

(From stage to stage.) "Stage after stage. Ease after difficulty, difficulty after ease, wealth after poverty, poverty after wealth, health after sickness, and sickness after health."

The Disapproval of Their Lack of Faith, giving Them Tidings of the Torment, and that the Ultimate Pleasure will be for the Believers

Allah said,

(What is the matter with them, that they believe not And when the Qur'an is recited to them, they fall not prostrate.) meaning, what prevents them from believing in Allah, His Messenger and the Last Day, and what is wrong with them that when Allah's Ayat and His Words are recited to them they do not prostrate due to awe, respect and reverence Concerning Allah's statement, (Nay, those who disbelieve deny.) meaning, from their mannerism is rejection, obstinacy, and opposition to the truth. (And Allah knows best what they gather,) Mujahid and Qatadah both said, "What they conceal in their chests."

(So, announce to them a painful torment.) meaning, `inform them, O Muhammad, that Allah has prepared for them a painful torment.' Then Allah says,

(Save those who believe and do righteous good deeds,) This is a clear exception meaning, `but those who believe.' This refers to those who believe in their hearts. Then the statement, "and do righteous good deeds," is referring to that which they do with their limbs.

(for them is a reward) meaning, in the abode of the Hereafter.

(that will never come to an end.) Ibn `Abbas said, "Without being decreased." Mujahid and Ad-Dahhak both said, "Without measure." The result of their statements is that it (the reward) is without end. This is as Allah says,

(A gift without an end.) (11:108) As-Suddi said, "Some of them have said that this means without end and without decrease." This is the end of the Tafsir of Surat Al-Inshiqaq. All praise and thanks are due to Allah, and He is the giver of success and freedom from error.

CHAPTER (SURAH) 85: AL-BUROOJ (THE MANSIONS OF THE STARS, CONSTELLATIONS), VERSES 001- 022

Surah: 85 Ayah: 1, Ayah: 2, Ayah: 3, Ayah: 4, Ayah: 5, Ayah: 6, Ayah: 7, Ayah: 8, Ayah: 9 & Ayah: 10

(بِسْمِ اللَّهِ الرَّحْمَـنِ الرَّحِيمِ)

In the Name of Allah, the Most Gracious, the Most Merciful.

Chapter 85: Al-Burooj (The Mansions Of The Stars, Constellations), Verses 001-022

﴿ وَٱلسَّمَآءِ ذَاتِ ٱلْبُرُوجِ ۝ ﴾

1. By the heaven, holding the big stars.

﴿ وَٱلْيَوْمِ ٱلْمَوْعُودِ ۝ ﴾

2. And by the Promised Day (i.e. the Day of Resurrection).

﴿ وَشَاهِدٍ وَمَشْهُودٍ ۝ ﴾

3. And by the Witnessing day (i.e. Friday), and by the Witnessed day (i.e. the day of 'Arafât (Hajj) the ninth of Dhul-Hîjjah);

﴿ قُتِلَ أَصْحَٰبُ ٱلْأُخْدُودِ ۝ ﴾

4. Cursed were the people of the Ditch (the story of the Boy and the King).

﴿ ٱلنَّارِ ذَاتِ ٱلْوَقُودِ ۝ ﴾

5. Of fire fed with fuel,

﴿ إِذْ هُمْ عَلَيْهَا قُعُودٌ ۝ ﴾

6. When they sat by it (fire),

﴿ وَهُمْ عَلَىٰ مَا يَفْعَلُونَ بِٱلْمُؤْمِنِينَ شُهُودٌ ۝ ﴾

7. And they witnessed what they were doing against the believers (i.e. burning them).

﴿ وَمَا نَقَمُوا۟ مِنْهُمْ إِلَّآ أَن يُؤْمِنُوا۟ بِٱللَّهِ ٱلْعَزِيزِ ٱلْحَمِيدِ ۝ ﴾

8. They had no fault except that they believed in Allâh, the All-Mighty, Worthy of all Praise!

﴿ ٱلَّذِى لَهُۥ مُلْكُ ٱلسَّمَٰوَٰتِ وَٱلْأَرْضِ ۚ وَٱللَّهُ عَلَىٰ كُلِّ شَىْءٍ شَهِيدٌ ۝ ﴾

9. To Whom belongs the dominion of the heavens and the earth! And Allâh is Witness over everything.

﴿ إِنَّ ٱلَّذِينَ فَتَنُوا۟ ٱلْمُؤْمِنِينَ وَٱلْمُؤْمِنَٰتِ ثُمَّ لَمْ يَتُوبُوا۟ فَلَهُمْ عَذَابُ جَهَنَّمَ وَلَهُمْ عَذَابُ ٱلْحَرِيقِ ۝ ﴾

10. Verily, those who put into trial the believing men and believing women (by torturing them and burning them), and then do not turn in repentance (to Allâh), then they will have the torment of Hell, and they will have the punishment of the burning Fire.

Transliteration

1. Waalssama-i thati alburooji 2. Waalyawmi almawAAoodi 3. Washahidin wamashhoodin 4. Qutila as-habu alukhdoodi 5. Alnnari thati alwaqoodi 6. Ith hum AAalayha quAAoodun 7. Wahum AAala ma yafAAaloona bialmu/mineena shuhoodun 8. Wama naqamoo minhum illa an yu/minoo biAllahi alAAazeezi alhameedi 9. Allathee lahu mulku alssamawati waal-ardi waAllahu AAala kulli shay-in shaheedun 10. Inna allatheena fatanoo almu/mineena waalmu/minati thumma lam yatooboo falahum AAathabu jahannama walahum AAathabu alhareeqi

Tafsir Ibn Kathir

The Interpretation of the Word Buruj Allah swears by the heaven and its Buruj.

The Buruj are the giant stars, as Allah says,

(Blessed is He Who has placed in the heaven Buruj, and has placed therein a great lamp (the sun), and a moon giving light.) (25:61) Ibn `Abbas, Mujahid, Ad-Dahhak, Al-Hasan, Qatadah and As-Suddi, all said, "Al-Buruj are the stars." Al-Minhal bin `Amr said,

(By the heaven holding the Buruj.) "The beautiful creation." Ibn Jarir chose the view that it means the positions of the sun and the moon, which are twelve Buruj. The sun travels through each one of these "Burj" (singular of Buruj) in one month. The moon travels through each one of these Burj in two-and-a-third days, which makes a total of twenty-eight positions, and it is hidden for two nights.

The Explanation of the Promised Day and the Witness and the Witnessed

Allah says,

(And by the Promised Day. And by the Witness, and by the Witnessed.) Ibn Abi Hatim recorded from Abu Hurayrah that the Messenger of Allah said,

«((وَالْيَوْمِ الْمَوْعُودِ)) يَوْمُ الْقِيَامَةِ (وَشَهِدَ) يَوْمُ الْجُمُعَةِ، وَمَا طَلَعَتْ شَمْسٌ وَلَا غَرَبَتْ عَلَى يَوْمٍ أَفْضَلَ مِنْ يَوْمِ الْجُمُعَةِ، وَفِيهِ سَاعَةٌ لَا يُوَافِقُهَا عَبْدٌ مُسْلِمٌ يَسْأَلُ اللهَ فِيهَا خَيْرًا إِلَّا أَعْطَاهُ إِيَّاهُ، وَلَا يَسْتَعِيذُ فِيهَا مِنْ شَرٍّ إِلَّا أَعَاذَهُ. (وَمَشْهُودٍ) يَوْمُ عَرَفَةَ»

(And by the Promised Day.)(This refers to the Day of Judgement. (And by the Witness.) This refers to Friday, and the sun does not rise or set on a day that is better than Friday. During it there is an hour that no Muslim servant catches while asking Allah from some good except that Allah will give it to him. He does not seek refuge from any evil in it except that Allah will protect him. (And by the Witnessed.)(This refers to the day of `Arafah (in Hajj).) Ibn Khuzaymah also recorded the same Hadith. It has also been recorded as a statement of Abu Hurayrah and it is similar (to this Hadith).

The Oppression of the People of the Ditch against the Muslims

Concerning Allah's statement,

(Cursed were (Qutila) the People of the Ditch (Ukhdud).) meaning, the companions of the Ukhdud were cursed. The plural of Ukhdud is Akhadid, which means ditches in the ground. This is information about a group of people who were among the disbelievers. They went after those among them who believed in Allah and they attempted to force them to give up their religion. However, the believers refused to recant, so they dug a ditch for them in the ground. Then they lit a fire in it and prepared some fuel for it in order to keep it ablaze. Then they tried to convince them (the believers) to apostate from their religion (again), but they still refused them. So they threw them into the fire. Thus, Allah says,

(Cursed were the People of the Ditch. Of fire fed with fuel. When they sat by it. And they witnessed what they were doing against the believers.) meaning, they were witnesses to what was done to these believers. Allah said,

(And they had no fault except that they believed in Allah, the Almighty, Worthy of all praise!) meaning, they did not commit any sin according to these people, except for their faith in Allah the Almighty, Who does not treat unjustly those who desire to be with Him. He is the Most Mighty and Most Praiseworthy in all of His statements, actions, legislation, and decrees. He decreed what happened to these servants of His at the hands of the disbelievers - and He is the Most Mighty, the Most Praiseworthy - even though the reason for this decree is unknown to many people. Then Allah says,

(To Whom belongs the dominion of the heavens and the earth!) Among His perfect Attributes is that He is the Owner of all of the heavens, the earth, whatever is in them, and whatever is between them.

(And Allah is Witness over everything.) meaning, nothing is concealed from Him in all of the heavens and the earth, nor is anything hidden from Him.

The Story of the Sorcerer, the Monk, the Boy and Those Who were forced to enter the Ditch

Imam Ahmad recorded from Suhayb that the Messenger of Allah said,

»كَانَ فِيمَنْ كَانَ قَبْلَكُمْ مَلِكٌ وَكَانَ لَهُ سَاحِرٌ، فَلَمَّا كَبِرَ السَّاحِرُ قَالَ

لِلْمَلِكِ: إِنِّي قَدْ كَبُرَ سِنِّي وَحَضَرَ أَجَلِي، فَادْفَعْ إِلَيَّ غُلَامًا لِأُعَلِّمَهُ السِّحْرَ، فَدَفَعَ إِلَيْهِ غُلَامًا فَكَانَ يُعَلِّمُهُ السِّحْرَ، وَكَانَ الْغُلَامُ عَلَى الرَّاهِبِ فَسَمِعَ مِنْ كَلَامِهِ فَأَعْجَبَهُ نَحْوُهُ وَكَلَامُهُ، وَكَانَ إِذَا أَتَى السَّاحِرَ ضَرَبَهُ وَقَالَ: مَا حَبَسَكَ؟ وَإِذَا أَتَى أَهْلَهُ ضَرَبُوهُ وَقَالُوا: مَا حَبَسَكَ؟ فَشَكَا ذَلِكَ إِلَى الرَّاهِبِ فَقَالَ: إِذَا أَرَادَ السَّاحِرُ أَنْ يَضْرِبَكَ فَقُلْ: حَبَسَنِي أَهْلِي، وَإِذَا أَرَادَ أَهْلُكَ أَنْ يَضْرِبُوكَ فَقُلْ: حَبَسَنِي السَّاحِرُ، قَالَ: فَبَيْنَمَا هُوَ ذَاتَ يَوْمٍ إِذْ أَتَى عَلَى دَابَّةٍ فَظِيعَةٍ عَظِيمَةٍ قَدْ حَبَسَتِ النَّاسَ فَلَا يَسْتَطِيعُونَ أَنْ يَجُوزُوا. فَقَالَ: الْيَوْمَ أَعْلَمُ أَمْرُ الرَّاهِبِ أَحَبُّ إِلَى اللهِ أَمْ أَمْرُ السَّاحِرِ؟ قَالَ فَأَخَذَ حَجَرًا فَقَالَ: اللَّهُمَّ إِنْ كَانَ أَمْرُ الرَّاهِبِ أَحَبَّ إِلَيْكَ وَأَرْضَى مِنْ أَمْرِ السَّاحِرِ فَاقْتُلْ هَذِهِ الدَّابَّةَ حَتَّى يَجُوزَ النَّاسُ، وَرَمَاهَا فَقَتَلَهَا وَمَضَى النَّاسُ.

(Among the people who came before you, there was a king who had a sorcerer, and when that sorcerer became old, he said to the king, "I have become old and my time is nearly over, so please send me a boy whom I can teach magic." So, he sent him a boy and the sorcerer taught him magic. Whenever the boy went to the sorcerer, he sat with a monk who was on the way and listened to his speech and admired them. So, when he went to the sorcerer, he passed by the monk and sat there with him; and on visiting the sorcerer the latter would thrash him. So, the boy complained about this to the monk. The monk said to him, "Whenever you are afraid of the sorcerer, say to him: `My people kept me busy.' And whenever you are afraid of your people, say to them: `The sorcerer kept me busy.'" So the boy carried on like that (for some time). Then a huge terrible creature appeared on the road and the people were unable to pass by. The boy said, "Today I shall know whether the sorcerer is better or the monk is better." So, he took a stone and said, "O Allah! If the deeds and actions of the monk are liked by You better than those of the sorcerer, then kill this creature so that the people can cross (the road)." Then he struck it with a stone killing it and the people passed by on the road.

فَأَخْبَرَ الرَّاهِبَ بِذَلِكَ فَقَالَ: أَيْ بُنَيَّ، أَنْتَ أَفْضَلُ مِنِّي وَإِنَّكَ سَتُبْتَلَى، فَإِنِ ابْتُلِيتَ فَلَا تَدُلَّ عَلَيَّ، فَكَانَ الْغُلَامُ يُبْرِئُ الْأَكْمَهَ وَالْأَبْرَصَ وَسَائِرَ الْأَدْوَاءِ

Chapter 85: Al-Burooj (The Mansions Of The Stars, Constellations), Verses 001-022

وَيَشْفِيهِمْ، وَكَانَ لِلْمَلِكِ جَلِيسٌ جَلِيسٌ فَعَمِيَ فَسَمِعَ بِهِ فَأَتَاهُ بِهَدَايَا كَثِيرَةٍ فَقَالَ: اشْفِنِي وَلَكَ مَا هَهُنَا أَجْمَعُ، فَقَالَ: مَا أَنَا أَشْفِي أَحَدًا، إِنَّمَا يَشْفِي اللهُ عَزَّ وَجَلَّ، فَإِنْ آمَنْتَ بِهِ دَعَوْتُ اللهَ فَشَفَاكَ، فَآمَنَ فَدَعَا اللهَ فَشَفَاهُ.

The boy came to the monk and informed him about it. The monk said to him, "O my son! Today you are better than I, and you have achieved what I see! You will be put to trial. And in case you are put to trial, do not inform (them) about me." The boy used to treat the people suffering from congenital blindness, leprosy, and other diseases. There was a courtier of the king who had become blind and he heard about the boy. He came and brought a number of gifts for the boy and said, "All these gifts are for you on the condition that you cure me." The boy said, "I do not cure anybody; it is only Allah who cures people. So, if you believe in Allah and supplicate to Him, He will cure you." So, he believed in and supplicated to Allah, and Allah cured him.

ثُمَّ أَتَى الْمَلِكَ فَجَلَسَ مِنْهُ نَحْوَ مَا كَانَ يَجْلِسُ فَقَالَ لَهُ الْمَلِكُ: يَا فُلَانُ، مَنْ رَدَّ عَلَيْكَ بَصَرَكَ؟ فَقَالَ: رَبِّي. قَالَ: أَنَا؟ فَقَالَ: لَا، رَبِّي وَرَبُّكَ اللهُ، قَالَ: وَلَكَ رَبٌّ غَيْرِي؟ قَالَ: نَعَمْ رَبِّي وَرَبُّكَ اللهُ، فَلَمْ يَزَلْ يُعَذِّبُهُ حَتَّى دَلَّ عَلَى الْغُلَامِ، فَبَعَثَ إِلَيْهِ فَقَالَ: أَيْ بُنَيَّ بَلَغَ مِنْ سِحْرِكَ أَنْ تُبْرِىءَ الْأَكْمَهَ وَالْأَبْرَصَ وَهَذِهِ الْأَدْوَاءَ قَالَ: مَا أَشْفِي أَحَدًا إِنَّمَا يَشْفِي اللهُ عَزَّ وَجَلَّ، قَالَ: أَنَا؟ قَالَ: لَا. قَالَ: أَوَلَكَ رَبٌّ غَيْرِي؟ قَالَ: رَبِّي وَرَبُّكَ اللهُ، فَأَخَذَهُ أَيْضًا بِالْعَذَابِ فَلَمْ يَزَلْ بِهِ حَتَّى دَلَّ عَلَى الرَّاهِبِ فَأُتِيَ بِالرَّاهِبِ فَقَالَ: ارْجِعْ عَنْ دِينِكَ فَأَبَى، فَوَضَعَ الْمِنْشَارَ فِي مَفْرِقِ رَأْسِهِ حَتَّى وَقَعَ شِقَّاهُ، وَقَالَ لِلْأَعْمَى: ارْجِعْ عَنْ دِينِكَ، فَأَبَى، فَوَضَعَ الْمِنْشَارَ فِي مَفْرِقِ رَأْسِهِ حَتَّى وَقَعَ شِقَّاهُ إِلَى الْأَرْضِ. وَقَالَ لِلْغُلَامِ: ارْجِعْ عَنْ دِينِكَ، فَأَبَى، فَبَعَثَ بِهِ مَعَ نَفَرٍ إِلَى جَبَلٍ كَذَا وَكَذَا وَقَالَ: إِذَا بَلَغْتُمْ ذُرْوَتَهُ فَإِنْ رَجَعَ عَنْ دِينِهِ وَإِلَّا فَدَهْدِهُوهُ، فَذَهَبُوا بِهِ فَلَمَّا عَلَوْا بِهِ الْجَبَلَ قَالَ: اللَّهُمَّ اكْفِنِيهِمْ بِمَا شِئْتَ، فَرَجَفَ بِهِمُ الْجَبَلُ فَدُهْدِهُوا أَجْمَعُونَ،

وَجَاءَ الْغُلَامُ يَتَلَمَّسُ حَتَّى دَخَلَ عَلَى الْمَلِكِ فَقَالَ: مَا فَعَلَ أَصْحَابُكَ؟ فَقَالَ: كَفَانِيهِمُ اللهُ تَعَالَى، فَبَعَثَ بِهِ مَعَ نَفَرٍ فِي قُرْقُورٍ فَقَالَ: إِذَا لَجَجْتُمْ بِهِ الْبَحْرَ فَإِنْ رَجَعَ عَنْ دِينِهِ، وَإِلَّا فَغَرِّقُوهُ فِي الْبَحْرِ، فَلَجَّجُوا بِهِ الْبَحْرَ فَقَالَ الْغُلَامُ: اللَّهُمَّ اكْفِنِيهِمْ بِمَا شِئْتَ، فَغَرِقُوا أَجْمَعُونَ.

Later, the courtier came to the king and sat at the place where he used to sit before. The king said, "Who gave you back your sight" The courtier replied, "My Lord." The king then said, "I did" The courtier said, "No, my Lord and your Lord - Allah" The king said, "Do you have another Lord beside me" The courtier said, "Yes, your Lord and my Lord is Allah." The king tortured him and did not stop until he told him about the boy. So, the boy was brought to the king and he said to him, "O boy! Has your magic reached to the extent that you cure congenital blindness, leprosy and other diseases" He said, "I do not cure anyone. Only Allah can cure." The king said, "Me" The boy replied, "No." The king asked, "Do you have another Lord besides me" The boy answered, "My Lord and your Lord is Allah." So, he tortured him also until he told about the monk. Then the monk was brought to him and the king said to him, "Abandon your religion." The monk refused and so the king ordered a saw to be brought which was placed in the middle of his head and he fell, sawn in two. Then it was said to the man who used to be blind, "Abandon your religion." He refused to do so, and so a saw was brought and placed in the middle of his head and he fell, sawn in two. Then the boy was brought and it was said to him, "Abandon your religion." He refused and so the king sent him to the top of such and such mountain with some people. He told the people, "Ascend up the mountain with him till you reach its peak, then see if he abandons his religion; otherwise throw him from the top." They took him and when they ascended to the top, he said, "O Allah! Save me from them by any means that You wish." So, the mountain shook and they all fell down and the boy came back walking to the king. The king said, "What did your companions (the people I sent with you) do" The boy said, "Allah saved me from them." So, the king ordered some people to take the boy on a boat to the middle of the sea, saying, "If he renounces his religion (well and good), but if he refuses, drown him." So, they took him out to sea and he said, "O Allah! Save me from them by any means that you wish." So they were all drowned in the sea.

وَجَاءَ الْغُلَامُ حَتَّى دَخَلَ عَلَى الْمَلِكِ فَقَالَ: مَا فَعَلَ أَصْحَابُكَ؟ فَقَالَ: كَفَانِيهِمُ اللهُ تَعَالَى ثُمَّ قَالَ لِلْمَلِكِ: إِنَّكَ لَسْتَ بِقَاتِلِي حَتَّى تَفْعَلَ مَا آمُرُكَ بِهِ، فَإِنْ أَنْتَ فَعَلْتَ مَا آمُرُكَ بِهِ قَتَلْتَنِي، وَإِلَّا فَإِنَّكَ لَا تَسْتَطِيعُ قَتْلِي، قَالَ:

Chapter 85: Al-Burooj (The Mansions Of The Stars, Constellations), Verses 001-022

وَمَا هُوَ؟ قَالَ: تَجْمَعُ النَّاسَ فِي صَعِيدٍ وَاحِدٍ ثُمَّ تَصْلُبُنِي عَلَى جِذْعٍ وَتَأْخُذُ سَهْمًا مِنْ كِنَانَتِي، ثُمَّ قُلْ: بِاسْمِ اللهِ رَبِّ الْغُلَامِ. فَإِنَّكَ إِذَا فَعَلْتَ ذَلِكَ قَتَلْتَنِي. فَفَعَلَ وَوَضَعَ السَّهْمَ فِي كَبِدِ قَوْسِهِ ثُمَّ رَمَاهُ وَقَالَ: بِاسْمِ اللهِ رَبِّ الْغُلَامِ، فَوَقَعَ السَّهْمُ فِي صُدْغِهِ، فَوَضَعَ الْغُلَامُ يَدَهُ عَلَى مَوْضِعِ السَّهْمِ وَمَاتَ، فَقَالَ النَّاسُ: آمَنَّا بِرَبِّ الْغُلَامِ. فَقِيلَ لِلْمَلِكِ: أَرَأَيْتَ مَا كُنْتَ تَحْذَرُ؟ فَقَدْ وَاللهِ نَزَلَ بِكَ، قَدْ آمَنَ النَّاسُ كُلُّهُمْ، فَأَمَرَ بِأَفْوَاهِ السِّكَكِ، فَخُدَّتْ فِيهَا الْأَخَادِيدُ وَأُضْرِمَتْ فِيهَا النِّيرَانُ، وَقَالَ: مَنْ رَجَعَ عَنْ دِينِهِ فَدَعُوهُ، وَإِلَّا فَأَقْحِمُوهُ فِيهَا، قَالَ: فَكَانُوا يَتَعَادُّونَ فِيهَا وَيَتَدَافَعُونَ، فَجَاءَتِ امْرَأَةٌ بِابْنٍ لَهَا تُرْضِعُهُ، فَكَأَنَّهَا تَقَاعَسَتْ أَنْ تَقَعَ فِي النَّارِ فَقَالَ الصَّبِيُّ: اصْبِرِي يَا أُمَّاهُ فَإِنَّكِ عَلَى الْحَقِّ»

Then the boy returned to the king and the king said, "What did your companions do" The boy replied, "Allah, saved me from them." Then he said to the king, "You will not be able to kill me until you do as I order you. And if you do as I order you, you will be able to kill me." The king asked, "And what is that" The boy said, "Gather the people in one elevated place and tie me to the trunk of a tree; then take an arrow from my quiver and say: `In the Name of Allah, the Lord of the boy.' If you do this, you will be able to kill me." So he did this, and placing an arrow in the bow, he shot it, saying, "In the Name of Allah, the Lord of the boy." The arrow hit the boy in the temple, and the boy placed his hand over the arrow wound and died. The people proclaimed, "We believe in the Lord of the boy!" Then it was said to the king, "Do you see what has happened That which you feared has taken place. By Allah, all the people have believed (in the Lord of the boy)." So he ordered that ditches be dug at the entrances to the roads and it was done, and fires were kindled in them. Then the king said, "Whoever abandons his religion, let him go, and whoever does not, throw him into the fire." They were struggling and scuffling in the fire, until a woman and her baby whom she was breast feeding came and it was as if she was being somewhat hesitant of falling into the fire, so her baby said to her, "Be patient mother! For verily, you are following the truth!") Muslim also recorded this Hadith at the end of the Sahih. Muhammad bin Ishaq bin Yasar related this story in his book of Sirah in another way that has some differences from that which has just been related. Then, after Ibn Ishaq explained that the people of Najran began following the religion of the boy after his murder, which was the religion of Christianity, he said, "Then (the king) Dhu

Nuwas came to them with his army and called them to Judaism. He gave them a choice to either accept Judaism or be killed, so they chose death. Thus, he had a ditch dug and burned (some of them) in the fire (in the ditch), while others he killed with the sword. He made an example of them (by slaughtering them) until he had killed almost twenty thousand of them. It was about Dhu Nuwas and his army that Allah revealed to His Messenger :

(Cursed were the People of the Ditch. Of fire fed with fuel. When they sat by it. And they witnessed what they were doing against the believers. And they had no fault except that they believed in Allah, the Almighty, Worthy of all praise! To Whom belongs the dominion of the heavens and the earth! And Allah is Witness over everything.) (85:4-9)" This is what Muhammad bin Ishaq said in his book of Sirah -- that the one who killed the People of the Ditch was Dhu Nuwas, and his name was Zur`ah. In the time of his kingdom he was called Yusuf. He was the son of Tuban As`ad Abi Karib, who was the Tubba` who invaded Al-Madinah and put the covering over the Ka`bah. He kept two rabbis with him from the Jews of Al-Madinah. After this some of the people of Yemen accepted Judaism at the hands of these two rabbis, as Ibn Ishaq mentions at length. So Dhu Nuwas killed twenty thousand people in one morning in the Ditch. Only one man among them escaped. He was known as Daws Dhu Tha`laban. He escaped on a horse and they set out after him, but they were unable to catch him. He went to Caesar, the emperor of Ash-Sham. So, Caesar wrote to An-Najashi, the King of Abyssinia. So, he sent with him an army of Abyssinian Christians, who were lead by Aryat and Abrahah. They rescued Yemen from the hands of the Jews. Dhu Nuwas tried to flee but eventually fell into the sea and drowned. After this, the kingdom of Abyssinia remained under Christian power for seventy years. Then the power was divested from the Christians by Sayf bin Dhi Yazin Al-Himyari when Kisra, the king of Persia sent an army there (to Yemen). He (the king) sent with him (Sayf Al-Himyari) those people who were in the prisons, and they were close to seven hundred in number. So, he (Sayf Al-Himyari) conquered Yemen with them and returned the kingdom back to the people of Himyar (Yemenis). We will mention a portion of this -- if Allah wills -- when we discuss the Tafsir of the Surah:

(Have you not seen how your Lord dealt with the Owners of the Elephant) (105:1)

The Punishment of the People of the Ditch

Allah said,

(Verily, those who put into trial the believing men and believing women,) meaning, they burned (them). This was said by Ibn `Abbas, Mujahid, Qatadah, Ad-Dahhak, and Ibn Abza.

(and then do not turn in repentance,) meaning, `they do not cease from what they are doing, and do not regret what they had done before.'

(then they will have the torment of Hell, and they will have the punishment of the burning Fire.) This is because the recompense is based upon the type of deed performed. Al-Hasan Al-Basri said, "Look at this generosity and kindness. These people killed Allah's Awliya' and He still invites them to make repentance and seek forgiveness."

Surah: 85 Ayah: 11, Ayah: 12, Ayah: 13, Ayah: 14, Ayah: 15, Ayah: 16, Ayah: 17, Ayah: 18, Ayah: 19, Ayah: 20, Ayah: 21 & Ayah: 22

﴿ إِنَّ ٱلَّذِينَ ءَامَنُواْ وَعَمِلُواْ ٱلصَّٰلِحَٰتِ لَهُمْ جَنَّٰتٌ تَجْرِى مِن تَحْتِهَا ٱلْأَنْهَٰرُ ذَٰلِكَ ٱلْفَوْزُ ٱلْكَبِيرُ ﴾

11. Verily, those who believe and do righteous good deeds, for them will be Gardens under which rivers flow (Paradise). That is the great success.

﴿ إِنَّ بَطْشَ رَبِّكَ لَشَدِيدٌ ﴾

12. Verily, (O Muhammad (peace be upon him)) the Seizure (punishment) of your Lord is severe. (See V.11:102).

﴿ إِنَّهُۥ هُوَ يُبْدِئُ وَيُعِيدُ ﴾

13. Verily, He it is Who begins (punishment) and repeats (punishment in the Hereafter) (or originates the creation of everything, and then repeats it on the Day of Resurrection).

﴿ وَهُوَ ٱلْغَفُورُ ٱلْوَدُودُ ﴾

14. And He is Oft-Forgiving, full of love (towards the pious who are real true believers of Islâmic Monotheism),

﴿ ذُو ٱلْعَرْشِ ٱلْمَجِيدُ ﴾

15. Owner of the throne, the Glorious,

﴿ فَعَّالٌ لِّمَا يُرِيدُ ﴾

16. (He is the) Doer of whatsoever He intends (or wills).

﴿ هَلْ أَتَىٰكَ حَدِيثُ ٱلْجُنُودِ ﴾

17. Has the story reached you of the hosts,

﴿ فِرْعَوْنَ وَثَمُودَ ﴾

18. Of Fir'aun (Pharaoh) and Thamûd?

﴿ بَلِ ٱلَّذِينَ كَفَرُواْ فِى تَكْذِيبٍ ﴾

19. Nay! The disbelievers (persisted) in denying (Prophet Muhammad (peace be upon him) and his Message of Islâmic Monotheism).

﴿ وَٱللَّهُ مِن وَرَآئِهِم مُّحِيطٌ ۞ ﴾

20. And Allâh encompasses them from behind! (i.e. all their deeds are within His Knowledge, and He will requite them for their deeds).

﴿ بَلْ هُوَ قُرْءَانٌ مَّجِيدٌ ۞ ﴾

21. Nay! This is a Glorious Qur'ân,

﴿ فِى لَوْحٍ مَّحْفُوظٍ ۞ ﴾

22. (Inscribed) in Al-Lauh Al-Mahfûz (The Preserved Tablet)!

Transliteration

11. Inna allatheena amanoo waAAamiloo alssalihati lahum jannatun tajree min tahtiha alanharu thalika alfawzu alkabeeru 12. Inna batsha rabbika lashadeedun 13. Innahu huwa yubdi-o wayuAAeedu 14. Wahuwa alghafooru alwadoodu 15. Thoo alAAarshi almajeedi 16. FaAAAAalun lima yureedu 17. Hal ataka hadeethu aljunoodi 18. FirAAawna wathamooda 19. Bali allatheena kafaroo fee taktheebin 20. WaAllahu min wara-ihim muheetun 21. Bal huwa qur-anun majeedun 22. Fee lawhin mahfoothin

Tafsir Ibn Kathir

The Reward of the Righteous, and the Harsh Seizing of the Disbelieving Enemies of Allah

Allah informs about His believing servants that

(for them will be Gardens under which rivers flow.) This is the opposite of what he has prepared for His enemies of Fire and Hell. Thus, He says,

(That is the supreme success.) Then Allah says,

(Verily, the punishment of your Lord is severe and painful.) meaning, indeed His punishment and His vengeance upon His enemies, who have rejected His Messengers, and opposed His command, is severe, great and strong. For verily, He is the Owner of power, Most Strong. He is the One that whatever He wants, then it will be however He wants it to be, in the matter of a blinking of an eye, or even swifter. Thus, Allah says,

(Verily, He it is Who begins and repeats.) meaning, from His perfect strength and power is that He begins the creation, and He repeats it just as He began it, without opposition or resistance.

(And He is Oft-Forgiving, Al-Wadud.) meaning, He forgives the sin of whoever repents to Him and humbles himself before Him, no matter what the sin may be. Ibn `Abbas and others have said about the name Al-Wadud, "It means Al-Habib (the Loving)."

(Owner of the Throne,) meaning, the Owner of the Mighty Throne that is above all of the creation. Then He says,

(Al-Majid (the Glorious).) This word has been recited in two different ways: either with a Dhammah over its last letter (Al-Majidu), which is an attribute of the Lord, or with a Kasrah under its last letter (Al-Majid), which is a description of the Throne. Nevertheless, both meanings are correct.

(Doer of what He intends.) meaning, whatever He wants He does it, and there is no one who can counter His ruling. He is not asked about what He does due to His greatness, His power, His wisdom and His justice. This is as we have related previously from Abu Bakr As-Siddiq, that it was said to him during the illness of (his) death, "Has a doctor seen you" He replied, "Yes." They said, "What did he say to you" He replied, "He said, `I am the Doer of whatever I intend.'" Concerning Allah's statement,

(Has the story reached you of the hosts. Of Fir`awn and Thamud) meaning, has the news reached you of what Allah caused to befall them of torment, and that He sent down upon them the punishment that no one was able to ward off from them This is the affirmation of His statement,

(Verily, the punishment of your Lord is severe and painful.) meaning, when He seizes the wrongdoer, He seizes him with a severe and painful punishment. It is the seizing punishment of One Most Mighty, and Most Powerful. Then Allah says,

(Nay! The disbelievers (persisted) in denying.) meaning, they are in doubt, suspicion, disbelief and rebellion.

(And Allah encompasses them from behind!) meaning, He has power over them, and is able to compel them. They cannot escape Him or evade Him.

(Nay! This is a Glorious Qur'an.) meaning, magnificent and noble.

(In Al-Lawh Al-Mahfuz!) meaning, among the most high gathering, guarded from any increase, decrease, distortion, or change. This is the end of the Tafsir of Surat Al-Buruj, and all praise and blessings are due to Allah.

INTRODUCTION TO CHAPTER (SURAH) 86: AT-TARIQ (THE MORNING STAR, THE NIGHTCOMER)

Ibn Kathir's Introduction

The Virtues of Surat At-Tariq

An-Nasa'i recorded that Jabir said, "Mu`adh lead the Maghrib prayer and he recited Al-Baqarah and An-Nisa'. So the Prophet said,

«أَفَتَّانٌ أَنْتَ يَا مُعَاذُ، مَا كَانَ يَكْفِيكَ أَنْ تَقْرَأَ بِالسَّمَاءِ وَالطَّارِقِ وَالشَّمْسِ وَضُحَاهَا وَنَحْوِهَا؟»

(Are you putting the people to trial O Mu`adh! Was it not sufficient for you to recite As-Sama'i wat-Tariq, and Ash-Shamsi wa Duhaha, and something like them)

CHAPTER (SURAH) 86: AT-TARIQ (THE MORNING STAR, THE NIGHTCOMER), VERSES 001- 017

Surah: 86 Ayah: 1, Ayah: 2, Ayah: 3, Ayah: 4, Ayah: 5, Ayah: 6, Ayah: 7, Ayah: 8, Ayah: 9, Ayah: 10

(بِسْمِ اللَّهِ الرَّحْمَـنِ الرَّحِيمِ)

In the Name of Allah, the Most Gracious, the Most Merciful.

﴿ وَٱلسَّمَآءِ وَٱلطَّارِقِ ۝ ﴾

1. By the heaven, and At-Târiq (the night-comer, i.e. the bright star);

﴿ وَمَآ أَدْرَىٰكَ مَا ٱلطَّارِقُ ۝ ﴾

2. And what will make you to know what At-Târiq (night-comer) is?

﴿ ٱلنَّجْمُ ٱلثَّاقِبُ ۝ ﴾

3. (It is) the star of piercing brightness;

﴿ إِن كُلُّ نَفْسٍ لَّمَّا عَلَيْهَا حَافِظٌ ۝ ﴾

4. There is no human being but has a protector over him (or her) (i.e. angels in charge of each human being guarding him, writing his good and bad deeds)

﴿ فَلْيَنظُرِ ٱلْإِنسَٰنُ مِمَّ خُلِقَ ۝ ﴾

5. So let man see from what he is created!

﴿ خُلِقَ مِن مَّآءٍ دَافِقٍ ۝ ﴾

6. He is created from a water gushing forth,

﴿ يَخْرُجُ مِنْ بَيْنِ ٱلصُّلْبِ وَٱلتَّرَآئِبِ ۝ ﴾

7. Proceeding from between the backbone and the ribs.

﴿ إِنَّهُۥ عَلَىٰ رَجْعِهِۦ لَقَادِرٌ ۝ ﴾

8. Verily, (Allâh) is Able to bring him back (to life)!

﴿ يَوْمَ تُبْلَى ٱلسَّرَآئِرُ ۝ ﴾

9. The Day when all the secrets (deeds, prayers, fasting, etc.) will be examined (as to their truth).

﴿ فَمَا لَهُۥ مِن قُوَّةٍ وَلَا نَاصِرٍ ۝ ﴾

10. Then he will have no power, nor any helper.

Transliteration

1. Waalssama-i waalttariqi 2. Wama adraka ma alttariqu 3. Alnnajmu alththaqibu 4. In kullu nafsin lamma AAalayha hafithun 5. Falyanthuri al-insanu mimma khuliqa 6. Khuliqa min ma-in dafiqin 7. Yakhruju min bayni alssulbi waalttara-ibi 8. Innahu AAala rajAAihi laqadirun 9. Yawma tubla alssara-iru 10. Fama lahu min quwwatin wala nasirin

Tafsir Ibn Kathir

Swearing by the Existence of Humanity surrounded by the Organized System of Allah

Allah swears by the heaven and what He has placed in it of radiant stars. Thus, He says,

(By the heaven, and At-Tariq;) Then He says,

(And what will make you to know what At-Tariq is) Then He explains it by His saying,

(The star of Ath-Thaqib.) Qatadah and others have said, "The star has been named Tariq because it is only seen at night and it is hidden during the day." His view is supported by what has been mentioned in the authentic Hadith that prohibits a man to come to his family Taruq. This means that he comes to them unexpectedly at nighttime. Concerning Allah's statement,

(Ath-Thaqib.) Ibn `Abbas said, "The illuminating." `Ikrimah said, "It is illuminating and it burns the Shaytan" Then Allah says,

(There is no human being but has a protector over him.) meaning, every soul has a guardian over it from Allah that protects it from the calamities. This is as Allah says,

(For Him, there are angels in succession, before and behind him. They guard him by the command of Allah.) (13:11)

How Man is created is a Proof of Allah's Ability to Return Him to Him

Allah says,

(So, let man see from what he is created!) This is alerting man to the weakness of his origin from which he was created. The intent of it is to guide man to accept (the reality of) the Hereafter, because whoever is able to begin the creation then he is also able to repeat it in the same way. This is as Allah says,

(And He it is Who originates the creation, then He will repeat it; and this is easier for Him.) (30:27) Then Allah says,

(He is created from a water gushing forth.) meaning, the sexual fluid that comes out bursting forth from the man and the woman. Thus, the child is produced from both of them by the permission of Allah. Due to this Allah says,

(Proceeding from between the backbone and the ribs.) meaning, the backbone (or loins) of the man and the ribs of the woman, which is referring to her chest. Shabib bin Bishr reported from `Ikrimah who narrated from Ibn `Abbas that he said,

(Proceeding from between the backbone and the ribs.) "The backbone of the man and the ribs of the woman. It (the fluid) is yellow and fine in texture. The child will not be born except from both of them (i.e., their sexual fluids)." Concerning Allah's statement,

(Verily, He is Able to bring him back (to life)!) This means that He is able to return this man that is created from fluid gushed forth. In other words, He is able to repeat his creation and resurrect him to the final abode. This is clearly possible, because whoever is able to begin the creation then he surely is able to repeat it. Indeed Allah has mentioned this proof in more than one place in the Qur'an.

On the Day of Judgement, Man will have no Power or Assistance

In this regard Allah says,

(The Day when all the secrets will be examined.) meaning, on the Day of Judgement the secrets will be tested. This means that they will be exposed and made manifest. Thus, the secret will be made open and that which is concealed will be well known. It is confirmed in the Two Sahihs on the authority of Ibn `Umar that the Messenger of Allah said,

«يُرْفَعُ لِكُلِّ غَادِرٍ لِوَاءٌ عِنْدَ اسْتِهِ يُقَالُ: هذِهِ غَدْرَةُ فُلَانِ بْنِ فُلَانٍ»

(Every betrayer will have a flag raised for him behind his back, and it will be said, `This is the betrayal of so-and-so, the son of so-and-so.') Concerning Allah's statement,

(Then he will have no) meaning, man on the Day of Judgement.

(any power) meaning, within himself.

(nor any helper.) meaning, from other than himself. This statement means that he will not be able to save himself from the torment of Allah, and nor will anyone else be able to save him.

Surah: 86 Ayah: 11, Ayah: 12, Ayah: 13, Ayah: 14, Ayah: 15, Ayah: 16 & Ayah: 17

﴿وَالسَّمَاءِ ذَاتِ الرَّجْعِ ۝﴾

11. By the sky (having rain clouds) which gives rain, again and again.

﴿وَالْأَرْضِ ذَاتِ الصَّدْعِ ۝﴾

12. And the earth which splits (with the growth of trees and plants).

﴿إِنَّهُ لَقَوْلٌ فَصْلٌ ۝﴾

13. Verily, this (the Qur'ân) is the Word that separates (the truth from falsehood, and commands strict laws for mankind to cut the roots of evil).

﴿وَمَا هُوَ بِالْهَزْلِ ۝﴾

14. And it is not a thing for amusement.

﴿إِنَّهُمْ يَكِيدُونَ كَيْدًا ۝﴾

15. Verily, they are but plotting a plot (against you O Muhammad (peace be upon him))

﴿وَأَكِيدُ كَيْدًا ۝﴾

16. And I (too) am planning a plan.

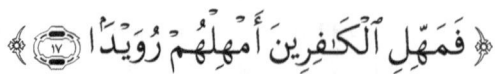

17. So give a respite to the disbelievers; deal you gently with them for a while.

Transliteration

11. Waalssama-i thati alrrajAAi 12. Waal-ardi thati alssadAAi 13. Innahu laqawlun faslun 14. Wama huwa bialhazli 15. Innahum yakeedoona kaydan 16. Waakeedu kaydan 17. Famahhili alkafireena amhilhum ruwaydan

Tafsir Ibn Kathir

Swearing to the Truthfulness of the Qur'an and the Failure of Those Who oppose it

Ibn `Abbas said, "Ar-raj` means rain." It has also been narrated from him that he said, "It means the clouds that contain rain." He also said,

(By the sky (having rain clouds) which gives rain, again and again.) "This means that it rains and then it rains (again)." Qatadah said, "It returns the sustenance of the servants (creatures) every year. Were it not for this, they would all be destroyed and so would their cattle."

(And the earth which splits.) Ibn `Abbas said, "Splitting to bring forth plant growths." This was also said by Sa`id bin Jubayr, `Ikrimah, Abu Malik, Ad-Dahhak, Al-Hasan, Qatadah, As-Suddi and others. Concerning Allah's statement,

(Verily, this is the Word that separates.) Ibn `Abbas said (Fasl is), "True." Qatadah also said the same. Someone else said, "A just ruling."

(And it is not a thing for amusement.) meaning, rather it is serious and true. Then Allah informs about the disbelievers saying that they reject Him and hinder others from His path. Allah says,

(Verily, they are but plotting a plot.) meaning, they plot against the people in their calling them to oppose the Qur'an. Then Allah says,

(So, give a respite to the disbelievers;) meaning, wait for them and do not be in haste concerning them.

(deal gently with them for a while.) meaning, a little while. This means that you will see what befalls them of torment, punishment and destruction. This is as Allah says,

(We let them enjoy for a little while, then in the end We shall oblige them to (enter) a great torment.) (31:24) This is the end of the Tafsir Surat At-Tariq, and unto Allah is all praise and thanks.

INTRODUCTION TO CHAPTER (SURAH) 87: AL-ALA (THE MOST HIGH, GLORY TO YOUR LORD IN THE HIGHEST)

Ibn Kathir's Introduction

The Virtues of Surat Al-A`la

This Surah was revealed in Makkah before the migration to Al-Madinah. The proof of this is what Al-Bukhari recorded from Al-Bara' bin `Azib, that he said, "The first people to come to us (in Al-Madinah) from the Companions of the Prophet were Mus`ab bin `Umayr and Ibn Umm Maktum, who taught us the Qur'an; then `Ammar, Bilal and Sa`d came. Then `Umar bin Al-Khattab came with a group of twenty people, after which the Prophet came. I have not seen the people of Al-Madinah happier with anything more than their happiness with his coming (to Al-Madinah). This was reached to such an extent that I saw the children and little ones saying, `This is the Messenger of Allah who has come.' Thus, he came, but he did not come until after I had already recited (i.e., learned how to recite)

(Glorify the Name of your Lord, the Most High.) (87:1) as well as other Surahs similar to it." It has been confirmed in the Two Sahihs that the Messenger of Allah said to Mu`adh,

«هَلَّا صَلَّيْتَ بِ (سَبِّحِ اسْمَ رَبِّكَ الْأَعْلَى) (وَالشَّمْسِ وَضُحَاهَا) (وَاللَّيْلِ إِذَا يَغْشَى)»

(Why didn't you recite "Glorify the Name of your Lord, the Most High,"; "By the sun and its brightness," and "By the night when it envelopes.") Imam Ahmad recorded from An-Nu`man bin Bashir that the Messenger of Allah recited

Surat Al-A`la (chapter 87) and Surat Al-Ghashiyh (chapter 88) in the two `Id prayers. If the `Id prayer fell on Friday, he would recite them in both prayers (`Id and Salat Al-Jumu`ah). Muslim also recorded this in his Sahih, as well as Abu Dawud, At-Tirmidhi, An-Nasa'i and Ibn Majah. The wording of Muslim and the Sunan compilers says, "He used to recite

Surat Al-A`la (chapter 87) and Surat Al-Ghashiyh (chapter 88) for the two `Ids and Jumu`ah. If they occurred on the same day, he would recite them in both of them." In his Musnad, Imam Ahmad recorded on the authority of Ubayy bin Ka`b, Abdullah bin `Abbas, `Abdur-Rahman bin Abza, and the Mother of the believers, `A'ishah, that the Messenger of Allah used to recite

(Glorify the Name of your Lord, the Most High.) and (Say: `O you who disbelieve.') and (Say: `He is Allah, the One.') `A'ishah added in her version that he would also recite the Mu`awwidhatayn (Al-Falaq and An-Nas).

CHAPTER (SURAH) 87: AL-ALA (THE MOST HIGH, GLORY TO YOUR LORD IN THE HIGHEST), VERSES 001- 019

Surah: 87 Ayah: 1, Ayah: 2, Ayah: 3, Ayah: 4, Ayah: 5, Ayah: 6, Ayah: 7, Ayah: 8, Ayah: 9, Ayah: 10, Ayah: 11, Ayah: 12 & Ayah: 13

(بِسْمِ اللَّهِ الرَّحْمَـنِ الرَّحِيمِ)

In the Name of Allah, the Most Gracious, the Most Merciful.

﴿ سَبِّحِ اسْمَ رَبِّكَ الْأَعْلَى ۝ ﴾

1. Glorify the Name of your Lord, the Most High,

﴿ الَّذِى خَلَقَ فَسَوَّىٰ ۝ ﴾

2. Who has created (everything), and then proportioned it.

﴿ وَالَّذِى قَدَّرَ فَهَدَىٰ ۝ ﴾

3. And Who has measured (preordainments for everything even to be blessed or wretched); then guided (i.e. showed mankind the right as well as the wrong paths, and guided the animals to pasture).

﴿ وَالَّذِى أَخْرَجَ الْمَرْعَىٰ ۝ ﴾

4. And Who brings out the pasturage,

﴿ فَجَعَلَهُ غُثَاءً أَحْوَىٰ ۝ ﴾

5. And then makes it dark stubble.

﴿ سَنُقْرِئُكَ فَلَا تَنسَىٰ ۝ ﴾

6. We shall make you to recite (the Qur'ân), so you (O Muhammad (peace be upon him)) shall not forget (it),

﴿ إِلَّا مَا شَاءَ ٱللَّهُ ۚ إِنَّهُۥ يَعْلَمُ ٱلْجَهْرَ وَمَا يَخْفَىٰ ۝ ﴾

7. Except what Allâh may will. He knows what is apparent and what is hidden.

﴿ وَنُيَسِّرُكَ لِلْيُسْرَىٰ ۝ ﴾

8. And We shall make easy for you (O Muhammad (peace be upon him)) the easy way (i.e. the doing of righteous deeds).

﴿ فَذَكِّرْ إِن نَّفَعَتِ ٱلذِّكْرَىٰ ۝ ﴾

9. Therefore remind (men) in case the reminder profits (them).

﴿ سَيَذَّكَّرُ مَن يَخْشَىٰ ۝ ﴾

10. The reminder will be received by him who fears (Allâh),

﴿ وَيَتَجَنَّبُهَا ٱلْأَشْقَى ۝ ﴾

11. But it will be avoided by the wretched,

﴿ ٱلَّذِى يَصْلَى ٱلنَّارَ ٱلْكُبْرَىٰ ۝ ﴾

12. Who will enter the great Fire (and will be made to taste its burning).

﴿ ثُمَّ لَا يَمُوتُ فِيهَا وَلَا يَحْيَىٰ ۝ ﴾

13. There he will neither die (to be in rest) nor live (a good living).

Transliteration

1. Sabbihi isma rabbika al-aAAla 2. Allathee khalaqa fasawwa 3. Waallathee qaddara fahada 4. Waallathee akhraja almarAAa 5. FajaAAalahu ghuthaan ahwa 6. Sanuqri-oka fala tansa 7. Illa ma shaa Allahu innahu yaAAlamu aljahra wama yakhfa 8. Wanuyassiruka lilyusra 9. Fathakkir in nafaAAati aththikra 10. Sayaththakkaru man yakhsha 11. Wayatajannabuha al-ashqa 12. Allathee yasla alnnara alkubra 13. Thumma la yamootu feeha wala yahya

Tafsir Ibn Kathir

The Command to pronounce Tasbih and its Response

Imam Ahmad recorded from Ibn `Abbas that whenever the Messenger of Allah would recite

(Glorify the Name of your Lord, the Most High.) he would say,

«سُبْحَانَ رَبِّيَ الْأَعْلَى»

(Glory to my Lord, the Most High.) Ibn Jarir recorded from Ibn Ishaq Al-Hamdani that whenever Ibn `Abbas would recite

(Glorify the Name of your Lord, the Most High.) he would say, "Glory to my Lord, the Most High," and whenever he would recite

(I swear by the Day of Resurrection.) (75:1) and then reach the end of it

(Is not He able to give life to the dead) (75:40) he would say, "Glory to You, of course." Qatadah said,

(Glorify the Name of your Lord, the Most High.) "It has been mentioned to us that whenever the Prophet of Allah used to recite it he would say,

«سُبْحَانَ رَبِّيَ الْأَعْلَى»

(Glory to my Lord, the Most High.)"

The Creation, the Decree, and the bringing forth of Vegetation

Allah says,

(Who has created, and then proportioned it.) meaning, He created that which has been created, and He fashioned every creation in the best of forms. Then Allah says,

(And Who has measured; and then guided.) Mujahid said, "He guided man to distress and happiness, and he guided the cattle to their pastures." This Ayah is similar to what Allah has said about Musa's statement to Fir`awn,

(Our Lord is He Who gave to each thing its form and nature, then guided it aright.) (20:50) meaning, He decreed a set measure and guided the creation to it. This is just as is confirmed in Sahih Muslim on the authority of `Abdullah bin `Amr that the Messenger of Allah said,

«إِنَّ اللهَ قَدَّرَ مَقَادِيرَ الْخَلَائِقِ قَبْلَ أَنْ يَخْلُقَ السَّمَوَاتِ وَالْأَرْضَ بِخَمْسِينَ أَلْفَ

Chapter 87: Al-Ala (The Most High), Verses 001-019

«سَنَةٍ وَكَانَ عَرْشُهُ عَلَى الْمَاءِ»

(Verily, Allah ordained the measure of all creation fifty thousand years before He created the heavens and the earth, and His Throne was over the water.) Concerning Allah's statement,

(And Who brings out the pasturage,) meaning, all types of vegetation and crops.

(And then makes it dark stubble.) Ibn `Abbas said, "Dried up and altered." It has been narrated that Mujahid, Qatadah and Ibn Zayd, all made similar statements.

The Prophet does not forget the Revelation

Allah says,

(We shall make you to recite,) meaning, `O Muhammad.'

(so you shall not forget (it),) This is Allah informing and promising him (the Prophet) that He will teach him a recitation that he will not forget.

(Except what Allah may will.) Qatadah said, "The Prophet did not forget anything except what Allah willed." It has been said that the meaning of Allah's statement,

(so you shall not forget,) is, "do not forget" and that which would be abrogated, is merely an exception to this. Meaning, `do not forget what We teach you to recite, except what Allah wills, which He removes and there is no sin on your leaving it off (not retaining it).' Concerning Allah's statement,

(He knows what is apparent and what is hidden.) meaning, He knows what the creatures do openly and what they hide, whether it be statements or deeds. None of that is hidden from Him. Then Allah says,

(And We shall make easy for you the easy.) meaning, `We will make good deeds and statements easy for you, and We will legislate such Law for you that is easy, tolerant, straight and just, with no crookedness, difficulty or hardship in it.'

The Command to remind

Allah then says,

(Therefore remind in case the reminder profits.) meaning, remind where reminding is beneficial. From here we get the etiquette of spreading knowledge, that it should not be wasted upon those who are not suitable or worthy of it. The Commander of the believers, `Ali said, "You do not tell people any statement that their intellects do not grasp except that it will be a Fitnah (trial) for some of them." He also said, "Tell people that which they know. Would you like for Allah and His Messenger to be rejected" Allah said:

(The reminder will be received by him who fears,) meaning, `he whose heart fears Allah and who knows that he is going to meet Him, will receive admonition from what you convey to him, O Muhammad.'

(But it will be avoided by the wretched, who will enter the great Fire. There he will neither die nor live.) meaning, he will not die and thus be allowed to rest, nor will he live a life that is beneficial to him. Instead, his life will be harmful to him, because it will be the cause of his feeling of the pain of torment and various types of punishments what he is being punished with. Imam Ahmad recorded from Abu Sa`id that the Messenger of Allah said,

«أَمَّا أَهْلُ النَّارِ الَّذِينَ هُمْ أَهْلُهَا لَا يَمُوتُونَ وَلَا يَحْيَوْنَ، وَأَمَّا أُنَاسٌ يُرِيدُ اللهُ بِهِمُ الرَّحْمَةَ فَيُمِيتُهُمْ فِي النَّارِ فَيَدْخُلُ عَلَيْهِمُ الشُّفَعَاءُ فَيَأْخُذُ الرَّجُلُ الضُّبَارَةَ فَيُنْبِتُهُمْ أَوْ قَالَ: يَنْبُتُونَ فِي نَهَرِ الْحَيَا، أَوْ قَالَ: الْحَيَاةِ، أَوْ قَالَ: الْحَيَوَانِ أَوْ قَالَ: نَهَرِ الْجَنَّةِ فَيَنْبُتُونَ نَبَاتَ الْحِبَّةِ فِي حَمِيلِ السَّيْلِ»

(Concerning the people of the Fire who are deserving of it, they will not die nor will they live. Regarding the people that Allah wants mercy for, He will cause them to die in the Fire. Then He will allow the intercessors to come to them, and a man will take his groups of supporters and plant them (or he said (they will be planted) in the River of Al-Haya (or he said (Al-Hayah, or Al-Hayawan, or Nahr Al-Jannah). Then they will sprout up like the sprouting of the seed on the moist bank of a flowing stream.) Then the Prophet said,

«أَمَا تَرَوْنَ الشَّجَرَةَ تَكُونُ خَضْرَاءَ، ثُمَّ تَكُونُ صَفْرَاءَ، ثُمَّ تَكُونُ خَضْرَاءَ؟»

(Haven't you all seen the tree that is green, then it turns yellow, then it turns green (again)) Abu Sa`id then said that some of those present said, "It is as if the Prophet used to live in the desert wilderness (i.e., due to his parables of nature)." Ahmad also recorded from Abu Sa`id that the Messenger of Allah said,

«أَمَّا أَهْلُ النَّارِ الَّذِينَ هُمْ أَهْلُهَا فَإِنَّهُمْ لَا يَمُوتُونَ فِيهَا وَلَا يَحْيَوْنَ، وَلَكِنْ أُنَاسٌ أَوْ كَمَا قَالَ تُصِيبُهُمُ النَّارُ بِذُنُوبِهِمْ أَوْ قَالَ: بِخَطَايَاهُمْ فَيُمِيتُهُمْ إِمَاتَةً حَتَّى إِذَا صَارُوا فَحْمًا أُذِنَ فِي الشَّفَاعَةِ، فَجِيءَ بِهِمْ ضَبَائِرَ ضَبَائِرَ فَبُثُّوا عَلَى أَنْهَارِ الْجَنَّةِ فَيُقَالُ: يَا أَهْلَ الْجَنَّةِ أَفِيضُوا عَلَيْهِمْ، فَيَنْبُتُونَ نَبَاتَ الْحِبَّةِ تَكُونُ فِي حَمِيلِ

«السَّيْل»

(Concerning the people of the Fire who will be dwellers of it, they will not die in it nor will they live. However, there will be a group of people - or as he said -(whom the Fire will burn due to their sins - or he said - (their wrongdoings. So, He will cause them to die until they become burnt coal. Then the intercession will be allowed and they will be brought group after group, and they will be scattered over the rivers of Paradise. Then it will be said: "O people of Paradise! Pour down upon them." Then they will sprout like the growing of the seed that is upon the moist bank of the flowing stream." Then, a man from among the people present said, "It is as if the Messenger of Allah used to live in the desert wilderness." Muslim also recorded this Hadith.

Surah: 87 Ayah: 14, Ayah: 15, Ayah: 16, Ayah: 17, Ayah: 18 & Ayah: 19

﴿ قَدْ أَفْلَحَ مَن تَزَكَّىٰ ۝ ﴾

14. Indeed whosoever purifies himself (by avoiding polytheism and accepting Islâmic Monotheism) shall achieve success,

﴿ وَذَكَرَ ٱسْمَ رَبِّهِۦ فَصَلَّىٰ ۝ ﴾

15. And remembers (glorifies) the Name of his Lord (worships none but Allâh), and prays (five compulsory prayers and Nawâfil - additional prayers).

﴿ بَلْ تُؤْثِرُونَ ٱلْحَيَوٰةَ ٱلدُّنْيَا ۝ ﴾

16. Nay, you prefer the life of this world,

﴿ وَٱلْءَاخِرَةُ خَيْرٌ وَأَبْقَىٰ ۝ ﴾

17. Although the Hereafter is better and more lasting.

﴿ إِنَّ هَٰذَا لَفِى ٱلصُّحُفِ ٱلْأُولَىٰ ۝ ﴾

18. Verily, this is in the former Scriptures -

19. The Scriptures of Ibrâhîm (Abraham) and Mûsa (Moses) (peace be upon them).

Transliteration

14. Qad aflaha man tazakka 15. Wathakara isma rabbihi fasalla 16. Bal tu/thiroona alhayata alddunya 17. Waal-akhiratu khayrun waabqa 18. Inna hatha lafee alssuhufi al-oola 19. Suhufi ibraheema wamoosa

Tafsir Ibn Kathir

A Statement concerning the People of Success

Allah says,

(Indeed whosoever purifies himself shall achieve success.) meaning, he purifies himself from despised characteristics and he follows what Allah has revealed to the Messenger.

(And remembers the Name of his Lord, and performs Salah.) meaning, he establishes the prayer in its appointed time, seeking the pleasure of Allah, obedience to His command, and implementation of His Law. We have already reported from the Commander of the believers, `Umar bin `Abdul-`Aziz, that he used to command the people to give the Sadaqat Al-Fitr, and he would recite this Ayah:

(Indeed whosoever purifies himself shall achieve success. And remembers the Name of his Lord, and performs Salah.) Abu Al-Ahwas said, "If someone comes to any of you begging, and he wants to pray, then he should give charity (Zakah) before he prays. For verily, Allah the Exalted says,

(Indeed whosoever purifies himself shall achieve success. And remembers the Name of his Lord, and performs Salah.)" Qatadah said concerning this Ayah,

(Indeed whosoever purifies himself shall achieve success. And remembers the Name of his Lord, and performs Salah (Fasalla).) "He purifies his wealth and pleases his Creator."

This World is Worthless in Comparison to the Hereafter

Then Allah says,

(Rather you prefer the life of this world.) meaning, `you give it precedence over the matter of the Hereafter, and you prefer it because of what it contains of usefulness and benefit for you in livelihood, and your returns (i.e., income, profitable gain).'

(Although the Hereafter is better and more lasting.) meaning, the reward of the final abode is better than the worldly life, and it is more lasting. For indeed, this worldly life is lowly and temporal, whereas the Hereafter is noble and eternal. Thus, how can an intelligent person prefer that which is short-lived over that which is eternal. How can he give importance to that which will soon pass away from him, while ignoring the importance of the abode of eternity and infinity. Imam Ahmad recorded from Abu Musa Al-Ash`ari that the Messenger of Allah said,

«مَنْ أَحَبَّ دُنْيَاهُ أَضَرَّ بِآخِرَتِهِ، وَمَنْ أَحَبَّ آخِرَتَهُ أَضَرَّ بِدُنْيَاهُ، فَآثِرُوا مَا يَبْقَى عَلَى مَا يَفْنَى»

(Whoever loves his worldly life, will suffer in his Hereafter, and whoever loves his worldly life, will suffer in his Hereafter, and whoever loves his Hereafter, will suffer in his worldly life. Therefore, chose that which is everlasting over that which is temporal.) Ahmad was alone in recording this Hadith.

The Scriptures of Ibrahim and Musa

Allah then says,

(Verily, this is in the former Scriptures -- the Scriptures of Ibrahim and Musa.) This Ayah is similar to Allah's statement in Surat An-Najm,

(Or is he not informed with what is in the Scriptures of Musa. And of Ibrahim who fulfilled (or conveyed) all that (Allah ordered him to do or convey): that no burdened person (with sins) shall bear the burden (sins) of another. And that man can have nothing but what he does. And that his deeds will be seen. Then he will be recompensed with a full and the best recompense. And that to your Lord is the End (Return of everything).) (53:36-42) And so forth, until the end of these Ayat. Abu `Aliyah said, "The story of this Surah is in the earlier Scriptures." Ibn Jarir preferred the view that the meaning of Allah's statement,

(Verily, this) is referring to His previous statement, (Indeed whosoever purifies himself shall achieve success. And remembers the Name of his Lord, and offers Salah. Rather you prefer the life of this world. Although the Hereafter is better and more lasting.) Then Allah says,

(Verily, this) meaning, the content of this discussion,

(in the former Scriptures, the Scriptures of Ibrahim and Musa.) This view that he (At-Tabari) has chosen is good and strong. Similar to it has been reported from Qatadah and Ibn Zayd. And Allah knows best. This is the end of the Tafsir of Surat Al-A`la (Sabbih). All praise and blessings are due to Allah, and He is the Giver of success and protection from error.

INTRODUCTION TO CHAPTER (SURAH) 88: AL-GHASHIYA (THE OVERWHELMING, THE PALL)

Ibn Kathir's Introduction

Reciting Surat Al-A`la and Al-Ghashiyah in the Friday Prayer

It has already been mentioned on the authority of An-Nu`man bin Bashir that the Messenger of Allah used to recite Surat Al-A`la (87) and Al-Ghashiyah in the `Id and Friday prayers. Imam Malik recorded that Ad-Dahhak bin Qays asked An-Nu`man bin Bashir, "What else did the Messenger of Allah recite on Friday along with Surat Al-Jumu`ah" An-Nu`man replied, "Al-Ghashiyah (88)." This narration has been recorded by Abu Dawud, An-Nasa'i, Muslim and Ibn Majah.

CHAPTER (SURAH) 88 AL-GHASHIYA THE OVERWHELMING, THE PALL, VERSES 001- 026

Surah: 88 Ayah: 1, Ayah: 2, Ayah: 3, Ayah: 4, Ayah: 5, Ayah: 6 & Ayah: 7

﴿بِسْمِ اللَّهِ الرَّحْمَـنِ الرَّحِيمِ﴾

In the Name of Allah, the Most Gracious, the Most Merciful.

﴿هَلْ أَتَـٰكَ حَدِيثُ ٱلْغَـٰشِيَةِ ۝﴾

1. Has there come to you the narration of the overwhelming (i.e. the Day of Resurrection)?

﴿وُجُوهٌ يَوْمَئِذٍ خَـٰشِعَةٌ ۝﴾

2. Some faces, that Day will be humiliated (in the Hell-fire, i.e. the faces of all disbelievers, Jews and Christians).

﴿عَامِلَةٌ نَّاصِبَةٌ ۝﴾

3. Laboring (hard in the worldly life by worshipping others besides Allâh), weary (in the Hereafter with humility and disgrace).

$$ \text{﴿ تَصْلَىٰ نَارًا حَامِيَةً ۝ ﴾} $$

4. They will enter in the hot blazing Fire.

$$ \text{﴿ تُسْقَىٰ مِنْ عَيْنٍ ءَانِيَةٍ ۝ ﴾} $$

5. They will be given to drink from a boiling spring,

$$ \text{﴿ لَّيْسَ لَهُمْ طَعَامٌ إِلَّا مِن ضَرِيعٍ ۝ ﴾} $$

6. No food will there be for them but a poisonous thorny plant,

$$ \text{﴿ لَّا يُسْمِنُ وَلَا يُغْنِى مِن جُوعٍ ۝ ﴾} $$

7. Which will neither nourish nor avail against hunger.

Transliteration

1. Hal ataka hadeethu alghashiyati 2. Wujoohun yawma-ithin khashiAAatun 3. AAamilatun nasibatun 4. Tasla naran hamiyatan 5. Tusqa min AAaynin aniyatin 6. Laysa lahum taAAamun illa min dareeAAin 7. La yusminu wala yughnee min jooAAin

Tafsir Ibn Kathir

The Day of Judgement and what will happen to the People of the Fire during it Al-Ghashiyah is one of the names of the Day of Judgement.

This was said by Ibn `Abbas, Qatadah and Ibn Zayd. It has been called this because it will overwhelm the people and overcome them. Allah then says,

(Some faces that Day will be Khashi`ah.) meaning, humiliated. This was said by Qatadah. Ibn `Abbas said, "They will be humble but this action will be of no benefit to them." Then Allah says,

(Laboring, weary.) meaning, they did many deeds and became weary in their performance, yet they will be cast into a blazing Fire on the Day of Judgement. Al-Hafiz Abu Bakr Al-Burqani narrated from Abu `Imran Al-Jawni that he said, " `Umar bin Al-Khattab passed by the monastery of a monk and he said: `O monk!' Then the monk came out, and `Umar looked at him and began to weep. Then it was said to him: `O Commander of the faithful! Why are you weeping' He replied: `I remembered the statement of Allah, the Mighty and Majestic, in His Book,

(Laboring, weary. They will enter into Fire, Hamiyah.) So that is what has made me cry.'" Al-Bukhari recorded that Ibn `Abbas said,

(Laboring, weary.) "The Christians." It is narrated that `Ikrimah and As-Suddi both said, "Laboring in the worldly life with disobedience, and weariness in the Fire from torment and perdition." Ibn `Abbas, Al-Hasan, and Qatadah all said,

(They will enter into Fire, Hamiyah) meaning, hot with intense heat.

(They will be given to drink from a boiling (Aniyah) spring.) meaning, its heat has reached its maximum limit and boiling point. This was said by Ibn `Abbas, Mujahid, Al-Hasan and As-Suddi. Concerning Allah's statement,

(No food will there be for them but from Dari`,) `Ali bin Abi Talhah reported from Ibn `Abbas that he said, "A tree from the Hellfire." Ibn `Abbas, Mujahid, `Ikrimah, Abu Al-Jawza' and Qatadah, all said, "It is Ash-Shibriq (a type of plant)." Qatadah said, "The Quraysh called it Ash-Shabraq in the spring and Ad-Dari` in the summer." `Ikrimah said, "It is a thorny tree which reaches down to the ground." Al-Bukhari related that Mujahid said, "Ad-Dari` is a plant that is called Ash-Shibriq. The people of the Hijaz call it Ad-Dari` when it dries, and it is poisonous." Ma`mar narrated that Qatadah said,

(No food will there be for them but from Dari`,) "This is Ash-Shibriq. When it dries it is called Ad-Dari`." Sa`id narrated from Qatadah that he said,

(No food will there be for them but Dari`,) "This is of the worst, most disgusting and loathsome of foods." Concerning Allah's statement,

(Which will neither nourish nor avail against hunger.) This means that the intent in eating it will not be achieved, and nothing harmful will be repelled by it.

Surah: 88 Ayah: 8, Ayah: 9, Ayah: 10, Ayah: 11, Ayah: 12, Ayah: 13, Ayah: 14, Ayah: 15 & Ayah: 16

﴿ وُجُوهٌ يَوْمَئِذٍ نَّاعِمَةٌ ۝ ﴾

8. (Other) faces that Day will be joyful,

﴿ لِّسَعْيِهَا رَاضِيَةٌ ۝ ﴾

9. Glad with their endeavor (for their good deeds which they did in this world, along with the true Faith of Islâmic Monotheism).

﴿ فِى جَنَّةٍ عَالِيَةٍ ۝ ﴾

10. In a lofty Paradise.

$$ ﴿ لَّا تَسْمَعُ فِيهَا لَاغِيَةً ﴾ $$

11. Where they shall neither hear harmful speech nor falsehood.

$$ ﴿ فِيهَا عَيْنٌ جَارِيَةٌ ﴾ $$

12. Therein will be a running spring.

$$ ﴿ فِيهَا سُرُرٌ مَّرْفُوعَةٌ ﴾ $$

13. Therein will be thrones raised high.

$$ ﴿ وَأَكْوَابٌ مَّوْضُوعَةٌ ﴾ $$

14. And cups set at hand.

$$ ﴿ وَنَمَارِقُ مَصْفُوفَةٌ ﴾ $$

15. And cushions set in rows.

$$ ﴿ وَزَرَابِيُّ مَبْثُوثَةٌ ﴾ $$

16. And rich carpets (all) spread out.

Transliteration

8. Wujoohun yawma-ithin naAAimatun 9. LisaAAyiha radiyatun 10. Fee jannatin AAaliyatin 11. La tasmaAAu feeha laghiyatan 12. Feeha AAaynun jariyatun 13. Feeha sururun marfooAAatun 14. Waakwabun mawdooAAatun 15. Wanamariqu masfoofatun 16. Wazarabiyyu mabthoothatun

Tafsir Ibn Kathir

The Condition of the People of Paradise on the Day of Judgement

After mentioning the situation of the wretched people, Allah changes the discussion to mention those who will be happy. He says,

(Faces that Day.) meaning, on the Day of Judgement.

(will be joyful,) meaning, pleasure will be noticeable in them (those faces). This will only occur due to their striving. Sufyan said,

(Glad with their endeavor.) "They will be pleased with their deeds." Then Allah says,

(In a lofty Paradise.) meaning, elevated and brilliant, secure in their dwellings.

(Where they shall neither hear harmful speech nor falsehood.) meaning, they will not hear in the Paradise that they will be in, any foolish word. This is as Allah says,

(They shall not hear therein any Laghw, but only Salam.) (19:62) Allah also says,

(Free from any Laghw, and free from sin.) (52:23) and He says,

(No Laghw will they hear therein, nor any sinful speech. But only the saying of: "Salam! Salam!") (56:25-26) Then Allah continues,

(Therein will be a running spring.) meaning, flowing freely. This is mentioned with the intent of emphasizing affirmation. It is not intended to mean that there is only one spring. So here it refers to springs collectively. Thus, the meaning is that in it (Paradise) are flowing springs. Ibn Abi Hatim recorded from Abu Hurayrah that the Messenger of Allah said,

«أَنْهَارُ الْجَنَّةِ تَفَجَّرُ مِنْ تَحْتِ تِلَالٍ أَوْ مِنْ تَحْتِ جِبَالِ الْمِسْكِ»

(The rivers of Paradise spring forth from beneath hills -- or mountains -- of musk.)

(Therein will be thrones raised high.) meaning, lofty, delightful, numerous couches, with elevated ceilings. Upon which will be seated wide-eyed, beautiful maidens. They have mentioned that whenever the friend of Allah wishes to sit on these lofty thrones, they (the thrones) will lower themselves for him.

(And cups set at hand.) meaning, drinking containers that are prepared and presented for whoever among their masters (i.e., the people of Paradise) wants them.

(And Namariq set in rows.) Ibn `Abbas said, "An-Namariq are pillows." This was also said by `Ikrimah, Qatadah, Ad-Dahhak, As-Suddi, Ath-Thawri and others. Concerning Allah's statement,

(And Zarabi, spread out (Mabthuthah).) Ibn `Abbas said, "Az-Zarabi are carpets." This was also said by Ad-Dahhak and others. Here the word Mabthuthah means placed here and there for whoever would like to sit upon them.

Chapter 88: Al-Ghashiya (The Overwhelming, The Pall), Verses 001-026

Surah: 88 Ayah: 17, Ayah: 18, Ayah: 19, Ayah: 20, Ayah: 21, Ayah: 22, Ayah: 23, Ayah: 24, Ayah: 25 & Ayah: 26

﴿ أَفَلَا يَنظُرُونَ إِلَى ٱلْإِبِلِ كَيْفَ خُلِقَتْ ۝ ﴾

17. Do they not look at the camels, how they are created?

﴿ وَإِلَى ٱلسَّمَآءِ كَيْفَ رُفِعَتْ ۝ ﴾

18. And at the heaven, how it is raised?

﴿ وَإِلَى ٱلْجِبَالِ كَيْفَ نُصِبَتْ ۝ ﴾

19. And at the mountains, how they are rooted (and fixed firm)?

﴿ وَإِلَى ٱلْأَرْضِ كَيْفَ سُطِحَتْ ۝ ﴾

20. And at the earth, how it is outspread?

﴿ فَذَكِّرْ إِنَّمَآ أَنتَ مُذَكِّرٌ ۝ ﴾

21. So remind them (O Muhammad (peace be upon him)) - you are only one who reminds.

﴿ لَّسْتَ عَلَيْهِم بِمُصَيْطِرٍ ۝ ﴾

22. You are not a dictator over them -

﴿ إِلَّا مَن تَوَلَّىٰ وَكَفَرَ ۝ ﴾

23. Save the one who turns away and disbelieves.

﴿ فَيُعَذِّبُهُ ٱللَّهُ ٱلْعَذَابَ ٱلْأَكْبَرَ ۝ ﴾

24. Then Allâh will punish him with the greatest punishment.

$$ \left\{ \text{إِنَّ إِلَيْنَا إِيَابَهُمْ} \text{ ﴿٢٥﴾} \right\} $$

25. Verily, to Us will be their return;

$$ \left\{ \text{ثُمَّ إِنَّ عَلَيْنَا حِسَابَهُم} \text{ ﴿٢٦﴾} \right\} $$

26. Then verily, for Us will be their reckoning.

Transliteration

17. Afala yanthuroona ila al-ibili kayfa khuliqat 18. Wa-ila alssama-i kayfa rufiAAat 19. Wa-ila aljibali kayfa nusibat 20. Wa-ila al-ardi kayfa sutihat 21. Fathakkir innama anta muthakkirun 22. Lasta AAalayhim bimusaytirin 23. Illa man tawalla wakafara 24. FayuAAaththibuhu Allahu alAAathaba al-akbara 25. Inna ilayna iyabahum 26. Thumma inna AAalayna hisabahum

Tafsir Ibn Kathir

The Exhortation to look at the Creation of the Camel, the Heaven, the Mountains and the Earth

Allah commands His servants to look at His creations that prove His power and greatness. He says,

(Do they not look at the camels, how they are created) Indeed it is an amazing creation, and the way it has been fashioned is strange. For it is extremely powerful and strong, yet gentle, carrying heavy loads. It allows itself to be guided by a weak rider. It is eaten, benefit is derived from its hair, and its milk is drunk. They are reminded of this because the most common domestic animal of the Arabs was the camel. Shurayh Al-Qadi used to say, "Come out with us so that we may look at the camels and how they were created, and at the sky and how it has been raised." Meaning, how Allah raised it in such magnificence above the ground. This is as Allah says,

(Have they not looked at the heaven above them, how we have made it and adorned it and there are no rifts on it) (50:6) Then Allah says,

(And at the mountains, how they are rooted) meaning, how they have been erected. For indeed they are firmly affixed so that the earth does not sway with its dwellers. And He made them with the benefits and minerals they contain.

(And at the earth, how it is outspread) meaning, how it has been spread out, extended and made smooth. Thus, He directs the bedouin to consider what he himself witnesses. His camel that he rides upon, the sky that is above his head, the mountain that faces him, and the earth that is under him, all of this is proof of the power of the Creator and Maker of these things. These things should lead him to see that He is the

Lord, the Most Great, the Creator, the Owner, and the Controller of everything. Therefore, He is the God other than Whom none deserves to be worshipped.

The Story of Dimam bin Tha`labah

These are the things Dimam swore by after questioning the Messenger of Allah . This can be seen in what Imam Ahmad recorded from Thabit, who reported that Anas said, "We were prohibited from asking the Messenger of Allah anything. Thus, it used to amaze us when an intelligent man from the people of the desert (bedouin Arabs) would come and ask him about something while we were listening. So a man from the people of the desert came and said, `O Muhammad! Verily, your messenger has come to us and he claims that you claim that Allah sent you.' He (the Prophet) said,

《صَدَقَ》

('He told the truth'.) The man said, 'Who created the heaven?' He (the Prophet) replied,

《اللهُ》

('Allah'.) The man said, 'Who created the earth?' He (the Prophet) replied,

《اللهُ》

('Allah'). The man said, `Who erected these mountains and placed in them whatever is in them?' He (the Prophet) replied, ('Allah'). Then the man said, 'By the One Who created the heaven, the earth, and erected these mountains, did Allah send you' He (the Prophet) said,

《نَعَم》

('Yes'.) The man then said, `Your messenger claims that we are obligated to pray five prayers during our day and night.' He (the Prophet) said,

《صَدَقَ》

('He told the truth'.) The man then said, `By He Who has sent you, did Allah command you with this' He (the Prophet) replied,

《نَعَم》

('Yes'.) The man then said, 'Your messenger also claims that we are obligated to give charity from our wealth.' He (the Prophet) said,

$$«صَدَق»$$

('He told the truth'.) Then the man said, 'By He Who has sent you, did Allah command you with this' He (the Prophet) replied,

$$«نَعَم»$$

('Yes'.) The man then said, 'Your messenger claims that we are obligated to perform pilgrimage (Hajj) to the House (the Ka`bah), for whoever is able to find a way there.' He (the Prophet) said,

$$«صَدَق»$$

('He told the truth'.) Then the man turned away to leave while saying, 'By He Who has sent you with the truth, I will not add anything to these things and I will not decrease anything from them.' The Prophet then said,

$$«إِنْ صَدَقَ لَيَدْخُلَنَّ الْجَنَّة»$$

('If he has spoken truthfully, he will certainly enter Paradise'.) This Hadith was recorded by Al-Bukhari, Muslim, Abu Dawud, At-Tirmidhi, An-Nasa'i and Ibn Majah.

The Messenger is only charged with delivering the Message

Allah says,

(So remind them -- you are only one who reminds. You are not a Musaytir over them) meaning, "O Muhammad! Remind the people with what you have been sent with to them."

(your duty is only to convey (the Message) and on Us is the reckoning.) (13:40) Then Allah says,

(You are not a Musaytir over them.) Ibn `Abbas, Mujahid and others said, "You are not a dictator over them." This means that you cannot create faith in their hearts. Ibn Zayd said, "You are not the one who can force them to have faith." Imam Ahmad recorded from Jabir that the Messenger of Allah said,

$$«أُمِرْتُ أَنْ أُقَاتِلَ النَّاسَ حَتَّى يَقُولُوا: لَا إِلَهَ إِلَّا اللهُ، فَإِذَا قَالُوهَا عَصَمُوا مِنِّي»$$

$$\text{دِمَاءَهُمْ وَأَمْوَالَهُمْ إِلَّا بِحَقِّهَا، وَحِسَابُهُمْ عَلَى اللهِ عَزَّ وَجَل}$$

(I have been commanded to fight the people until they say La ilaha illallah (none has the right to be worshipped except Allah). So if they say that, they have safeguarded their blood and wealth from me - except for what is rightfully due from it - and their reckoning is with Allah, the Mighty and Majestic.)" Then he recited,

(So remind them - you are only one who reminds. You are not a dictator over them -) This is how Muslim recorded this Hadith in his Book of Faith, and At-Tirmidhi and An-Nasa'i also recorded it in their Sunans in the Books of Tafsir. This Hadith can be found in both of the Two Sahihs.

The Threat for Whoever turns away from the Truth

Concerning Allah's statement,

(Save the one who turns away and disbelieves.) meaning, he turns away from acting upon its pillars, and he disbelieves in the truth with his heart and his tongue. This is similar to Allah's statement,

(So he neither believed nor prayed! But on the contrary, he belied and turn away!) (75:31-32) Thus, Allah says,

(Then Allah will punish him with the greatest punishment.) Allah then says,

(Verily, to Us will be their return;) meaning, their place of return and their resort.

(Then verily, for Us will be their reckoning.) meaning, `We will reckon their deeds for them and requite them for those deeds.' If they did good, they will receive good, and if they did evil, they will receive evil. This is the end of the Tafsir of Surat Al-Ghashiyah.

INTRODUCTION TO CHAPTER (SURAH) 89: AL-FAJR (THE DAWN, DAYBREAK)

Ibn Kathir's Introduction

Recitation of Surat Al-Fajr in the Prayer

An-Nasa'i recorded a narration from Jabir that Mu`adh prayed a prayer and a man came and joined him in the prayer. Mu`adh made the prayer long, so the man went and prayed (alone) at the side of the Masjid, and then left. When Mu`adh was informed of this he said, "(He is) a hypocrite." He (Mu`adh) then informed the Messenger of Allah of what happened. The Prophet then asked the young man (about it) and he replied, "O Messenger of Allah! I came to pray with him, but he made the prayer too long for me. So I left him and prayed at the side of the Masjid. Then I went to feed my she-camel." The Messenger of Allah then said,

«أَفَتَّانٌ يَا مُعَاذُ؟ أَيْنَ أَنْتَ مِنْ (سَبِّحِ اسْمَ رَبِّكَ الأَعْلَى) (وَالشَّمْسِ وَضُحَاهَا) (وَالْفَجْرِ) (وَاللَّيْلِ إِذَا يَغْشَى)»

(Are you causing trouble Mu`adh Why don't you recite (`Glorify the Name of your Lord the Most High'), (`By the sun and its brightness'), (`By the dawn'), (and (`By the night as it envelops'))

CHAPTER (SURAH) 89: AL-FAJR (THE DAWN, DAYBREAK), VERSES 001-030

Surah: 89 Ayah: 1, Ayah: 2, Ayah: 3, Ayah: 4, Ayah: 5, Ayah: 6, Ayah: 7, Ayah: 8, Ayah: 9, Ayah: 10, Ayah: 11, Ayah: 12, Ayah: 13 & Ayah: 14

(بِسْمِ اللَّهِ الرَّحْمَـنِ الرَّحِيمِ)

In the Name of Allah, the Most Gracious, the Most Merciful.

﴿ وَٱلْفَجْرِ ۝ ﴾

1. By the dawn;

﴿ وَلَيَالٍ عَشْرٍ ۝ ﴾

2. By the ten nights (i.e. the first ten days of the month of Dhul-Hîjjah),

﴿ وَٱلشَّفْعِ وَٱلْوَتْرِ ۝ ﴾

3. And by the even and the odd (of all the creations of Allâh).

﴿ وَٱلَّيْلِ إِذَا يَسْرِ ۝ ﴾

4. And by the night when it departs.

﴿ هَلْ فِى ذَٰلِكَ قَسَمٌ لِّذِى حِجْرٍ ۝ ﴾

Chapter 89: Al-Fajr (The Dawn, Daybreak), Verses 001-030

5. There is indeed in them (the above oaths) sufficient proofs for men of understanding (and that, they should avoid all kinds of sins and disbeliefs)!

﴿ أَلَمْ تَرَ كَيْفَ فَعَلَ رَبُّكَ بِعَادٍ ۝ ﴾

6. Saw you (O Muhammad (peace be upon him)) not how your Lord dealt with 'Âd (people)?

﴿ إِرَمَ ذَاتِ ٱلْعِمَادِ ۝ ﴾

7. Of Iram (who were very tall) like (lofty) pillars,

﴿ ٱلَّتِى لَمْ يُخْلَقْ مِثْلُهَا فِى ٱلْبِلَٰدِ ۝ ﴾

8. The like of which were not created in the land?

﴿ وَثَمُودَ ٱلَّذِينَ جَابُوا۟ ٱلصَّخْرَ بِٱلْوَادِ ۝ ﴾

9. And (with) Thamûd (people), who hewed out rocks in the valley (to make dwellings)?

﴿ وَفِرْعَوْنَ ذِى ٱلْأَوْتَادِ ۝ ﴾

10. And (with) Fir'aun (Pharaoh) who had the stakes (to torture men by binding them to stakes)?

﴿ ٱلَّذِينَ طَغَوْا۟ فِى ٱلْبِلَٰدِ ۝ ﴾

11. Who did transgress beyond the bounds in the lands (in the disobedience of Allâh).

﴿ فَأَكْثَرُوا۟ فِيهَا ٱلْفَسَادَ ۝ ﴾

12. And made therein much mischief.

$$\text{﴿ فَصَبَّ عَلَيْهِمْ رَبُّكَ سَوْطَ عَذَابٍ ﴾}$$

13. So your Lord poured on them different kinds of severe torment.

$$\text{﴿ إِنَّ رَبَّكَ لَبِالْمِرْصَادِ ﴾}$$

14. Verily, your Lord is Ever Watchful (over them).

Transliteration

1. Waalfajri 2. Walayalin AAashrin 3. WaalshshafAAi waalwatri 4. Waallayli itha yasri 5. Hal fee thalika qasamun lithee hijrin 6. Alam tara kayfa faAAala rabbuka biAAadin 7. Irama thati alAAimadi 8. Allatee lam yukhlaq mithluha fee albiladi 9. Wathamooda allatheena jaboo alssakhra bialwadi 10. WafirAAawna thee al-awtadi 11. Allatheena taghaw fee albiladi 12. Faaktharoo feeha alfasada 13. Fasabba AAalayhim rabbuka sawta AAathabin 14. Inna rabbaka labialmirsadi

Tafsir Ibn Kathir

The Explanation of Al-Fajr and what comes after it

Concerning Al-Fajr, it is well known that it is the morning. This was said by `Ali, Ibn `Abbas, `Ikrimah, Mujahid and As-Suddi. It has been reported from Masruq and Muhammad bin Ka`b that Al-Fajr refers to the day of Sacrifice (An-Nahr) in particular, and it is the last of the ten nights. `The ten nights' refers to the (first) ten days of Dhul-Hijjah. This was said by Ibn `Abbas, Ibn Zubayr, Mujahid and others among the Salaf and the latter generations. It has been confirmed in Sahih Al-Bukhari from Ibn `Abbas that the Prophet said,

«مَا مِنْ أَيَّامٍ الْعَمَلُ الصَّالِحُ أَحَبُّ إِلَى اللهِ فِيهِنَّ مِنْ هَذِهِ الْأَيَّامِ»

(There are no days in which righteous deeds are more beloved to Allah than these days.) meaning the ten days of Dhul-Hijjah. They said, "Not even fighting Jihad in the way of Allah" He replied,

«وَلَا الْجِهَادُ فِي سَبِيلِ اللهِ، إِلَّا رَجُلًا خَرَجَ بِنَفْسِهِ وَمَالِهِ ثُمَّ لَمْ يَرْجِعْ مِنْ ذَلِكَ بِشَيْءٍ»

(Not even Jihad in the way of Allah; except for a man who goes out (for Jihad) with his self and his wealth, and he does not return with any of that.)

Chapter 89: Al-Fajr (The Dawn, Daybreak), Verses 001-030

Explanation of Night

Concerning Allah's statement,

(And by the night when it departs.) Al-`Awfi reported from Ibn `Abbas that he said, "When it goes away." `Abdullah bin Zubayr said,

(And by the night when it departs.) "As some parts of it remove other parts of it." Mujahid, Abu Al-`Aliyah, Qatadah, and Malik who reported it from Zayd bin Aslam and Ibn Zayd, they all said;

(And by the night when it departs.) "When it moves along." Concerning Allah's statement,

(There is indeed in them sufficient proofs for men with Hijr!) meaning, for he who possesses intellect, sound reasoning, understanding and religious discernment. The intellect has only been called Hijr because it prevents the person from doing that which is not befitting of him of actions and statement. From this we see the meaning of Hijr Al-Bayt because it prevents the person performing Tawaf from clinging the wall facing Ash-Sham. Also the term Hijr Al-Yamamah (the cage of the pigeon) is derived from this meaning (i.e., prevention). It is said, "Hajara Al-Hakim so-and-so (The judge passed a judgement preventing so-and-so)," when his judgement prevents the person from his liberty (i.e., of freely utilizing his wealth). Allah says,

(And they will say: "Hijr Mahjur.") (25:22) All of these examples are different cases but their meanings are quite similar. The oath that is referred to here is about the times of worship and the acts of worship themselves, such as Hajj, Salah and other acts of worship that Allah's pious, obedient, servants who fear Him and are humble before Him, seeking His Noble Face, perform in order to draw nearer to Him.

Mentioning the Destruction of `Ad

After mentioning these people, and their worship and obedience, Allah says,

(Saw you not how your Lord dealt with `Ad) These were people who were rebellious, disobedient, arrogant, outside of His obedience, deniers of His Messengers and rejectors of His Scriptures. Thus, Allah mentions how He destroyed them, annihilated them and made them legends to be spoken of and an exemplary lesson of warning. He says,

(Saw you not how your Lord dealt with `Ad Iram of the pillars,) These were the first people of `Ad. They were the descendants of `Ad bin Iram bin `Aws bin Sam bin Nuh. This was said by Ibn Ishaq. They are those to whom Allah sent His Messenger Hud. However, they rejected and opposed him. Therefore, Allah saved him and those who believed with him from among them, and He destroyed others with a furious, violent wind.

(Which Allah imposed on them for seven nights and eight days in succession, so that you could see men lying overthrown, as if they were hollow trunks of date palms! Do you see any remnants of them) (69: 7-8) Allah mentioned their story in the Qur'an in more than one place, so that the believers may learn a lesson from their demise. Allah then says,

(Iram of the pillars.) This is an additional explanation that adds clarification who they actually were. Concerning His saying,

(of the pillars.) is because they used to live in trellised houses that were raised with firm pillars. They were the strongest people of their time in their physical stature, and they were the mightiest people in power. Thus, Hud reminded them of this blessing, and he directed them to use this power in the obedience of their Lord Who had created them. He said,

(And remember that He made you successors after the people of Nuh and increased you amply in stature. So remember the graces from Allah so that you may be successful.)(7:69) Allah also said,

(As for 'Ad, they were arrogant in the land without right, and they said: "Who is mightier than us in strength" See they not that Allah Who created them was mightier in strength than them.) (41:15) And Allah says here,

(The like of which were not created in the land) meaning, there had been none created like them in their land, due to their strength, power and their great physical stature. Mujahid said, "Iram was an ancient nation who were the first people of `Ad." Qatadah bin Di`amah and As-Suddi both said, "Verily, Iram refers to the House of the kingdom of `Ad." This latter statement is good and strong. Concerning Allah's statement,

(The like of which were not created in the land) Ibn Zayd considered the pronoun of discussion here to refer to the pillars, due to their loftiness. He said, "They built pillars among the hills, the likes of which had not been constructed in their land before." However, Qatadah and Ibn Jarir considered the pronoun of discussion to refer to the tribe (of `Ad), meaning that there was no tribe that had been created like this tribe in the land - meaning during their time. And this latter view is the correct position. The saying of Ibn Zayd and those who follow his view is a weak one, because if He intended that, He would have said "The like of which were not produced in the land." But He said:

(The like of which were not created in the land.) Then Allah says,

(And Thamud, who hewed (Jabu) rocks in the valley) meaning, they cut the rocks in the valley. Ibn `Abbas said, "They carved them and they hewed them." This was also said by Mujahid, Qatadah, Ad-Dahhak and Ibn Zayd. From this terminology it is said (in the Arabic language), "the hewing of leopard skin" when it is torn, and "The hewing of a garment" when it is opened. The word `Jayb' (pocket or opening in a garment) also comes from Jabu. Allah says,

(And you hew in the mountains, houses with great skill.) (26:149)

A Mention of Fir`awn

Allah then says,

(And Fir`awn with Al-Awtad) Al-`Awfi reported from Ibn `Abbas that he said, "Al-Awtad are the armies who enforced his commands for him." It has also been said that Fir`awn used to nail their hands and their feet into pegs (Awtad) of iron that he would hang them from. A similar statement was made by Mujahid when he said, "He used to nail the people (up) on pegs." Sa`id bin Jubayr, Al-Hasan and As-Suddi all said the same thing. Allah said,

(Who did transgress beyond bounds in the lands. And made therein much mischief.) meaning, they rebelled, were arrogant, and went about making corruption in the land, and harming the people.

(So, your Lord poured on them different kinds of severe torment.) meaning, He sent down a torment upon them from the sky and caused them to be overcome by a punishment that could not be repelled from the people who were criminals.

The Lord is Ever Watchful

Concerning Allah's statement,

(Verily, your Lord is Ever Watchful.) Ibn `Abbas said, "He hears and He sees." This means that He watches over His creation in that which they do, and He will reward them in this life and in the Hereafter based upon what each of them strove for. He will bring all of the creation before Him and He will judge them with justice. He will requit each of them with that which he deserves, for He is far removed from injustice and tyranny.

> Surah: 89 Ayah: 15, Ayah: 16, Ayah: 17, Ayah: 18, Ayah: 19 & Ayah: 20

﴿ فَأَمَّا ٱلْإِنسَـٰنُ إِذَا مَا ٱبْتَلَىٰهُ رَبُّهُۥ فَأَكْرَمَهُۥ وَنَعَّمَهُۥ فَيَقُولُ رَبِّىٓ أَكْرَمَنِ ﴾

15. As for man, when his Lord tries him by giving him honor and bounties, then he says (in exultation): "My Lord has honored me."

﴿ وَأَمَّآ إِذَا مَا ٱبْتَلَىٰهُ فَقَدَرَ عَلَيْهِ رِزْقَهُۥ فَيَقُولُ رَبِّىٓ أَهَـٰنَنِ ﴾

16. But when He tries him by straitening his means of life, he says: "My Lord has humiliated me!"

﴿ كَلَّا بَل لَّا تُكْرِمُونَ ٱلْيَتِيمَ ۝ ﴾

17. Nay! But you treat not the orphans with kindness and generosity (i.e. you neither treat them well, nor give them their exact right of inheritance)!

﴿ وَلَا تَحَـٰضُّونَ عَلَىٰ طَعَامِ ٱلْمِسْكِينِ ۝ ﴾

18. And urge not one another on the feeding of Al-Miskîn (the poor)!

﴿ وَتَأْكُلُونَ ٱلتُّرَاثَ أَكْلًا لَّمًّا ۝ ﴾

19. And you devour inheritance all with greed.

﴿ وَتُحِبُّونَ ٱلْمَالَ حُبًّا جَمًّا ۝ ﴾

20. And you love wealth with much love.

Transliteration

15. Faamma al-insanu itha ma ibtalahu rabbuhu faakramahu wanaAAAAamahu fayaqoolu rabbee akramani 16. Waamma itha ma ibtalahu faqadara AAalayhi rizqahu fayaqoolu rabbee ahanani   17. Kalla bal la tukrimoona alyateema   18. Wala tahaddoona AAala taAAami almiskeeni 19. Wata/kuloona altturatha aklan lamman 20. Watuhibboona almala hubban jamman

Tafsir Ibn Kathir

Wealth and Poverty are both a Test and Honor or Disgrace for the Servant

Allah refutes man in his belief that if Allah gives Him abundant provisions to test him with it, it is out of His honor for him. But this is not the case, rather it is a trial and a test, as Allah says,

(Do they think that in wealth and children with which We enlarge them. We hasten unto them with good things. Nay, but they perceive not.) (23:55-56) Likewise, from another angle, if Allah tests him and tries him by curtailing his sustenance, he believes that is because Allah is humiliating him. As Allah says,

(But no!) meaning, the matter is not as he claims, neither in this nor in that. For indeed Allah gives wealth to those whom He loves as well as those whom He does not love. Likewise, He withholds sustenance from those whom He loves and those whom He does not love. The point is that Allah should be obeyed in either circumstance. If

Chapter 89: Al-Fajr (The Dawn, Daybreak), Verses 001-030

one is wealthy, he should thank Allah for that, and if he is poor, he should exercise patience.

From the Evil that the Servant does regarding Wealth

Allah said,

(But you treat not the orphans with kindness and generosity!) This contains the command to honor him (the orphan). Abu Dawud recorded from Sahl bin Sa`id that the Messenger of Allah said,

«أَنَا وَكَافِلُ الْيَتِيمِ كَهَاتَيْنِ فِي الْجَنَّةِ»

(The guardian of the orphan and I will be like these two in Paradise.) And he put his two fingers together - the middle finger and the index finger.

(And urge not one another on the feeding of the Miskin!) meaning, they do not command that the poor and the needy be treated with kindness, nor do they encourage each other to do so.

(And you devour the Turath) meaning, the inheritance.

(devouring with greed.) meaning, however they can get it, whether lawful or forbidden.

(And you love wealth with love Jamma.) meaning, in abundance. This increases some of them in their wickedness.

Surah: 89 Ayah: 21, Ayah: 22, Ayah: 23, Ayah: 24, Ayah: 25, Ayah: 26, Ayah: 27, Ayah: 28, Ayah: 29 & Ayah: 30

﴿ كَلَّا إِذَا دُكَّتِ ٱلْأَرْضُ دَكًّا دَكًّا ﴾

21. Nay! When the earth is ground to powder.

﴿ وَجَآءَ رَبُّكَ وَٱلْمَلَكُ صَفًّا صَفًّا ﴾

22. And your Lord comes with the angels in rows.

﴿ وَجِا۟ىٓءَ يَوْمَئِذٍ بِجَهَنَّمَ يَوْمَئِذٍ يَتَذَكَّرُ ٱلْإِنسَـٰنُ وَأَنَّىٰ لَهُ ٱلذِّكْرَىٰ ﴾

23. And Hell will be brought near that Day. On that Day will man remember, but how will that remembrance (then) avail him?

﴿ يَقُولُ يَٰلَيْتَنِى قَدَّمْتُ لِحَيَاتِى ۞ ﴾

24. He will say: "Alas! Would that I had sent forth (good deeds) for (this) my life!"

﴿ فَيَوْمَئِذٍ لَّا يُعَذِّبُ عَذَابَهُۥ أَحَدٌ ۞ ﴾

25. So on that Day none will punish as He will punish.

﴿ وَلَا يُوثِقُ وَثَاقَهُۥ أَحَدٌ ۞ ﴾

26. And none will bind (the wicked, disbelievers and polytheists) as He will bind.

﴿ يَٰٓأَيَّتُهَا ٱلنَّفْسُ ٱلْمُطْمَئِنَّةُ ۞ ﴾

27. (It will be said to the pious - believers of Islamic Monotheism): "O (you) the one in (complete) rest and satisfaction!

﴿ ٱرْجِعِىٓ إِلَىٰ رَبِّكِ رَاضِيَةً مَّرْضِيَّةً ۞ ﴾

28. "Come back to your Lord well-pleased (yourself) and well-pleasing (unto Him)!

﴿ فَٱدْخُلِى فِى عِبَٰدِى ۞ ﴾

29. "Enter you then among My (honored) slaves,

﴿ وَٱدْخُلِى جَنَّتِى ۞ ﴾

30. "And enter you My Paradise!"

Transliteration

21. Kalla itha dukkati al-ardu dakkan dakkan 22. Wajaa rabbuka waalmalaku saffan saffan 23. Wajee-a yawma-ithin bijahannama yawma-ithin yatathakkaru al-insanu waanna lahu alththikra 24. Yaqoolu ya laytanee qaddamtu lihayatee 25. Fayawma-ithin la yuAAaththibu AAathabahu ahadun 26. Wala yoothiqu wathaqahu ahadun 27. Ya ayyatuha alnnafsu almutma-innatu 28. IrjiAAee ila rabbiki radiyatan mardiyyatan 29. Faodkhulee fee AAibadee 30. Waodkhulee jannatee

Tafsir Ibn Kathir

On the Day of Judgement Everyone will be recompensed according to what He did of Good or Evil

Allah informs of what will happen on the Day of Judgement of the great horrors. He says,

(Nay!) meaning, truly.

(When the earth is flatened, Dakkan Dakka.) meaning, the earth and the mountains will be flattened, leveled and made even, and the creatures will rise from their graves for their Lord.

(And your Lord comes) meaning, for the session of Judgement between His creatures. This is after they requested the best of the Sons of Adam -- Muhammad -- to intercede with Allah. This will occur only after they have requested the other great Messengers, one after another. Yet, all of them will say, "I cannot do that for you." This will continue until the beseeching of the men reaches Muhammad , and he will say, "I will do it, I will do it." So he will go and seek to intercede with Allah as the session of Judgement will have come, and Allah will allow him to intercede for that (the Judgement). This will be the first of the intercessions, and it is the praiseworthy station that has already been discussed in Surat Subhan (Al-Isra'). So Allah will come for the session of Judgement as He wills, and the angels will also come, lined up in rows upon rows before Him. Then Allah says,

(And Hell will be brought near that Day.) In his Sahih, Imam Muslim bin Al-Hajjaj recorded that `Abdullah bin Mas`ud said that the Messenger of Allah said,

«يُؤْتَى بِجَهَنَّمَ يَوْمَئِذٍ لَهَا سَبْعُونَ أَلْفَ زِمَامٍ مَعَ كُلِّ زِمَامٍ سَبْعُونَ أَلْفَ مَلَكٍ يَجُرُّونَهَا»

(Hell will be brought on near that Day and it will have seventy thousand leashes, and each leash will have seventy thousand angels pulling it.) At-Tirmidhi also recorded the same narration. Allah said:

(On that Day will man remember,) meaning, his deeds, and what he did before in his past and recent times.

(but how will that remembrance avail him) meaning, how can remembrance then benefit him

(He will say: "Alas! Would that I had sent forth for my life!") meaning, if he was a disobedient person, he will be sorry for the acts of disobedience he committed. If he was an obedient person, he will wish that he performed more acts of obdedience. This is similar to what Imam Ahmad bin Hanbal recorded from Muhammad bin Abi `Amirah, who was one of the Companions of the Messenger of Allah . He said, "If a servant fell down on his face (in prostration) from the day that he was born until the day he died as an old man, in obedience to Allah, he would scorn this act on the Day of Judgement. He would wish to be returned to this life so that he could earn more reward and compensation." Allah then says,

(So on that Day none will punish as He will punish.) meaning, there is no one more severely punished than those whom Allah punishes for disobeying Him.

(And none will bind as He will bind.) meaning, there is no one who is more severely punished and bound than those the Az-Zabaniyah punish the disbelievers in their Lord. This is for the criminals and the wrongdoers among the creatures. In reference to the pure and tranquil soul -- which is always at rest and abiding by the truth it will be said to it,

(O tranquil soul! Come back to your Lord.) meaning, to His company, His reward and what He has prepared for His servants in His Paradise.

(well-pleased) meaning, within itself.

(well-pleasing.) meaning, pleased with Allah, and He will be pleased with it and gratify it.

(Enter then among My servants,) meaning, among their ranks.

(And enter My Paradise!) This will be said to it at the time of death and on the Day of Judgement. This is like the angels giving glad tiding to the believer at his time of death and when he rises from his grave. Likewise is this statement here. Ibn Abi Hatim recorded from Ibn `Abbas concerning Allah's statement,

(O tranquil soul! Come back to your Lord, well-pleased and well-pleasing!) He said, "This Ayah was revealed while Abu Bakr was sitting (with the Prophet). So he said, `O Messenger of Allah! There is nothing better than this!' The Prophet then replied,

»أَمَا إِنَّهُ سَيُقَالُ لَكَ هَذَا«

(This will indeed be said to you.)" This is the end of the Tafsir of Surat Al-Fajr, and all praise and blessings are due to Allah.

CHAPTER (SURAH) 90: AL-BALAD (THE CITY, THIS COUNTRYSIDE), VERSES 001- 020

Surah: 90 Ayah: 1, Ayah: 2, Ayah: 3, Ayah: 4, Ayah: 5, Ayah: 6, Ayah: 7, Ayah: 8, Ayah: 9 & Ayah: 10

(بِسْمِ اللَّهِ الرَّحْمَـنِ الرَّحِيمِ)

In the Name of Allah, the Most Gracious, the Most Merciful.

Chapter 90: Al-Balad (The City), Verses 001-020

$$﴿ لَا أُقْسِمُ بِهَٰذَا ٱلْبَلَدِ ۝ ﴾$$

1. I swear by this city (Makkah);

$$﴿ وَأَنتَ حِلٌّ بِهَٰذَا ٱلْبَلَدِ ۝ ﴾$$

2. And you are free (from sin, and to punish the enemies of Islâm on the Day of the conquest) in this city (Makkah).

$$﴿ وَوَالِدٍ وَمَا وَلَدَ ۝ ﴾$$

3. And by the begetter (i.e. Adam (peace be upon him)) and that which he begot (i.e. his progeny).

$$﴿ لَقَدْ خَلَقْنَا ٱلْإِنسَٰنَ فِي كَبَدٍ ۝ ﴾$$

4. Verily, We have created man in toil.

$$﴿ أَيَحْسَبُ أَن لَّن يَقْدِرَ عَلَيْهِ أَحَدٌ ۝ ﴾$$

5. Thinks he that none can overcome him?

$$﴿ يَقُولُ أَهْلَكْتُ مَالًا لُّبَدًا ۝ ﴾$$

6. He says (boastfully): "I have wasted wealth in abundance!"

$$﴿ أَيَحْسَبُ أَن لَّمْ يَرَهُۥ أَحَدٌ ۝ ﴾$$

7. Thinks he that none sees him?

$$﴿ أَلَمْ نَجْعَل لَّهُۥ عَيْنَيْنِ ۝ ﴾$$

8. Have We not made for him a pair of eyes,

$$\left\{ \text{وَلِسَانًا وَشَفَتَيْنِ} \; \textcircled{9} \right\}$$

9. And a tongue and a pair of lips?

$$\left\{ \text{وَهَدَيْنَاهُ النَّجْدَيْنِ} \; \textcircled{10} \right\}$$

10. And shown him the two ways (good and evil)?

Transliteration

1. La oqsimu bihatha albaladi 2. Waanta hillun bihatha albaladi 3. Wawalidin wama walada 4. Laqad khalaqna al-insana fee kabadin 5. Ayahsabu an lan yaqdira AAalayhi ahadun 6. Yaqoolu ahlaktu malan lubadan 7. Ayahsabu an lam yarahu ahadun 8. Alam najAAal lahu AAaynayni 9. Walisanan washafatayni 10. Wahadaynahu alnnajdayni

Tafsir Ibn Kathir

Swearing by the Sanctity of Makkah and Other Things that Man was created in Hardship

Here Allah has sworn by Makkah, the Mother of the Towns, addressing its resident (during the non-sacred months,) free in this city in order to draw his attention to the significance of its sanctity when its people are in the state of sanctity. Khusayf reported from Mujahid;

(Nay! I swear by this city;) "The word "La" (Nay) refers to the refutation against them (Quraish). I swear by this city." Shabib bin Bishr narrated from `Ikrimah, from Ibn `Abbas that he said,

(Nay! I swear by this city;) "This means Makkah." Concerning the Ayah:

(And you are free in this city.) he (Ibn `Abbas) said, "O Muhammad! It is permissable for you to fight in it." Similar was reported from Sa`id bin Jubayr, Abu Salih, `Atiyah, Ad-Dahhak, Qatadah, As-Suddi and Ibn Zayd. Al-Hasan Al-Basri said, "Allah made it lawful (to fight in) for him (the Prophet) for one hour of a day." The meaning of what they have said was mentioned in a Hadith that is agreed- upon as being authentic. In it the Prophet said,

«إِنَّ هَذَا الْبَلَدَ حَرَّمَهُ اللهُ يَوْمَ خَلَقَ السَّموَاتِ وَالْأَرْضَ، فَهُوَ حَرَامٌ بِحُرْمَةِ اللهِ إِلَى يَوْمِ الْقِيَامَةِ لَا يُعْضَدُ شَجَرُهُ وَلَا يُخْتَلَى خَلَاهُ، وَإِنَّمَا أُحِلَّتْ لِي سَاعَةٌ مِنْ نَهَارٍ، وَقَدْ عَادَتْ حُرْمَتُهَا الْيَوْمَ كَحُرْمَتِهَا بِالْأَمْسِ، أَلَا فَلْيُبَلِّغِ الشَّاهِدُ

Chapter 90: Al-Balad (The City), Verses 001-020

«الْغَائِبَ»

(Verily, Allah made this city sacred on the Day that He created the heavens and the earth. Therefore, it is sacred by the sanctity of Allah until the Day of Judgement. Its trees should not be uprooted, and its bushes and grasses should not be removed. And it was only made lawful for me (to fight in) for one hour of a day. Today its sanctity has been restored just as it was sacred yesterday. So, let the one who is present inform those who are absent.) In another wording of this Hadith, he said,

«فَإِنْ أَحَدٌ تَرَخَّصَ بِقِتَالِ رَسُولِ اللهِ فَقُولُوا: إِنَّ اللهَ أَذِنَ لِرَسُولِهِ وَلَمْ يَأْذَنْ لَكُمْ»

(So, if anyone tries to use the fighting of the Messenger (to conquer Makkah) as an excuse (to fight there), then tell him that Allah permitted it for His Messenger and He has not permitted it for you.) Concerning Allah's statement,

(And by the begetter and that which he begot.) Mujahid, Abu Salih, Qatadah, Ad-Dahhak, Sufyan Ath-Thawri, Sa`id bin Jubayr, As-Suddi, Al-Hasan Al-Basri, Khusayf, Shurahbil bin Sa`d and others have said, "Meaning, by the begetter, Adam, and that which he begot is his children." This view that Mujahid and his companions have chosen is good and strong. This is supported by the fact that Allah swears by the Mother of the Towns, which are dwellings. Then after it He swears by the dwellers therein, who is Adam, the father of mankind, and his children. Abu `Imran Al-Jawni said, "It refers to Ibrahim and his progeny." Ibn Jarir recorded this statement as did Ibn Abi Hatim. Ibn Jarir preferred the view that it is general and it refers to every father and his children. This meaning is also acceptable. Allah then says,

(Verily, We have created man in Kabad.) Ibn Abi Najih and Jurayj reported from `Ata, from Ibn `Abbas concerning the phrase `in Kabad', "He was created while in hardship. Don't you see him" Then he mentioned his birth and the sprouting of his teeth. Mujahid said,

(in Kabad.) "A drop of sperm, then a clot, then a lump of flesh, enduring in his creation." Mujahid then said, "This is similar to Allah's statement,

(His mother bears him with hardship. And she brings him forth with hardship.) (46:15) and she breast-feeds him with hardship, and his livelihood is a hardship. So he endures all of this." Sa`id bin Jubayr said,

(Verily, We have created man in Kabad.) "In hardship and seeking livelihood." `Ikrimah said, "In hardship and long-suffering." Qatadah said, "In difficulty." It is reported from Al-Hasan that he said, "Enduring the hardships of the world by life and the severity of the Hereafter."

Man is encompassed by Allah and His Bounties

Allah says,

(Does he think that none can overcome him) Al-Hasan Al-Basri said,

(Does he think that none can overcome him) "Meaning no one is able to take his wealth." Qatadah said,

(Does he think that none can overcome him) "The Son of Adam thinks that he will not be asked about this wealth of his -- how he earned and how he spent it." Allah said:

(He says: "I have wasted wealth in abundance!") This means, the Son of Adam says, "I spent an abundance of wealth." Mujahid, Al-Hasan, Qatadah, As-Suddi and others have said this.

(Does he think that none sees him) Mujahid said, "Does he think that Allah, the Mighty and Majestic, does not see him." Others among the Salaf have said similar to this. Allah said;

(Have We not made for him two eyes) meaning, for him to see with them.

(And a tongue) meaning, for him to speak with, and so that he can express that which is inside of him.

(and two lips) In order to help him with speaking, eating food, and beautifying his face and his mouth.

The Ability to distinguish between Good and Evil is also a Blessing

(And shown him the two ways) This refers to the two paths. Sufyan Ath-Thawri narrated from `Asim, from Zirr, from `Abdullah bin Mas`ud that he said,

(And shown him the two ways) "The good and the evil." Similar to this has been reported from `Ali, Ibn `Abbas, Mujahid, `Ikrimah, Abu Wa'il, Abu Salih, Muhammad bin Ka`b, Ad-Dahhak, and `Ata' Al-Khurasani among others. Similar to this Ayah is Allah's statement,

(Verily, We have created man from Nutfah Amshaj, in order to try him: so We made him hearer and seer. Verily, We showed him the way, whether he be grateful or ungrateful.) (76:2-3)

> **Surah: 90 Ayah: 11, Ayah: 12, Ayah: 13, Ayah: 14, Ayah: 15, Ayah: 16, Ayah: 17, Ayah: 18, Ayah: 19 & Ayah: 20**

﴿ فَلَا ٱقۡتَحَمَ ٱلۡعَقَبَةَ ۝ ﴾

11. But he has not attempted to pass on the path that is steep (i.e. the path which will lead to goodness and success).

﴿ وَمَآ أَدْرَىٰكَ مَا ٱلْعَقَبَةُ ۞ ﴾

12. And what will make you know the path that is steep?

﴿ فَكُّ رَقَبَةٍ ۞ ﴾

13. (It is) freeing a neck (slave)

﴿ أَوْ إِطْعَـٰمٌ فِى يَوْمٍ ذِى مَسْغَبَةٍ ۞ ﴾

14. Or giving food in a day of hunger (famine),

﴿ يَتِيمًا ذَا مَقْرَبَةٍ ۞ ﴾

15. To an orphan near of kin.

﴿ أَوْ مِسْكِينًا ذَا مَتْرَبَةٍ ۞ ﴾

16. Or to a Miskîn (poor) cleaving to dust (out of misery).

﴿ ثُمَّ كَانَ مِنَ ٱلَّذِينَ ءَامَنُوا۟ وَتَوَاصَوْا۟ بِٱلصَّبْرِ وَتَوَاصَوْا۟ بِٱلْمَرْحَمَةِ ۞ ﴾

17. Then he became one of those who believed in the Islamic Monotheism) and recommended one another to perseverance and patience, and (also) recommended one another to pity and compassion.

﴿ أُو۟لَـٰٓئِكَ أَصْحَـٰبُ ٱلْمَيْمَنَةِ ۞ ﴾

18. They are those on the Right Hand (i.e. the dwellers of Paradise),

﴿ وَٱلَّذِينَ كَفَرُوا۟ بِـَٔايَـٰتِنَا هُمْ أَصْحَـٰبُ ٱلْمَشْـَٔمَةِ ۞ ﴾

19. But those who disbelieved in Our Ayât (proofs, evidences, verses, lessons, signs, revelations, etc.), they are those on the Left Hand (the dwellers of Hell).

$$﴿ عَلَيْهِمْ نَارٌ مُّؤْصَدَةٌ ﴾$$

20. The Fire will be shut over them (i.e. they will be enveloped by the Fire without any opening or window or outlet.

Transliteration

11. Fala iqtahama alAAaqabata 12. Wama adraka ma alAAaqabatu 13. Fakku raqabatin 14. Aw itAAamun fee yawmin thee masghabatin 15. Yateeman tha maqrabatin 16. Aw miskeenan tha matrabatin 17. Thumma kana mina allatheena amanoo watawasaw bialssabri watawasaw bialmarhamati 18. Ola-ika as-habu almaymanati 19. Waallatheena kafaroo bi-ayatina hum as-habu almash-amati 20. AAalayhim narun mu/sadatun

Tafsir Ibn Kathir

The Encouragement to traverse upon the Path of Goodness

Ibn Zayd said,

(But he has not attempted to pass on the path that is steep.) "This means, will he not traverse upon the path which contains salvation and good Then He explains this path by his saying,

(And what will make you know the path that is steep Freeing a neck, or giving food.)" Imam Ahmad recorded from Sa`id bin Marjanah that he heard Abu Hurayrah saying that the Messenger of Allah said,

«مَنْ أَعْتَقَ رَقَبَةً مُؤْمِنَةً أَعْتَقَ اللهُ بِكُلِّ إِرْبٍ أَيْ عُضْوٍ مِنْهَا إِرْبًا مِنْهُ مِنَ النَّارِ حَتَّى إِنَّهُ لَيُعْتِقُ بِالْيَدِ الْيَدَ، وَبِالرِّجْلِ الرِّجْلَ، وَبِالْفَرْجِ الْفَرْجَ»

(Whoever frees a believing slave, Allah will free for every limb (of the slave) one of his limbs from the Fire. This is to such an extent that He (Allah) will free a hand for a hand, a leg for a leg, and a private part for a private part.) `Ali bin Al-Husayn then said (to Sa`id), "Did you hear this from Abu Hurayrah" Sa`id replied, "Yes." Then `Ali bin Al-Husayn said to a slave boy that he owned who was the swiftest of his servants, "Call Mutarrif!" So when the slave was brought before him he said, "Go, for you are free for the Face of Allah." Al-Bukhari, Muslim, At-Tirmidhi, An-Nasa'i, all recorded this Hadith from Sa`id bin Marjanah. Imam Ahmad recorded from `Amr bin `Abasah that the Prophet said,

«مَنْ بَنَى مَسْجِدًا لِيُذْكَرَ اللهُ فِيهِ بَنَى اللهُ لَهُ بَيْتًا فِي الْجَنَّةِ وَمَنْ أَعْتَقَ نَفْسًا مُسْلِمَةً كَانَتْ فِدْيَتَهُ مِنْ جَهَنَّمَ وَمَنْ شَابَ شَيْبَةً فِي الْإِسْلَامِ كَانَتْ لَهُ نُورًا

Chapter 90: Al-Balad (The City), Verses 001-020

يَوْمَ الْقِيَامَةِ»

(Whoever builds a Masjid so that Allah may be remembered in it, Allah will build a house for him in Paradise; and whoever frees a Muslim person, then it will be his ransom from Hell; and whoever grows grey in Islam, then it will be a light for him on the Day of Judgement.) According to another route of transmission, Ahmad recorded from Abu Umamah, who reported from `Amr bin `Abasah that As-Sulami said to him, "Narrate a Hadith to us that you heard from the Messenger of Allah, without any deficiency or mistakes." He (`Amr) said, "I heard him saying,

«مَنْ وُلِدَ لَهُ ثَلَاثَةُ أَوْلَادٍ فِي الْإِسْلَامِ فَمَاتُوا قَبْلَ أَنْ يَبْلُغُوا الْحِنْثَ أَدْخَلَهُ اللهُ الْجَنَّةَ بِفَضْلِ رَحْمَتِهِ إِيَّاهُمْ، وَمَنْ شَابَ شَيْبَةً فِي سَبِيلِ اللهِ كَانَتْ لَهُ نُورًا يَوْمَ الْقِيَامَةِ، وَمَنْ رَمَى بِسَهْمٍ فِي سَبِيلِ اللهِ بَلَغَ بِهِ الْعَدُوَّ أَصَابَ أَوْ أَخْطَأَ كَانَ لَهُ عِتْقُ رَقَبَةٍ، وَمَنْ أَعْتَقَ رَقَبَةً مُؤْمِنَةً أَعْتَقَ اللهُ بِكُلِّ عُضْوٍ مِنْهُ عُضْوًا مِنْهُ مِنَ النَّارِ، وَمَنْ أَنْفَقَ زَوْجَيْنِ فِي سَبِيلِ اللهِ فَإِنَّ لِلْجَنَّةِ ثَمَانِيَةَ أَبْوَابٍ يُدْخِلُهُ اللهُ مِنْ أَيِّ بَابٍ شَاءَ مِنْهَا»

(Whoever has three children born to him in Islam, and they die before reaching the age of puberty, Allah will enter him into Paradise by virtue of His mercy to them. And whoever grows gray in the way of Allah (fighting Jihad), then it will be a light for him on the Day of Judgement. And whoever shoots an arrow in the way of Allah (fighting Jihad) that reaches the enemy, whether it hits or misses, he will get the reward of freeing a slave. And whoever frees a believing slave, then Allah will free each of his limbs from the Fire for every limb that the slave has. And whoever equipped two riding animals in the way of Allah (for fighting Jihad), then indeed Paradise has eight gates, and Allah will allow him to enter any of them he choses.)" Ahmad recorded this Hadith from different routes of transmission that are good and strong, and all praise is due to Allah. Allah said,

(Or giving food in a day full of Masghabah,) Ibn `Abbas said, "Of hunger." `Ikrimah, Mujahid, Ad-Dahhak, Qatadah and others all said the same. The word `Saghb' means hunger. Then Allah says,

(To an orphan) meaning, he gives food on a day like this to an orphan.

(near of kin.) meaning, who is related to him. Ibn `Abbas, `Ikrimah, Al-Hasan, Ad-Dahhak and As-Suddi all said this. This is similar to what was related in a Hadith that was collected by Imam Ahmad on the authority of Salman bin `Amir who said that he heard the Messenger of Allah say,

«الصَّدَقَةُ عَلَى الْمِسْكِينِ صَدَقَةٌ وَعَلَى ذِي الرَّحِمِ اثْنَتَانِ: صَدَقَةٌ وَصِلَةٌ»

(Charity given to the poor person is counted as one charity, while if it is given to a relative it is counted as two: charity and connecting the ties (of kinship).) At-Tirmidhi and An-Nasa'i both recorded this Hadith and its chain of narration is authentic. Then Allah says,

(Or to a Miskin cleaving to dust (Dha Matrabah).) meaning, poor, miserable, and clinging to the dirt. It means those who are in a state of destitution. Ibn `Abbas said, "Dha Matrabah is that who is dejected in the street and who has no house or anything else to protect him against the dirt." Allah said;

(Then he became one of those who believed) meaning, then, along with these beautiful and pure characteristics, he was a believer in his heart, seeking the reward of that from Allah. This is as Allah says,

(And whoever desires the Hereafter and strives for it, with the necessary effort due for it while he is believer, then such are the ones whose striving shall be appreciated.) (17:19) Allah also says,

(Whoever works righteousness -- whether male or female -- while being a true believer....) (16:97) Allah says,

(and recommended one another to patience, and recommended one another to compassion.) meaning, he was from the believers who worked righteous deeds, and advised each other to be patient with the harms of the people, and to be merciful with them. This is similar to what has been related in the noble Hadith,

«الرَّاحِمُونَ يَرْحَمُهُمُ الرَّحْمنُ، ارْحَمُوا مَنْ فِي الْأَرْضِ يَرْحَمْكُمْ مَنْ فِي السَّمَاءِ»

(The merciful people will be treated with mercy by the Most Merciful (Allah). Be merciful to those who are on the earth and He Who is above the heavens will be merciful to you.) In another Hadith he said,

«لَا يَرْحَمُ اللهُ مَنْ لَا يَرْحَمِ النَّاسَ»

(Allah will not be merciful with whoever is not merciful with the people.) Abu Dawud recorded from `Abdullah bin `Amr that he narrated (from the Prophet),

«مَنْ لَمْ يَرْحَمْ صَغِيرَنَا وَيَعْرِفْ حَقَّ كَبِيرِنَا فَلَيْسَ مِنَّا»

(Whoever does not show mercy to our children, nor does he recognize the right of our elders, then he is not of us.) Then Allah says,

(They are those on the Right,) meaning, those who have these characteristics are the companions of the Right Hand.

The Companions of the Left Hand and Their Recompense

Then Allah says,

(But those who disbelieved in Our Ayat, they are those on the Left.) meaning, the companions of the Left Hand.

(Upon them Fire will Mu'sadah.) meaning, it will be sealed over them and there will be no way for them to avoid it, nor will they have any way out. Abu Hurayrah, Ibn `Abbas, `Ikrimah, Sa`id bin Jubayr, Mujahid, Muhammad bin Ka`b Al-Qurazi, `Atiyah Al-`Awfi, Al-Hasan, Qatadah and As-Suddi, all said,

(Mu'sadah.) "This means shut." Ibn `Abbas said, "Its doors will be closed." Ad-Dahhak said,

(Mu'sadah.) "It will be sealed over them and it will have no door." Qatadah said,

(Mu'sadah.) "It will be shut and there will be no light in it, no crevice (escape), and no way out of it forever." This is the end of the Tafsir of Surat Al-Balad, and all praise and blessings are due to Allah.

INTRODUCTION TO CHAPTER (SURAH) 91: ASH-SHAMS (THE SUN)

Ibn Kathir's Introduction

Recitation of Surah Ash-Shams wa Duhaha in the `Isha' Prayer The Hadith of Jabir which was recorded in the Two Sahihs has already been mentioned. In it the Messenger of Allah said to Mu`adh,

«هَلَّا صَلَّيْتَ بِ (سَبِّحِ اسْمَ رَبِّكَ الْأَعْلَى) (وَالشَّمْسِ وَضُحَاهَا) (وَاللَّيْلِ إِذَا يَغْشَى) »

(Why didn't you pray with (the recitation of) (Glorify the Name of your Lord the Most High) (87), (By the sun and Duhaha) (91), and (By the night as it envelops) (92))

CHAPTER (SURAH) 91: ASH-SHAMS (THE SUN), VERSES 001- 015

Surah: 91 Ayah: 1, Ayah: 2, Ayah: 3, Ayah: 4, Ayah: 5, Ayah: 6, Ayah: 7, Ayah: 8, Ayah: 9 & Ayah: 10

(بِسْمِ اللَّهِ الرَّحْمَـنِ الرَّحِيمِ)

In the Name of Allah, the Most Gracious, the Most Merciful.

﴿ وَٱلشَّمْسِ وَضُحَىٰهَا ۝ ﴾

1. By the sun and its brightness.

﴿ وَٱلْقَمَرِ إِذَا تَلَىٰهَا ۝ ﴾

2. By the moon as it follows it (the sun).

﴿ وَٱلنَّهَارِ إِذَا جَلَّىٰهَا ۝ ﴾

3. By the day as it shows up (the sun's) brightness.

﴿ وَٱلَّيْلِ إِذَا يَغْشَىٰهَا ۝ ﴾

4. By the night as it conceals it (the sun).

﴿ وَٱلسَّمَآءِ وَمَا بَنَىٰهَا ۝ ﴾

5. By the heaven and Him Who built it.

﴿ وَٱلْأَرْضِ وَمَا طَحَىٰهَا ۝ ﴾

6. By the earth and Him Who spread it.

﴿ وَنَفْسٍ وَمَا سَوَّىٰهَا ۝ ﴾

7. By Nafs (Adam or a person or a soul), and Him Who perfected him in proportion;

﴿ فَأَلْهَمَهَا فُجُورَهَا وَتَقْوَىٰهَا ۝ ﴾

8. Then He showed him what is wrong for him and what is right for him.

Chapter 91: Ash-Shams (The Sun), Verses 001-015

﴿ قَدْ أَفْلَحَ مَن زَكَّىٰهَا ۝ ﴾

9. Indeed he succeeds who purifies his own self (i.e. obeys and performs all that Allâh ordered, by following the true Faith of Islâmic Monotheism and by doing righteous good deeds).

﴿ وَقَدْ خَابَ مَن دَسَّىٰهَا ۝ ﴾

10. And indeed he fails who corrupts his own self (i.e. disobeys what Allâh has ordered by rejecting the true Faith of Islâmic Monotheism or by following polytheism or by doing every kind of evil wicked deeds).

Transliteration

1. Waalshshamsi waduhaha 2. Waalqamari itha talaha 3. Waalnnahari itha jallaha 4. Waallayli itha yaghshaha 5. Waalssama-i wama banaha 6. Waal-ardi wama tahaha 7. Wanafsin wama sawwaha 8. Faalhamaha fujooraha wataqwaha 9. Qad aflaha man zakkaha 10. Waqad khaba man dassaha

Tafsir Ibn Kathir

Allah swears by His Creation that the Person Who purifies Himself will be Successful and the Person Who corrupts Himself will fail

Mujahid said,

(By the sun and Duhaha.) "This means, by its light." Qatadah said,

(wa Duhaha.) "The whole day." Ibn Jarir said, "The correct view is what has been said, `Allah swears by the sun and its daytime, because the clear light of the sun is daytime.'"

(By the moon as it Talaha.) Mujahid said, "It follows it (the sun)." Al-`Awfi reported from Ibn `Abbas that he said,

(By the moon as it Talaha.) "It follows the day." Qatadah said, "`as it Talaha (follows it)' is referring to the night of the Hilal (the new crescent moon). When the sun goes down, the Hilal is visible." Concerning Allah's statement,

(By the day as it Jallaha.) Mujahid said, "When it illuminates." Thus, Mujahid said,

(By the day as it Jallaha.) "This is similar to Allah's statement,

(By the day as it Tajalla.) (92:2)" And they have said concerning Allah's statement,

(By the night as it Yaghshaha.) meaning, when it covers the sun, which takes place when sun disappears and the horizons become dark. Concerning Allah's statement,

(By the heaven and Ma Banaha.) The meaning here could be for descriptive purposes, meaning "By the heaven and its construction." This was said by Qatadah. It could also mean "By the heaven and its Constructor." This was stated by Mujahid. Both views are interrelated, and construction means raising. This is as Allah says,

(With Hands did We construct the heaven.) (51:47) meaning, with strength.

(Verily, We are able to extend the vastness of space thereof. And We have spread out the earth: how excellent a spreader are We!) (51:47-48) This is also similar to Allah's statement,

(By the earth and Ma Tahaha.) Mujahid said, "Tahaha means He spread it out." Al-`Awfi reported from Ibn `Abbas that he said,

(and Ma Tahaha.) "This means what He created in it." `Ali bin Abi Talhah reported from Ibn `Abbas that he said, "Tahaha means that He proportioned it." Mujahid, Qatadah, Ad-Dahhak, As-Suddi, Ath-Thawri, Abu Salih and Ibn Zayd all said that

(Tahaha) means, He spread it out. Allah then says,

(By Nafs, and Ma Sawwaha (Who apportioned it).) meaning, He created it sound and well-proportioned upon the correct nature (Al-Fitrah). This is as Allah says,

(So set you your face towards the religion, Hanif. Allah's Fitrah with which He has created mankind. No change let there be in the Khalqillah.) (30:30) The Messenger of Allah said,

«كُلُّ مَوْلُودٍ يُولَدُ عَلَى الْفِطْرَةِ فَأَبَوَاهُ يُهَوِّدَانِهِ أَوْ يُنَصِّرَانِهِ أَوْ يُمَجِّسَانِهِ، كَمَا تُولَدُ الْبَهِيمَةُ بَهِيمَةً جَمْعَاءَ، هَلْ تُحِسُّونَ فِيهَا مِنْ جَدْعَاءَ؟»

(Every child that is born, is born upon the Fitrah, but his parents make him a Jew, a Christian, or a Zoroastrian. This is just as the animal is born, complete with all of its parts. Do you notice any mutilation in it) Both Al-Bukhari and Muslim recorded this Hadith from Abu Hurayrah. In Sahih Muslim, it has been narrated from `Iyad bin Himar Al-Mujashi`i that the Messenger of Allah said,

«يَقُولُ اللهُ عَزَّ وَجَلَّ: إِنِّي خَلَقْتُ عِبَادِي حُنَفَاءَ فَجَاءَتْهُمُ الشَّيَاطِينُ فَاجْتَالَتْهُمْ عَنْ دِينِهِم»

(Allah the Mighty and Majestic says, "Verily I created My servants Hunafa' (as monotheists), but then the devils came to them and distracted them from their religion.") Then Allah says,

Chapter 91: Ash-Shams (The Sun), Verses 001-015

(Then He showed it its Fujur and its Taqwa.) meaning, He showed him to his transgression and his Taqwa. This means that He clarified that for it and He guided it to what has been ordained for him. Ibn `Abbas said,

(Then He showed it its Fujur and its Taqwa.) "He explained the good and the evil to it (the soul)." Mujahid, Qatadah, Ad-Dahhak and Ath-Thawri all said the same. Sa`id bin Jubayr said, "He gave him inspiration (to see what was) good and evil." Ibn Zayd said, "He made its Fujur and its Taqwa inside of it." Ibn Jarir recorded from Abul-Aswad Ad-Dili that he said, "`Imran bin Husayn said to me, `Do you think that what the people do, and what they strive for is a thing that is pre-ordained and predestined for them, or is it a thing which is only written after the Message comes to them from the Prophet , when there will be an evidence against them' I said, `Rather it is something preordained upon them.' Then he said, `Is that an injustice' Then I became extremely frightened of him (due to what he was saying), and I said to him, `There is nothing except that He (Allah) created it and possesses it in His Hand. He is not asked about what He does, while they (His creation) will be asked.' He (`Imran) then said, `May Allah guide you! I only asked you about that in order to inform you that a man from Muzaynah or Juhaynah tribe came to the Allah's Messenger and asked him: "O Messenger of Allah! Do you consider the actions of mankind and their struggles to be preordained for them and written for them from Qadr, or something written for them only after the Message came to them from their Prophet, when there will be an evidence against them" He (the Prophet) replied:

»بَلْ شَيْءٌ قَدْ قُضِيَ عَلَيْهِمْ«

(Rather it is something preordained for them.) So the man said, "Then what is the point of our actions" The Prophet replied,

»مَنْ كَانَ اللهُ خَلَقَهُ لِإِحْدَى الْمَنْزِلَتَيْنِ يُهَيِّئُهُ لَهَا، وَتَصْدِيقُ ذَلِكَ فِي كِتَابِ اللهِ تَعَالَى: (وَنَفْسٍ وَمَا سَوَّاهَا – فَأَلْهَمَهَا فُجُورَهَا وَتَقْوَاهَا)«

(Whoever Allah created for one of the two positions (Paradise or Hell), He makes it easy for him (to attain). The proof of that is in the Book of Allah (By Nafs, and Ma Sawwaha (Who apportioned it). Then He showed it its Fujur and its Taqwa).)" Ahmad and Muslim both recorded this Hadith. Allah then says,

(Indeed he succeeds who purifies it. And indeed he fails who Dassaha.) This could mean that whoever purifies himself by obedience to Allah, then he will be successful. This is as Qatadah said, "He cleanses it from the lowly and despicable characteristics." Similar to this has been reported from Mujahid, `Ikrimah and Sa`id bin Jubayr.

(And indeed he fails who Dassaha.) meaning, to conceal it. This means that he makes it dull, and he disregards it by neglecting to allow it to receive guidance. He treats it in this manner until he performs acts of disobedience and he abandons obedience of Allah. It also could mean that he is indeed successful whose soul Allah purifies, and he has failed whose soul Allah corrupts. This is like what was reported by Al-`Awfi and `Ali bin Abi Talhah from Ibn `Abbas. At-Tabarani recorded that Ibn `Abbas said, "The Messenger of Allah used to stop whenever he recited this Ayah,

(By Nafs, and Ma Sawwaha (Who apportioned it). Then He showed it its Fujur and its Taqwa.) Then he would say,

«اللَّهُمَّ آتِ نَفْسِي تَقْوَاهَا، أَنْتَ وَلِيُّهَا وَمَوْلَاهَا، وَخَيْرُ مَنْ زَكَّاهَا»

(O Allah! Give my soul its good. You are its Guardian and Master, and the best to purify it.)" Another Hadith Imam Ahmad recorded that Zayd bin Arqam said that the Messenger of Allah said,

«اللَّهُمَّ إِنِّي أَعُوذُ بِكَ مِنَ الْعَجْزِ وَالْكَسَلِ، وَالْهَرَمِ وَالْجُبْنِ وَالْبُخْلِ وَعَذَابِ الْقَبْرِ. اللَّهُمَّ آتِ نَفْسِي تَقْوَاهَا، وَزَكِّهَا أَنْتَ خَيْرُ مَنْ زَكَّاهَا، أَنْتَ وَلِيُّهَا وَمَوْلَاهَا. اللَّهُمَّ إِنِّي أَعُوذُ بِكَ مِنْ قَلْبٍ لَا يَخْشَعُ، وَمِنْ نَفْسٍ لَا تَشْبَعُ، وَعِلْمٍ لَا يَنْفَعُ، وَدَعْوَةٍ لَا يُسْتَجَابُ لَهَا»

(O Allah! Verily, I seek refuge with You from weakness, laziness, senility (of old age), cowardliness, stinginess and the torment of the grave. O Allah! Give my soul its good and purify it, for You are the best to purify it. You are its Guardian and Master. O Allah! Verily, I seek refuge with You from a heart that is not humble, a soul that is not satisfied, knowledge that does not benefit and a supplication that is not answered.) Zayd then said, "The Messenger of Allah used to teach us these (words) and we now teach them to you." Muslim also recorded this Hadith.

Surah: 91 Ayah: 11, Ayah: 12, Ayah: 13, Ayah: 14 & Ayah: 15

﴿ كَذَّبَتْ ثَمُودُ بِطَغْوَاهَا ﴾

11. Thamûd (people) denied (their Prophet) through their transgression (by rejecting the true Faith of Islâmic Monotheism, and by following polytheism, and by committing every kind of sin).

﴿ إِذِ انبَعَثَ أَشْقَاهَا ﴾

12. When the most wicked man among them went forth (to kill the she-camel).

Chapter 91: Ash-Shams (The Sun), Verses 001-015

﴿ فَقَالَ لَهُمْ رَسُولُ ٱللَّهِ نَاقَةَ ٱللَّهِ وَسُقْيَٰهَا ۞ ﴾

13. But the Messenger of Allâh (Sâlih (peace be upon him)) said to them: "Be cautious! (Fear the evil end). That is the she-camel of Allâh! (Do not harm it) and bar it not from having its drink!"

﴿ فَكَذَّبُوهُ فَعَقَرُوهَا فَدَمْدَمَ عَلَيْهِمْ رَبُّهُم بِذَنۢبِهِمْ فَسَوَّىٰهَا ۞ ﴾

14. Then they denied him and they killed it. So their Lord destroyed them because of their sin, and made them equal in destruction (i.e. all grades of people, rich and poor, strong and weak, etc.)!

﴿ وَلَا يَخَافُ عُقْبَٰهَا ۞ ﴾

15. And He (Allâh) feared not the consequences thereof.

Transliteration

11. Kaththabat thamoodu bitaghwaha 12. Ithi inbaAAatha ashqaha 13. Faqala lahum rasoolu Allahi naqata Allahi wasuqyaha 14. Fakaththaboohu faAAaqarooha fadamdama AAalayhim rabbuhum bithanbihim fasawwaha 15. Wala yakhafu AAuqbaha

Tafsir Ibn Kathir

The Rejection of Thamud and Allah's Destruction of Them

Allah informs that Thamud rejected their Messenger because of the injustice and transgression they practiced. This was said by Mujahid, Qatadah and others. Therefore, this resulted in a rejection in their hearts for the guidance and conviction their Messenger came to them with.

(When their most wicked went forth.) meaning, the most wicked person of the tribe, and he was Qudar bin Salif, the one who killed the she-camel. He was leader of the tribe of Thamud, and he is the one whom Allah refers to in His saying,

(But they called their comrade and he took (a sword) and killed (her).) (54:29) This man was mighty and respected among his people. He was of noble lineage and a leader who was obeyed. This is just as Imam Ahmad recorded from `Abdullah bin Zam`ah. He said that the Messenger of Allah gave a sermon in which he mentioned the she-camel and he mentioned the man who killed her. Then he said,

«(إِذِ انۢبَعَثَ أَشْقَٰهَا)»

«انْبَعَثَ لَهَا رَجُلٌ عَارِمٌ عَزِيزٌ مَنِيعٌ فِي رَهْطِهِ مِثْلُ أَبِي زَمْعَة»

((When their most wicked went forth.)(A strong and mighty man who was invincible among his tribe, like Abu Zam`ah, went forth to her.) This Hadith was recorded by Al-Bukhari in his Book of Tafsir, and Muslim in his Book of the Description of the Hellfire. At-Tirmidhi and An-Nasa'i both recorded it in their Sunans in their Books of Tafsir.

The Story of Salih's She-Camel

Allah then says,

(But the Messenger of Allah said to them) referring to Salih.

(That is the she-camel of Allah!) meaning, `beware of touching the she-camel of Allah with any harm.'

(and its drink!) meaning, `do not transgress against her in her drinking, for she has been allocated a day to drink and you have been allocated a day to drink, as is known to you.' Then Allah says,

(Then they denied him and they killed it.) which means they rejected what he came with. This resulted in them killing the she-camel that Allah had brought out of the rock as a sign for them and a proof against them.

(So their Lord destroyed them because of their sin,) meaning, He became angry with them and He annihilated them.

(Fasawwaha!) meaning, He made the punishment descend upon them all equally. Qatadah said, "It has reached us that the leader of tribe of Thamud did not kill the she-camel until their youth, their elderly, their males and their females all pledged allegiance to him. So when the people cooperated in killing her, Allah destroyed them all with the same punishment due to their sin." Allah said,

(And He feared not) it has also been recited as (So He feared not)

(the consequences thereof.) Ibn `Abbas said, "Allah does not fear any consequences from anyone else." Mujahid, Al-Hasan, Bakr bin `Abdullah Al-Muzani and others all said the same. This is the end of the Tafsir of Surat Ash-Shams, and all praise and thanks are due to Allah.

INTRODUCTION TO CHAPTER (SURAH) 92: AL-LAIL (THE NIGHT)

Ibn Kathir's Introduction

The Recitation of Surat Al-Layl in the `Isha' Prayer

The statement of the Prophet to Mu`adh has already preceded, where he said,

«فَهَلَّا صَلَّيْتَ بِ (سَبِّحِ اسْمَ رَبِّكَ الْأَعْلَى) (وَالشَّمْسِ وَضُحَاهَا) (وَاللَّيْلِ إِذَا يَغْشَى)»

(Why did you not pray with (the recitation of) (Glorify the Name of your Lord the Most High) (87), and (By the sun and Duhaha) (91), and (By the night as it envelops) (92))

CHAPTER (SURAH) 92: AL-LAIL (THE NIGHT), VERSES 001- 021

Surah: 92 Ayah: 1, Ayah: 2, Ayah: 3, Ayah: 4, Ayah: 5, Ayah: 6, Ayah: 7, Ayah: 8, Ayah: 9, Ayah: 10 & Ayah: 11

(بِسْمِ اللَّهِ الرَّحْمَـنِ الرَّحِيمِ)

In the Name of Allah, the Most Gracious, the Most Merciful.

﴿ وَٱلَّيْلِ إِذَا يَغْشَىٰ ۝ ﴾

1. By the night as it envelops.

﴿ وَٱلنَّهَارِ إِذَا تَجَلَّىٰ ۝ ﴾

2. By the day as it appears in brightness.

﴿ وَمَا خَلَقَ ٱلذَّكَرَ وَٱلْأُنثَىٰ ۝ ﴾

3. By Him Who created male and female.

﴿ إِنَّ سَعْيَكُمْ لَشَتَّىٰ ۝ ﴾

4. Certainly, your efforts and deeds are diverse (different in aims and purposes);

﴿ فَأَمَّا مَنْ أَعْطَىٰ وَٱتَّقَىٰ ۝ ﴾

5. As for him who gives (in charity) and keeps his duty to Allâh and fears Him,

﴿ وَصَدَّقَ بِٱلْحُسْنَىٰ ۝ ﴾

6. And believes in Al-Husnâ.

﴿ فَسَنُيَسِّرُهُ لِلْيُسْرَىٰ ۝ ﴾

7. We will make smooth for him the path of ease (goodness).

﴿ وَأَمَّا مَن بَخِلَ وَٱسْتَغْنَىٰ ۝ ﴾

8. But he who is greedy miser and thinks himself self-sufficient.

﴿ وَكَذَّبَ بِٱلْحُسْنَىٰ ۝ ﴾

9. And belies Al-Husnâ.

﴿ فَسَنُيَسِّرُهُ لِلْعُسْرَىٰ ۝ ﴾

10. We will make smooth for him the path for evil.

﴿ وَمَا يُغْنِى عَنْهُ مَالُهُ إِذَا تَرَدَّىٰ ۝ ﴾

11. And what will his wealth avail him when he goes down (in destruction).

Transliteration

1. Waallayli itha yaghsha 2. Waalnnahari itha tajalla 3. Wama khalaqa alththakara waal-ontha 4. Inna saAAyakum lashatta 5. Faamma man aAAta waittaqa 6. Wasaddaqa bialhusna 7. Fasanuyassiruhu lilyusra 8. Waamma man bakhila waistaghna 9. Wakaththaba bialhusna 10. Fasanuyassiruhu lilAAusra 11. Wama yughnee AAanhu maluhu itha taradda

Tafsir Ibn Kathir

Swearing by the Diversity of Mankind in Their Efforts and informing of the Different Results of that

Allah swears by saying:

(By the night as it envelops.) meaning, when it covers the creation with its darkness.

Chapter 92: Al-Lail (The Night), Verses 001-021

(By the day as it appears.) meaning, with its light and its radiance.

(By Him Who created male and female.) This is similar to Allah's saying,

(And We have created you in pairs.) (78:8) It is also similar to saying,

(And of everything We have created pairs.) (51:49) And just as these things that are being sworn by are opposites, likewise that which this swearing is about are opposing things. This is why Allah says,

(Certainly, your efforts and deeds are diverse.) meaning, the actions of the servants that they have performed are also opposites and diverse. Therefore, there are those who do good and there are those who do evil. Allah then says,

(As for him who gives and has Taqwa.) meaning, he gives what he has been commanded to give and he fears Allah in his affairs.

(And believes in Al-Husna.) meaning, in the compensation for that. This was said by Qatadah. Khusayf said, "In the reward." Then Allah says,

(We will make smooth for him the path of ease.) Ibn `Abbas said, "Meaning for goodness." Thus, Allah says,

(But he who is greedy) meaning, with that which he has.

(and thinks himself self-sufficient,) `Ikrimah reported that Ibn `Abbas said, "This means he is stingy with his wealth and considers himself to be in no need of his Lord, the Mighty and Majestic." This was recorded by Ibn Abi Hatim.

(And denies Al-Husna.) meaning, the recompense in the abode of the Hereafter.

(We will make smooth for him the path to evil.) meaning, the path of evil. This is as Allah says,

(And We shall turn their hearts and their eyes away, as they refused to believe therein for the first time, and We shall leave them in their trespass to wander blindly.) (6:110) And there are many Ayat with this meaning, proving that Allah rewards those who intend good with success, while whoever intends evil is abandoned, and all of this is in accordance with a preordained decree. There are also many Hadiths that prove this.

The Narration of Abu Bakr As-Siddiq

Imam Ahmad recorded from Abu Bakr that he said to the Messenger of Allah , "O Messenger of Allah! Do we act according to what has already been decided, or is the matter just beginning (i.e., still undecided)" He replied,

《بَلْ عَلَى أَمْرٍ قَدْ فُرِغَ مِنْهُ》

(Indeed it is according to what has already been decided.) Then Abu Bakr said, "Then what (good) are deeds, O Messenger of Allah" He replied,

«كُلٌّ مُيَسَّرٌ لِمَا خُلِقَ لَهُ»

(Everyone will find it easy to do such deeds that will lead him to what he was created for.)

The Narration of `Ali

Al-Bukhari recorded from `Ali bin Abi Talib that they (the Companions) were with the Messenger of Allah at the cemetery of Baqi` Al-Gharqad for a funeral, when the Prophet said,

«مَا مِنْكُمْ مِنْ أَحَدٍ إِلَّا وَقَدْ كُتِبَ مَقْعَدُهُ مِنَ الْجَنَّةِ وَمَقْعَدُهُ مِنَ النَّارِ»

(There is none among you except that his place has already been written, a seat in Paradise and a seat in the Hellfire.) They said, "O Messenger of Allah! Should we depend on this" He replied,

«اعْمَلُوا، فَكُلٌّ مُيَسَّرٌ لِمَا خُلِقَ لَهُ»

(Perform deeds for everyone will have the deeds of what he was created for (Paradise or Hell) made easy for him.) Then he recited the Ayah

(As for him who gives and has Taqwa, and believes in Al-Husna. We will make smooth for him the path of ease.)" until the Ayah:

(the path to evil) He (Imam Al-Bukhari) also recorded another similar narration from `Ali bin Abi Talib in which he said, "We were at a funeral in the cemetery of Baqi` Al-Gharqad when the Messenger of Allah came and sat down. So we came and sat around him and he had a stick with him. Then he bowed his head and he began to scratch the ground with his stick. He then said,

«مَا مِنْكُمْ مِنْ أَحَدٍ أَوْ مَا مِنْ نَفْسٍ مَنْفُوسَةٍ إِلَّا كُتِبَ مَكَانُهَا مِنَ الْجَنَّةِ وَالنَّارِ، وَإِلَّا قَدْ كُتِبَتْ شَقِيَّةً أَوْ سَعِيدَةً»

(There is not anyone among you -- or is not a single soul (that has been created) -- except that his place has been written in Paradise or in the Fire, and it has been written that he will be miserable or happy.) A man said, "O Messenger of Allah! Should we just depend on what has been written for us and give up performing deeds For whoever of us is of the people of happiness then he will be of the people of

Chapter 92: Al-Lail (The Night), Verses 001-021

happiness, and whoever among us is of the people of misery then he will be of the people of misery." The Prophet replied,

»أَمَّا أَهْلُ السَّعَادَةِ فَيُيَسَّرُونَ لِعَمَلِ أَهْلِ السَّعَادَةِ، وَأَمَّا أَهْلُ الشَّقَاءِ فَيُيَسَّرُونَ إِلَى عَمَلِ أَهْلِ الشَّقَاءِ، ثُمَّ قَرَأَ:

(Those people who are the people of happiness, they will have the deeds of the people of happiness made easy for them. And those people who are the people of misery, they will have the deeds of the people of misery made easy for them.) Then he recited the Ayah:

(As for him who gives and has Taqwa, and believes in Al-Husna. We will make smooth for him the path of ease (goodness). But he who is greedy and thinks himself self-sufficient, and belies Al-Husna. We will make smooth for him the path to evil.)) The other compilers of the Group have also recorded this Hadith.

The Narration of `Abdullah bin `Umar

Imam Ahmad recorded from Ibn `Umar that `Umar said, "O Messenger of Allah! Do you think that the deeds that we do are a matter that is already predetermined or are they something just beginning or new" The Prophet replied,

»فِيمَا قَدْ فُرِغَ مِنْهُ، فَاعْمَلْ يَا ابْنَ الْخَطَّابِ، فَإِنَّ كُلًّا مُيَسَّرٌ، أَمَّا مَنْ كَانَ مِنْ أَهْلِ السَّعَادَةِ فَإِنَّهُ يَعْمَلُ لِلسَّعَادَةِ، وَأَمَّا مَنْ كَانَ مِنْ أَهْلِ الشَّقَاءِ فَإِنَّهُ يَعْمَلُ لِلشَّقَاءِ«

(It is something that has already been predetermined. Therefore, work deeds, O son of Al-Khattab! For verily, each person will have things made easy for him. So whoever is from the people of happiness, then he will work deeds for happiness, and whoever is from the people of misery, then he will work deeds for misery.)" This Hadith has been recorded by At-Tirmidhi in the Book of Al-Qadar and he said "Hasan Sahih." Another Hadith Narrated by Jabir Ibn Jarir recorded from Jabir bin `Abdullah that he said, "O Messenger of Allah! Are we performing deeds for something that has already been predetermined or is the matter based upon what we are just doing (now)" The Prophet replied,

»لِأَمْرٍ قَدْ فُرِغَ مِنْهُ«

(It is a matter that has been predetermined.) Then Suraqah said, "Then what is the purpose of deeds" The Messenger of Allah then said,

«كُلُّ عَامِلٍ مُيَسَّرٌ لِعَمَلِهِ»

(Everyone who does deeds will have his deeds made easy for him.) Muslim also recorded this Hadith. Ibn Jarir recorded from `Amir bin `Abdullah bin Az-Zubayr that he said, "Abu Bakr used to free servants upon their acceptance of Islam in Makkah. He used to free the elderly and the women when they accepted Islam. So his father said to him, `O my son! I see that you are freeing people who are weak. But if you freed strong men they could stand with you, defend you and protect you.' Abu Bakr replied, `O my father! I only want -- and I think he said -- what is with Allah.' Some people of my family have told me this Ayah was revealed about him:

(As for him who gives and has Taqwa, and believes in Al-Husna. We will make smooth for him the path of ease.)" Then Allah says,

(And what will his wealth avail him when he goes down) Mujahid said, "This means when he dies." Abu Salih and Malik said -- narrating from Zayd bin Aslam, "When he goes down into the Fire."

Surah: 92 Ayah: 12, Ayah: 13, Ayah: 14, Ayah: 15, Ayah: 16, Ayah: 17, Ayah: 18, Ayah: 19, Ayah: 20 & Ayah: 21

﴿ إِنَّ عَلَيْنَا لَلْهُدَىٰ ﴾

12. Truly! On Us it is (to give) guidance.

﴿ وَإِنَّ لَنَا لَلْآخِرَةَ وَالْأُولَىٰ ﴾

13. And truly, unto Us (belong) the last (Hereafter) and the first (this world).

﴿ فَأَنذَرْتُكُمْ نَارًا تَلَظَّىٰ ﴾

14. Therefore I have warned you of a blazing Fire (Hell).

﴿ لَا يَصْلَاهَا إِلَّا الْأَشْقَى ﴾

15. None shall enter it save the most wretched.

﴿ الَّذِى كَذَّبَ وَتَوَلَّىٰ ﴾

16. Who denies and turns away.

﴿ وَسَيُجَنَّبُهَا ٱلْأَتْقَى ۝ ﴾

17. And Al-Muttaqûn (the pious and righteous - see V.2:2) will be far removed from it (Hell).

﴿ ٱلَّذِى يُؤْتِى مَالَهُۥ يَتَزَكَّىٰ ۝ ﴾

18. He who spends his wealth for increase in self-purification,

﴿ وَمَا لِأَحَدٍ عِندَهُۥ مِن نِّعْمَةٍ تُجْزَىٰٓ ۝ ﴾

19. And who has (in mind) no favor from anyone to be paid back,

﴿ إِلَّا ٱبْتِغَآءَ وَجْهِ رَبِّهِ ٱلْأَعْلَىٰ ۝ ﴾

20. Except to seek the Countenance of his Lord, the Most High.

﴿ وَلَسَوْفَ يَرْضَىٰ ۝ ﴾

21. He surely will be pleased (when he will enter Paradise).

Transliteration

12. Inna AAalayna lalhuda   13. Wa-inna lana lal-akhirata waal-oola   14. Faanthartukum naran talaththa   15. La yaslaha illa al-ashqa   16. Allathee kaththaba watawalla 17. Wasayujannabuha al-atqa   18. Allathee yu/tee malahu yatazakka   19. Wama li-ahadin AAindahu min niAAmatin tujza   20. Illa ibtighaa wajhi rabbihi al-aAAla 21. Walasawfa yarda

Tafsir Ibn Kathir

The Matter of Guidance and other than it is in the Hand of Allah, and Allah's Warning about the Hellfire

Qatadah said,

(Truly, on Us is (to give) guidance.) "This means, We will explain what is lawful and what is prohibited." Others have said that it means, "Whoever traverses upon the path of guidance, then he will reach Allah (i.e., in the Hereafter)." They consider this Ayah like Allah's saying,

(And upon Allah is the responsibility to explain the Straight path.) (16:9) This has been mentioned by Ibn Jarir. Allah said;

(And truly, unto Us (belong) the last (Hereafter) and the first (this world).) This means, `they both belong to Us and I (Allah) am in complete control of them.' Then Allah says,

(Therefore I have warned you of a Fire Talazza.) Mujahid said, "Blazing." Imam Ahmad recorded from Simak bin Harb that he heard An-Nu`man bin Bashir giving a sermon, in which he said, "I heard the Messenger of Allah giving a sermon, in which he said:

»أَنْذَرْتُكُمُ النَّارَ«

(I have warned you of the Fire.) And he said it in such a voice that if a man was in the marketplace he could hear it from where I am standing now. And he said it (with such force) that the garment that was on his shoulder fell down to his feet." Imam Ahmad recorded from Abu Ishaq that he heard An-Nu`man bin Bashir giving a sermon, in which he said, "I heard the Messenger of Allah saying,

»إِنَّ أَهْوَنَ أَهْلِ النَّارِ عَذَابًا يَوْمَ الْقِيَامَةِ رَجُلٌ تُوضَعُ فِي أَخْمَصِ قَدَمَيْهِ جَمْرَتَانِ يَغْلِي مِنْهُمَا دِمَاغُهُ«

(Verily, the person to be punished lightest of the people of the Fire on the Day of Judgement will be a man who will have placed on the soles of his feet two coals that will cause his brain to boil.)" Imam Al-Bukhari also recorded this narration. Muslim recorded that Abu Ishaq narrated from An-Nu`man bin Bashir that the Messenger of Allah said,

»إِنَّ أَهْوَنَ أَهْلِ النَّارِ عَذَابًا مَنْ لَهُ نَعْلَانِ وَشِرَاكَانِ مِنْ نَارٍ يَغْلِي مِنْهُمَا دِمَاغُهُ كَمَا يَغْلِي الْمِرْجَلُ، مَا يَرَى أَنَّ أَحَدًا أَشَدُّ مِنْهُ عَذَابًا، وَإِنَّهُ لَأَهْوَنُهُمْ عَذَابًا«

(Verily, the lightest punishment received by the people of the Hellfire will be a man who will have two sandals whose straps will be made of fire that will cause his brain to boil just as a cauldron boils. Yet he will not think that anyone is receiving a torment more severe than him, even though he will be receiving the lightest punishment of them.) Allah says,

Chapter 92: Al-Lail (The Night), Verses 001-021

(None shall enter it save the most wretched.) meaning, none will enter surrounded by it on all sides except the most wretched. Then Allah explains who this (the most wretched) is by His saying,

(Who denies) meaning, in his heart.

(and turns away.) meaning, from acting with his limbs and performing deeds according to their pillars. Imam Ahmad recorded from Abu Hurayrah that the Messenger of Allah said,

«كُلُّ أُمَّتِي يَدْخُلُ الْجَنَّةَ يَوْمَ الْقِيَامَةِ إِلَّا مَنْ أَبَى»

(All of my followers will enter Paradise on the Day of Judgement except for whoever refuses.) They (the Companions) said, "Who would refuse, O Messenger of Allah" He replied,

«مَنْ أَطَاعَنِي دَخَلَ الْجَنَّةَ، وَمَنْ عَصَانِي فَقَدْ أَبَى»

(Whoever obeys me, he will enter Paradise, and whoever disobeys me, then he has refused.) Al-Bukhari also recorded this Hadith. Allah then says,

(And those with Taqwa will be far removed from it.) meaning, the righteous, pure, most pious person will be saved from the Fire. Then He explains who he is by His saying,

(He who gives of his wealth for self-purification.) meaning, he spends his wealth in obedience of his Lord in order to purify himself, his wealth and whatever Allah has bestowed upon him of religion and worldly things.

(And who has (in mind) no favor from anyone to be paid back.) meaning, giving his wealth is not done so that he may gain some favor from someone wherein they return some good to him, and therefore he gives to get something in return. He only spends his wealth

(to seek the Face of his Lord, the Most High) meaning, hoping to attain the blessing of seeing Him in the final abode in the Gardens of Paradise. Allah then says,

(He, surely, will be pleased.) meaning, indeed those with these characteristics will be pleased.

The Cause of this Revelation and the Virtue of Abu Bakr

Many of the scholars of Tafsir have mentioned that these Ayat were revealed about Abu Bakr As-Siddiq. Some of them even mentioned that there is a consensus among the Qur'anic commentators concerning this. There is no doubt that he is included in the meaning of these Ayat, and that he is the most deserving of the Ummah to be described with these characteristics in general, for indeed, the wording of these Ayat is general. As in Allah's saying,

(And those with Taqwa will be far removed from it. He who gives of his wealth for self-purification. And who has (in mind) no favor from anyone to be paid back.) However, he (Abu Bakr) was the first and foremost of this Ummah to have all of these characteristics and other praiseworthy characteristics as well. For verily, he was truthful, pious, generous, charitable, and he always spent his wealth in obedience of His Master (Allah) and in aiding the Messenger of Allah . How many Dirhams and Dinars did he spend seeking the Face of His Most Noble Lord. And did not consider any of the people as owning him some favor that he needed to get compensation for. Rather, his virtue and kindness was even shown towards leaders and chiefs from all the other tribes as well. This is why `Urwah bin Mas`ud, who was the chief of the Thaqif tribe, said to him on the day of the Treaty of Hudaybiyyah, "By Allah, if I did not owe you a debt, which I have not paid you back for, I would have responded to you (i.e., your call to Islam)." Abu Bakr As-Siddiq became angry with him for saying such a thing (i.e., I owe you something). So if this was his position with the chiefs of the Arabs and the heads of the tribes, then what about those other than them. Thus, Allah says,

(And who has (in mind) no favor from anyone to be paid back. Except to seek the Face of his Lord, the Most High. He, surely, will be pleased.) And in the Two Sahihs it is recorded that the Messenger of Allah said,

«مَنْ أَنْفَقَ زَوْجَيْنِ فِي سَبِيلِ اللهِ دَعَتْهُ خَزَنَةُ الْجَنَّةِ يَاعَبْدَاللهِ، هَذَا خَيْرٌ»

(Whoever equipped two riding animals in the way of Allah, the Gatekeepers of Paradise will call to him saying, "O servant of Allah! This is good.") So Abu Bakr said, "O Messenger of Allah! The one who is called from them will not have any need. Will there be anyone who will be called from all of them" The Prophet replied,

«نَعَمْ، وَأَرْجُو أَنْ تَكُونَ مِنْهُم»

(Yes, and I hope that you will be one of them.) This is the end of the Tafsir of Surat Al-Layl, and all praise and thanks are due to Allah.

CHAPTER (SURAH) 93: AD-DHUHA (THE MORNING HOURS, MORNING BRIGHT), VERSES 001- 011

Surah: 93 Ayah: 1, Ayah: 2, Ayah: 3, Ayah: 4, Ayah: 5, Ayah: 6, Ayah: 7, Ayah: 8, Ayah: 9, Ayah: 10 & Ayah: 11

(بِسْمِ اللهِ الرَّحْمَنِ الرَّحِيمِ)

In the Name of Allah, the Most Gracious, the Most Merciful.

﴿ وَٱلضُّحَىٰ ۝ ﴾

1. By the forenoon (after sunrise).

﴿ وَٱلَّيْلِ إِذَا سَجَىٰ ۝ ﴾

2. And by the night when it darkens (and stand still).

﴿ مَا وَدَّعَكَ رَبُّكَ وَمَا قَلَىٰ ۝ ﴾

3. Your Lord (O Muhammad (peace be upon him)) has neither forsaken you nor hates you.

﴿ وَلَلْآخِرَةُ خَيْرٌ لَّكَ مِنَ ٱلْأُولَىٰ ۝ ﴾

4. And indeed the Hereafter is better for you than the present (life of this world).

﴿ وَلَسَوْفَ يُعْطِيكَ رَبُّكَ فَتَرْضَىٰ ۝ ﴾

5. And verily, your Lord will give you (all good) so that you shall be well-pleased.

﴿ أَلَمْ يَجِدْكَ يَتِيمًا فَـَٔاوَىٰ ۝ ﴾

6. Did He not find you (O Muhammad (peace be upon him)) an orphan and gave you a refuge?

﴿ وَوَجَدَكَ ضَآلًّا فَهَدَىٰ ۝ ﴾

7. And He found you unaware (of the Qur'ân, its laws, and Prophethood) and guided you?

﴿ وَوَجَدَكَ عَآئِلًا فَأَغْنَىٰ ۝ ﴾

8. And He found you poor and made you rich (self-sufficient with self-contentment)?

﴿ فَأَمَّا ٱلْيَتِيمَ فَلَا تَقْهَرْ ۝ ﴾

9. Therefore, treat not the orphan with oppression.

﴿ وَأَمَّا ٱلسَّآئِلَ فَلَا تَنْهَرْ ۝ ﴾

10. And repulse not the beggar.

﴿ وَأَمَّا بِنِعْمَةِ رَبِّكَ فَحَدِّثْ ۝ ﴾

11. And proclaim the Grace of your Lord (i.e. the Prophethood and all other Graces).

Transliteration

1. Waaldduha 2. Waallayli itha saja 3. Ma waddaAAaka rabbuka wama qala 4. Walal-akhiratu khayrun laka mina al-oola 5. Walasawfa yuAAteeka rabbuka fatarda 6. Alam yajidka yateeman faawa 7. Wawajadaka dallan fahada 8. Wawajadaka AAa-ilan faaghna 9. Faamma alyateema fala taqhar 10. Waamma alssa-ila fala tanhar 11. Waamma biniAAmati rabbika fahaddith

Tafsir Ibn Kathir

The Reason for the Revelation of Surat Ad-Duha

Imam Ahmad recorded from Jundub that he said, "The Prophet became ill, so he did not stand for prayer for a night or two. Then a woman came and said, `O Muhammad! I think that your devil has finally left you.' So Allah revealed,

(By the forenoon. By the night when it darkens. Your Lord has neither forsaken you nor hates you.)" Al-Bukhari, Muslim, At-Tirmidhi, An-Nasa'i, Ibn Abi Hatim and Ibn Jarir, all recorded this Hadith. This Jundub (who narrated it) is Ibn `Abdullah Al-Bajali Al-`Alaqi. In a narration from Al-Aswad bin Qays, he said that he heard Jundub say that Jibril was slow in coming to the Messenger of Allah . So the idolators said, "Muhammad's Lord has abandoned him." So Allah revealed,

(By the forenoon. By the night when it darkens. Your Lord has neither forsaken you nor hates you.)

(By the forenoon. By the night when it darkens.) Al-`Awfi reported from Ibn `Abbas, "When the Qur'an was revealed to the Messenger of Allah , Jibril was delayed from coming to him for a number of days (on one occasion). Therefore, the Messenger of Allah was affected by this. Then the idolators began to say, `His Lord has abandoned him and hates him.' So Allah revealed,

(Your Lord has neither forsaken you nor hates you.)" In this, Allah is swearing by the forenoon and the light that He has placed in it.

(By the night when it darkens (Saja).) meaning, it settles, darkens meaning, it settles, darkens and overcomes them. This was said by Mujahid, Qatadah, Ad-Dahhak, Ibn Zayd and others. This is a clear proof of the power of the Creator of this (light) and that (darkness). This is as Allah says,

(By the night as it envelops. By the Day as it appears.) (92:1-2) Allah also says,

((He is the) Cleaver of the daybreak. He has appointed the night for resting, and the sun and the moon for reckoning. Such is the measuring of the Almighty, the All-Knowing.) (6:96) Allah then says,

(Your Lord has neither forsaken you) meaning, `He has not abandoned you.'

(nor hates (Qala) you.) meaning, `He does not hate you.'

The Hereafter is Better Than This First Life

(And indeed the Hereafter is better for you than the present.) meaning, the abode of the Hereafter is better for you than this current abode. For this reason the Messenger of Allah used to be the most abstinent of the people concerning the worldly things, and he was the greatest of them in his disregard for worldly matters. This is well known by necessity from his biography. When the Prophet was given the choice at the end of his life between remaining in this life forever and then going to Paradise, or moving on to the company of Allah, he chose that which is with Allah over this lowly world. Imam Ahmad recorded that `Abdullah bin Mas`ud said, "The Messenger of Allah was lying down on a straw mat and it left marks on his side. Then when he woke up he began to rub his side. So I said, `O Messenger of Allah! Will you allow us to spread something soft over this straw mat' He replied,

«مَالِي وَلِلدُّنْيَا، إِنَّمَا مَثَلِي وَمَثَلُ الدُّنْيَا كَرَاكِبٍ ظَلَّ تَحْتَ شَجَرَةٍ ثُمَّ رَاحَ وَتَرَكَهَا»

(I have nothing to do with this world. The parable of me and this world is like a rider who rests in the shade of a tree, then he passes on and leaves it.)" At-Tirmidhi and Ibn Majah both recorded this Hadith by way of Al-Mas`udi. At-Tirmidhi said, "Hasan Sahih."

The Numerous Bounties of the Hereafter are waiting for the Messenger of Allah

Then Allah says,

(And verily, your Lord will give you so that you shall be well-pleased.) meaning, in the final abode Allah will give him until He pleases him concerning his followers, and in that which He has prepared for him from His generosity. From this will be the River of Al-Kawthar, which will have domes of hollowed pearls on its banks, and the mud on its banks will be the strongest frangrance of musk, as will be mentioned. Imam Abu

`Amr Al-Awza`i recorded that Ibn `Abbas said, "The Messenger of Allah was shown that which his Ummah would be blessed with after him, treasure upon treasure. So he was pleased with that. Then Allah revealed,

(And verily, your Lord will give you so that you shall be well-pleased.) So, Allah will give him in Paradise one million palaces, and each palace will contain whatever he wishes of wives and servants." This was recorded by Ibn Jarir and Ibn Abi Hatim from his route of transmission. This chain of narration is authentic to Ibn `Abbas, and statements like this can only be said from that which is Tawqif.

A Mention of some of Allah's Favors upon the Messenger Enumerating His favors upon His Messenger, Muhammad

Allah says;

(Did He not find you an orphan and gave you a refuge) This refers to the fact that his father died while his mother was still pregnant with him, and his mother, Aminah bint Wahb died when he was only six years old. After this he was under the guardianship of his grandfather, `Abdul-Muttalib, until he died when Muhammad was eight years old. Then his uncle, Abu Talib took responsibility for him and continued to protect him, assist him, elavate his status, honor him, and even restrain his people from harming him when he was forty years of age and Allah commissioned him with the prophethood. Even with this, Abu Talib continued to follow the religion of his people, worshipping idols. All of this took place by the divine decree of Allah and His decree is most excellent. Until Abu Talib died a short time before the Hijrah. After this (Abu Talib's death) the foolish and ignorant people of the Quraysh began to attack him, so Allah chose for him to migrate away from them to the city of Al-Aws and Al-Khazraj among those who helped him (in Al-Madinah). Allah caused his Sunnah to be spread in the most perfect and complete manner. Then, when he arrived at their city, they gave him shelter, supported him, defended him and fought before him (against the enemies of Islam) -- may Allah be pleased with all of them. All of this was from Allah's protection for him, guarding over him and caring for him. Then Allah says,

(He found you unaware and guided you) This is similar to Allah's saying,

(And thus We have sent to you a Ruh from Our command. you knew not what is the Book, nor what is Faith. But We have made it a light wherewith We guide whosoever of our servants We will...) (42:52) Allah says,

(And He found you poor and made you rich) meaning, `you were poor having dependents, so Allah made you wealthy and independent of all others besides Him.' Thus, Allah combined for him the two positions: the one who is poor and patient, and the one who is wealthy and thankful. In the Two Sahihs it has been recorded from Abu Hurayrah that the Messenger of Allah said,

«لَيْسَ الْغِنَى عَنْ كَثْرَةِ الْعَرَضِ، وَلَكِنَّ الْغِنَى غِنَى النَّفْسِ»

(Wealth is not determined by abundance of possessions, but wealth is the richness of the soul.) In Sahih Muslim, it is recorded from `Abdullah bin `Amr that the Messenger of Allah said,

«قَدْ أَفْلَحَ مَنْ أَسْلَمَ وَرُزِقَ كَفَافًا وَقَنَّعَهُ اللهُ بِمَا آتَاه»

(Whoever accepts Islam, is provided with his basic needs, and Allah makes him content with what He has given him, then he will be successful.)

How should this Bounty be responded to

Then Allah says, (Therefore, treat not the orphan with oppression.) meaning, `just as you were an orphan and Allah sheltered you, then do not oppress the orphan.' In other words, `do not humiliate him, scorn him or despise him. Rather, you should be kind and gentle to him.' Qatadah said, "Be like a merciful father to the orphan."

(And repulse not the one who asks.) meaning, `just as you were astray and Allah guided you, then do not scorn the one who asks for knowledge seeking to be guided.' Ibn Ishaq said, (And repulse not the one who asks.) "This means do not be oppressive, arrogant, wicked, or mean to the weak among Allah's servants." Qatadah said, "This means respond to the poor with mercy and gentleness."

(And proclaim the grace of your Lord.) meaning, `just as you were poor and needy, and Allah made you wealthy, then tell about Allah's favor upon you.' Abu Dawud recorded from Abu Hurayrah that the Prophet said,

«لَا يَشْكُرُ اللهَ مَنْ لَا يَشْكُرُ النَّاس»

(Whoever is not thankful to the people, then he is not thankful to Allah.) At-Tirmidhi also recorded this Hadith and he said, "Sahih". Abu Dawud recorded from Jabir that the Prophet said,

«مَنْ أُبْلِيَ بَلَاءً فَذَكَرَهُ فَقَدْ شَكَرَهُ، وَمَنْ كَتَمَهُ فَقَدْ كَفَرَه»

(Whoever overcomes some test (i.e., calamity) and mentions it (to others), then he is indeed thankful. And whoever conceals it, then indeed he was ungrateful.) Abu Dawud was alone in recording this Hadith. This is the end of the Tafsir of Surat Ad-Duha, and unto Allah is due all praise and thanks.

CHAPTER 94: AL-INSHIRAH (SOLACE, CONSOLATION, RELIEF), VERSES 001- 008

Surah: 94 Ayah: 1, Ayah: 2, Ayah: 3, Ayah: 4, Ayah: 5, Ayah: 6, Ayah: 7 & Ayah: 8

﴿بِسْمِ اللَّهِ الرَّحْمَـٰنِ الرَّحِيمِ﴾

In the Name of Allah, the Most Gracious, the Most Merciful.

﴿أَلَمْ نَشْرَحْ لَكَ صَدْرَكَ ۝﴾

1. Have We not opened your breast for you (O Muhammad (peace be upon him))

﴿وَوَضَعْنَا عَنكَ وِزْرَكَ ۝﴾

2. And removed from you your burden.

﴿ٱلَّذِىٓ أَنقَضَ ظَهْرَكَ ۝﴾

3. Which weighed down your back?

﴿وَرَفَعْنَا لَكَ ذِكْرَكَ ۝﴾

4. And have We raised high your fame?

﴿فَإِنَّ مَعَ ٱلْعُسْرِ يُسْرًا ۝﴾

5. Verily, along with every hardship is relief,

﴿إِنَّ مَعَ ٱلْعُسْرِ يُسْرًا ۝﴾

6. Verily, along with every hardship is relief (i.e. there is one hardship with two reliefs, so one hardship cannot overcome two reliefs).

Chapter 94: Al-Inshirah (Solace, Consolation, Relief), Verses 001-008

$$\{ \text{فَإِذَا فَرَغْتَ فَانصَبْ} \; \textcircled{\tiny 7} \}$$

7. So when you have finished (your occupation), devote yourself for Allâh's worship.

$$\{ \text{وَإِلَىٰ رَبِّكَ فَارْغَب} \; \textcircled{\tiny 8} \}$$

8. And to your Lord (Alone) turn (all your) intentions and hopes.

Transliteration

1. Alam nashrah laka sadraka   2. WawadaAAna AAanka wizraka   3. Allathee anqada thahraka   4. WarafaAAna laka thikraka   5. Fa-inna maAAa alAAusri yusran   6. Inna maAAa alAAusri yusran   7. Fa-itha faraghta fainsab   8. Wa-ila rabbika fairghab

Tafsir Ibn Kathir

The Meaning of opening the Breast

Allah says,

(Have We not opened your breast for you) meaning, `have We not opened your chest for you.' This means, `We illuminated it, and We made it spacious, vast and wide.' This is as Allah says,

(And whomsoever Allah wills to guide, He opens his breast to Islam.) (6:125) And just as Allah expanded his chest, He also made His Law vast, wide, accommodating and easy, containing no difficulty, hardship or burden.

A Discussion of Allah's Favor upon His Messenger Concerning Allah's statement,

(And removed from you your burden.) This means

(That Allah may forgive you your sins of the past and the future.) (48:2)

(Which weighed down your back) Al-Inqad means the sound. And more than one of the Salaf has said concerning Allah's saying,

(Which weighed down your back) meaning, `its burden weighed heavy upon you.'

INTRODUCTION TO CHAPTER (SURAH) 95: AT-TIN (THE FIG, THE FIGTREE)

Ibn Kathir's Introduction

The Recitation of Surat At-Tin in the Prayer while traveling

Malik and Shu`bah narrated from `Adi bin Thabit, who narrated that Al-Bara' bin `Azib said, "The Prophet used to recite in one of his Rak`ahs while traveling `At-Tin waz-Zaytun' (Surat At-Tin), and I have never heard anyone with a nicer voice or recitation than him." The Group has recorded this Hadith in their books.

CHAPTER (SURAH) 95: AT-TIN (THE FIG, THE FIGTREE), VERSES 001- 008

Surah: 95 Ayah: 1, Ayah: 2, Ayah: 3, Ayah: 4, Ayah: 5, Ayah: 6, Ayah: 7 & Ayah: 8

(بِسْمِ اللَّهِ الرَّحْمَـنِ الرَّحِيمِ)

In the Name of Allah, the Most Gracious, the Most Merciful.

﴿ وَٱلتِّينِ وَٱلزَّيْتُونِ ۝ ﴾

1. By the fig, and the olive.

﴿ وَطُورِ سِينِينَ ۝ ﴾

2. By Mount Sinai.

﴿ وَهَـذَا ٱلْبَلَدِ ٱلْأَمِينِ ۝ ﴾

3. By this city of security (Makkah).

﴿ لَقَدْ خَلَقْنَا ٱلْإِنسَـٰنَ فِىٓ أَحْسَنِ تَقْوِيمٍ ۝ ﴾

4. Verily, We created man in the best stature (mould).

﴿ ثُمَّ رَدَدْنَٰهُ أَسْفَلَ سَٰفِلِينَ ۝ ﴾

5. Then We reduced him to the lowest of the low.

﴿ إِلَّا ٱلَّذِينَ ءَامَنُواْ وَعَمِلُواْ ٱلصَّٰلِحَٰتِ فَلَهُمْ أَجْرٌ غَيْرُ مَمْنُونٍ ۝ ﴾

6. Save those who believe (in Islâmic Monotheism) and do righteous deeds. Then they shall have a reward without end (Paradise).

﴿ فَمَا يُكَذِّبُكَ بَعْدُ بِٱلدِّينِ ۝ ﴾

7. Then what (or who) causes you (O disbelievers) to deny the Recompense (i.e. Day of Resurrection)?

﴿ أَلَيْسَ ٱللَّهُ بِأَحْكَمِ ٱلْحَٰكِمِينَ ۝ ﴾

8. Is not Allâh the Best of judges?

Transliteration

1. Waalttteeni waalzzaytooni 2. Watoori seeneena 3. Wahatha albaladi al-ameeni 4. Laqad khalaqna al-insana fee ahsani taqweemin 5. Thumma radadnahu asfala safileena 6. Illa allatheena amanoo waAAamiloo alssalihati falahum ajrun ghayru mamnoonin 7. Fama yukaththibuka baAAdu bialddeeni 8. Alaysa Allahu bi-ahkami alhakimeena

Tafsir Ibn Kathir

The Explanation of At-Tin and what comes after it

Al-`Awfi reported from Ibn `Abbas that what is meant by At-Tin is the Masjid of Nuh that was built upon Mount Al-Judi. Mujahid said, "It is this fig that you have."

(By Az-Zaytun.) Ka`b Al-Ahbar, Qatadah, Ibn Zayd and others have said, "It is the Masjid of Jerusalem (Bayt Al-Maqdis)." Mujahid and `Ikrimah said, "It is this olive which you press (to extract the oil)."

(By Tur Sinin.) Ka`b Al-Ahbar and several others have said, "It is the mountain upon which Allah spoke to Musa."

(By this city of security.) meaning Makkah. This was said by Ibn `Abbas, Mujahid, `Ikrimah, Al-Hasan, Ibrahim An-Nakha`i, Ibn Zayd and Ka`b Al-Ahbar. There is no difference of opinion about this. Some of the Imams have said that these are three different places, and that Allah sent a Messenger to each of them from the Leading Messengers, who delivered the Great Codes of Law. The first place is that of the fig and the olive, which was Jerusalem, where Allah sent `Isa bin Maryam. The second place is Mount Sinin, which is Mount Sinai where Allah spoke to Musa bin `Imran. The third place is Makkah, and it is the city of security where whoever enters is safe. It is also the city in which Muhammad was sent. They have said that these three places are mentioned at the end of the Tawrah. The verse says, "Allah has come from Mount Sinai - meaning the one upon which Allah spoke to Musa bin `Imran; and shined from Sa`ir - meaning the mountain of Jerusalem from which Allah sent `Isa; and appeared from the mountains of Faran - meaning the mountains of Makkah from which Allah sent `Isa; and appeared from the mountains of Faran - meaning the mountains of Makkah from which Allah sent Muhammad ." Thus, He mentioned them in order to inform about them based upon their order of existence in time. This is why He swore by a noble place, then by a nobler place, and then by a place that is the nobler than both of them.

Man becoming Lowly even though He was created in the Best Form

and the Result of that Allah says,

(Verily, We created man in the best form.) This is the subject being sworn about, and it is that Allah created man in the best image and form, standing upright with straight limbs that He beautified.

(Then We reduced him to the lowest of the low.) meaning, to the Hellfire. This was said by Mujahid, Abu Al-`Aliyah, Al-Hasan, Ibn Zayd and others. Then after this attractiveness and beauty, their destination will be to the Hell-fire if they disobey Allah and belie the Messengers. This is why Allah says,

(Save those who believe and do righteous deeds.) Some have said,

(Then We reduced him to the lowest of the low.) "This means decrepit old age." This has been reported from Ibn `Abbas and `Ikrimah. `Ikrimah even said, "Whoever gathers the Qur'an (i.e., he memorizes it all), then he will not be returned to decrepit old age." Ibn Jarir preferred this explanation. Even if this was the meaning, it would not be correct to exclude the believers from this, because some of them are also overcome by the senility of old age. Thus, the meaning here is what we have already mentioned (i.e., the first view), which is similar to Allah's saying,

(By Al-`Asr. Verily man is in loss, except those who believe and perform righteous deeds.) (103:1-3) Concerning Allah's statement, (Then they shall have a reward without end.) meaning, that will not end, as we have mentioned previously. Then Allah says, (Then what causes you to deny) meaning, `O Son of Adam!'

(after this the Recompense) meaning, `in the recompense that will take place in the Hereafter. For indeed you know the beginning, and you know that He Who is able to begin (the creation) is also able to repeat it which is easier. So what is it that makes you deny the final return in the Hereafter after you have known this' Then Allah says,

Chapter 95: At-Tin (The Fig, The Figtree), Verses 001-008

(Is not the Allah the best of judges) meaning, `is He not the best of judges, Who does not oppress or do any injustice to anyone' And from His justice is that He will establish the Judgement, and He will give retribution to the person who was wronged in this life against whoever wronged him. This is the end of the Tafsir of Surat wat-Tin waz-Zaytun and all praise and thanks are due to Allah.

CHAPTER (SURAH) 96: AL-ALAQ (THE CLOT, READ), VERSES 001-019

Surah: 96 Ayah: 1, Ayah: 2, Ayah: 3, Ayah: 4 & Ayah: 5

(بِسْمِ اللَّهِ الرَّحْمَـنِ الرَّحِيمِ)

In the Name of Allah, the Most Gracious, the Most Merciful.

﴿ اقْرَأْ بِاسْمِ رَبِّكَ الَّذِى خَلَقَ ۝ ﴾

1. Read! In the Name of your Lord Who has created (all that exists).

﴿ خَلَقَ الْإِنسَـنَ مِنْ عَلَقٍ ۝ ﴾

2. He has created man from a clot (a piece of thick coagulated blood).

﴿ اقْرَأْ وَرَبُّكَ الْأَكْرَمُ ۝ ﴾

3. Read! And your Lord is the Most Generous.

﴿ الَّذِى عَلَّمَ بِالْقَلَمِ ۝ ﴾

4. Who has taught (the writing) by the pen.

﴿ عَلَّمَ الْإِنسَـنَ مَا لَمْ يَعْلَمْ ۝ ﴾

5. He has taught man that which he knew not.

Transliteration

1. Iqra/ bi-ismi rabbika allathee khalaqa 2. Khalaqa al-insana min AAalaqin 3. Iqra/ warabbuka al-akramu 4. Allathee AAallama bialqalami 5. AAallama al-insana ma lam yaAAlam

Tafsir Ibn Kathir

The Beginning of the Prophethood of Muhammad and the First of the Qur'an revealed

Imam Ahmad recorded that `A'ishah said: The first thing that began happening with the Messenger of Allah from the revelation was dreams that he would see in his sleep that would come true. He would not see any dream except that it would come true just like the (clearness of) the daybreak in the morning. Then seclusion became beloved to him. So, he used to go to the cave of Hira' and devote himself to worship there for a number of nights, and he would bring provisions for that. Then he would return to Khadijah and replenish his provisions for a similar number of nights. This continued until the revelation suddenly came to him while he was in the cave of Hira'. The angel came to him while he was in the cave and said, "Read!" The Messen- ger of Allah said,

《فَقُلْتُ: مَا أَنَا بِقَارِىءٍ》

(I replied: "I am not one who reads.) Then he said, "So he (the angel) seized me and pressed me until I could no longer bear it. Then he released me and said: `Read!' So I replied: `I am not one who reads.' So, he pressed me a second time until I could no longer bear it. Then he released me and said:

(Read in the Name of your Lord who has created.) until he reached the Ayah,

(That which he knew not.)" So he returned with them (those Ayat) and with his heart trembling until he came (home) to Khadijah, and he said,

《زَمِّلُونِي زَمِّلُونِي》

(Wrap me up, wrap me up!) So they wrapped him up until his fear went away. After that he told Khadijah everything that had happened (and said),

《قَدْ خَشِيتُ عَلَى نَفْسِي》

(I fear that something may happen to me.) Khadijah replied, "Never! By Allah, Allah will never disgrace you. You keep good relations with your relatives, you speak the truth, you help the poor and the destitute, you serve your guests generously, and you help the deserving, calamity afflicted people." Khadijah then accompanied him to her cousin Waraqah bin Nawfal bin Asad bin `Abdul-`Uzza bin Qusay, who, during the period of ignorance became a Christian and used to scribe the Scriptures in Arabic. He would write from the Injil in Hebrew as much as Allah willed for him to write. He was an old man and had lost his eyesight. Khadijah said to him, "O my cousin! Listen to the story of your nephew." Waraqah asked, "O my nephew! What have you seen" Allah's Messenger described what he saw. Waraqah said, "This is An-Namus whom

Allah had sent to Musa. I wish I was young and could live until the time when your people would drive you out." Allah's Messenger asked,

«أَوَ مُخْرِجِيَّ هُمْ؟»

(Will they drive me out) Waraqah replied in the affirmative and said, "Anyone who came with something similar to what you have brought, was treated with hostility and enmity; and if I should remain alive till that day then I would firmly support you." But Waraqah did not remain. He died and the revelation paused until Allah's Messenger became sad according to what we were told. Due to this grief he set out a number of times with the intent of throwing himself from the mountain tops. However, every time he would reach the peak of a mountain to throw himself from it, Jibril would appear to him and say, "O Muhammad! You are truly the Messenger of Allah!" Therefore, his worry would be eased, his soul would be settled and he would return (down from the mountain). Then, when the revelation did not come again for a long time, he set out as he had done before. So when he reached the peak of the mountain, Jibril appeared to him again and said to him the same as he had said before." This Hadith has been recorded in the Two Sahihs by way of Az-Zuhri. We have already discussed this Hadith's chain of narration, its text and its meanings at length in the beginning of our explanation of Sahih Al-Bukhari. Therefore, whoever would like to read it, it is researched there, and all praise and blessings are due to Allah. So the first thing that was revealed of the Qur'an were these noble and blessed Ayat. They are the first mercy that Allah bestowed upon His servants and the first bounty that Allah favored them with.

The Honor and Nobility of Man is in His Knowledge

These Ayat inform of the beginning of man's creation from a dangling clot, and that out of Allah's generosity He taught man that which he did not know. Thus, Allah exalted him and honored him by giving him knowledge, and it is the dignity that the Father of Humanity, Adam, was distinguished with over the angels. Knowledge sometimes is in the mind, sometimes on the tongue, and sometimes in writing with the fingers. Thus, it may be intellectual, spoken and written. And while the last (written) necessitates the first two (intellectual and spoken), the reverse is not true. For this reason Allah says, (Read! And your Lord is the Most Generous. Who has taught by the pen. He has taught man that which he knew not.) There is a narration that states, "Record knowledge by writing." There is also a saying which states, "Whoever acts according to what he knows, Allah will make him inherit knowledge that he did not know."

Surah: 96 Ayah: 6, Ayah: 7, Ayah: 8, Ayah: 9, Ayah: 10, Ayah: 11, Ayah: 12, Ayah: 13, Ayah: 14, Ayah: 15, Ayah: 16, Ayah: 17, Ayah: 18 & Ayah: 19

﴿ كَلَّا إِنَّ ٱلْإِنسَٰنَ لَيَطْغَىٰٓ ۝ ﴾

6. Nay! Verily, man does transgress (in disbelief and evil deed).

﴿ أَن رَّءَاهُ ٱسْتَغْنَىٰٓ ۝ ﴾

7. Because he considers himself self-sufficient.

﴿ إِنَّ إِلَىٰ رَبِّكَ ٱلرُّجْعَىٰٓ ۝ ﴾

8. Surely, unto your Lord is the return.

﴿ أَرَءَيْتَ ٱلَّذِى يَنْهَىٰ ۝ ﴾

9. Have you (O Muhammad (peace be upon him)) seen him (i.e. Abû Jahl) who prevents

﴿ عَبْدًا إِذَا صَلَّىٰٓ ۝ ﴾

10. A slave (Muhammad (peace be upon him)) when he prays?

﴿ أَرَءَيْتَ إِن كَانَ عَلَى ٱلْهُدَىٰٓ ۝ ﴾

11. Tell me if he (Muhammad (peace be upon him)) is on the guidance (of Allâh)?

﴿ أَوْ أَمَرَ بِٱلتَّقْوَىٰٓ ۝ ﴾

12. Or enjoins piety?

﴿ أَرَءَيْتَ إِن كَذَّبَ وَتَوَلَّىٰٓ ۝ ﴾

13. Tell me if he (Abû Jahl) denies (the truth, i.e. this Qur'ân), and turns away!

﴿ أَلَمْ يَعْلَم بِأَنَّ ٱللَّهَ يَرَىٰ ۝ ﴾

14. Knows he not that Allâh does see (what he does)?

Chapter 96: Al-Alaq (The Clot, Read), Verses 001-019

﴿ كَلَّا لَئِن لَّمْ يَنتَهِ لَنَسْفَعًا بِالنَّاصِيَةِ ۝ ﴾

15. Nay! If he (Abû Jahl) ceases not, We will catch him by the forelock -

﴿ نَاصِيَةٍ كَاذِبَةٍ خَاطِئَةٍ ۝ ﴾

16. A lying, sinful forelock!

﴿ فَلْيَدْعُ نَادِيَهُ ۝ ﴾

17. Then, let him call upon his council (of helpers).

﴿ سَنَدْعُ الزَّبَانِيَةَ ۝ ﴾

18. We will call out the guards of Hell (to deal with him)!

﴿ كَلَّا لَا تُطِعْهُ وَاسْجُدْ وَاقْتَرِب ۩ ۝ ﴾

19. Nay! (O Muhammad (peace be upon him))! Do not obey him (Abû Jahl). Fall prostrate and draw near to Allâh!

Transliteration

6. Kalla inna al-insana layatgha 7. An raahu istaghna 8. Inna ila rabbika alrrujAAa 9. Araayta allathee yanha 10. AAabdan itha salla 11. Araayta in kana AAala alhuda 12. Aw amara bialttaqwa 13. Araayta in kaththaba watawalla 14. Alam yaAAlam bi-anna Allaha yara 15. Kalla la-in lam yantahi lanasfaAAan bialnnasiyati 16. Nasiyatin kathibatin khati-atin 17. FalyadAAu nadiyahu 18. SanadAAu alzzabaniyata 19. Kalla la tutiAAhu waosjud waiqtarib

Tafsir Ibn Kathir

The Threat against Man's Transgression for the sake of Wealth

Allah informs that man is very pleased, most evil, scornful and transgressive when he considers himself self-sufficient and having an abundance of wealth. Then Allah threatens, warns and admonishes him in His saying,

(Surely, unto your Lord is the return.) meaning, `unto Allah is the final destination and return, and He will hold you accountable for your wealth, as to where you obtained it from and how did you spend it.'

Scolding of Abu Jahl and the Threat of seizing Him

Then Allah says,

(Have you seen him who prevents. A servant when he prays) This was revealed about Abu Jahl, may Allah curse him. He threatened the Prophet for performing Salah at the Ka`bah. Thus, Allah firstly admonished him with that which was better by saying,

(Have you seen if he is on the guidance.) meaning, `do you think this man whom you are preventing is upon the straight path in his action, or

(Or enjoins Taqwa) in his statements Yet, you rebuke him and threaten him due to his prayer.' Thus, Allah says,

(Knows he not that Allah sees) meaning, doesn't this person who is preventing this man who is following correct guidance know that Allah sees him and hears his words, and He will compensate him in full for what he has done Then Allah says by way of warning and threatening,

(Nay! If he ceases not,) meaning, if he does not recant from his discord and obstinacy,

(We will scorch his forehead.) meaning, `indeed We will make it extremely black on the Day of Judgement.' Then He says,

(A lying, sinful forehead!) meaning, the forehead of Abu Jahl is lying in its statements and sinful in its actions.

(Then let him call upon his council.) meaning, his people and his tribe. In other words, let him call them in order to seek help from them.

(We will call out the guards of Hell!) `And they are the angels of torment. This is so that he may know who will win -- Our group or his group' Al-Bukhari recorded that Ibn `Abbas said, "Abu Jahl said, `If I see Muhammad praying at the Ka`bah, I will stomp on his neck.' So this reached the Prophet, who said,

«لَئِنْ فَعَلَ لَأَخَذَتْهُ الْمَلَائِكَةُ»

(If he does, he will be seized by the angels.)" This Hadith was also recorded by At-Tirmidhi and An-Nasa'i in their Books of Tafsir. Likewise, it has been recorded by Ibn Jarir. Ahmad, At-Tirmidhi, An-Nasa'i and Ibn Jarir, all recorded it from Ibn `Abbas with the following wording: "The Messenger of Allah was praying at the Maqam (prayer station of Ibrahim) when Abu Jahl bin Hisham passed by him and said, `O Muhammad! Haven't I prevented you from this' He threatened the Prophet and thus, the Messenger of Allah became angry with him and reprimanded him. Then he said, `O Muhammad! What can you threaten me with By Allah, I have the most kinsmen of this valley with me in the large.' Then Allah revealed,

Chapter 96: Al-Alaq (The Clot, Read), Verses 001-019

(Then let him call upon his council. We will call out the guards of Hell!)" Ibn `Abbas then said, "If he had called his people, the angels of torment would have seized him at that very instant." At-Tirmidhi said, "Hasan Sahih." Ibn Jarir recorded from Abu Hurayrah that Abu Jahl said, "Does Muhammad cover his face with dust (i.e., from prostration) while he is among you all" They (the people) replied, "Yes." Then he said, "By Al-Lat and Al-`Uzza, if I see him praying like this, I will stomp on his neck, and I will certainly put his face in the dust." So the Messenger of Allah came and he began praying, which made it possible for Abu Jahl to stomp on his neck. Then the people became surprised at him (Abu Jahl) because he began retreating on his heels and covering himself with his hands. Then it was said to him, "What's the matter with you" He replied, "Verily, between me and him is a ditch of fire, monsters and wings." Then the Messenger of Allah said,

«لَوْ دَنَا مِنِّي لَاخْتَطَفَتْهُ الْمَلَائِكَةُ عُضْوًا عُضْوًا»

(If he had come near me, the angels would have snatched him limb by limb.) The narrator added; "Allah revealed an Ayah, but I do not know whether it is concerning the Hadith of Abu Hurayrah or not:

(Nay! Verily, man does transgress.) to the end of the Surah." Imam Ahmad bin Hanbal, Muslim, An-Nasa'i and Ibn Abi Hatim all recorded this Hadith.

Amusement for the Prophet

Then Allah says,

(Nay! Do not obey him.) meaning, `O Muhammad! Do not obey him in what he is forbidding from such as steadfastness in worship and performing worship in abundance. Pray wherever you wish and do not worry about him. For indeed Allah will protect you and help you, and He will defend you against the people.'

(Fall prostrate and draw near (to Allah)!) This is just like what has been confirmed in the Sahih of Muslim on the authority of Abu Salih who reported from Abu Hurayrah that the Messenger of Allah said,

«أَقْرَبُ مَا يَكُونُ الْعَبْدُ مِنْ رَبِّهِ وَهُوَ سَاجِدٌ، فَأَكْثِرُوا الدُّعَاءَ»

(The closest that a servant can be to his Lord is when he is in prostration. Therefore, make abundant supplications (i.e., while prostrating).)" It has also been mentioned previously that the Messenger of Allah used to prostrate when he recited

(When the heaven is split asunder.) (84:1) and

(Read! In the Name of your Lord Who has created.) (96:1) This is the end of the Tafsir of Surah Iqra' (Surat Al-`Alaq). Unto Allah is due all praise and thanks, and He is the Giver of success and protection against error.

CHAPTER (SURAH) 97: AL-QADR (POWER, FATE), VERSES 001- 005

Surah: 97 Ayah: 1, Ayah: 2, Ayah: 3, Ayah: 4 & Ayah: 5

$$\text{(بِسْمِ اللَّهِ الرَّحْمَـٰنِ الرَّحِيمِ)}$$

In the Name of Allah, the Most Gracious, the Most Merciful.

$$\text{﴿ إِنَّا أَنزَلْنَاهُ فِي لَيْلَةِ الْقَدْرِ ﴾}$$

1. Verily! We have sent it (this Qur'ân) down in the night of Al-Qadr (Decree)

$$\text{﴿ وَمَا أَدْرَاكَ مَا لَيْلَةُ الْقَدْرِ ﴾}$$

2. And what will make you know what the night of Al-Qadr (Decree) is?

$$\text{﴿ لَيْلَةُ الْقَدْرِ خَيْرٌ مِّنْ أَلْفِ شَهْرٍ ﴾}$$

3. The night of Al-Qadr (Decree) is better than a thousand months (i.e. worshipping Allâh in that night is better than worshipping Him a thousand months, i.e. 83 years and 4 months).

$$\text{﴿ تَنَزَّلُ الْمَلَائِكَةُ وَالرُّوحُ فِيهَا بِإِذْنِ رَبِّهِم مِّن كُلِّ أَمْرٍ ﴾}$$

4. Therein descend the angels and the Rûh (Jibrîl (Gabriel)) by Allâh's Permission with all Decrees,

$$\text{﴿ سَلَامٌ هِيَ حَتَّىٰ مَطْلَعِ الْفَجْرِ ﴾}$$

5. (All that night), there is Peace (and Goodness from Allâh to His believing slaves) until the appearance of dawn.

Transliteration

1. Inna anzalnahu fee laylati alqadri 2. Wama adraka ma laylatu alqadri 3. Laylatu alqadri khayrun min alfi shahrin 4. Tanazzalu almala-ikatu waalrroohu feeha bi-ithni rabbihim min kulli amrin 5. Salamun hiya hatta matlaAAi alfajri

Tafsir Ibn Kathir

The Virtues of the Night of Al-Qadr (the Decree)

Allah informs that He sent the Qur'an down during the Night of Al-Qadr, and it is a blessed night about which Allah says,

(We sent it down on a blessed night.) (44:3) This is the Night of Al-Qadr and it occurs during the month of Ramadan. This is as Allah says,

(The month of Ramadan in which was revealed the Qur'an.) (2:185) Ibn `Abbas and others have said, "Allah sent the Qur'an down all at one time from the Preserved Tablet (Al-Lawh Al-Mahfuz) to the House of Might (Baytul-`Izzah), which is in the heaven of this world. Then it came down in parts to the Messenger of Allah based upon the incidents that occurred over a period of twenty-three years." Then Allah magnified the status of the Night of Al-Qadr, which He chose for the revelation of the Mighty Qur'an, by His saying,

(And what will make you know what the Night of Al-Qadr is The Night of Al-Qadr is better than a thousand months.) Imam Ahmad recorded that Abu Hurayrah "When Ramadan would come, the Messenger of Allah would say,

«قَدْ جَاءَكُمْ شَهْرُ رَمَضَانَ، شَهْرٌ مُبَارَكٌ، افْتَرَضَ اللهُ عَلَيْكُمْ صِيَامَهُ، تُفْتَحُ فِيهِ أَبْوَابُ الْجَنَّةِ، وَتُغْلَقُ فِيهِ أَبْوَابُ الْجَحِيمِ، وَتُغَلُّ فِيهِ الشَّيَاطِينُ، فِيهِ لَيْلَةٌ خَيْرٌ مِنْ أَلْفِ شَهْرٍ، مَنْ حُرِمَ خَيْرَهَا فَقَدْ حُرِمَ»

(Verily, the month of Ramadan has come to you all. It is a blessed month, which Allah has obligated you all to fast. During it the gates of Paradise are opened, the gates of Hell are closed and the devils are shackled. In it there is a night that is better than one thousand months. Whoever is deprived of its good, then he has truly been deprived.)" An-Nasa'i recorded this same Hadith. Aside from the fact that worship during the Night of Al-Qadr is equivalent to worship performed for a period of one thousand months, it is also confirmed in the Two Sahihs from Abu Hurayrah that the Messenger of Allah said,

«مَنْ قَامَ لَيْلَةَ الْقَدْرِ إِيمَانًا وَاحْتِسَابًا غُفِرَ لَهُ مَا تَقَدَّمَ مِنْ ذَنْبِهِ»

(Whoever stands (in prayer) during the Night of Al-Qadr with faith and expecting reward (from Allah), he will be forgiven for his previous sins.)

The Descent of the Angels and the Decree for Every Good during the Night of Al-Qadr

Allah says,

(Therein descend the angels and the Ruh by their Lord's permission with every matter.) meaning, the angels descend in abundance during the Night of Al-Qadr due to its abundant blessings. The angels descend with the descending of blessings and mercy, just as they descend when the Qur'an is recited, they surround the circles of Dhikr (remembrance of Allah) and they lower their wings with true respect for the student of knowledge. In reference to Ar-Ruh, it is said that here it means the angel Jibril. Therefore, the wording of the Ayah is a method of adding the name of the distinct object (in this case Jibril) separate from the general group (in this case the angels). Concerning Allah's statement,

(with every matter.) Mujahid said, "Peace concerning every matter." Sa`id bin Mansur said, `Isa bin Yunus told us that Al-A`mash narrated to them that Mujahid said concerning Allah's statement,

(There is peace) "It is security in which Shaytan cannot do any evil or any harm." Qatadah and others have said, "The matters are determined during it, and the times of death and provisions are measured out (i.e., decided) during it." Allah says,

(Therein is decreed every matter of decree.) (44:4) Then Allah says,

(There is peace until the appearance of dawn.) Sa`id bin Mansur said, "Hushaym narrated to us on the authority of Abu Ishaq, who narrated that Ash-Sha`bi said concerning Allah's statement,

(With every matter, there is a peace until the appearance of dawn.) `The angels giving the greetings of peace during the Night of Al-Qadr to the people in the Masjids until the coming of Fajr (dawn).'" Qatadah and Ibn Zayd both said concerning Allah's statement,

(There is peace.) "This means all of it is good and there is no evil in it until the coming of Fajr (dawn)."

Specifying the Night of Decree and its Signs

This is supported by what Imam Ahmad recorded from `Ubadah bin As-Samit that the Messenger of Allah said,

«لَيْلَةُ الْقَدْرِ فِي الْعَشْرِ الْبَوَاقِي، مَنْ قَامَهُنَّ ابْتِغَاءَ حِسْبَتِهِنَّ فَإِنَّ اللهَ يَغْفِرُ لَهُ مَا تَقَدَّمَ مِنْ ذَنْبِهِ وَمَا تَأَخَّرَ، وَهِيَ لَيْلَةُ وِتْرٍ: تِسْعٍ أَوْ سَبْعٍ أَوْ خَامِسَةٍ أَوْ ثَالِثَةٍ أَوْ آخِرِ لَيْلَةٍ»

(The Night of Al-Qadr occurs during the last ten (nights). Whoever stands for them (in prayer) seeking their reward, then indeed Allah will forgive his previous sins and his latter sins. It is an odd night: the ninth, or the seventh, or the fifth, or the third or the last night (of Ramadan).) The Messenger of Allah also said,

Chapter 97: Al-Qadr (Power, Fate), Verses 001-005

«إِنَّ أَمَارَةَ لَيْلَةِ الْقَدْرِ أَنَّهَا صَافِيَةٌ بَلْجَةٌ، كَأَنَّ فِيهَا قَمَرًا سَاطِعًا، سَاكِنَةٌ سَاجِيَةٌ، لَا بَرْدَ فِيهَا وَلَا حَرَّ، وَلَا يَحِلُّ لِكَوْكَبٍ يُرْمَى بِهِ فِيهَا حَتَّى يُصْبِحَ، وَإِنَّ أَمَارَتَهَا أَنَّ الشَّمْسَ صَبِيحَتَهَا تَخْرُجُ مُسْتَوِيَةً لَيْسَ لَهَا شُعَاعٌ، مِثْلَ الْقَمَرِ لَيْلَةَ الْبَدْرِ، وَلَا يَحِلُّ لِلشَّيْطَانِ أَنْ يَخْرُجَ مَعَهَا يَوْمَئِذٍ»

(Verily, the sign of the Night of Al-Qadr is that it is pure and glowing as if there were a bright, tranquil, calm moon during it. It is not cold, nor is it hot, and no shooting star is permitted until morning. Its sign is that the sun appears on the morning following it smooth having no rays on it, just like the moon on a full moon night. Shaytan is not allowed to come out with it (the sun) on that day.) This chain of narration is good. In its text there is some oddities and in some of its wordings there are things that are objectionable. Abu Dawud mentioned a section in his Sunan that he titled, "Chapter: Clarification that the Night of Al-Qadr occurs during every Ramadan." Then he recorded that `Abdullah bin `Umar said, "The Messenger of Allah was asked about the Night of Al-Qadr while I was listening and he said,

«هِيَ فِي كُلِّ رَمَضَان»

(It occurs during every Ramadan.)" The men of this chain of narration are all reliable, but Abu Dawud said that Shu`bah and Sufyan both narrated it from Ishaq and they both considered it to be a statement of the Companion (Ibn `Umar, and thus not the statement of the Prophet). It has been reported that Abu Sa`id Al-Khudri said, "The Messenger of Allah performed I`tikaf during the first ten nights of Ramadan and we performed I`tikaf with him. Then Jibril came to him and said, `That which you are seeking is in front of you.' So the Prophet performed I`tikaf during the middle ten days of Ramadan and we also performed I`tikaf with him. Then Jibril came to him and said; `That which you are seeking is ahead of you.' So the Prophet stood up and gave a sermon on the morning of the twentieth of Ramadan and he said,

«مَنْ كَانَ اعْتَكَفَ مَعِيَ فَلْيَرْجِعْ فَإِنِّي رَأَيْتُ لَيْلَةَ الْقَدْرِ، وَإِنِّي أُنْسِيتُهَا، وَإِنَّهَا فِي الْعَشْرِ الْأَوَاخِرِ فِي وِتْرٍ، وَإِنِّي رَأَيْتُ كَأَنِّي أَسْجُدُ فِي طِينٍ وَمَاء»

(Whoever performed I`tikaf with me, let him come back (for I`tikaf again), for verily I saw the Night of Al-Qadr, and I was caused to forget it, and indeed it is during the last ten (nights). It is during an odd night and I saw myself as if I were prostrating in mud and water.) The roof of the Masjid was made of dried palm-tree leaves and we did not see anything (i.e., clouds) in the sky. But then a patch of wind-driven clouds came and it rained. So the Prophet lead us in prayer until we saw the traces of mud and water on the forehead of the Messenger of Allah , which confirmed his dream." In one narration it adds that this occurred on the morning of the twenty-first night (meaning the next morning). They both (Al-Bukhari and Muslim) recorded it in the Two Sahihs. Ash-Shafi`i said, "This Hadith is the most authentic of what has been reported." It has also been said that it is on the twenty-third night due to a Hadith narrated from `Abdullah bin Unays in Sahih Muslim. It has also been said that it is on the twenty-fifth night due to what Al-Bukhari recorded from Ibn `Abbas that the Messenger of Allah said,

«الْتَمِسُوهَا فِي الْعَشْرِ الْأَوَاخِرِ مِنْ رَمَضَانَ فِي تَاسِعَةٍ تَبْقَى، فِي سَابِعَةٍ تَبْقَى، فِي خَامِسَةٍ تَبْقَى»

(Seek it in the last ten (nights) of Ramadan. In the ninth it still remains, in the seventh it still remains, in the fifth it still remains.) Many have explained this Hadith to refer to the odd nights, and this is the most apparent and most popular explanation. It has also been said that it occurs on the twenty-seventh night because of what Muslim recorded in his Sahih from Ubay bin Ka`b that the Messenger of Allah mentioned that it was on the twenty-seventh night. Imam Ahmad recorded from Zirr that he asked Ubayy bin Ka`b, "O Abu Al-Mundhir! Verily, your brother Ibn Mas`ud says whoever stands for prayer (at night) the entire year, will catch the Night of Al-Qadr." He (Ubayy) said, "May Allah have mercy upon him. Indeed he knows that it is during the month of Ramadan and that it is the twenty-seventh night." Then he swore by Allah. Zirr then said, "How do you know that" Ubayy replied, "By a sign or an indication that he (the Prophet) informed us of. It rises that next day having no rays on it -- meaning the sun." Muslim has also recorded it. It has been said that it is the night of the twenty-ninth. Imam Ahmad bin Hanbal recorded from `Ubadah bin As-Samit that he asked the Messenger of Allah about the Night of Decree and he replied,

«فِي رَمَضَانَ فَالْتَمِسُوهَا فِي الْعَشْرِ الْأَوَاخِرِ، فَإِنَّهَا فِي وِتْرٍ إِحْدَى وَعِشْرِينَ، أَوْ ثَلَاثٍ وَعِشْرِينَ، أَوْ خَمْسٍ وَعِشْرِينَ، أَوْ سَبْعٍ وَعِشْرِينَ، أَوْ تِسْعٍ وَعِشْرِينَ، أَوْ فِي آخِرِ لَيْلَةٍ»

(Seek it in Ramadan in the last ten nights. For verily, it is during the odd nights, the twenty-first, or the twenty-third, or the twenty-fifth, or the twenty-seventh, or the twenty-ninth, or during the last night.) Imam Ahmad also recorded from Abu Hurayrah that the Messenger of Allah said about the Night of Al-Qadr,

«إِنَّهَا لَيْلَةُ سَابِعَةٍ أَوْ تَاسِعَةٍ وَعِشْرِينَ، وَإِنَّ الْمَلَائِكَةَ تِلْكَ اللَّيْلَةَ فِي الْأَرْضِ

$$\text{«أَكْثَرُ مِنْ عَدَدِ الْحَصَى»}$$

(Verily, it is during the twenty-seventh or the twenty-ninth night. And verily, the angels who are on the earth during that night are more numerous than the number of pebbles.) Ahmad was alone in recording this Hadith and there is nothing wrong with its chain of narration. At-Tirmidhi recorded from Abu Qilabah that he said, "The Night of Al-Qadr moves around (i.e., from year to year) throughout the last ten nights." This view that At-Tirmidhi mentions from Abu Qilabah has also been recorded by Malik, Ath-Thawri, Ahmad bin Hanbal, Ishaq bin Rahuyah, Abu Thawr, Al-Muzani, Abu Bakr bin Khuzaymah and others. It has also been related from Ash-Shafi`i, and Al-Qadi reported it from him, and this is most likely. And Allah knows best.

Supplication during the Night of Decree

It is recommended to supplicate often during all times, especially during the month of Ramadan, in the last ten nights, and during the odd nights of it even more so. It is recommended that one say the following supplication a lot: "O Allah! Verily, You are the Oft-Pardoning, You love to pardon, so pardon me." This is due to what Imam Ahmad recorded from `A'ishah, that she said, "O Messenger of Allah! If I find the Night of Al-Qadr what should I say" He replied,

$$\text{«قُولِي: اللَّهُمَّ إِنَّكَ عَفُوٌّ تُحِبُّ الْعَفْوَ فَاعْفُ عَنِّي»}$$

(Say: "O Allah! Verily, You are the Oft-Pardoning, You love to pardon, so pardon me.") At-Tirmidhi, An-Nasa'i and Ibn Majah have all recorded this Hadith. At-Tirmidhi said, "This Hadith is Hasan Sahih." Al-Hakim recorded it in his Mustadrak (with a different chain of narration) and he said that it is authentic according to the criteria of the two Shaykhs (Al-Bukhari and Muslim). An-Nasa'i also recorded it. This is the end of the Tafsir of Surah Laylat Al-Qadr, and all praise and blessings are due to Allah.

INTRODUCTION TO CHAPTER (SURAH) 98: AL-BAYYINA (THE CLEAR PROOF, EVIDENCE)

Ibn Kathir's Introduction

The Messenger of Allah recited this Surah to Ubayy

Imam Ahmad recorded from Anas bin Malik that the Messenger of Allah said to Ubayy bin Ka`b,

$$\text{«إِنَّ اللهَ أَمَرَنِي أَنْ أَقْرَأَ عَلَيْكَ}$$

$$\text{(لَمْ يَكُنِ الَّذِينَ كَفَرُوا مِنْ أَهْلِ الْكِتَبِ)»}$$

(Verily, Allah has commanded me to recite to you (Those who disbelieve from among the People of the Scripture.)) Ubayy said, "He (Allah) mentioned me by name to you" The Prophet replied,

«نَعَم»

(Yes.) So he (Ubayy) cried. Al-Bukhari, Muslim, At-Tirmidhi and An-Nasa'i all recorded this Hadith from Shu`bah.

CHAPTER (SURAH) 98: AL-BAYYINA (THE CLEAR PROOF, EVIDENCE), VERSES 001- 008

Surah: 98 Ayah: 1, Ayah: 2, Ayah: 3, Ayah: 4 & Ayah: 5

(بِسْمِ اللَّهِ الرَّحْمَـنِ الرَّحِيمِ)

In the Name of Allah, the Most Gracious, the Most Merciful.

﴿ لَمْ يَكُنِ الَّذِينَ كَفَرُوا مِنْ أَهْلِ الْكِتَابِ وَالْمُشْرِكِينَ مُنفَكِّينَ حَتَّى تَأْتِيَهُمُ الْبَيِّنَةُ ۝ ﴾

1. Those who disbelieve from among the people of the Scripture (Jews and Christians) and among Al-Mushrikûn, were not going to leave (their disbelief) until there came to them clear evidence.

﴿ رَسُولٌ مِّنَ اللَّهِ يَتْلُوا صُحُفًا مُّطَهَّرَةً ۝ ﴾

2. A Messenger (Muhammad (peace be upon him)) from Allâh, reciting (the Qur'ân) purified pages (purified from Al-Bâtil (falsehood))

﴿ فِيهَا كُتُبٌ قَيِّمَةٌ ۝ ﴾

3. Wherein are correct and straight laws from Allâh.

﴿ وَمَا تَفَرَّقَ الَّذِينَ أُوتُوا الْكِتَابَ إِلَّا مِنْ بَعْدِ مَا جَاءَتْهُمُ الْبَيِّنَةُ ۝ ﴾

4. And the people of the Scripture (Jews and Christians) differed not until after there came to them clear evidence (i.e. Prophet Muhammad (peace be upon him) and whatever was revealed to him).

﴿ وَمَآ أُمِرُوٓاْ إِلَّا لِيَعْبُدُواْ ٱللَّهَ مُخْلِصِينَ لَهُ ٱلدِّينَ حُنَفَآءَ وَيُقِيمُواْ ٱلصَّلَوٰةَ وَيُؤْتُواْ ٱلزَّكَوٰةَ ۚ وَذَٰلِكَ دِينُ ٱلْقَيِّمَةِ ۞ ﴾

5. And they were commanded not, but that they should worship Allâh, and worship none but Him Alone (abstaining from ascribing partners to Him), and perform As-Salât (Iqâmat-as-Salât) and give Zakât, and that is the right religion.

Transliteration

1. Lam yakuni allatheena kafaroo min ahli alkitabi waalmushrikeena munfakkeena hatta ta/tiyahumu albayyinatu 2. Rasoolun mina Allahi yatloo suhufan mutahharatan 3. Feeha kutubun qayyimatun 4. Wama tafarraqa allatheena ootoo alkitaba illa min baAAdi ma jaat-humu albayyinatu 5. Wama omiroo illa liyaAAbudoo Allaha mukhliseena lahu alddeena hunafaa wayuqeemoo alssalata wayu/too alzzakata wathalika deenu alqayyimati

Tafsir Ibn Kathir

Mentioning the Situation of the Disbelievers among the People of the Scripture and the Idolators

As for the People of the Scripture, they are the Jews and the Christians, and the idolators are the worshippers of idols and fire among the Arabs and the non-Arabs. Mujahid said, they are not going

(to leave) "Meaning, they will not be finished until the truth becomes clear to them." Qatadah also said the same thing.

(until there came to them the Bayyinah.) meaning, this Qur'an. This is why Allah says,

(Those who disbelieve from among the People of the Scripture and idolators, were not going to leave until there came to them the Bayyinah.) Then He explains what the Bayyinah is by His saying,

(A Messenger from Allah, reciting purified pages.) meaning, Muhammad and the Magnificent Qur'an he recites, which is written down among the most high gathering in purified pages. This is similar to Allah's statement,

(In Records held in honor. Exalted, purified, in the hands of scribes (angels). Honorable and obedient.) (80:13-16) Then Allah says,

(Wherein are upright Books.) Ibn Jarir said, "Meaning in the purified pages are Books from Allah that are upright, just and straight. They have no mistakes in them because they are from Allah, the Mighty and Majestic."

The Differing only occurred after the Knowledge came

Allah says,

(And the People of the Scripture differed not until after there came to them the Bayyinah.) This is similar to Allah's statement,

(And be not as those who divided and differed among themselves after the Bayyinat came to them. It is they for whom there is an awful torment.) (3:105) This refers to the people of those divinely revealed Scriptures that were sent down to the nations that were before us. After Allah established the proofs and evidences against them, they divided and differed concerning that which Allah had intended in their Scriptures, and they had many differences. This is like what has been reported in a Hadith that has many routes of transmission,

«إِنَّ الْيَهُودَ اخْتَلَفُوا عَلَى إِحْدَى وَسَبْعِينَ فِرْقَةً، وَإِنَّ النَّصَارَى اخْتَلَفُوا عَلَى ثِنْتَيْنِ وَسَبْعِينَ فِرْقَةً، وَسَتَفْتَرِقُ هَذِهِ الْأُمَّةُ عَلَى ثَلَاثٍ وَسَبْعِينَ فِرْقَةً، كُلُّهَا فِي النَّارِ إِلَّا وَاحِدَةً»

(Verily, the Jews differed until they became seventy-one sects. And verily, the Christians differed until they became seventy-two sects. And this Ummah will divide into seventy-three sects, and all of them will be in the Fire except one.) They said, "Who are they, O Messenger of Allah" He replied,

«مَا أَنَا عَلَيْهِ وَأَصْحَابِي»

((Those who are upon) what I and my Companions are upon.)

The Command of Allah was merely that They make their Religion solely for Him

Allah says,

(And they were commanded not, but that they should worship Allah, making religion purely for Him alone,) This is similar to Allah's statement,

(And We did not send any Messenger before you but We revealed to him: La ilaha illa Ana.) (21:25) Thus, Allah says,

(Hunafa') meaning, avoiding Shirk and being truly devout to Tawhid. This is like Allah's statement,

(And Verily, We have sent among every Ummah a Messenger (proclaiming): "Worship Allah, and avoid the Taghut (false deities).") (16:36) A discussion of the word Hanif has already been mentioned previously and in Surat Al-An`am, so there is no need to repeat it here.

(and perform Salah) And this is the best of the physical forms of worship.

(and give Zakah,) This is doing good to the poor and the needy.

(and that is the right religion.) meaning, the upright and just religion, or the nation that is straight and balanced.

Surah: 98 Ayah: 6, Ayah: 7 & Ayah: 8

﴿ إِنَّ ٱلَّذِينَ كَفَرُوا۟ مِنْ أَهْلِ ٱلْكِتَٰبِ وَٱلْمُشْرِكِينَ فِى نَارِ جَهَنَّمَ خَٰلِدِينَ فِيهَآ ۚ أُو۟لَٰٓئِكَ هُمْ شَرُّ ٱلْبَرِيَّةِ ۝ ﴾

6. Verily, those who disbelieve (in the religion of Islâm, the Qur'ân and Prophet Muhammad (peace be upon him)) from among the people of the Scripture (Jews and Christians) and Al-Mushrikûn will abide in the Fire of Hell. They are the worst of creatures.

﴿ إِنَّ ٱلَّذِينَ ءَامَنُوا۟ وَعَمِلُوا۟ ٱلصَّٰلِحَٰتِ أُو۟لَٰٓئِكَ هُمْ خَيْرُ ٱلْبَرِيَّةِ ۝ ﴾

7. Verily, those who believe (in the Oneness of Allâh, and in His Messenger Muhammad (peace be upon him) including all obligations ordered by Islâm) and do righteous good deeds, they are the best of creatures.

﴿ جَزَآؤُهُمْ عِندَ رَبِّهِمْ جَنَّٰتُ عَدْنٍ تَجْرِى مِن تَحْتِهَا ٱلْأَنْهَٰرُ خَٰلِدِينَ فِيهَآ أَبَدًا ۖ رَّضِىَ ٱللَّهُ عَنْهُمْ وَرَضُوا۟ عَنْهُ ۚ ذَٰلِكَ لِمَنْ خَشِىَ رَبَّهُۥ ۝ ﴾

8. Their reward with their Lord is 'Adn (Eden) Paradise (Gardens of Eternity), underneath which rivers flow. They will abide therein forever, Allâh will be pleased with them, and they with Him. That is for him who fears his Lord.

Transliteration

6. Inna allatheena kafaroo min ahli alkitabi waalmushrikeena fee nari jahannama khalideena feeha ola-ika hum sharru albariyyati 7. Inna allatheena amanoo waAAamiloo alssalihati ola-ika hum khayru albariyyati 8. Jazaohum AAinda rabbihim

jannatu AAadnin tajree min tahtiha al-anharu khalideena feeha abadan radiya Allahu AAanhum waradoo AAanhu thalika liman khashiya rabbahu

Tafsir Ibn Kathir

Mentioning the Worse and Best of Creation and Their Recompense

Allah informs of what will happen to the wicked disbelievers among the People of the Scripture and the idolators who oppose the Allah's divinely revealed Books and the Prophets whom He sent. He says that they will be in the fire of Hell on the Day of Judgement and they will abide therein forever. This means that they will remain in it and they will have no way out of it and they will not cease being in it.

(They are the worst of creatures.) meaning, they are the worst creation that Allah has fashioned and created. Then Allah informs about the situation of the righteous people who believed in their hearts and performed righteous deeds with their bodies. He says that they are the best of creation. Abu Hurayrah and a group of the scholars have used this Ayah as a proof that the believers have a status among the creatures that is better than the angels. This is because Allah says,

(They are the best of creatures.) Then Allah says,

(Their reward with their Lord) meaning, on the Day of Judgement.

(is Eternal Gardens underneath which rivers flow. They will abide therein forever,) meaning, having no end, no break and no conclusion.

(Allah will be pleased with them, and they well-pleased with Him.) The condition of Him being pleased with them is more illustri- ous than all of the everlasting delights that they will be given.

(and they well-pleased with Him.) Due to the comprehensive favors He has given them. Then Allah says, (That is for him who fears his Lord.) meaning, this is the reward that will be attained by those who revere Allah and fear Him as He deserves to be feared. This is the person who worships Allah as if he sees Him, and he knows that even though he does not see Him, indeed Allah sees him. Imam Ahmad recorded from Abu Hurayrah that the Messenger of Allah said,

«أَلَا أُخْبِرُكُمْ بِخَيْرِ الْبَرِيَّةِ؟»

(Shall I not inform you of the best of creation) They said, "Of course, O Messenger of Allah!" He said,

«رَجُلٌ آخِذٌ بِعِنَانِ فَرَسِهِ فِي سَبِيلِ اللهِ، كُلَّمَا كَانَتْ هَيْعَةٌ اسْتَوَى عَلَيْهِ. أَلَا أُخْبِرُكُمْ بِخَيْرِ الْبَرِيَّةِ»

(A man who takes the reins of his horse in the way of Allah, and whenever there is a fearful cry from the enemy, he climbs upon it. Shall I not inform you of the best of creation) They said, "Of course, O Messenger of Allah!" He said,

«رَجُلٌ فِي ثُلَّةٍ مِنْ غَنَمِهِ، يُقِيمُ الصَّلَاةَ وَيُؤْتِي الزَّكَاةَ. أَلَا أُخْبِرُكُمْ بِشَرِّ الْبَرِيَّةِ؟»

(A man who has a flock of sheep and he establishes the prayer and gives the obligatory charity. Shall I not inform you of the worst of creation) They said, "Of course." He said,

«الَّذِي يُسْأَلُ بِاللهِ وَلَا يُعْطِي بِهِ»

(The person who is asked by Allah and he does not give by Him.) This is the end of the Tafsir of Surat Lam Yakun (Al-Bayyinah), and all praise and thanks are due to Allah.

INTRODUCTION TO CHAPTER (SURAH) 99: AZ-ZALZALA (THE EARTHQUAKE)

Ibn Kathir's Introduction

The Virtues of Surat Az-Zalzalah

Imam Ahmad recorded from `Abdullah bin `Amr that he said, "A man came to the Messenger of Allah and said, `Teach me what to recite, O Messenger of Allah!' The Prophet said,

«اقْرَأْ ثَلَاثًا مِنْ ذَوَاتِ الر»

(Recite three from those (which begin) with the letters Alif, Lam, Ra') The man then said to him, `I have become old in age, my heart has hardened and my tongue has become harsh.' The Prophet said,

«فَاقْرَأْ مِنْ ذَوَاتِ حم»

(Then recite from those (which begin) with the letters Ha-Mim.) The man said the same thing as he had said before, so the Prophet said,

«اقْرَأْ ثَلَاثًا مِنَ الْمُسَبِّحَاتِ»

(Recite three from the Musabbihat.) The man again said the same thing as he had said before. Then the man said, `Rather give me something to recite that is comprehensive (of all of these), O Messenger of Allah.' So the Prophet told him to recite

(When the earth quakes with its Zilzal.) Then when he (the Prophet) finished reciting the Surah to him the man said, `By He Who has sent you you with the truth as a Prophet, I will never add anything else to it.' Then the man turned away and left, and the Prophet said,

»أَفْلَحَ الرُّوَيْجِلُ، أَفْلَحَ الرُّوَيْجِلُ«

(The little man has been successful, the little man has been successful.) Then the Prophet said,

»عَلَيَّ بِه«

(Bring him back to me.) So the man came to him and the Prophet said to him,

»أُمِرْتُ بِيَوْمِ الْأَضْحَى جَعَلَهُ اللهُ عِيدًا لِهَذِهِ الْأُمَّةِ«

(I have also been commanded to celebrate `Id Al-Adha, which Allah has made a celebration for this Ummah.) The man said `What do you think if I am only able to acquire a borrowed milking she-camel -- should I slaughter it' The Prophet said,

»لَا، وَلَكِنَّكَ تَأْخُذُ مِنْ شَعْرِكَ وَتُقَلِّمُ أَظَافِرَكَ وَتَقُصُّ شَارِبَكَ وَتَحْلِقُ عَانَتَكَ فَذَاكَ تَمَامُ أُضْحِيَّتِكَ عِنْدَ اللهِ عَزَّ وَجَلَّ«

(No. But you should cut your hair, clip your nails, trim your mustache, shave your pubic area and that will be the completion of your sacrifice with Allah, the Mighty and Majestic.)" Abu Dawud and An-Nasa'i recorded this (Hadith.

CHAPTER (SURAH) 99: AZ-ZALZALA (THE EARTHQUAKE), VERSES 001-008

Surah: 99 Ayah: 1, Ayah: 2, Ayah: 3, Ayah: 4, Ayah: 5, Ayah: 6, Ayah: 7 & Ayah: 8

(بِسْمِ اللَّهِ الرَّحْمَـنِ الرَّحِيمِ)

In the Name of Allah, the Most Gracious, the Most Merciful.

Chapter 99: Az-Zalzala (The Earthquake), Verses 001-008

﴿ إِذَا زُلْزِلَتِ ٱلْأَرْضُ زِلْزَالَهَا ۝ ﴾

1. When the earth is shaken with its (final) earthquake.

﴿ وَأَخْرَجَتِ ٱلْأَرْضُ أَثْقَالَهَا ۝ ﴾

2. And when the earth throws out its burdens,

﴿ وَقَالَ ٱلْإِنسَٰنُ مَا لَهَا ۝ ﴾

3. And man will say: "What is the matter with it?"

﴿ يَوْمَئِذٍ تُحَدِّثُ أَخْبَارَهَا ۝ ﴾

4. That Day it will declare its information (about all what happened over it of good or evil).

﴿ بِأَنَّ رَبَّكَ أَوْحَىٰ لَهَا ۝ ﴾

5. Because your Lord will inspire it.

﴿ يَوْمَئِذٍ يَصْدُرُ ٱلنَّاسُ أَشْتَاتًا لِّيُرَوْاْ أَعْمَٰلَهُمْ ۝ ﴾

6. That Day mankind will proceed in scattered groups that they may be shown their deeds.

﴿ فَمَن يَعْمَلْ مِثْقَالَ ذَرَّةٍ خَيْرًا يَرَهُۥ ۝ ﴾

7. So whosoever does good equal to the weight of an atom (or a small ant), shall see it.

﴿ وَمَن يَعْمَلْ مِثْقَالَ ذَرَّةٍ شَرًّا يَرَهُۥ ۝ ﴾

8. And whosoever does evil equal to the weight of an atom (or a small ant), shall see it.

Transliteration

1. Itha zulzilati al-ardu zilzalaha 2. Waakhrajati al-ardu athqalaha 3. Waqala al-insanu ma laha 4. Yawma-ithin tuhaddithu akhbaraha 5. Bi-anna rabbaka awha laha 6. Yawma-ithin yasduru alnnasu ashtatan liyuraw aAAmalahum 7. Faman yaAAmal mithqala tharratin khayran yarahu 8. Waman yaAAmal mithqala tharratin sharran yarahu

Tafsir Ibn Kathir

The Day of Judgement, what will take place during it, the Condition of the Earth and the Condition of the People

Ibn `Abbas said, (When the earth quakes with its Zilzal.) "This means that it will move from beneath it." (And when the earth throws out its burdens.) meaning, it will throw forth that which is in it of the dead. More than one of the Salaf have said this and it is similar to Allah's statement, (O mankind! Have Taqwa of your Lord! Verily, the earthquake (Zalzalah) of the Hour is a terrible thing.) (22:1) This is also similar to His saying, (And when the earth is stretched forth, and has cast out all that was in it and became empty.) (84:3-4) Muslim recorded in his Sahih from Abu Hurayrah that the Messenger of Allah said,

«تُلْقِي الْأَرْضُ أَفْلَاذَ كَبِدِهَا أَمْثَالَ الْأُسْطُوَانِ مِنَ الذَّهَبِ وَالْفِضَّةِ، فَيَجِيءُ الْقَاتِلُ فَيَقُولُ فِي هَذَا قَتَلْتُ، وَيَجِيءُ الْقَاطِعُ فَيَقُولُ فِي هَذَا قَطَعْتُ رَحِمِي، وَيَجِيءُ السَّارِقُ فَيَقُولُ: فِي هَذَا قُطِعَتْ يَدِي، ثُمَّ يَدَعُونَهُ فَلَا يَأْخُذُونَ مِنْهُ شَيْئًا»

(The earth will throw out the pieces of its liver (its contents). Gold and silver will come out like columns. A murderer will come and say, `I killed for this' The one who broke the ties of kinship will say, `For this I severed the ties of kinship' The thief will say, `For this I got my hands amputated' Then they will leave it there and no one will take anything from it.)" Then Allah says, (And man will say: "What is the matter with it") meaning, he will be baffled by its situation after it used to be stable, settled and firm, and he used to be settled upon its surface. This refers to the alteration of the state of things and the earth moving and shaking. There will come to it inescapable quaking that Allah prepared for it. Then it will throw out its dead people -- from the first to the last generations. At that time the people will be baffled by the events and the earth changing into other than the earth, and the heavens as well. Then they will be presented before Allah, the One, the Irresistible. Concerning Allah's statement, (That Day it will declare its information.) meaning, it will speak of what the people did upon its surface. Imam Ahmad, At-Tirmidhi and Abu `Abdur-Rahman An-Nasa'i all recorded a Hadith from Abu Hurayrah -- and in the wording of An-Nasa'i's version it states -- that he said, "The Messenger of Allah recited this Ayah, (That Day it will declare its information.) Then he said,

«أَتَدْرُونَ مَا أَخْبَارُهَا؟»

(Do you know what is its information) They said, `Allah and His Messenger know best.' He said,

«فَإِنَّ أَخْبَارَهَا أَنْ تَشْهَدَ عَلَى كُلِّ عَبْدٍ وَأَمَةٍ بِمَا عَمِلَ عَلَى ظَهْرِهَا أَنْ تَقُولَ: عَمِلَ كَذَا وَكَذَا يَوْمَ كَذَا وَكَذَا، فَهَذِهِ أَخْبَارُهَا»

(Verily, its information is that it will testify against every male and female servant, about what they did upon its surface. It will say that he did such and such on such and such day. So this is its information.)" Then At-Tirmidhi said, "This Hadith is Sahih Gharib." Concerning Allah's statement, (Because your Lord will inspire it.) It is apparent that the implied meaning here is that He will permit it (the earth). Shabib bin Bishr narrated from `Ikrimah that Ibn `Abbas said, (That Day it will declare its information.) "Its Lord will say to it, `Speak.' So it will speak." Mujahid commented (on "inspire it"), " He commands it (i.e., to speak). " Al-Qurazi said, "He will command it to separate from them." Then Allah says, (That Day mankind will proceed in scattered groups (Ashtat)) meaning, they will return from the station of the Judgement in separate groups. This means that they will be divided into types and categories: between those who are miserable and those who are happy, and those who are commanded to go to Paradise and those who are commanded to go to the Hellfire. As-Suddi said, "Ashtat means sects." Allah said, (that they may be shown their deeds.) meaning, so that they may act and be rewarded for what they did in this life of good and evil.

The Recompense for Every Minute Deed Therefore

Allah goes on to say, (So whosoever does good equal to the weight of a speck of dust shall see it. And whosoever does evil equal to the weight of speck of dust shall see it.) Al-Bukhari recorded from Abu Hurayrah that the Messenger of Allah said,

«الْخَيْلُ لِثَلَاثَةٍ، لِرَجُلٍ أَجْرٌ، وَلِرَجُلٍ سِتْرٌ، وَعَلَى رَجُلٍ وِزْرٌ. فَأَمَّا الَّذِي لَهُ أَجْرٌ فَرَجُلٌ رَبَطَهَا فِي سَبِيلِ اللهِ فَأَطَالَ طِيَلَهَا فِي مَرْجٍ أَوْ رَوْضَةٍ، فَمَا أَصَابَتْ فِي طِيَلِهَا ذَلِكَ فِي الْمَرْجِ وَالرَّوْضَةِ كَانَ لَهُ حَسَنَاتٍ، وَلَوْ أَنَّهَا قَطَعَتْ طِيَلَهَا فَاسْتَنَّتْ شَرَفًا أَوْ شَرَفَيْنِ كَانَتْ آثَارُهَا وَأَرْوَاثُهَا حَسَنَاتٍ لَهُ، وَلَوْ أَنَّهَا مَرَّتْ بِنَهَرٍ فَشَرِبَتْ مِنْهُ وَلَمْ يُرِدْ أَنْ يَسْقِيَ بِهِ كَانَ ذَلِكَ حَسَنَاتٍ لَهُ، وَهِيَ لِذَلِكَ

«الرَّجُلِ أَجْرٌ. وَرَجُلٌ رَبَطَهَا تَغَنِّيًا وَتَعَفُّفًا وَلَمْ يَنْسَ حَقَّ اللهِ فِي رِقَابِهَا وَلَا ظُهُورِهَا فَهِيَ لَهُ سِتْرٌ، وَرَجُلٌ رَبَطَهَا فَخْرًا وَرِيَاءً وَنِوَاءً فَهِيَ عَلَى ذَلِكَ وِزْرٌ»

(The horses are for three. For one man they are a reward, for another man they are a shield, and for another man they are a burden. In reference to the man for whom they are a reward, he is the man who keeps them to be used in the way of Allah. Thus, they spend their entire life grazing in the pasture or garden (waiting in preparation for Jihad). So whatever afflicts them during that lengthy period in the pasture or garden, it will be counted as good deeds for him. Then, if their lengthy period is ended and they are used for a noble battle or two, their hoof prints and their dung are counted as good deeds for him.

When they passed through a stream from which they did drink, though he (their owner) does not intend to quench their thirst, yet, it would be counted as good deeds, Therefore, they are a reward for that man. A man who keeps them to maintain himself and to be independent of others (i.e., begging, etc.), and he does not forget the right of Allah upon their necks and their backs (i.e., their Zakah), then they are a shield for him (from the Hellfire). A man who keeps them in order to boast, brag and show off, then they are a burden for him (on Judgement Day).) So the Messenger of Allah was then asked about the donkeys and he said,

«مَا أَنْزَلَ اللهُ فِيهَا شَيْئًا إِلَّا هَذِهِ الْآيَةَ الْفَاذَّةَ الْجَامِعَةَ

(فَمَن يَعْمَلْ مِثْقَالَ ذَرَّةٍ خَيْراً يَرَهُ - وَمَن يَعْمَلْ مِثْقَالَ ذَرَّةٍ شَرّاً يَرَهُ)»

(Allah has not revealed anything concerning them except this single, comprehensive Ayah: (So whosoever does good equal to the weight of a speck of dust shall see it. And whosoever does evil equal to the weight of speck of dust shall see it.)) Muslim also recorded this Hadith. In Sahih Al-Bukhari, it is recorded from `Adi that the Prophet said,

«اتَّقُوا النَّارَ وَلَوْ بِشِقِّ تَمْرَةٍ، وَلَوْ بِكَلِمَةٍ طَيِّبَةٍ»

(Fear (ward off) the Fire, even if by giving half a date in charity, and even by saying a single word of good.) In the Sahih as well, he (`Adi) narrated (from the Prophet):

«لَا تَحْقِرَنَّ مِنَ الْمَعْرُوفِ شَيْئًا وَلَوْ أَنْ تُفْرِغَ مِنْ دَلْوِكَ فِي إِنَاءِ الْمُسْتَسْقِي، وَلَوْ

«أَنْ تَلْقَى أَخَاكَ وَوَجْهُكَ إِلَيْهِ مُنْبَسِطٌ»

(Do not under rate any good act, even if it is offering drinking water from your bucket to one who is seeking a drink, or meeting your brother with a cheerful face.) It is also recorded in the Sahih that the Prophet said,

«يَا مَعْشَرَ نِسَاءِ الْمُؤْمِنَاتِ، لَا تَحْقِرَنَّ جَارَةٌ لِجَارَتِهَا وَلَوْ فِرْسَنَ شَاةٍ»

(O party of believing women! None of you should belittle a gift sent by your neighbor, even if it is a Firsan of a sheep.) The word Firsan in this Hadith means its hoof. In another Hadith he said,

«رُدُّوا السَّائِلَ وَلَوْ بِظِلْفٍ مُحْرَقٍ»

(Give something to the beggar, even if it is a burnt hoof.) It has been reported from `A'ishah that she gave a single grape in charity and then she said, "To how much dust is it equivelent" Imam Ahmad recorded from `Awf bin Al-Harith bin At-Tufayl that `A'ishah told him that the Prophet used to say,

«يَا عَائِشَةُ، إِيَّاكِ وَمُحَقَّرَاتِ الذُّنُوبِ، فَإِنَّ لَهَا مِنَ اللهِ طَالِبًا»

(O `A'ishah! Beware of the sins that are belittled, for indeed they will be taken account of by Allah.) This Hadith was recorded by An-Nasa'i and Ibn Majah. Imam Ahmad recorded from `Abdullah bin Mas`ud that the Messenger of Allah said,

«إِيَّاكُمْ وَمُحَقَّرَاتِ الذُّنُوبِ، فَإِنَّهُنَّ يَجْتَمِعْنَ عَلَى الرَّجُلِ حَتَّى يُهْلِكْنَهُ»

(Beware of the sins that are belittled. For verily, they are gathered in a man until they destroy him.) And indeed the Messenger of Allah made an example of them (sins that are taken lightly) by saying that they are like a people who settle in barren land. Then their leader comes and orders the men to go out one at a time and each bring back a stick until they have gathered a large number of sticks. Then they kindled a fire and burned everything that they threw into it.

This is the end of the Tafsir of Surat Idha Zulzilat (Az-Zalzalah) and all praise and thanks are due to Allah.

CHAPTER (SURAH) 100: AL-ADIYAT (THE COURSER, THE CHARGERS), VERSES 001- 0011

Surah: 100 Ayah: 1, Ayah: 2, Ayah: 3, Ayah: 4, Ayah: 5, Ayah: 6, Ayah: 7, Ayah: 8, Ayah: 9, Ayah: 10 & Ayah: 11

(بِسْمِ اللَّهِ الرَّحْمَـنِ الرَّحِيمِ)

In the Name of Allah, the Most Gracious, the Most Merciful.

﴿ وَٱلْعَـٰدِيَـٰتِ ضَبْحًا ۝ ﴾

1. By the (steeds) that run, with panting,

﴿ فَٱلْمُورِيَـٰتِ قَدْحًا ۝ ﴾

2. Striking sparks of fire (by their hooves).

﴿ فَٱلْمُغِيرَٰتِ صُبْحًا ۝ ﴾

3. And scouring to the raid at dawn.

﴿ فَأَثَرْنَ بِهِ نَقْعًا ۝ ﴾

4. And raise the dust in clouds the while.

﴿ فَوَسَطْنَ بِهِ جَمْعًا ۝ ﴾

5. And penetrating forthwith as one into the midst (of the foe).

﴿ إِنَّ ٱلْإِنسَـٰنَ لِرَبِّهِ لَكَنُودٌ ۝ ﴾

6. Verily, man (disbeliever) is ungrateful to his Lord.

﴿ وَإِنَّهُ عَلَىٰ ذَٰلِكَ لَشَهِيدٌ ۝ ﴾

Chapter 100: Al-Adiyat (The Courser, The Chargers), Verses 001-011

7. And to that he bears witness (by his deeds).

﴿ وَإِنَّهُۥ لِحُبِّ ٱلْخَيْرِ لَشَدِيدٌ ۝ ﴾

8. And verily, he is violent in the love of wealth.

﴿ ۞ أَفَلَا يَعْلَمُ إِذَا بُعْثِرَ مَا فِى ٱلْقُبُورِ ۝ ﴾

9. Knows he not that when the contents of the graves are poured forth (all mankind is resurrected)?

﴿ وَحُصِّلَ مَا فِى ٱلصُّدُورِ ۝ ﴾

10. And that which is in the breasts (of men) is made known.

﴿ إِنَّ رَبَّهُم بِهِمْ يَوْمَئِذٍ لَّخَبِيرٌ ۝ ﴾

11. Verily, that Day (i.e. the Day of Resurrection) their Lord will be Well-Acquainted with them (as to their deeds and will reward them for their deeds).

Transliteration

1. WaalAAadiyati dabhan 2. Faalmooriyati qadhan 3. Faalmugheerati subhan 4. Faatharna bihi naqAAan 5. Fawasatna bihi jamAAan 6. Inna al-insana lirabbihi lakanoodun 7. Wa-innahu AAala thalika lashaheedun 8. Wa-innahu lihubbi alkhayri lashadeedun 9. Afala yaAAlamu itha buAAthira ma fee alquboori 10. Wahussila ma fee alssudoori 11. Inna rabbahum bihim yawma-ithin lakhabeerun

Tafsir Ibn Kathir

Swearing by the Horses of War about the Ungratefulness of Man and His Zeal for Wealth

Allah swears by the horses when they are made to gallop into battle in His path (i.e., Jihad), and thus they run and pant, which is the sound that is heard from the horse when it runs.

(Striking sparks of fire.) meaning, the striking of their hooves on the rocks, which causes sparks of fire to fly from them.

(And scouring to the raid at dawn.) meaning, the raid that is carried out in the early morning time. This is just as the Messenger of Allah used to perform raids in the early morning. He would wait to see if he heard the Adhan (call to prayer) from the people.

If he heard it he would leave them alone, and if he didn't hear it he would attack. Then Allah says,

(And raise the dust in clouds the while.) meaning, dust at the place of the battle with the horses.

(And penetrating forthwith as one into the midst.) means, then are all in the middle of that spot, together. Allah's saying;

(And scouring to the raid at dawn.) Ibn `Abbas, Mujahid and Qatadah, all said, "This means the invasion of the horses in the morning in the way of Allah." And His statement,

(And raise the dust in clouds the while.) This is the place in which the attack takes place. The dust is stirred up by it. And His statement,

(And penetrating forthwith as one into the midst.) Al-`Awfi narrated from Ibn `Abbas, `Ata, `Ikrimah, Qatadah and Ad-Dahhak that they all said, "This means into the midst of the disbelieving enemy." Concerning Allah's statement,

(Verily, man is ungrateful (Kanud) to his Lord.) This is the subject what is being sworn about, and it means that he (man) is ungrateful for the favors of His Lord and he rejects them. Ibn `Abbas, Mujahid, Ibrahim An-Nakha`i, Abu Al-Jawza', Abu Al-`Aliyah, Abu Ad-Duha, Sa`id bin Jubayr, Muhammad bin Qays, Ad-Dahhak, Al-Hasan, Qatadah, Ar-Rabi` bin Anas and Ibn Zayd all said, "Al-Kanud means ungrateful." Al-Hasan said, "Al-Kanud is the one who counts the calamities (that befall him) and he forgets Allah's favors."

Concerning Allah's statement,

(And to that He bears witness.) Qatadah and Sufyan Ath-Thawri both said, "And indeed Allah is a witness to that." It is also possible that the pronoun (He) could be referring to man. This was said by Muhammad bin Ka`b Al-Qurazi. Thus, its meaning would be that man is a witness himself to the fact that he is ungrateful. This is obvious in his condition, meaning this is apparent from his statements and deeds. This is as Allah says,

(It is not for the idolators, to maintain the Masajid of Allah, while they witness disbelief against themselves.) (9:17) Allah said;

(And verily, he is violent in the love of wealth.) meaning, and indeed in his love of the good, which is wealth, he is severe. There are two opinions concerning this. One of them is that it means that he is severe. There are two opinions concerning this. One of them is that it means that he is severe in his love of wealth. The other view is that it means he is covetous and stingy due to the love of wealth. However, both views are correct.

The Threat about the Hereafter

Then Allah encourages abstinence from worldly things and striving for the Hereafter, and He informs of what the situation will be after this present condition, and what man will face of horrors. He says,

(Knows he not that when the contents of the graves are poured forth) meaning, the dead that are in it will be brought out.

(And that which is in the breasts shall be made known) Ibn `Abbas and others have said, "This means what was in their souls would be exposed and made apparent."

(Verily, that Day their Lord will be Well-Acquainted with them.) meaning, He knows all of that they used to do, and He will compensate them for it with the most deserving reward. He does not do even the slightest amount of injustice. This is the end of the Tafsir of Surat Al-`Adiyat, and all praise and thanks are due to Allah.

CHAPTER (SURAH) 101: AL-QARIA (THE CALAMITY, THE STUNNING BLOW, THE DISASTER), VERSES 001-0011

Surah: 101 Ayah: 1, Ayah: 2, Ayah: 3, Ayah: 4, Ayah: 5, Ayah: 6, Ayah: 7, Ayah: 8, Ayah: 9, Ayah: 10 & Ayah: 11

(بِسْمِ اللَّهِ الرَّحْمَـنِ الرَّحِيمِ)

In the Name of Allah, the Most Gracious, the Most Merciful.

﴿ ٱلْقَارِعَةُ ۝ ﴾

1. Al-Qâri'ah (the striking Hour i.e. the Day of Resurrection).

﴿ مَا ٱلْقَارِعَةُ ۝ ﴾

2. What is the striking (Hour)?

﴿ وَمَآ أَدْرَىٰكَ مَا ٱلْقَارِعَةُ ۝ ﴾

3. And what will make you know what the striking (Hour) is?

﴿ يَوْمَ يَكُونُ ٱلنَّاسُ كَٱلْفَرَاشِ ٱلْمَبْثُوثِ ۝ ﴾

4. It is a Day whereon mankind will be like moths scattered about.

$$ \text{﴿ وَتَكُونُ ٱلْجِبَالُ كَٱلْعِهْنِ ٱلْمَنفُوشِ ۝ ﴾} $$

5. And the mountains will be like carded wool.

$$ \text{﴿ فَأَمَّا مَن ثَقُلَتْ مَوَٰزِينُهُۥ ۝ ﴾} $$

6. Then as for him whose balance (of good deeds) will be heavy,

$$ \text{﴿ فَهُوَ فِى عِيشَةٍ رَّاضِيَةٍ ۝ ﴾} $$

7. He will live a pleasant life (in Paradise).

$$ \text{﴿ وَأَمَّا مَنْ خَفَّتْ مَوَٰزِينُهُۥ ۝ ﴾} $$

8. But as for him whose balance (of good deeds) will be light,

$$ \text{﴿ فَأُمُّهُۥ هَاوِيَةٌ ۝ ﴾} $$

9. He will have his home in Hâwiyah (pit, i.e. Hell).

$$ \text{﴿ وَمَآ أَدْرَىٰكَ مَا هِيَهْ ۝ ﴾} $$

10. And what will make you know what it is?

$$ \text{﴿ نَارٌ حَامِيَةٌ ۝ ﴾} $$

11. (It is) a fiercely blazing Fire!

Transliteration

1. AlqariAAatu 2. Ma alqariAAatu 3. Wama adraka ma alqariAAatu 4. Yawma yakoonu alnnasu kaalfarashi almabthoothi 5. Watakoonu aljibalu kaalAAihni almanfooshi 6. Faamma man thaqulat mawazeenuhu 7. Fahuwa fee AAeeshatin radiyatin 8. Waamma man khaffat mawazeenuhu 9. Faommuhu hawiyatun 10. Wama adraka ma hiyah 11. Narun hamiyatun

Tafsir Ibn Kathir

Al-Qari`ah is one of the names of the Day of Judgement, like Al-Haqqah, At-Tammah, As-Sakhkhah, Al-Ghashiyah and other names.

Then Allah intensifies concern and fright for it by saying,

(And what will make you know what Al-Qari`ah is) Then He explains this by saying,

(It is a Day whereon mankind will be like moths scattered about.) meaning, in their scattering, their dividing, their coming and their going, all due to being bewildered at what is happening to them, they will be like scattered moths. This is like Allah's statement,

(As if they were locusts spread abroad.) (54:7) Allah said,

(And the mountains will be like wool, carded.) meaning, they will become like carded wool that has began to wear out (fade away) and be torn apart. Mujahid, `Ikrimah, Sa`id bin Jubayr, Al-Hasan, Qatadah, `Ata' Al-Khurasani, Ad-Dahhak and As-Suddi have all said,

(like wool (`Ihn).) "Woolen." Then Allah informs about the results received by those who performed the deeds, and the honor and disgrace they will experience based upon their deeds. He says,

(Then as for him whose Balance will be heavy.) meaning, his good deeds are more than his bad deeds.

(He will live a pleasant life.) meaning, in Paradise.

(But as for him whose Balance will be light.) meaning, his bad deeds are more than his good deeds. Then Allah says,

(His mother will be Hawiyah.) It has been said that this means he will be falling and tumbling headfirst into the fire of Hell, and the expression `his mother' has been used to refer to his brain (as it is the mother of his head). A statement similar to this has been reported from Ibn `Abbas, `Ikrimah, Abu Salih and Qatadah. Qatadah said, "He will fall into the Hellfire on his head." Abu Salih made a similar statement when he said, "They will fall into the Fire on their heads." It has also been said that it means his mother that he will return to and end up with in the Hereafter will be Hawiyah, which is one of the names of the Hellfire. Ibn Jarir said, "Al-Hawiyah is only called his mother because he will have no other abode except for it." Ibn Zayd said, "Al-Hawiyah is the Fire, and it will be his mother and his abode to which he will return, and where he will be settled." Then he recited the Ayah,

(Their abode will be the Fire.) (3:151) Ibn Abi Hatim said that it has been narrated from Qatadah that he said, "It is the Fire, and it is their abode." Thus, Allah says in explaining the meaning of Al-Hawiyah,

(And what will make you know what it is). Allah's statement

(A fire Hamiyah!) meaning, extreme heat. It is a heat that is accompanied by a strong flame and fire. It is narrated from Abu Hurayrah that the Prophet said,

«نَارُ بَنِي آدَمَ الَّتِي تُوقِدُونَ، جُزْءٌ مِنْ سَبْعِينَ جُزْءًا مِنْ نَارِ جَهَنَّم»

(The fire of the Children of Adam that you all kindle is one part of the seventy parts of the fire of Hell.) They (the Companions) said, "O Messenger of Allah! Isn't it sufficient" He replied,

«إِنَّهَا فُضِّلَتْ عَلَيْهَا بِتِسْعَةٍ وَسِتِّينَ جُزْءًا»

(It is more than it by sixty-nine times.) This has been recorded by Al-Bukhari and Muslim.

In some of the wordings he stated,

«إِنَّهَا فُضِّلَتْ عَلَيْهَا بِتِسْعَةٍ وَسِتِّينَ جُزْءًا، كُلُّهُنَّ مِثْلُ حَرِّهَا»

(It is more than it by sixty-nine times, each of them is like the heat of it.) It has been narrated in a Hadith that Imam Ahmad recorded from Abu Hurayrah that the Prophet said,

«إِنَّ أَهْوَنَ أَهْلِ النَّارِ عَذَابًا مَنْ لَهُ نَعْلَانِ، يَغْلِي مِنْهُمَا دِمَاغُه»

(Verily, the person who will receive the lightest torment of the people of the Hellfire will be a man who will have two sandals that will cause his brain to boil.)"

It has been confirmed in the

Two Sahihs that the Messenger of Allah said,

«اشْتَكَتِ النَّارُ إِلَى رَبِّهَا فَقَالَتْ: يَا رَبِّ أَكَلَ بَعْضِي بَعْضًا، فَأَذِنَ لَهَا بِنَفَسَيْنِ: نَفَسٍ فِي الشِّتَاءِ، وَنَفَسٍ فِي الصَّيْفِ، فَأَشَدُّ مَا تَجِدُونَ فِي الشِّتَاءِ مِنْ بَرْدِهَا، وَأَشَدُّ مَا تَجِدُونَ فِي الصَّيْفِ مِنْ حَرِّهَا»

(The Hellfire complained to its Lord and said, "O Lord! Some parts of me devour other parts of me." So He (Allah) permitted it to take two breaths: one breath in the winter and one breath in the summer. Thus, the most severe cold that you experience in the winter is from its cold, and the most severe heat that you experience in the summer is from its heat.)

In the Two Sahihs it is recorded that he said,

«إِذَا اشْتَدَّ الْحَرُّ فَأَبْرِدُوا عَنِ الصَّلَاةِ، فَإِنَّ شِدَّةَ الْحَرِّ مِنْ فَيْحِ جَهَنَّمَ»

(When the heat becomes intense pray the prayer when it cools down, for indeed the intense heat is from the breath of Hell.)

This is the end of the Tafsir of Surat Al-Qari`ah, and all praise and thanks are due to Allah.

CHAPTER (SURAH) 102: AT-TAKATHUR (RIVALRY IN WORLD INCREASE, COMPETITION), VERSES 001-008

Surah: 102 Ayah: 1, Ayah: 2, Ayah: 3, Ayah: 4, Ayah: 5, Ayah: 6, Ayah: 7 & Ayah: 8

(بِسْمِ اللَّهِ الرَّحْمَـنِ الرَّحِيمِ)

In the Name of Allah, the Most Gracious, the Most Merciful.

﴿ أَلْهَـٰكُمُ ٱلتَّكَاثُرُ ۝ ﴾

1. The mutual rivalry (for piling up of worldly things) diverts you,

﴿ حَتَّىٰ زُرْتُمُ ٱلْمَقَابِرَ ۝ ﴾

2. Until you visit the graves (i.e. till you die).

﴿ كَلَّا سَوْفَ تَعْلَمُونَ ۝ ﴾

3. Nay! You shall come to know!

﴿ ثُمَّ كَلَّا سَوْفَ تَعْلَمُونَ ۝ ﴾

4. Again, Nay! You shall come to know!

$$\text{﴿ كَلَّا لَوْ تَعْلَمُونَ عِلْمَ ٱلْيَقِينِ ﴾}$$

5. Nay! If you knew with a sure knowledge (the end result of piling up, you would not have occupied yourselves in worldly things).

$$\text{﴿ لَتَرَوُنَّ ٱلْجَحِيمَ ﴾}$$

6. Verily, You shall see the blazing Fire (Hell)!

$$\text{﴿ ثُمَّ لَتَرَوُنَّهَا عَيْنَ ٱلْيَقِينِ ﴾}$$

7. And again, you shall see it with certainty of sight!

$$\text{﴿ ثُمَّ لَتُسْأَلُنَّ يَوْمَئِذٍ عَنِ ٱلنَّعِيمِ ﴾}$$

8. Then, on that Day you shall be asked about the delight (you indulged in, in this world)!

Transliteration

1. Alhakumu alttakathuru 2. Hatta zurtumu almaqabira 3. Kalla sawfa taAAlamoona 4. Thumma kalla sawfa taAAlamoona 5. Kalla law taAAlamoona AAilma alyaqeeni 6. Latarawunna aljaheema 7. Thumma latarawunnaha AAayna alyaqeeni 8. Thumma latus-alunna yawma-ithin AAani alnnaAAeemi

Tafsir Ibn Kathir

The Result of Loving the World and Heedlessness of the Hereafter

Allah says that all are preoccupied by love of the world, its delights and its adornments, and this distracts you from seeking the Hereafter and desiring it. This delays you until death comes to you and you visit the graves, thus becoming its inhabitants. In Sahih Al-Bukhari, it is recorded in the Book of Ar-Riqaq (Narrations that soften the Heart) from Anas bin Malik, who reported that Ubayy bin Ka`b said, "We used to think that this was a part of the Qur'an until the Ayah was revealed which says;

(The mutual increase diverts you.)" He was referring to the Hadith in which the Prophet said,

$$\text{«لَوْ كَانَ لِابْنِ آدَمَ وَادٍ مِنْ ذَهَبٍ»}$$

Chapter 102: At-Takathur (Rivalry In World Increase, Competition), Verses 001-008   207

(If the Son of Adam had a valley of gold, he would desire another like it...) Imam Ahmad recorded from `Abdullah bin Ash-Shikhkhir that he said, "I came to the Messenger of Allah while he was saying,

»﴿أَلْهَاكُمُ التَّكَاثُرُ﴾«

يَقُولُ ابْنُ آدَمَ: مَالِي مَالِي، وَهَلْ لَكَ مِنْ مَالِكَ إِلَّا مَا أَكَلْتَ فَأَفْنَيْتَ، أَوْ لَبِسْتَ فَأَبْلَيْتَ، أَوْ تَصَدَّقْتَ فَأَمْضَيْتَ؟«

((The mutual increase diverts you.)" He was referring to the Hadith in which the Prophet said,

«لَوْ كَانَ لِابْنِ آدَمَ وَادٍ مِنْ ذَهَبٍ»

(If the Son of Adam had a valley of gold, he would desire another like it...) Imam Ahmad recorded from `Abdullah bin Ash-Shikhkhir that he said, "I came to the Messenger of Allah while he was saying,

»﴿أَلْهَاكُمُ التَّكَاثُرُ﴾«

يَقُولُ ابْنُ آدَمَ: مَالِي مَالِي، وَهَلْ لَكَ مِنْ مَالِكَ إِلَّا مَا أَكَلْتَ فَأَفْنَيْتَ، أَوْ لَبِسْتَ فَأَبْلَيْتَ، أَوْ تَصَدَّقْتَ فَأَمْضَيْتَ؟«

((The mutual increase diverts you.)(The Son of Adam says, "My wealth, my wealth." But do you get anything (of benefit) from your wealth except for that which you ate and you finished it, or that which you clothed yourself with and you wore it out, or that which you gave as charity and you have spent it)" Muslim, At-Tirmidhi and An-Nasa'i also recorded this Hadith. Muslim recorded in his Sahih from Abu Hurayrah that the Messenger of Allah said,

«يَقُولُ الْعَبْدُ: مَالِي مَالِي، وَإِنَّمَا لَهُ مِنْ مَالِهِ ثَلَاثٌ: مَا أَكَلَ فَأَفْنَى، أَوْ لَبِسَ فَأَبْلَى، أَوْ تَصَدَّقَ فَأَمْضَى، وَمَا سِوَى ذَلِكَ فَذَاهِبٌ وَتَارِكُهُ لِلنَّاسِ»

(The servant says "My wealth, my wealth." Yet he only gets three (benefits) from his wealth: that which he eats and finishes, that which he eats and finishes, that which he wears until it is worn out, or that which he gives in charity and it is spent. Everything else other than that will go away and leave him for the people.) Muslim was alone in recording this Hadith. Al-Bukhari recorded from Anas bin Malik that the Messenger of Allah said,

«يَتْبَعُ الْمَيِّتَ ثَلَاثَةٌ، فَيَرْجِعُ اثْنَانِ وَيَبْقَى مَعَهُ وَاحِدٌ: يَتْبَعُهُ أَهْلُهُ وَمَالُهُ وَعَمَلُهُ، فَيَرْجِعُ أَهْلُهُ وَمَالُهُ، وَيَبْقَى عَمَلُهُ»

(Three things follow the deceased person, and two of them return while one remains behind with him. The things which follow him are his family, his wealth and his deeds. His family and his wealth return while his deeds remain.) This Hadith has also been recorded by Muslim, At-Tirmidhi and An-Nasa'i. Imam Ahmad recorded from Anas that the Prophet said,

«يَهْرَمُ ابْنُ آدَمَ وَيَبْقَى مِنْهُ اثْنَتَانِ: الْحِرْصُ وَالْأَمَلُ»

(The Son of Adam becomes old with senility, but yet two things remain with him: greed and hope.) Both of them (Al-Bukhari and Muslim) recorded this Hadith in the Two Sahihs.

The Threat of seeing Hell and being questioned about the Delights

(Nay! you shall come to know! Again nay! you shall come to know!) Al-Hasan Al-Basri said, "This is a threat after a threat." Ad-Dahhak said,

(Nay! you shall come to know!) "Meaning, `O you disbelievers.'

(Again nay! you shall come to know!) meaning, `O you believers.'" Then Allah says,

(Nay! you shall come to know! Again nay! you shall come to know!) Al-Hasan Al-Basri said, "This is a threat after a threat." Ad-Dahhak said,

(Nay! you shall come to know!) "Meaning, `O you disbelievers.'

(Again nay! you shall come to know!) meaning, `O you believers.'" Then Allah says,

(Nay! If you knew with a sure knowledge.) meaning, `if you knew with true knowledge, you would not be diverted by rivalry for wealth away from seeking the abode of the Hereafter until you reach the graves.' Then Allah says,

(Verily, you shall see the blazing Fire! And again you shall see it with certainty of sight!) This is the explanation of the previous threat which was in Allah's saying,

(Nay! you shall come to know! Again nay! you shall come to know!) Thus, Allah threatens them with this situation, which is what the people of the Fire will see. It is a Fire, which if it exhaled one breath, every angel who is near (to Allah) and every Prophet who was sent would all fall down on their knees due to fear, awe and the sight of its horrors. This is based upon what has been reported in the narrations concerning it. Allah then says,

(Then on that Day you shall be asked about the delights!) meaning, `on that Day you all will be questioned concerning your gratitude towards the favors that Allah blessed you with, such as health, safety, sustenance and other things. You will be asked did you return His favors by being thankful to Him and worshipping Him.' Ibn Jarir recorded that Al-Husayn bin `Ali As-Suda'i narrated to him from Al-Walid bin Al-Qasim, who reported from Yazid bin Kaysan, who reported from Abi Hazim, who reported from Abu Hurayrah that he said, "Once while Abu Bakr and `Umar were sitting, the Prophet came to them and said,

«مَا أَجْلَسَكُمَا هٰهُنَا؟»

(What has caused you two to sit here) They replied, `By He Who has sent you with the truth, nothing has brought us out of our houses except hunger.' The Prophet said,

«وَالَّذِي بَعَثَنِي بِالْحَقِّ مَا أَخْرَجَنِي غَيْرُهُ»

(By He Who has sent me with the truth, nothing has brought me out other than this.) So they went until they came to the house of a man from the Ansar, and the woman of the house received them. The Prophet said to her,

«أَيْنَ فُلَانٌ؟»

(Where is so-and-so) She replied, `He went to fetch some drinking water for us.' So the man came carrying his bucket and he said, `Welcome. Nothing has visited the servants (of Allah) better than a Prophet who has visited me today.' Then he hung his bucket near a palm tree, and climbed it and returned to them with a cluster of dates. So the Prophet said,

«أَلَا كُنْتَ اجْتَنَيْتَ؟»

Why didn't you pick (some of them)) The man replied, `I wanted you to choose with your own eyes.' Then he took a blade (to slaughter a sheep) and the Prophet said,

«إِيَّاكَ وَالْحَلُوبَ»

(Do not slaughter one that gives milk.) So he slaughtered a sheep for them that day and they all ate. Then the Prophet said,

«لَتُسْأَلُنَّ عَنْ هَذَا يَوْمَ الْقِيَامَةِ، أَخْرَجَكُمْ مِنْ بُيُوتِكُمُ الْجُوعُ، فَلَمْ تَرْجِعُوا حَتَّى أَصَبْتُمْ هَذَا، فَهَذَا مِنَ النَّعِيمِ»

(You will be asked about this on the Day of Judgement. Hunger caused you to come out of your homes and you did not return until you had eaten this meal. So this is from the delights.)" Muslim also recorded this Hadith. It has been confirmed in Sahih Al-Bukhari and the Sunans of At-Tirmidhi, An-Nasa'i and Ibn Majah from Ibn `Abbas that the Messenger of Allah said,

«نِعْمَتَانِ مَغْبُونٌ فِيهِمَا كَثِيرٌ مِنَ النَّاسِ: الصِّحَّةُ وَالْفَرَاغُ»

(Two favors are treated unjustly by most people: health and free time.) This means that the people are lacking gratitude for these two favors. They do fulfill their obligations to them. Therefore, whoever does not maintain the right that is obligatory upon him, then he is unjust. Imam Ahmad recorded from Abu Hurayrah that the Prophet said,

«يَقُولُ اللهُ عَزَّ وَجَلَّ قَالَ عفان: يَوْمَ الْقِيَامَةِ: يَا ابْنَ آدَمَ، حَمَلْتُكَ عَلَى الْخَيْلِ وَالْإِبِلِ، وَزَوَّجْتُكَ النِّسَاءَ، وَجَعَلْتُكَ تَرْبَعُ وَتَرْأَسُ، فَأَيْنَ شُكْرُ ذَلِكَ؟»

(Allah the Mighty and Majestic says on the Day of Judgement, "O Son of Adam! I made you ride upon the horses and camels, I gave you women to marry, and I made you reside and rule (in the earth). So where is the thanks for that") Ahmad was alone in recording this Hadith in this manner. This is the end of the Tafsir of Surat At-Takathur, and all praise and blessings are due to Allah.

INTRODUCTION TO CHAPTER (SURAH) 103: AL-ASR (THE DECLINING DAY, EVENTIDE, THE EPOCH)

Ibn Kathir's Introduction

How `Amr bin Al-`As was aware of the Qur'an's Miracle due to this Surah

They have mentioned that `Amr bin Al-`As went to visit Musaylimah Al-Kadhdhab after the Messenger of Allah was commissioned (as a Prophet) and before `Amr had accepted Islam. Upon his arrival, Musaylimah said to him, "What has been revealed to your friend (Muhammad) during this time" `Amr said, "A short and concise Surah has been revealed to him." Musaylimah then said, "What is it" `Amr replied;

(By Al-`Asr. Verily, man is in loss. Except those who believe and do righteous deeds, and recommend one another to the truth, and recommend one another to patience.)

So Musaylimah thought for a while. Then he said, "Indeed something similar has also been revealed to me." `Amr asked him, "What is it" He replied, "O Wabr (a small, furry mammal; hyrax), O Wabr! You are only two ears and a chest, and the rest of you is digging and burrowing." Then he said, "What do you think, O `Amr" So `Amr said to him, "By Allah! Verily, you know that I know you are lying." I saw that Abu Bakr Al-Khara'iti mentioned a chain of narration for part of this story, or what was close to its meaning, in volume two of his famous book Masawi' ul-Akhlaq. The Wabr is a small animal that resembles a cat, and the largest thing on it is its ears and its torso, while the rest of it is ugly. Musayli- mah intended by the composition of these nonsensical verses to produce something which would oppose the Qur'an. Yet, it was not even convin- cing to the idol wor- shipper of that time. At-Tabarani recorded from `Abdullah bin Hisn Abi Madinah that he said, "Whenever two men from the Companions of the Messenger of Allah used to meet, they would not part until one of them had recited Surat Al-`Asr in its entirety to the other, and one of them had given the greetings of peace to the other." Ash-Shafi`i said, "If the people were to ponder on this Surah, it would be sufficient for them."

CHAPTER (SURAH) 103: AL-ASR (THE DECLINING DAY, EVENTIDE, THE EPOCH), VERSES 001-003

Surah: 103 Ayah: 1, Ayah: 2 & Ayah: 3

(بِسْمِ اللَّهِ الرَّحْمَـنِ الرَّحِيمِ)

In the Name of Allah, the Most Gracious, the Most Merciful.

﴿ وَٱلْعَصْرِ ۝ ﴾

1. By Al-'Asr (the time).

﴿ إِنَّ ٱلْإِنسَـٰنَ لَفِى خُسْرٍ ۝ ﴾

2. Verily, man is in loss,

﴿ إِلَّا ٱلَّذِينَ ءَامَنُوا۟ وَعَمِلُوا۟ ٱلصَّـٰلِحَـٰتِ وَتَوَاصَوْا۟ بِٱلْحَقِّ وَتَوَاصَوْا۟ بِٱلصَّبْرِ

۝ ﴾

3. Except those who believe (in Islâmic Monotheism) and do righteous good deeds, and recommend one another to the truth (i.e. order one another to perform all kinds of good deeds (Al-Ma'ruf) which Allâh has ordained, and abstain from all

kinds of sins and evil deeds (Al-Munkar which Allâh has forbidden), and recommend one another to patience (for the sufferings, harms, and injuries which one may encounter in Allâh's Cause during preaching His religion of Islâmic Monotheism or Jihâd).

Transliteration

1. WaalAAasri 2. Inna al-insana lafee khusrin 3. Illa allatheena amanoo waAAamiloo alssalihati watawasaw bialhaqqi watawasaw bialssabri

Tafsir Ibn Kathir

Al-`Asr is the time in which the movements of the Children of Adam occur, whether good or evil.

Malik narrated from Zayd bin Aslam that he said, "It is the evening." However, the first view is the popular opinion. Thus, Allah swears by this, that man is in Khusr, which means in loss and destruction.

(Except those who believe and do righteous good deeds) So Allah makes an exception, among the species of man being in loss, for those who believe in their hearts and work righteous deeds with their limbs.

(And recommend one another to the truth,) This is to perform acts of obedience and avoid the forbidden things.

(And recommend one another to patience.) meaning, with the plots, the evils, and the harms of those who harm people due to their commanding them to do good and forbidding them from evil. This is the end of the Tafsir of Surat Al-`Asr, and all praise and thanks are due to Allah.

CHAPTER (SURAH) 104: AL-HUMAZA (THE TRADUCER, THE GOSSIPMONGER), VERSES 001-009

Surah: 104 Ayah: 1, Ayah: 2, Ayah: 3, Ayah: 4, Ayah: 5, Ayah: 6, Ayah: 7, Ayah: 8 & Ayah: 9

(بِسْمِ اللَّهِ الرَّحْمَـنِ الرَّحِيمِ)

In the Name of Allah, the Most Gracious, the Most Merciful.

﴿ وَيْلٌ لِّكُلِّ هُمَزَةٍ لُّمَزَةٍ ۝ ﴾

1. Woe to every slanderer and backbiter.

Chapter 104: Al-Humaza (The Traducer, The Gossipmonger), Verses 001-009

﴿ ٱلَّذِى جَمَعَ مَالًا وَعَدَّدَهُۥ ۝ ﴾

2. Who has gathered wealth and counted it.

﴿ يَحْسَبُ أَنَّ مَالَهُۥٓ أَخْلَدَهُۥ ۝ ﴾

3. He thinks that his wealth will make him last forever!

﴿ كَلَّا ۖ لَيُنۢبَذَنَّ فِى ٱلْحُطَمَةِ ۝ ﴾

4. Nay! Verily, he will be thrown into the crushing Fire.

﴿ وَمَآ أَدْرَىٰكَ مَا ٱلْحُطَمَةُ ۝ ﴾

5. And what will make you know what the crushing Fire is?

﴿ نَارُ ٱللَّهِ ٱلْمُوقَدَةُ ۝ ﴾

6. The fire of Allâh, kindled,

﴿ ٱلَّتِى تَطَّلِعُ عَلَى ٱلْأَفْـِٔدَةِ ۝ ﴾

7. Which leaps up over the hearts,

﴿ إِنَّهَا عَلَيْهِم مُّؤْصَدَةٌ ۝ ﴾

8. Verily, it shall be closed upon them,

﴿ فِى عَمَدٍ مُّمَدَّدَةٍ ۝ ﴾

9. In pillars stretched forth (i.e. they will be punished in the Fire with pillars).

Transliteration

1. Waylun likulli humazatin lumazatin 2. Allathee jamaAAa malan waAAaddadahu 3. Yahsabu anna malahu akhladahu 4. Kalla layunbathanna fee alhutamati 5. Wama adraka ma alhutamatu 6. Naru Allahi almooqadatu 7. Allatee tattaliAAu AAala al-afidati 8. Innaha AAalayhim mu/sadatun 9. Fee AAamadin mumaddadatin

Tafsir Ibn Kathir

Al-Hammaz refers to (slander) by speech, and Al-Lammaz refers to (slander) by action. This means that the person finds fault with people and belittles them. An explanation of this has already preceded in the discussion of Allah's statement,

(Hammaz, going about with slander) (68:11) Ibn `Abbas said, "Humazah Lumazah means one who reviles and disgraces (others)." Mujahid said, "Al-Humazah is with the hand and the eye, and Al-Lumazah is with the tongue." Then Allah says,

(Who has gathered wealth and counted it.) meaning, he gathers it piling some of it on top of the rest and he counts it up. This is similar to Allah's saying,

(And collect (wealth) and hide it.) (70:18) This was said by As-Suddi and Ibn Jarir. Muhammad bin Ka`b said concerning Allah's statement,

(gathered wealth and counted it.) "His wealth occupies his time in the day, going from this to that. Then when the night comes he sleeps like a rotting corpse." Then Allah says,

(He thinks that his wealth will make him last forever!) meaning, he thinks that gathering wealth will make him last forever in this abode (the worldly life).

(But no!) meaning, the matter is not as he claims, nor as he reckons. Then Allah says,

(Verily, he will be thrown into Al-Hutamah.) meaning, the person who gathered wealth and counted it, will be thrown into Al-Hutamah, which is one of the descriptive names of the Hellfire. This is because it crushes whoever is in it. Thus, Allah says,

(And what will make you know what Al-Hutamah is The fire of Allah, Al-Muqadah, which leaps up over the hearts.) Thabit Al-Bunani said, "It will burn them all the way to their hearts while they are still alive." Then he said, "Indeed the torment will reach them." Then he cried. Muhammad bin Ka`b said, "It (the Fire) will devour every part of his body until it reaches his heart and comes to the level of his throat, then it will return to his body."

Concerning Allah's statement,

(Verily, it shall Mu'sadah upon them.) meaning, covering, just as was mentioned in the Tafsir of Surat Al-Balad (see 90:20). Then Allah says,

(In pillars stretched forth.) "Atiyah Al-`Awfi said, "Pillars of Iron." As-Suddi said, "Made of fire." Al-`Awfi reported from Ibn `Abbas, "He will make them enter pillars stretched forth, meaning there will be columns over them, and they will have chains on their necks, and the gates (of Hell) will be shut upon them." This is the end of the Tafsir of Surat Al-Humazah, and all praise and thanks are due to Allah.

CHAPTER (SURAH) 105: AL-FIL (THE ELEPHANT), VERSES 001-005

Surah: 105 Ayah: 1, Ayah: 2, Ayah: 3, Ayah: 4 & Ayah: 5

﴿بِسْمِ اللَّهِ الرَّحْمَـنِ الرَّحِيمِ﴾

In the Name of Allah, the Most Gracious, the Most Merciful.

﴿ أَلَمْ تَرَ كَيْفَ فَعَلَ رَبُّكَ بِأَصْحَـبِ ٱلْفِيلِ ۝ ﴾

1. Have you (O Muhammad (peace be upon him)) not seen how your Lord dealt with the owners of the Elephant? (The elephant army which came from Yemen under the command of Abrahah Al-Ashram intending to destroy the Ka'bah at Makkah).

﴿ أَلَمْ يَجْعَلْ كَيْدَهُمْ فِى تَضْلِيلٍ ۝ ﴾

2. Did He not make their plot go astray?

﴿ وَأَرْسَلَ عَلَيْهِمْ طَيْرًا أَبَابِيلَ ۝ ﴾

3. And He sent against them birds, in flocks,

﴿ تَرْمِيهِم بِحِجَارَةٍ مِّن سِجِّيلٍ ۝ ﴾

4. Striking them with stones of Sijjîl (baked clay).

﴿ فَجَعَلَهُمْ كَعَصْفٍ مَّأْكُولٍ ۝ ﴾

5. And He made them like (an empty field of) stalks (of which the corn has been eaten up by cattle).

Transliteration

1. Alam tara kayfa faAAala rabbuka bi-as-habi alfeeli 2. Alam yajAAal kaydahum fee tadleelin 3. Waarsala AAalayhim tayran ababeela 4. Tarmeehim bihijaratin min sijjeelin 5. FajaAAalahum kaAAasfin ma/koolin

Tafsir Ibn Kathir

This is one of the favors Allah did for the Quraysh. He saved them from the People of the Elephant who had tried to tear down the Ka`bah and wipe out all traces of its existence. Allah destroyed them, defeated them, thwarted their plans, made their efforts in vain and sent them back routed. They were people who were Christians, and thus, their religion was closer to the True Religion (Islam) than the idolatry of the Quraysh. However, this was a means of giving a sign and preparing the way for the coming of the Messenger of Allah . For verily, he was born during that same year according to the most popular opinion. So the tongue of destiny was saying, "We will not help you, O people of Quraysh, because of any status you may have over the Ethiopians (Abyssinians). We are only helping you in order to defend the Ancient House (the Ka`bah), which We will honor, magnify, and venerate by sending the unlettered Prophet, Muhammad , the Finality of all Prophets."

A Summary of the Story of the People of the Elephant

This is the story of the people of the Elephant, in brief, and summarized. It has already been mentioned in the story of the People of the Ditch that Dhu Nuas, the last king of Himyar, a polytheist -- was the one who ordered killing the People of the Ditch. They were Christians and their number was approximately twenty thousand. None of them except a man named Daws Dhu Tha`laban escaped. He fled to Ash-Sham where he sought protection from Caesar, the emperor of Ash-Sham, who was also a Christian. Caesar wrote to An-Najashi, the king of Ethiopia (Abyssinia), who was closer to the home of the man. An-Najashi sent two governors with him: Aryat and Abrahah bin As-Sabah Abu Yaksum, along with a great army. The army entered Yemen and began searching the houses and looting in search of the king of Himyar (Dhu Nuwas). Dhu Nuwas was eventually killed by drowning in the sea. Thus, the Ethiopians were free to rule Yemen, with Aryat and Abrahah as its governors. However, they continually disagreed about matters, attacked each other, fought each other and warred against each other, until one of them said to the other, "There is no need for our two armies to fight. Instead let us fight each other (in a duel) and the one who kills the other will be the ruler of Yemen." So the other accepted the challenge and they held a duel. Behind each man was a channel of water (to keep either from fleeing). Aryat gained the upper hand and struck Abrahah with his sword, splitting his nose and mouth, and slashing his face. But `Atawdah, Abrahah's guard, attacked Aryat and killed him. Thus, Abrahah returned wounded to Yemen where he was treated for his injuries and recovered. He thus became the commander of the Abyssinian army in Yemen.

Then the king of Abyssinia, An-Najashi wrote to him, blaming him for what had happened (between him and Aryat) and threatened him, saying that he swore to tread on the soil of Yemen and cut off his forelock. Therefore, Abrahah sent a messenger with gifts and precious objects to An-Najashi to appease him and flatter him, and a sack containing soil from Yemen and a piece of hair cut from his forelock. He said in his letter to the king, "Let the king walk upon this soil and thus fulfill his oath, and this is my forelock hair that I send to you." When An-Najashi received this, he was pleased with Abrahah and gave him his approval. Then Abrahah wrote to An-Najashi saying that he would build a church for him in Yemen the like of which had never been built before. Thus, he began to build a huge church in San`a', tall and beautifully crafted and decorated on all sides. The Arabs called it Al-Qullays because of its great height, and because if one looked at it, his cap would be in danger of falling off as he tilted his head back. Then Abrahah Al-Ashram decided to force the Arabs to make their pilgrimage to this magnificent church, just as they had performed pilgrimage to the Ka`bah in Makkah. He announced this in his kingdom (Yemen), but it was rejected by the Arab tribes of `Adnan and Qahtan. The Quraysh were infuriated by it, so much so that one of them journeyed to the church and entered it one night. He then relieved himself in the church and ran away (escaping the people). When its custodians saw what he had done, they reported it to their king, Abrahah, saying; "One of the Quraysh has done this in anger over their House in whose place you have appointed this church." Upon hearing this, Abrahah swore to march to the House of Makkah (the Ka`bah) and destroy it stone by stone. Muqatil bin Sulayman mentioned that a group of young men from the Quraysh entered the church and started a fire in it on an extremely windy day. So the church caught on fire and collapsed to the ground. Due to this Abrahah prepared himself and set out with a huge and powerful army so that none might prevent him from carrying out his mission. He took along a great, powerful elephant that had a huge body the like of which had never been seen before. This elephant was called Mahmud and it was sent to Abrahah from An-Najashi, the king of Abyssinia, particularly for this expedition. It has also been said that he had eight other elephants with him; their number was also reported to be twelve, plus the large one, Mahmud -- and Allah knows best. Their intention was to use this big elephant to demolish the Ka`bah. They planned to do this by fastening chains to the pillars of the Ka`bah and placing the other ends around the neck of the elephant. Then they would make the elephant pull on them in order to tear down the walls of the Ka`bah all at one time. When the Arabs heard of Abrahah's expedition, they considered it an extremely grave matter. They held it to be an obligation upon them to defend the Sacred House and repel whoever intended a plot against it. Thus, the noblest man of the people of Yemen and the greatest of their chiefs set out to face him (Abrahah). His name was Dhu Nafr. He called his people, and whoever would respond to his call among the Arabs, to go to war against Abrahah and fight in defense of the Sacred House. He called the people to stop Abrahah's plan to demolish and tear down the Ka`bah. So the people responded to him and they entered into battle with Abrahah, but he defeated them. This was due to Allah's will and His intent to honor and venerate the Ka`bah.

Dhu Nafr was captured and taken along with the army of Abrahah.

The army continued on its way until it came to the land of Khath`am where it was confronted by Nufayl bin Habib Al-Kath`ami along with his people, the Shahran and Nahis tribes. They fought Abrahah but he defeated them and captured Nufayl bin Habib. Initially he wanted to kill him, but he forgave him and took him as his guide to show him the way to Al-Hijaz.

When they approached the area of At-Ta'if, its people -- the people of Thaqif -- went out to Abrahah. They wanted to appease him because they were fearful for their place of worship, which they called Al-Lat. Abrahah was kind to them and they sent a man named Abu Righal with him as a guide. When they reached a place known as Al-Mughammas, which is near Makkah, they settled there. Then he sent his troops on a foray to capture the camels and other grazing animals of the Makkans, which they did, including about two hundred camels belonging to `Abdul-Muttalib. The leader of this particular expedition was a man named Al-Aswad bin Mafsud. According to what Ibn Ishaq mentioned, some of the Arabs used to satirize him (because of the part he played in this historical in this historical incident). Then Abrahah sent an emissary named Hanatah Al-Himyari to enter Makkah, commanding him to bring the head of the Quraysh to him. He also commanded him to inform him that the king will not fight the people of Makkah unless they try to prevent him from the destruction of the Ka`bah. Hanatah went to the city and he was directed to `Abdul-Muttalib bin Hashim, to whom he relayed Abrahah's message. `Abdul-Muttalib replied, "By Allah! We have no wish to fight him, nor are we in any position to do so. This is the Sacred House of Allah, and the house of His Khalil, Ibrahim, and if He wishes to prevent him (Abrahah) from (destroying) it, it is His House and His Sacred Place (to do so). And if He lets him approach it, by Allah, We have no means to defend it from him." So Hanatah told him, "Come with me to him (Abrahah)." And so `Abdul-Muttalib went with him. When Abrahah saw him, he was impressed by him, because `Abdul-Muttalib was a large and handsome man. So Abrahah descended from his seat and sat with him on a carpet on the ground. Then he asked his translator to say to him, "What do you need" `Abdul-Muttalib replied to the translator, "I want the king to return my camels which he has taken from me which are two hundred in number." Abrahah then told his translator to tell him, "I was impressed by you when I first saw you, but now I withdraw from you after you have spoken to me. You are asking me about two hundred camels which I have taken from you and you leave the matter of a house which is (the foundation of) religion and the religion of your fathers, which I have come to destroy and you do not speak to me about it" `Abdul-Muttalib said to him, "Verily, I am the lord of the camels. As for the House, it has its Lord Who will defend it." Abrahah said, "I cannot be prevented (from destroying it)." `Abdul-Muttalib answered, "Then do so." It is said that a number of the chiefs of the Arabs accompanied `Abdul-Muttalib and offered Abrahah a third of the wealth of the tribe of Tihamah if he would withdraw from the House, but he refused and returned `Abdul-Muttalib's camels to him. `Abdul-Muttalib then returned to his people and ordered them to leave Makkah and seek shelter at the top of the mountains, fearful of the excesses which might be committed by the army against them. Then he took hold of the metal ring of the door of the Ka`bah, and along with a number of Quraysh, he called upon Allah to give them victory over Abrahah and his army. `Abdul-Muttalib said, while hanging on to the ring of the Ka`bah's door, "There is no matter more important to any man right now than the defense of his livestock and property. So, O my Lord! Defend Your property. Their cross and their cunning will not be victorious over your cunning by the time morning comes." According to Ibn Ishaq, then `Abdul-Muttalib let go of the metal ring of the door of the Ka`bah, and they left Makkah and ascended to the mountains tops. Muqatil bin Sulayman mentioned that they left one hundred animals (camels) tied near the Ka`bah hoping that some of the army would take some of them without a right to do so, and thus bring about the vengeance of Allah upon themselves.

When morning came, Abrahah prepared to enter the sacred city of Makkah. He prepared the elephant named Mahmud. He mobilized his army, and they turned the elephant towards the Ka`bah. At that moment Nufayl bin Habib approached it and stood next to it, and taking it by its ear, he said, "Kneel, Mahmud! Then turn around and return directly to whence you came. For verily, you are in the Sacred City of Allah." Then he released the elephant's ear and it knelt, after which Nufayl bin Habib left and hastened to the mountains. Abrahah's men beat the elephant in an attempt to make it rise, but it refused. They beat it on its head with axes and used hooked staffs to pull it out of its resistance and make it stand, but it refused. So they turned him towards Yemen, and he rose and walked quickly. Then they turned him towards Ash-Sham and he did likewise. Then they turned him towards the east and he did the same thing. Then they turned him towards Makkah and he knelt down again. Then Allah sent against them the birds from the sea, like swallows and herons. Each bird carried three stones the size of chickpeas and lentils, one in each claw and one in its beak. Everyone who was hit by them was destroyed, though not all of them were hit. They fled in panic along the road asking about the whereabouts of Nufayl that he might point out to them the way home. Nufayl, however, was at the top of the mountain with the Quraysh and the Arabs of the Hijaz observing the wrath which Allah had caused to descend on the people of the elephant. Nufayl then began to say, "Where will they flee when the One True God is the Pursuer For Al-Ashram is defeated and not the victor. Ibn Ishaq reported that Nufayl said these lines of poetry at that time,

"Didn't you live with continued support We favored you all with a revolving eye in the morning (i.e., a guide along the way). If you saw, but you did not see it at the side of the rock covered mountain that which we saw. Then you will excuse me and praise my affair, and do not grieve over what is lost between us. I praised Allah when I saw the birds, and I feared that the stones might be thrown down upon us. So all the people are asking about the whereabouts of Nufayl, as if I have some debt that I owe the Abyssinians." `Ata' bin Yasar and others have said that all of them were not struck by the torment at this hour of retribution. Rather some of them were destroyed immediately, while others were gradually broken down limb by limb while trying to escape. Abrahah was of those who was broken down limb by limb until he eventually died in the land of Khath`am. Ibn Ishaq said that they left (Makkah) being struck down and destroyed along every path and at every water spring. Abrahah's body was afflicted by the pestilence of the stones and his army carried him away with them as he was falling apart piece by piece, until they arrived back in San`a'. When they arrived there he was but like the baby chick of a bird. And he did not die until his heart fell out of his chest. So they claim. Ibn Ishaq said that when Allah sent Muhammad with the prophethood, among the things that he used to recount to the Quraysh as blessings that Allah had favored them with of His bounties, was His defending them from the attack of the Abyssinians. Due to this they (the Quraysh) were allowed to remain (safely in Makkah) for a period of time. Thus, Allah said,

(Have you not seen how your Lord dealt with the Owners of the Elephant Did He not make their plot go astray And He sent against them birds, in flocks (Ababil). Striking them with stones of Sijjil. And He made them like `Asf, Ma'kul.)

(For the Ilaf of the Quraysh, their Ilaf caravans, in winter and in summer. So, let them worship the Lord of this House, Who has fed them against hunger, and has made them safe from fear.) (106:1-4) meaning, that Allah would not alter their situation because Allah wanted good for them if they accepted Him. Ibn Hisham said, "Al-Ababil are the groups, as the Arabs do not speak of just one (bird)." He also said, "As for As-Sijjil, Yunus An-Nahwi and Abu `Ubaydah have informed me that according to the Arabs, it means something hard and solid." He then said, "Some of the commentators have mentioned that it is actually two Persian words that the Arabs have made into one word. The two words are Sanj and Jil, Sanj meaning stones, and Jil meaning clay. The rocks are of these two types: stone and clay." He continued saying, "Al-`Asf are the leaves of the crops that are not gathered. One of them is called `Asfah." This is the end of what he mentioned. Hammad bin Salamah narrated from `Asim, who related from Zirr, who related from `Abdullah and Abu Salamah bin `Abdur-Rahman that they said,

(birds Ababil.) "In groups." Ibn `Abbas and Ad-Dahhak both said, "Ababil means some of them following after others." Al-Hasan Al-Basri and Qatadah both said, "Ababil means many." Mujahid said, "Ababil means in various, successive groups." Ibn Zayd said, "Ababil means different, coming from here and there. They came upon them from everywhere." Al-Kasa'i said, "I heard some of the grammarians saying, "The singular of Ababil is Ibil." Ibn Jarir recorded from Ishaq bin `Abdullah bin Al-Harith bin Nawfal that he said concerning Allah's statement,

(And He sent against them birds, Ababil.) "This means in divisions just as camels march in divisions (in their herds)." It is reported that Ibn `Abbas said,

(And He sent against them birds, Ababil.) "They had snouts like the beaks of birds and paws like the paws of dogs." It has been reported that `Ikrimah said commenting on Allah's statement,

(birds, Ababil.) "They were green birds that came out of the sea and they had heads like the heads of predatory animals." It has been reported from `Ubayd bin `Umayr that he commented:

(birds, Ababil.) "They were black birds of the sea that had stones in their beaks and claws." And the chains of narration (for these statements) are all authentic. It is reported from `Ubayd bin `Umayr that he said, "When Allah wanted to destroy the People of the Elephant, he sent birds upon them that came from sea swallows. Each of the birds was carrying three small stones -- two stones with its feet and one stone in its beak. They came until they gathered in rows over their heads. Then they gave a loud cry and threw what was in their claws and beaks. Thus, no stone fell upon the head of any man except that it came out of his behind (i.e., it went through him), and it did not fall on any part of his body except that it came out from the opposite side. Then Allah sent a severe wind that struck the stones and increased them in force. Thus, they were all destroyed."

Concerning Allah's statement,

And He made them like `Asf, Ma'kul.) Sa`id bin Jubayr said, "This means straw, which the common people call Habbur." In a report from Sa`id he said, "The leaves of wheat." He also said, "Al-`Asf is straw, and Al-Ma'kul refers to the fodder that is cut for animals." Al-Hasan Al-Basri said the same thing. Ibn `Abbas said, "Al-`Asf is the shell of the grain, just like the covering of wheat." Ibn Zayd said, "Al-`Asf are the leaves of vegetation and produce. When the cattle eat it they defecate it out and it becomes dung." The meaning of this is that Allah destroyed them, annihilated them and repelled them in their plan and their anger. They did not achieve any good. He made a mass destruction of them, and not one of them returned (to their land) to relate what happened except that he was wounded. This is just like what happened to their king, Abrahah. For indeed he was split open, exposing his heart when he reached his land of San`a'. He informed the people of what happened to them and then he died. His son Yaksum became the king after him, and then Yaksum's brother, Masruq bin Abrahah succeeded him. Then Sayf bin Dhi Yazan Al-Himyari went to Kisra (the king of Persia) and sought his help against the Abyssinians. Therefore, Kisra dispatched some of his army with Sayf Al-Himyari to fight with him against the Abyssinians. Thus, Allah returned their kingdom to them (i.e., the Arabs of Yemen) along with all the sovereignty their fathers possessed. Then large delegations of Arabs came to him (Sayf Al-Himyari) to congratulate him for their victory. We have mentioned previously in the Tafsir of Surat Al-Fath that when the Messenger of Allah approached the mountain pass that would lead him to the Quraysh on the Day of Al-Hudaybiyyah, his she-camel knelt down. Then the people attempted to make her get up but she refused. So, the people said, "Al-Qaswa' has become stubborn." The Prophet replied,

«مَا خَلَأَتِ الْقَصْوَاءُ، وَمَا ذَاكَ لَهَا بِخُلُقٍ، وَلَكِنْ حَبَسَهَا حَابِسُ الْفِيلِ»

(Al-Qaswa' has not become stubborn, for that is not part of her character. Rather, she has been stopped by He Who restrained the Elephant (of Abrahah).) Then he said,

«وَالَّذِي نَفْسِي بِيَدِهِ لَا يَسْأَلُونِي الْيَوْمَ خُطَّةً يُعَظِّمُونَ فِيهَا حُرُمَاتِ اللهِ إِلَّا أَجَبْتُهُمْ إِلَيْهَا»

(I swear by He in Whose Hand is my soul, they (the Quraysh) will not ask me for any matter (of the treaty) in which the sacred things of Allah are honored except that I will agree with them on it.) Then he beckoned the she-camel to rise and she stood up. This Hadith is of those that Al-Bukhari was alone in recording. It has been recorded in the Two Sahihs that on the Day of the conquest of Makkah, the Messenger of Allah said,

«إِنَّ اللهَ حَبَسَ عَنْ مَكَّةَ الْفِيلَ، وَسَلَّطَ عَلَيْهَا رَسُولَهُ وَالْمُؤْمِنِينَ، وَإِنَّهُ قَدْ عَادَتْ حُرْمَتُهَا الْيَوْمَ كَحُرْمَتِهَا بِالْأَمْسِ، أَلَا فَلْيُبَلِّغِ الشَّاهِدُ الْغَائِبَ»

(Verily, Allah restrained the Elephant from Makkah, and He has given His Messenger and the believers authority over it. And indeed its sacredness has returned just as it was sacred yesterday. So, let those who are present inform those who are absent.) This is the end of the Tafsir of Surat Al-Fil, and all praise and thanks are due to Allah.

CHAPTER (SURAH) 106: QURAISH (WINTER, QURAYSH), VERSES 001-004

Surah: 106 Ayah: 1, Ayah: 2, Ayah: 3 & Ayah: 4

(بِسْمِ اللَّهِ الرَّحْمَـٰنِ الرَّحِيمِ)

In the Name of Allah, the Most Gracious, the Most Merciful.

﴿ لِإِيلَـٰفِ قُرَيْشٍ ۝ ﴾

1. (It is a great Grace and Protection from Allâh), for the taming of the Quraish,

﴿ إِۦلَـٰفِهِمْ رِحْلَةَ ٱلشِّتَآءِ وَٱلصَّيْفِ ۝ ﴾

2. (And with all those Allâh's Grace and Protections for their taming, We cause) the (Quraish) caravans to set forth safe in winter (to the south), and in summer (to the north without any fear),

﴿ فَلْيَعْبُدُوا۟ رَبَّ هَـٰذَا ٱلْبَيْتِ ۝ ﴾

3. So let them worship (Allâh) the Lord of this House (the Ka'bah in Makkah).

﴿ ٱلَّذِىٓ أَطْعَمَهُم مِّن جُوعٍ وَءَامَنَهُم مِّنْ خَوْفٍۭ ۝ ﴾

4. (He) Who has fed them against hunger, and has made them safe from fear.

Transliteration

1. Li-eelafi qurayshin 2. Eelafihim rihlata alshshita-i waalssayfi 3. FalyaAAbudoo rabba hatha albayti 4. Allathee atAAamahum min jooAAin waamanahum min khawfin

Tafsir Ibn Kathir

This Surah has been separated from the one that preceded it in the primary Mushaf (the original copy of `Uthman).

They (the Companions) wrote "In the Name of Allah, the Most Gracious, the Most Merciful" on the line (i.e., the space) between these two Surahs. They did this even though this Surah is directly related to the one which precedes it, as Muhammad bin

Chapter 106: Quraish (Winter, Quraysh), Verses 001-004

Ishaq and `Abdur-Rahman bin Zayd bin Aslam have both clarified. This is because the meaning of both of them is, "We have prevented the Elephant from entering Makkah and We have destroyed its people in order to gather (Ilaf) the Quraysh, which means to unite them and bring them together safely in their city." It has also been said that the meaning of this (Ilaf) is what they would gather during their journey in the winter to Yemen and in the summer to Ash-Sham through trade and other than that. Then they would return to their city in safety during their journeys due to the respect that the people had for them because they were the residents of Allah's sanctuary. Therefore, whoever knew them would honor them. Even those who came to them and traveled with them, would be safe because of them. This was their situation during their journeys and travels during their winter and summer. In reference to their living in the city, then it is as Allah said,

(Have they not seen that We have made it a secure sanctuary, while men are being snatched away from all around them) (29:67) Thus, Allah says,

(For the Ilaf of the Quraysh. Their Ilaf) This is a subject that has been transferred from the first sentence in order to give it more explanation. Thus, Allah says,

(Their Ilaf caravans, in winter and in summer.) Ibn Jarir said, "The correct opinion is that the letter Lam is a prefix that shows amazement. It is as though He (Allah) is saying, `You should be amazed at the uniting (or taming) of the Quraysh and My favor upon them in that.'" He went on to say, "This is due to the consensus of the Muslims that they are two separate and independent Surahs." Then Allah directs them to be grateful for this magnificent favor in His saying,

(So, let them worship the Lord of this House.) meaning, then let them single Him out for worship, just as He has given them a safe sanctuary and a Sacred House. This is as Allah says,

(I have been commanded only to worship the Lord of this city, Who has sanctified it and to Whom belongs everything. And I am commanded to be from among the Muslims.) (27:91) Then Allah says,

(Who has fed them against hunger,) meaning, He is the Lord of the House and He is the One Who feeds them against hunger.

(And has made them safe from fear.) meaning, He favors them with safety and gentleness, so they should single Him out for worship alone, without any partner. They should not worship any idol, rival or statue besides Him. Therefore, whoever accepts this command, Allah will give him safety in both this life and the Hereafter. However, whoever disobeys Him, He will remove both of them from him. This is as Allah says,

(And Allah puts forward the example of a township, that dwelt secure and well-content: its provision coming to it in abundance from every place, but it denied the favors of Allah. So, Allah made it taste extreme of hunger and fear, because of that which they used to do. And verily, there had come unto them a Messenger from among themselves, but they denied him, so the torment overtook them while they were wrongdoers.) (16:112-113) This is the end of the Tafsir of Surah Quraysh, and all praise and thanks are due to Allah.

CHAPTER (SURAH) 107: AL-MAUN (SMALL KINDNESSES, ALMSGIVING, HAVE YOU SEEN), VERSES 001-007

Surah: 107 Ayah: 1, Ayah: 2, Ayah: 3, Ayah: 4, Ayah: 5, Ayah: 6 & Ayah: 7

(بِسْمِ اللَّهِ الرَّحْمَـنِ الرَّحِيمِ)

In the Name of Allah, the Most Gracious, the Most Merciful.

﴿ أَرَءَيْتَ ٱلَّذِى يُكَذِّبُ بِٱلدِّينِ ۝ ﴾

1. Have you seen him who denies the Recompense?

﴿ فَذَٰلِكَ ٱلَّذِى يَدُعُّ ٱلْيَتِيمَ ۝ ﴾

2. That is he who repulses the orphan (harshly),

﴿ وَلَا يَحُضُّ عَلَىٰ طَعَامِ ٱلْمِسْكِينِ ۝ ﴾

3. And urges not on the feeding of Al-Miskîn (the poor),

﴿ فَوَيْلٌ لِّلْمُصَلِّينَ ۝ ﴾

4. So woe unto those performers of Salât (prayers) (hypocrites),

﴿ ٱلَّذِينَ هُمْ عَن صَلَاتِهِمْ سَاهُونَ ۝ ﴾

5. Those who delay their Salât (prayer from their stated fixed times).

﴿ ٱلَّذِينَ هُمْ يُرَآءُونَ ۝ ﴾

6. Those who do good deeds only to be seen (of men),

Chapter 107: Al-Maun (Small Kindnesses, Almsgiving), Verses 001-007

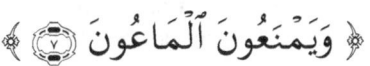

7. And prevent Al-Mâ'ûn (small kindnesses like salt, sugar, water).

Transliteration

1.Aaayta allathee yukaththibu bialddeeni 2. Fathalika allathee yaduAAAAu alyateema 3. Wala yahuddu AAala taAAami almiskeeni 4. Fawaylun lilmusalleena 5. Allatheena hum AAan salatihim sahoona 6. Allatheena hum yuraoona 7. WayamnaAAoona almaAAoona

Tafsir Ibn Kathir

Allah says, "O Muhammad! Have you seen the one who denies the Din"

Here the word Din means the Hereafter, the Recompense and the Final Reward.

(That is he who repulses the orphan,) meaning, he is the one who oppresses the orphan and does not give him his just due. He does not feed him, nor is he kind to him.

(And urges not the feeding of Al-Miskin.) This is as Allah says,

(Nay! But you treat not the orphans with kindness and generosity! And urge not one another on the feeding of Al-Miskin!) (89:17-18) meaning, the poor man who has nothing to sustain him and suffice his needs. Then Allah says,

(So, woe unto those performers of Salah, those who with their Salah are Sahun.) Ibn `Abbas and others have said, "This means the hypocrites who pray in public but do not pray in private." Thus, Allah says,

(unto those performers of Salah,) They are those people who pray and adhere to the prayer, yet they are mindless of it. This may either be referring to its act entirely, as Ibn `Abbas said, or it may be referring to performing it in its stipulated time that has been legislated Islamically. This means that the person prays it completely outside of its time.

This was said by Masruq and Abu Ad-Duha.

`Ata' bin Dinar said, "All praise is due to Allah, the One Who said,

(with their Salah are Sahun.) and He did not say, `those who are absent minded in their prayer.'" It could also mean the first time of the prayer, which means they always delay it until the end of its time, or they usually do so. It may also refer to not fulfilling its pillars and conditions, and in the required manner. It could also mean performing it with humility and contemplation of its meanings. The wording of the Ayah comprises all of these meanings. However, whoever has any characteristic of this that we have mentioned then a portion of this Ayah applies to him. And whoever has all of these characteristics, then he has completed his share of this Ayah, and the hypocrisy of actions is fulfilled in him. This is just as is confirmed in the Two Sahihs that the Messenger of Allah said,

«تِلْكَ صَلَاةُ الْمُنَافِقِ، تِلْكَ صَلَاةُ الْمُنَافِقِ، تِلْكَ صَلَاةُ الْمُنَافِقِ، يَجْلِسُ يَرْقُبُ الشَّمْسَ، حَتَّى إِذَا كَانَتْ بَيْنَ قَرْنَيِ الشَّيْطَانِ قَامَ فَنَقَرَ أَرْبَعًا، لَا يَذْكُرُ اللهَ فِيهَا إِلَّا قَلِيلًا»

(This is the prayer of the hypocrite, this is the prayer of the hypocrite, this is the prayer of the hypocrite. He sits watching the sun until it is between the two horns of Shaytan. Then he stands and pecks four (Rak`ahs) and he does not remember Allah (in them) except very little.) This Hadith is describing the end of the time for the `Asr prayer, which is the middle prayer as is confirmed by a text (Hadith). This is the time in which it is disliked to pray. Then this person stands to pray it, pecking in it like the pecking of a crow. He does not have tranquility or humility in it at all. Thus, the Prophet said,

«لَا يَذْكُرُ اللهَ فِيهَا إِلَّا قَلِيلًا»

(He does not remember Allah (in them) except very little.) He probably only stands to pray it so that the people will see him praying, and not seeking the Face of Allah. This is just as if he did not pray at all. Allah says,

(Verily, the hypocrites seek to deceive Allah, but it is He Who deceives them. And when they stand up with laziness and to be seen of men, and they do not remember Allah but little.) (4:142) and Allah says here,

(Those who do good deeds only to be seen,) Imam Ahmad recorded from `Amr bin Murrah that he said, "We were sitting with Abu `Ubaydah when the people mentioned showing-off. A man known as Abu Yazid said, "I heard `Abdullah bin `Amr saying that the Messenger of Allah said,

«مَنْ سَمَّعَ النَّاسَ بِعَمَلِهِ، سَمَّعَ اللهُ بِهِ سَامِعَ خَلْقِهِ، وَحَقَّرَهُ وَصَغَّرَهُ»

(Whoever tries to make the people hear of his deed, Allah, the One Who hears His creation, will hear it and make him despised and degraded.)" from what is related to his statement,

(Those who do good deeds only to be seen.) is that whoever does a deed solely for Allah, but the people come to know about it, and he is pleased with that, then this is not considered showing off. Allah said:

(And withhold Al-Ma`un.) This means that they do not worship their Lord well, nor do they treat His creation well. They do not even lend that which others may benefit from and be helped by, even though the object will remain intact and be returned to them. These people are even stingier when it comes to giving Zakah and different types of charity that bring one closer to Allah. Al-Mas`udi narrated from Salamah bin Kuhayl who reported from Abu Al-`Ubaydin that he asked Ibn Mas`ud about Al-Ma`un and he said, "It is what the people give to each other, like an axe, a pot, a bucket and similar items." This is the end of the Tafsir of Surat Al-Ma`un, and all praise and thanks are due to Allah.

CHAPTER (SURAH) 108: AL-KAUTHER (ABUNDANCE, PLENTY), VERSES 001-003

Surah: 108 Ayah: 1, Ayah: 2 & Ayah: 3

﴿بِسْمِ اللَّهِ الرَّحْمَـنِ الرَّحِيمِ﴾

In the Name of Allah, the Most Gracious, the Most Merciful.

﴿إِنَّا أَعْطَيْنَـكَ ٱلْكَوْثَرَ ۝﴾

1. Verily, We have granted you (O Muhammad (peace be upon him)) Al-Kauthar (a river in Paradise).

﴿فَصَلِّ لِرَبِّكَ وَٱنْحَرْ ۝﴾

2. Therefore turn in prayer to your Lord and sacrifice (to Him only).

﴿إِنَّ شَانِئَكَ هُوَ ٱلْأَبْتَرُ ۝﴾

3. For he who hates you (O Muhammad (peace be upon him)) he will be cut off (from every good thing in this world and in the Hereafter).

Transliteration

1. Inna aAAtaynaka alkawthara 2. Fasalli lirabbika wainhar 3. Inna shani-aka huwa al-abtaru

Tafsir Ibn Kathir

Muslim, Abu Dawud and An-Nasa'i, all recorded from Anas that he said, "While we were with the Messenger of Allah in the Masjid, he dozed off into a slumber. Then he lifted his head smiling. We said, `O Messenger of Allah! What has caused you to laugh' He said,

«لَقَدْ أُنْزِلَتْ عَلَيَّ آنِفًا سُورَةٌ»

(Verily, a Surah was just revealed to me.) Then he recited,

(Verily, We have granted you Al-Kawthar. Therefore turn in prayer to your Lord and sacrifice. For he who hates you, he will be cut off.) Then he said,

«أَتَدْرُونَ مَا الْكَوْثَرُ؟»

(Do you all know what is Al-Kawthar) We said, `Allah and His Messenger know best.' He said,

«فَإِنَّهُ نَهَرٌ وَعَدَنِيهِ رَبِّي عَزَّ وَجَلَّ، عَلَيْهِ خَيْرٌ كَثِيرٌ، هُوَ حَوْضٌ تَرِدُ عَلَيْهِ أُمَّتِي يَوْمَ الْقِيَامَةِ، آنِيَتُهُ عَدَدُ النُّجُومِ فِي السَّمَاءِ، فَيُخْتَلَجُ الْعَبْدُ مِنْهُمْ فَأَقُولُ: رَبِّ إِنَّهُ مِنْ أُمَّتِي، فَيَقُولُ: إِنَّكَ لَا تَدْرِي مَا أَحْدَثَ بَعْدَكَ»

(Verily, it is a river that my Lord, the Mighty and Majestic, has promised me and it has abundant goodness. It is a pond where my Ummah will be brought to on the Day of Judgement. Its containers are as numerous as the stars in the sky. Then a servant of Allah from among them will be (prevented from it) and I will say: "O Lord! Verily, he is from my Ummah (followers)." Then He (Allah) will say: "Verily, you do not know what he introduced (or innovated) after you.)" This is the wording of Muslim. Ahmad recorded this Hadith from Muhammad bin Fudayl, who reported from Al-Mukhtar bin Fulful, who reported it from Anas bin Malik. Imam Ahmad also recorded from Anas that the Messenger of Allah said,

«دَخَلْتُ الْجَنَّةَ فَإِذَا أَنَا بِنَهْرٍ حَافَتَاهُ خِيَامُ اللُّؤْلُؤِ، فَضَرَبْتُ بِيَدِي إِلَى مَا يَجْرِي فِيهِ الْمَاءُ، فَإِذَا مِسْكٌ أَذْفَرُ، قُلْتُ: مَا هَذَا يَا جِبْرِيلُ؟ قَالَ: هَذَا الْكَوْثَرُ الَّذِي أَعْطَاكَهُ اللَّهُ عَزَّ وَجَلَّ»

(I entered Paradise and I came to a river whose banks had tents made of pearls. So I thrust my hand into its flowing water and found that it was the strongest (smell) of musk. So I asked, "O Jibril! What is this" He replied, "This is Al-Kawthar which Allah, the Mighty and Majestic has given you.") Al-Bukhari recorded this in his Sahih, and so did Muslim, on the authority of Anas bin Malik. In their version Anas said, "When the Prophet was taken up to the heaven, he said,

«أَتَيْتُ عَلَى نَهْرٍ حَافَتَاهُ قِبَابُ اللُّؤْلُؤِ الْمُجَوَّفِ فَقُلْتُ: مَا هَذَا يَا جِبْرِيلُ؟ قَالَ: هَذَا الْكَوْثَرُ»

(I came to a river whose banks had domes of hollowed pearl. I said: "O Jibril! What is this" He replied: "This is Al-Kawthar.")" This is the wording of Al-Bukhari. Ahmad recorded from Anas that a man said, "O Messenger of Allah! What is Al-Kawthar" He replied,

«هُوَ نَهْرٌ فِي الْجَنَّةِ أَعْطَانِيهِ رَبِّي، لَهُوَ أَشَدُّ بَيَاضًا مِنَ اللَّبَنِ، وَأَحْلَى مِنَ الْعَسَلِ، فِيهِ طُيُورٌ أَعْنَاقُهَا كَأَعْنَاقِ الْجُزُرِ»

(It is a river in Paradise which my Lord has given me. It is whiter than milk and sweeter than honey. There are birds in it whose necks are (long) like carrots.) `Umar said, "O Messenger of Allah! Verily, they (the birds) will be beautiful." The Prophet replied,

«آكِلُهَا أَنْعَمُ مِنْهَا يَا عُمَر»

(The one who eats them (i.e., the people of Paradise) will be more beautiful than them, O `Umar.) Al-Bukhari recorded from Sa`id bin Jubayr that Ibn `Abbas said about Al-Kawthar, "It is the good which Allah gave to him (the Prophet)." Abu Bishr said, "I said to Sa`id bin Jubayr, `Verily, people are claiming that it is a river in Paradise.'" Sa`id replied, `The river which is in Paradise is part of the goodness which Allah gave him.'" Al-Bukhari also recorded from Sa`id bin Jubayr that Ibn `Abbas said, "Al-Kawthar is the abundant goodness." This explanation includes the river and other things as well. Because the word Al-Kawthar comes from the word Kathrah (abundance) and it (Al-Kawthar) linguistically means an abundance of goodness. So from this goodness is the river (in Paradise). Imam Ahmad recorded from Ibn `Umar that the Messenger of Allah said,

«الْكَوْثَرُ نَهْرٌ فِي الْجَنَّةِ حَافَتَاهُ مِنْ ذَهَبٍ، وَالْمَاءُ يَجْرِي عَلَى اللُّؤْلُؤِ، وَمَاؤُهُ أَشَدُّ بَيَاضًا مِنَ اللَّبَنِ، وَأَحْلَى مِنَ الْعَسَلِ»

(Al-Kawthar is a river in Paradise whose banks are of gold and it runs over pearls. Its water is whiter than milk and sweeter than honey.) This Hadith was recorded in this manner by At-Tirmidhi, Ibn Majah, Ibn Abi Hatim and Ibn Jarir. At-Tirmidhi said, "Hasan Sahih." Then Allah says,

(Therefore turn in prayer to your Lord and sacrifice.) meaning, `just as We have given you the abundant goodness in this life and the Hereafter -- and from that is the river that has been described previously -- then make your obligatory and optional prayer, and your sacrifice (of animals) solely and sincerely for your Lord. Woship Him alone and do not associate any partner with him. And sacrifice pronouncing His Name alone, without ascribing any partner to Him.' This is as Allah says,

(Say: "Verily, my Salah, my sacrifice, my living, and my dying are for Allah, the Lord of all that exists. He has no partner. And of this I have been commanded, and I am the first of the Muslims.") (6:162-163) Ibn `Abbas, `Ata,' Mujahid, `Ikrimah and Al-Hasan all said, "This means with this the Budn should be sacrificed." Qatadah, Muhammad bin Ka`b Al-Qurazi, Ad-Dahhak, Ar-Rabi`, `Ata' Al-Khurasani, Al-Hakam, Isma`il bin Abi Khalid and others from the Salaf have all said the same. This is the opposite of the way of the idolators, prostrating to other than Allah and sacrificing in other than His Name. Allah says,

(And do not eat from what Allah's Name has not been pronounced over, indeed that is Fisq.) (6:121)

The Enemy of the Prophet is Cut Off

Allah says,

(For he who hates you, he will be cut off.) meaning, `indeed he who hates you, O Muhammad, and he hates what you have come with of guidance, truth, clear proof and manifest light, he is the most cut off, meanest, lowliest person who will not be remembered. Ibn `Abbas, Mujahid, Sa`id bin Jubayr and Qatadah all said, "This Ayah was revealed about Al-`As bin Wa'il. Whenever the Messenger of Allah would be mentioned (in his presence) he would say, `Leave him, for indeed he is a man who is cut off having no descendants. So when he dies he will not be remembered.' Therefore, Allah revealed this Surah." Shamir bin `Atiyah said, "This Surah was revealed concerning `Uqbah bin Abi Mu`ayt." Ibn `Abbas and `Ikrimah have both said, "This Surah was revealed about Ka`b bin Al-Ashraf and a group of the disbelievers of the Quraysh." Al-Bazzar recorded that Ibn `Abbas said, "Ka`b bin Al-Ashraf came to Makkah and the Quraysh said to him, `You are the leader of them (the people). What do you think about this worthless man who is cut off from his people He claims that he is better than us while we are the people of the place of pilgrimage, the people of custodianship (of the Ka`bah), and the people who supply water to the pilgrims.' He replied, `You all are better than him.' So Allah revealed,

(For he who hates you, he will be cut off.)" This is how Al-Bazzar recorded this incident and its chain of narration is authentic. It has been reported that `Ata' said, "This Surah was revealed about Abu Lahab when a son of the Messenger of Allah died. Abu Lahab went to the idolators and said, `Muhammad has been cut off (i.e., from progeny) tonight.' So concerning this Allah revealed,

(For he who hates you, he will be cut off.)" As-Suddi said, "When the male sons of a man died the people used to say, `He has been cut off.' So, when the sons of the Messenger of Allah

died they said, `Muhammad has been cut off.' Thus, Allah revealed,

(For he who hates you, he will be cut off.)" So they thought in their ignorance that if his sons died, his remembrance would be cut off. Allah forbid! To the contrary, Allah preserved his remembrance for all the world to see, and He obligated all the servants to follow his Law. This will continue for all of time until the Day of Gathering and the coming of the Hereafter. May the blessings of Allah and His peace be upon him forever until the Day of Assembling. This is the end of the Tafsir of Surat Al-Kawthar, and all praise and blessings are due to Allah.

INTRODUCTION TO CHAPTER (SURAH) 109: AL-KAFIROON (THE DISBELIEVERS, ATHEISTS)

Ibn Kathir's Introduction

The Recitation of these Surahs in the Optional Prayers

It has been confirmed in Sahih Muslim from Jabir that the Messenger of Allah recited this Surah (Al-Kafirun) and

(Say: "He is Allah One.") (112:1) in the two Rak`ahs of Tawaf. It is also recorded in Sahih Muslim in a Hadith of Abu Hurayrah that the Messenger of Allah recited these two Surahs in the two Rak`ahs (optional prayer) of the Morning prayer. Imam Ahmad recorded from Ibn `Umar that the Messenger of Allah recited in the two Rak`ahs before the Morning prayer and the two Rak`ahs after the Sunset prayer on approximately ten or twenty different occasions,

(Say: "O Al-Kafirun!") and

(Say: " He is Allah One.") (112:1) Ahmad also recorded that Ibn `Umar said, "I watched the Prophet twenty-four or twenty-five times reciting in the two Rak`ahs before the Morning prayer and the two Rak`ahs after the Sunset prayer,

(Say: "O Al-Kafirun!") and

(Say: "He is Allah One.") (112:1)" Ahmad recorded that Ibn `Umar said, "I watched the Prophet for a month and he would recite in the two Rak`ahs before the Morning prayer,

(Say: "O Al-Kafirun.") and

(Say: "He is Allah One.") (112:1)" This was also recor- ded by At-Tirmidhi, Ibn Majah and An-Nasa'i. At-Tirmidhi said, "Hasan." It has already been mentioned previously in a Hadith that it (Surat Al-Kafirun) is equivalent to a fourth of the Qur'an and Az-Zalzalah is equivalent to a fourth of the Qur'an.

CHAPTER (SURAH) 109: AL-KAFIROON THE DISBELIEVERS, ATHEISTS, VERSES 001-006

Surah: 109 Ayah: 1, Ayah: 2, Ayah: 3, Ayah: 4, Ayah: 5 & Ayah: 6

(بِسْمِ اللَّهِ الرَّحْمَـنِ الرَّحِيمِ)

In the Name of Allah, the Most Gracious, the Most Merciful.

﴿ قُلْ يَـٰأَيُّهَا ٱلْكَـٰفِرُونَ ۝ ﴾

1. Say (O Muhammad (peace be upon him) to these Mushrikûn and Kâfirûn): "O Al-Kâfirûn (disbelievers in Allâh, in His Oneness, in His Angels, in His Books, in His Messengers, in the Day of Resurrection, and in Al-Qadar.)!

﴿ لَآ أَعْبُدُ مَا تَعْبُدُونَ ۝ ﴾

2. "I worship not that which you worship,

﴿ وَلَآ أَنتُمْ عَـٰبِدُونَ مَآ أَعْبُدُ ۝ ﴾

3. "Nor will you worship that which I worship.

﴿ وَلَآ أَنَا۠ عَابِدٌ مَّا عَبَدتُّمْ ۝ ﴾

4. "And I shall not worship that which you are worshipping.

﴿ وَلَآ أَنتُمْ عَـٰبِدُونَ مَآ أَعْبُدُ ۝ ﴾

5. "Nor will you worship that which I worship.

﴿ لَكُمْ دِينُكُمْ وَلِىَ دِينِ ۝ ﴾

6. "To you be your religion, and to me my religion (Islâmic Monotheism)."

Chapter 109: Al-Kafiroon (The Disbelievers, Atheists), Verses 001-006

Transliteration

1. Qul ya ayyuha alkafiroona 2. La aAAbudu ma taAAbudoona 3. Wala antum AAabidoona ma aAAbudu 4. Wala ana AAabidun ma AAabadtum 5. Wala antum AAabidoona ma aAAbudu 6. Lakum deenukum waliya deeni

Tafsir Ibn Kathir

The Declaration of Innocence from Shirk

This Surah is the Surah of disavowal from the deeds of the idolators. It commands a complete disavowal of that. Allah's statement,

(Say: "O disbelievers!") includes every disbeliever on the face of the earth, however, this statement is particularly directed towards the disbelievers of the Quraysh. It has been said that in their ignorance they invited the Messenger of Allah to worship their idols for a year and they would (in turn) worship his God for a year. Therefore, Allah revealed this Surah and in it

He commanded His Messenger to disavow himself from their religion completely

Allah said,

(I worship not that which you worship.) meaning, statues and rival gods.

(Nor will you worship whom I worship.) and He is Allah Alone, Who has no partner. So the word Ma (what) here means Man (who). Then Allah says,

(And I shall not worship that which you are worshipping. Nor will you worship whom I worship.) meaning, `I do not worship according to your worship, which means that I do not go along with it or follow it. I only worship Allah in the manner in which He loves and is pleased with.' Thus, Allah says,

(Nor will you worship whom I worship.) meaning, `you do not follow the commands of Allah and His Legislation in His worship. Rather, you have invented something out of the promptings of your own souls.' This is as Allah says,

(They follow but a guess and that which they themselves desire, whereas there has surely come to them the guidance from their Lord!) (53:23) Therefore, the disavowal is from all of what they are involved. For certainly the worshipper must have a god whom he worships and set acts of worship that he follows to get to him. So the Messenger and his followers worship Allah according to what He has legislated. This is why the statement of Islam is "There is no God worthy of being worshipped except Allah, and Muhammad is the Messenger of Allah." This means that there is no (true) object of worship except Allah and there is no path to Him (i.e., way of worshipping Him) other than that which the Messenger came with. The idolators worship other than Allah, with acts of worship that Allah has not allowed. This is why the Messenger said to them,

(To you be your religion, and to me my religion.) This is similar to Allah's statement,

(And if they belie you, say: "For me are my deeds and for you are your deeds! You are innocent of what I do, and I am innocent of what you do!") (10:41) and He said,

(To us our deeds, and to you your deeds.) (28:55) Al-Bukhari said, "It has been said,

(To you be your religion.) means disbelief.

(and to me my religion.) means, Islam. This is the end of the Tafsir of Surat Qul ya Ayyuhal-Kafirun.

INTRODUCTION TO CHAPTER (SURAH) 110: AN-NASR (SUCCOUR, DIVINE SUPPORT)

Ibn Kathir's Introduction

The Virtues of Surat An-Nasr

It has been mentioned previously that it (Surat An-Nasr) is equivalent to one-fourth of the Qur'an and that Surat Az-Zalzalah is equivalent to one-fourth of the Qur'an. An-Nasa'i recorded from `Ubaydullah bin `Abdullah bin `Utbah that Ibn `Abbas said to him, "O Ibn `Utbah! Do you know the last Surah of the Qur'an that was revealed" He answered, "Yes, it was

(When there comes the help of Allah and the Conquest.) (110:1)" He (Ibn `Abbas) He (Ibn `Abbas) said, "You have spoken truthfully."

CHAPTER (SURAH) 110: AN-NASR (SUCCOUR, DIVINE SUPPORT), VERSES 001-003

Surah: 110 Ayah: 1, Ayah: 2 & Ayah: 3

(بِسْمِ اللَّهِ الرَّحْمَـنِ الرَّحِيمِ)

In the Name of Allah, the Most Gracious, the Most Merciful.

﴿ إِذَا جَآءَ نَصْرُ ٱللَّهِ وَٱلْفَتْحُ ۝ ﴾

1. When there comes the Help of Allâh (to you, O Muhammad (peace be upon him) against your enemies) and the conquest (of Makkah).

﴿ وَرَأَيْتَ ٱلنَّاسَ يَدْخُلُونَ فِى دِينِ ٱللَّهِ أَفْوَاجًا ۝ ﴾

2. And you see that the people enter Allâh's religion (Islâm) in crowds.

Chapter 110: An-Nasr (Succour, Divine Support), Verses 001-003

$$ \text{﴿ فَسَبِّحْ بِحَمْدِ رَبِّكَ وَٱسْتَغْفِرْهُ ۚ إِنَّهُ كَانَ تَوَّابًۢا ۝ ﴾} $$

3. So glorify the Praises of your Lord, and ask for His Forgiveness. Verily, He is the One Who accepts the repentance and forgives.

Transliteration

1. Itha jaa nasru Allahi waalfathu 2. Waraayta alnnasa yadkhuloona fee deeni Allahi afwajan 3. Fasabbih bihamdi rabbika waistaghfirhu innahu kana tawwaban

Tafsir Ibn Kathir

This Surah informs of the Completion of the Life of Allah's Messenger

Al-Bukhari recorded from Ibn `Abbas that he said, "Umar used to bring me into the gatherings with the old men of (the battle of) Badr. However, it was as if one of them felt something in himself (against my attending). So he said, `Why do you (`Umar) bring this (youth) to sit with us when we have children like him (i.e., his age)' So `Umar replied, `Verily, he is among those whom you know. Then one day he called them and invited me to sit with them, and I do not think that he invited me to be among them that day except to show them. So he said, `What do you say about Allah's statement, (When there comes the help of Allah and the Conquest.)' Some of them said, `We were commanded to praise Allah and seek His forgiveness when He helps us and gives us victory.' Some of them remained silent and did not say anything. Then he (`Umar) said to me, `Is this what you say, O Ibn `Abbas' I said, `No.' He then said, `What do you say' I said, `It was the end of the life of Allah's Messenger that Allah was informing him of. Allah said, (When there comes the help of Allah and the Conquest.) which means, that is a sign of the end of your life.

(So, glorify the praises of your Lord, and ask His forgiveness. Verily, He is the One Who accepts the repentance and Who forgives.)' So, `Umar bin Al-Khattab said, `I do not know anything about it other than what you have said.'" Al-Bukhari was alone in recording this Hadith. Imam Ahmad recorded from Ibn `Abbas that he said, "When (When there comes the help of Allah and the Conquest.) was revealed, the Messenger of Allah said,

$$ \text{«نُعِيَتْ إِلَيَّ نَفْسِي»} $$

(My death has been announced to me.) And indeed he died during that year." Ahmad was alone in recording this Hadith. Al-Bukhari recorded that `A'ishah said, "The Messenger of Allah used to say often in his bowing and prostrating,

$$ \text{«سُبْحَانَكَ اللَّهُمَّ رَبَّنَا وَبِحَمْدِكَ اللَّهُمَّ اغْفِرْ لِي»} $$

(Glory to You, O Allah, our Lord, and praise be to You. O Allah, forgive me.) He did this as his interpretation of the Qur'an (i.e., showing its implementation)." The rest of the group has also recorded this Hadith except for At-Tirmidhi. Imam Ahmad recorded from Masruq that `A'ishah said, "The Messenger of Allah used to often say towards the end of his life,

«سُبْحَانَ اللهِ وَبِحَمْدِهِ، أَسْتَغْفِرُ اللهَ وَأَتُوبُ إِلَيْهِ»

(Glory to Allah, and praise be unto Him. I seek Allah's forgiveness and I repent to Him.) And he said,

«إِنَّ رَبِّي كَانَ أَخْبَرَنِي أَنِّي سَأَرَى عَلَامَةً فِي أُمَّتِي، وَأَمَرَنِي إِذَا رَأَيْتُهَا أَنْ أُسَبِّحَ بِحَمْدِهِ وَأَسْتَغْفِرَهُ، إِنَّهُ كَانَ تَوَّابًا، فَقَدْ رَأَيْتُهَا:

(إِذَا جَاءَ نَصْرُ اللَّهِ وَالْفَتْحُ - وَرَأَيْتَ النَّاسَ يَدْخُلُونَ فِي دِينِ اللَّهِ أَفْوَاجاً - فَسَبِّحْ بِحَمْدِ رَبِّكَ وَاسْتَغْفِرْهُ إِنَّهُ كَانَ تَوَّابًا)»

(Verily, my Lord has informed me that I will see a sign in my Ummah and He has commanded me that when I see it, I should glorify His praises and seek His forgiveness, for He is the One Who accepts repentance. And indeed I have seen it (i.e., the sign). (When there comes the help of Allah and the Conquest (Al-Fath). And you see that the people enter Allah's religion in crowds. So glorify the praises of your Lord, and ask His forgiveness. Verily, He is the One Who accepts the repentance and Who forgives.))" Muslim also recorded this Hadith. The meaning of Al-Fath here is the conquest of Makkah, and there is only one view concerning it. For indeed the different areas of the Arabs were waiting for the conquest of Makkah before they would accept Islam. They said, "If he (Muhammad is victorious over his people, then he is a (true) Prophet." So when Allah gave him victory over Makkah, they entered into the religion of Allah (Islam) in crowds. Thus, two years did not pass (after the conquest of Makkah) before the peninsula of the Arabs was laden with faith. And there did not remain any of the tribes of the Arabs except that they professed (their acceptance) of Islam. And all praise and blessings are due to Allah. Al-Bukhari recorded in his Sahih that `Amr bin Salamah said, "When Makkah was conquered, all of the people rushed to the Messenger of Allah to profess their Islam. The various regions were delaying their acceptance of Islam until Makkah was conquered. The people used to say, `Leave him and his people alone. If he is victorious over them he is a (true) Prophet.'" We have researched the war expedition for conquest of Makkah in our book As-Surah. Therefore, whoever wishes he may review it there. And all praise and blessings are due to Allah. Imam Ahmad recorded from Abu `Ammar that a neighbor of Jabir bin `Abdullah told him, "I returned from a journey and Jabir bin `Abdullah came and greeted me. So I began to talk with him about the divisions among the people and what they had started doing. Thus, Jabir began to cry and he said, `I heard the Messenger of Allah saying,

《إِنَّ النَّاسَ دَخَلُوا فِي دِينِ اللَّهِ أَفْوَاجًا، وَسَيَخْرُجُونَ مِنْهُ أَفْوَاجًا》

(Verily, the people have entered into the religion of Allah in crowds and they will also leave it in crowds.)"

This is the end of the Tafsir of Surat An-Nasr, and all praise and blessings are due to Allah.

CHAPTER (SURAH) 111: AL-MASADD (PALM FIBRE, THE FLAME), VERSES 001-005

Surah: 111 Ayah: 1, Ayah: 2, Ayah: 3, Ayah: 4 & Ayah: 5

(بِسْمِ اللَّهِ الرَّحْمَـنِ الرَّحِيمِ)

In the Name of Allah, the Most Gracious, the Most Merciful.

﴿ تَبَّتْ يَدَا أَبِي لَهَبٍ وَتَبَّ ۝ ﴾

1. Perish the two hands of Abû Lahab (an uncle of the Prophet) and perish he!

﴿ مَا أَغْنَىٰ عَنْهُ مَالُهُ وَمَا كَسَبَ ۝ ﴾

2. His wealth and his children will not benefit him!

﴿ سَيَصْلَىٰ نَارًا ذَاتَ لَهَبٍ ۝ ﴾

3. He will be burnt in a Fire of blazing flames!

﴿ وَامْرَأَتُهُ حَمَّالَةَ الْحَطَبِ ۝ ﴾

4. And his wife, too, who carries wood (thorns of Sadân which she used to put on the way of the Prophet (peace be upon him) or used to slander him).

﴿ فِي جِيدِهَا حَبْلٌ مِّن مَّسَدٍ ۝ ﴾

5. In her neck is a twisted rope of Masad (palm fiber).

Transliteration

1. Tabbat yada abee lahabin watabba 2. Ma aghna AAanhu maluhu wama kasaba 3. Sayasla naran thata lahabin 4. Waimraatuhu hammalata alhatabi 5. Fee jeediha hablun min masadin

Tafsir Ibn Kathir

The Reason for the Revelation of this Surah and the Arrogance of Abu Lahab toward the Messenger of Allah

Al-Bukhari recorded from Ibn `Abbas that the Prophet went out to the valley of Al-Batha and he ascended the mountain. Then he cried out,

«يَا صَبَاحَاه»

(O people, come at once!) So the Quraysh gathered around him. Then he said,

«أَرَأَيْتُمْ إِنْ حَدَّثْتُكُمْ أَنَّ الْعَدُوَّ مُصَبِّحُكُمْ، أَوْ مُمَسِّيكُمْ أَكُنْتُمْ تُصَدِّقُونِّي»

(If I told you all that the enemy was going to attack you in the morning, or in the evening, would you all believe me) They replied, "Yes." Then he said,

«فَإِنِّي نَذِيرٌ لَكُمْ بَيْنَ يَدَيْ عَذَابٍ شَدِيد»

(Verily, I am a warner (sent) to you all before the coming of a severe torment.) Then Abu Lahab said, "Have you gathered us for this May you perish!" Thus, Allah revealed,

(Perish the two hands of Abu Lahab and perish he!) to the end of the Surah. In another narration it states that he stood up dusting of his hands and said, "Perish you for the rest of this day! Have you gathered us for this" Then Allah revealed,

(Perish the two hands of Abu Lahab and perish he!) The first part is a supplication against him and the second is information about him. This man Abu Lahab was one of the uncles of the Messenger of Allah. His name was `Abdul-`Uzza bin Abdul-Muttalib. His surname was Abu `Utaybah and he was only called Abu Lahab because of the brightness of his face. He used to often cause harm to the Messenger of Allah . He hated and scorned him and his religion. Imam Ahmad recorded from Abu Az-Zinad that a man called Rabi`ah bin `Abbad from the tribe of Bani Ad-Dil, who was a man of pre-Islamic ignorance who accepted Islam, said to him, "I saw the Prophet in the time of pre-Islamic ignorance in the market of Dhul-Majaz and he was saying,

«يَا أَيُّهَا النَّاسُ، قُولُوا: لَا إِلَهَ إِلَّا اللهُ تُفْلِحُوا»

Chapter 111: Al-Masadd (Palm Fibre, The Flame), Verses 001-005   239

(O people! Say there is no god worthy of worship except Allah and you will be successful.) The people were gathered around him and behind him there was a man with a bright face, squint (or cross) eyes and two braids in his hair. He was saying, "Verily, he is an apostate (from our religion) and a liar!" This man was following him (the Prophet) around wherever he went. So, I asked who was he and they (the people) said, "This is his uncle, Abu Lahab." Ahmad also recorded this narration from Surayj, who reported it from Ibn Abu Az-Zinad, who reported it from his father (Abu Zinad) who mentioned this same narration. However in this report, Abu Zinad said, "I said to Rabi`ah, `Were you a child at that time' He replied, `No. By Allah, that day I was most intelligent, and I was the strongest blower of the flute (for music).'" Ahmad was alone in recording this Hadith. Concerning Allah's statement,

(His wealth and his children (Kasab) will not benefit him!) Ibn `Abbas and others have said,

(and his children (Kasab) will not benefit him!) "Kasab means his children." A similar statement has been reported from `A'ishah, Mujahid, `Ata', Al-Hasan and Ibn Sirin. It has been mentioned from Ibn Mas`ud that when the Messenger of Allah called his people to faith, Abu Lahab said, "Even if what my nephew says is true, I will ransom myself (i.e., save myself) from the painful torment on the Day of Judgement with my wealth and my children." Thus, Allah revealed,

(His wealth and his children will not benefit him!) Then Allah says,

(He will enter a Fire full of flames!) meaning, it has flames, evil and severe burning.

The Destiny of Umm Jamil, the Wife of Abu Lahab

(And his wife too, who carries wood.) His wife was among the leading women of the Quraysh and she was known as Umm Jamil. Her name was `Arwah bint Harb bin Umayyah and she was the sister of Abu Sufyan. She was supportive of her husband in his disbelief, rejection and obstinacy. Therefore, she will be helping to administer his punishment in the fire of Hell on the Day of Judgement. Thus, Allah says,

(Who carries wood. In her neck is a twisted rope of Masad.) meaning, she will carry the firewood and throw it upon her husband to increase that which he is in (of torment), and she will be ready and prepared to do so.

(In her neck is a twisted rope of Masad.) Mujahid and `Urwah both said, "From the palm fiber of the Fire." Al-`Awfi narrated from Ibn `Abbas, `Atiyah Al-Jadali, Ad-Dahhak and Ibn Zayd that she used to place thorns in the path of the Messenger of Allah . Al-Jawhari said, "Al-Masad refers to fibers, it is also a rope made from fibers or palm leaves. It is also made from the skins of camels or their furs. It is said (in Arabic) Masadtul-Habla and Amsaduhu Masadan, when you tightly fasten its twine." Mujahid said,

(In her neck is a twisted rope of Masad.) "This means a collar of iron." Don't you see that the Arabs call a pulley cable a Masad

A Story of Abu Lahab's Wife harming the Messenger of Allah

Ibn Abi Hatim said that his father and Abu Zur`ah both said that `Abdullah bin Az-Zubayr Al-Humaydi told them that Sufyan informed them that Al-Walid bin Kathir related from Ibn Tadrus who reported that Asma' bint Abi Bakr said, "When

(Perish the two hands of Abu Lahab and perish he)!) was revealed, the one-eyed Umm Jamil bint Harb came out wailing, and she had a stone in her hand. She was saying, `He criticizes our father, and his religion is our scorn, and his command is to disobey us.' The Messenger of Allah was sitting in the Masjid (of the Ka`bah) and Abu Bakr was with him. When Abu Bakr saw her he said, `O Messenger of Allah! She is coming and I fear that she will see you.' The Messenger of Allah replied,

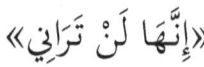

(Verily, she will not see me.) Then he recited some of the Qur'an as a protection for himself. This is as Allah says,

(And when you recite the Qur'an, We put between you and those who believe not in the Hereafter, an invisible veil.) (17:45) So she advanced until she was standing in front of Abu Bakr and she did not see the Messenger of Allah . She then said, `O Abu Bakr! Verily, I have been informed that your friend is making defamatory poetry about me.' Abu Bakr replied, `Nay! By the Lord of this House (the Ka`bah) he is not defaming you.' So she turned away saying, `Indeed the Quraysh know that I am the daughter of their leader.'" Al-Walid or another person said in a different version of this Hadith, "So Umm Jamil stumbled over her waist gown while she was making circuits (Tawaf) around the House (the Ka`bah) and she said, `Cursed be the reviler.' Then Umm Hakim bint `Abdul-Muttalib said, `I am a chaste woman so I will not speak abusively and I am refined so I do not know. Both of us are children of the same uncle. And after all the Quraysh know best."

This is the end of the Tafsir of this Surah, and all praise and blessings are due to Allah.

INTRODUCTION TO CHAPTER (SURAH) 112: AL-IKHLAS (SINCERITY)

Ibn Kathir's Introduction

The Reason for the Revelation of this Surah and its Virtues

Imam Ahmad recorded from Ubayy bin Ka`b that the idolators said to the Prophet , "O Muhammad! Tell us the lineage of your Lord." So Allah revealed

(Say: "He is Allah, One. Allah He begets not, nor was He begotten. And there is non comparable to Him.") Similar was recorded by At-Tirmidhi and Ibn Jarir and they added in their narration that he said,

Chapter 112: Al-Ikhlas (Sincerity), Verses 001-004

"(As-Samad) is One Who does not give birth, nor was He born, because there is nothing that is born except that it will die, and there is nothing that dies except that it leaves behind inheritance, and indeed Allah does not die and He does not leave behind any inheritance.

(And there is none comparable to Him.) This means that there is none similar to Him, none equal to Him and there is nothing at all like Him." Ibn Abi Hatim also recorded it and At-Tirmidhi mentioned it as a Mursal narration. Then At-Tirmidhi said, "And this is the most correct."

A Hadith on its Virtues

Al-Bukhari reported from `Amrah bint `Abdur-Rahman, who used to stay in the apartment of `A'ishah, the wife of the Prophet, that `A'ishah said, "The Prophet sent a man as the commander of a war expedition and he used to lead his companions in prayer with recitation (of the Qur'an). And he would complete his recitation with the recitation of `Say: He is Allah, One.' So when they returned they mentioned that to the Prophet and he said,

《سَلُوهُ لِأَيِّ شَيْءٍ يَصْنَعُ ذَلِكَ؟》

(Ask him why does he do that.) So they asked him and he said, `Because it is the description of Ar-Rahman and I love to recite it. So the Prophet said,

《أَخْبِرُوهُ أَنَّ اللهَ تَعَالَى يُحِبُّهُ》

(Inform him that Allah the Most High loves him.)" This is how Al-Bukhari recorded this Hadith in his Book of Tawhid. Muslim and An-Nasa'i also recorded it. In his Book of Salah, Al-Bukhari recorded that Anas said, "A man from the Ansar used to lead the people in prayer in the Masjid of Quba'. Whenever he began a Surah in the recitation of the prayer that he was leading them, he would start by reciting `Say: He is Allah, One' until he completed the entire Surah. Then he would recite another Surah along with it (after it). And used to do this in every Rak`ah. So his companions spoke to him about this saying; `Verily, you begin the prayer with this Surah. Then you think that it is not sufficient for you unless you recite another Surah as well. So you should either recite it or leave it and recite another Surah instead.' The man replied, `I will not leave it off. If you want me to continue leading you (in prayer), I will do this; and if you all do not like it, I will leave you (i.e., I will stop leading you).' They used to consider him to be of the best of them to lead them in prayer and they did not want anyone else to lead them other than him. So, when the Prophet came they informed him of this information and he said,

《يَا فُلَانُ، مَا يَمْنَعُكَ أَنْ تَفْعَلَ مَا يَأْمُرُكَ بِهِ أَصْحَابُكَ، وَمَا حَمَلَكَ عَلَى لُزُومِ هَذِهِ السُّورَةِ فِي كُلِّ رَكْعَةٍ؟》

(O so-and-so! What prevents you from doing what your companions are commanding you to do, and what makes you adhere to the recitation of this Surah in every Rak`ah) The man said, `Verily, I love it.' The Prophet replied,

《حُبُّكَ إِيَّاهَا أَدْخَلَكَ الْجَنَّةَ》

(Your love of it will cause you to enter Paradise.) This was recorded by Al-Bukhari, with a disconnected chain, but in a manner indicating his approval.

A Hadith that mentions this Surah is equivalent to a Third of the Qur'an

Al-Bukhari recorded from Abu Sa`id that a man heard another man reciting

(Say: "He is Allah, One.") and he was repeating over and over. So when morning came, the man went to the Prophet and mentioned that to him, and it was as though he was belittling it. The Prophet said,

《وَالَّذِي نَفْسِي بِيَدِهِ إِنَّهَا لَتَعْدِلُ ثُلُثَ الْقُرْآنِ》

(By He in Whose Hand is my soul, verily it is equivalent to a third of the Qur'an.) Abu Dawud and An-Nasa'i also recorded it. Another Hadith Al-Bukhari recorded from Abu Sa`id, may Allah be pleased with him, that the Messenger of Allah said to his Companions,

《أَيَعْجِزُ أَحَدُكُمْ أَنْ يَقْرَأَ ثُلُثَ الْقُرْآنِ فِي لَيْلَةٍ؟》

(Is one of you not able to recite a third of the Qur'an in a single night) This was something that was difficult for them and they said, "Which of us is able to do that, O Messenger of Allah" So he replied,

《اللهُ الْوَاحِدُ الصَّمَدُ ثُلُثُ الْقُرْآنِ》

("Allah is the One, As-Samad" is a third of the Qur'an.) Al-Bukhari was alone in recording this Hadith.

Another Hadith that its Recitation necessitates Admission into Paradise

Imam Malik bin Anas recorded from `Ubayd bin Hunayn that he heard Abu Hurayrah saying, "I went out with the Prophet and he heard a man reciting `Say: He is Allah, the One.' So the Messenger of Allah said,

《وَجَبَتْ》

(It is obligatory.) I asked, `What is obligatory' He replied,

Chapter 112: Al-Ikhlas (Sincerity), Verses 001-004

«الْجَنَّةُ»

(Paradise.)" At-Tirmidhi and An-Nasa'i also recorded it by way of Malik, and At-Tirmidhi said, "Hasan Sahih Gharib. We do not know of it except as a narration of Malik." The Hadith in which the Prophet said,

«حُبُّكَ إِيَّاهَا أَدْخَلَكَ الْجَنَّةَ»

(Your love of it will cause you to enter Paradise.) has already been mentioned.

A Hadith about repeating this Surah

`Abdullah bin Imam Ahmad recorded from Mu`adh bin `Abdullah bin Khubayb, who reported that his father said, "We became thirsty and it had become dark while we were waiting for the Messenger of Allah to lead us in prayer. Then, when he came out he took me by my hand and said,

«قُلْ»

(Say.) Then he was silent. Then he said again,

«قُلْ»

(Say.) So I said, `What should I say' He said,

«(قُلْ هُوَ اللَّهُ أَحَدٌ) وَالْمُعَوِّذَتَيْنِ حِينَ تُمْسِي وَحِينَ تُصْبِحُ ثَلَاثًا، تَكْفِيكَ كُلَّ يَوْمٍ مَرَّتَيْنِ»

(Say: "He is Allah, One,") and the two Surahs of Refuge (Al-Falaq and An-Nas) when you enter upon the evening and the morning three times (each). They will be sufficient for you two times every day.)" This Hadith was also recorded by Abu Dawud, At-Tirmidhi and An-Nasa'i. At-Tirmidhi said, "Hasan Sahih Gharib." An-Nasa'i also recorded through another chain of narrators with the wording,

«يَكْفِيكَ كُلَّ شَيْءٍ»

(They will suffice you against everything.)

Another Hadith about supplicating with it by Allah's Names

In his Book of Tafsir, An-Nasa'i recorded from `Abdullah bin Buraydah, who reported from his father that he entered the Masjid with the Messenger of Allah , and there was a man praying and supplicating saying, "O Allah! Verily, I ask you by my testifying that there is no God worthy of worship except You. You are the One, the Self-Sufficient Sustainer of all, Who does not give birth, nor were You born, and there is none comparable to Him."

A Hadith about seeking a Cure by these Surahs

Al-Bukhari recorded from `A'ishah that whenever the Prophet would go to bed every night, he would put his palms together and blow into them. Then he would recite into them (his palms), `Say: He is Allah, One', `Say: I seek refuge with the Lord of Al-Falaq', and `Say: I seek refuge with the Lord of mankind.' Then he would wipe whatever he was able to of his body with them (his palms). He would begin wiping his head and face with them and the front part of his body. He would do this (wiping his body) three times. The Sunan compilers also recorded this same Hadith.

CHAPTER (SURAH) 112: AL-IKHLAS (SINCERITY), VERSES 001-004

Surah: 112 Ayah: 1, Ayah: 2, Ayah: 3 & Ayah: 4

(بِسْمِ اللَّهِ الرَّحْمَـنِ الرَّحِيمِ)

In the Name of Allah, the Most Gracious, the Most Merciful.

﴿ قُلْ هُوَ ٱللَّهُ أَحَدٌ ۝ ﴾

1. Say (O Muhammad (peace be upon him)) "He is Allâh, (the) One.

﴿ ٱللَّهُ ٱلصَّمَدُ ۝ ﴾

2. "Allâh-us-Samad (allah The Self-Sufficient Master, Whom all creatures need, (He neither eats nor drinks))

﴿ لَمْ يَلِدْ وَلَمْ يُولَدْ ۝ ﴾

3. "He begets not, nor was He begotten.

﴿ وَلَمْ يَكُن لَّهُ كُفُوًا أَحَدٌ ۝ ﴾

4. "And there is none co-equal or comparable unto Him."

Transliteration

1. Qul huwa Allahu ahadun 2. Allahu alssamadu 3. Lam yalid walam yooladu 4. Walam yakun lahu kufuwan ahadun

Tafsir Ibn Kathir

The reason for the revelation of this Surah has already been mentioned. `Ikrimah said, "When the Jews said, `We worship `Uzayr, the son of Allah,' and the Christians said, `We worship the Messiah (`Isa), the son of Allah,' and the Zoroastrians said, `We worship the sun and the moon,' and the idolators said, `We worship idols,' Allah revealed to His Messenger ,

(Say: "He is Allah, One.") meaning, He is the One, the Singular, Who has no peer, no assistant, no rival, no equal and none comparable to Him. This word (Al-Ahad) cannot be used for anyone in affirmation except Allah the Mighty and Majestic, because He is perfect in all of His attributes and actions. Concerning His saying,

(Allah As-Samad.) `Ikrimah reported that Ibn `Abbas said, "This means the One Who all of the creation depends upon for their needs and their requests." `Ali bin Abi Talhah reported from Ibn `Abbas, "He is the Master Who is perfect in His sovereignty, the Most Noble Who is perfect in His nobility, the Most Magnificent Who is perfect in His magnificence, the Most Forbearing Who is perfect in His forbearance, the All-Knowing Who is perfect in His knowledge, and the Most Wise Who is perfect in His wisdom. He is the One Who is perfect in all aspects of nobility and authority. He is Allah, glory be unto Him. These attributes are not befitting anyone other than Him. He has no coequal and nothing is like Him. Glory be to Allah, the One, the Irresistible." Al-A`mash reported from Shaqiq, who said that Abu Wa'il said,

(As-Samad.) is the Master Whose control is complete."

Allah is Above having Children and procreating

Then Allah says,

(He begets not, nor was He begotten. And there is none comparable to Him.) meaning, He does not have any child, parent or spouse. Mujahid said,

(And there is none comparable to Him.) "This means He does not have a spouse." This is as Allah says,

(He is the Originator of the heavens and the earth. How can He have children when He has no wife He created all things.) (6:101) meaning, He owns everything and He created everything. So how can He have a peer among His creatures who can be equal to Him, or a relative who can resemble Him Glorified, Exalted and far removed is Allah from such a thing. Allah says,

(And they say: Ar-Rahman has begotten a son. Indeed you have brought forth (said) a terrible evil thing. Whereby the heavens are almost torn, and the earth is split asunder, and the mountains fall in ruins, that they ascribe a son to Ar-Rahman. But it is not suitable for Ar-Rahman that He should beget a son. There is none in the heavens and the earth but comes unto Ar-Rahman as a slave. Verily, He knows each one of them, and has counted them a full counting. And all of them will come to Him alone on the Day of Resurrection.) (19:88-95) And Allah says,

(And they say: "Ar-Rahman has begotten a son. Glory to Him! They are but honored servants. They speak not until He has spoken, and they act on His command.) (21:26-27) Allah also says,

(And they have invented a kinship between Him and the Jinn, but the Jinn know well that they have indeed to appear before Him. Glorified is Allah! (He is free) from what they attribute unto Him!) (37:158-159) In Sahih Al-Bukhari, it is recorded (that that the Prophet said),

«لَا أَحَدَ أَصْبَرُ عَلَى أَذًى سَمِعَهُ مِنَ اللهِ، يَجْعَلُونَ لَهُ وَلَدًا، وَهُوَ يَرْزُقُهُمْ وَيُعَافِيهِم»

(There is no one more patient with something harmful that he hears than Allah. They attribute a son to Him, while it is He Who gives them sustenance and cures them.) Al-Bukhari also recorded from Abu Hurayrah that the Prophet said,

«قَالَ اللهُ عَزَّ وَجَلَّ: كَذَّبَنِي ابْنُ آدَمَ وَلَمْ يَكُنْ لَهُ ذَلِكَ، وَشَتَمَنِي وَلَمْ يَكُنْ لَهُ ذَلِكَ، فَأَمَّا تَكْذِيبُهُ إِيَّايَ فَقَوْلُهُ: لَنْ يُعِيدَنِي كَمَا بَدَأَنِي، وَلَيْسَ أَوَّلُ الْخَلْقِ بِأَهْوَنَ عَلَيَّ مِنْ إِعَادَتِهِ، وَأَمَّا شَتْمُهُ إِيَّايَ فَقَوْلُهُ: اتَّخَذَ اللهُ وَلَدًا، وَأَنَا الْأَحَدُ الصَّمَدُ، لَمْ أَلِدْ وَلَمْ أُولَدْ، وَلَمْ يَكُنْ لِي كُفُوًا أَحَد»

(Allah the Mighty and Majestic says, "The Son of Adam denies Me and he has no right to do so, and he abuses Me and he has no right to do so. In reference to his denial of Me, it is his saying: `He (Allah) will never re-create me like He created me before.' But the re-creation of him is easier than his original creation. As for his cursing Me, it is his saying: `Allah has taken a son.' But I am the One, the Self-Sufficient Master. I do not give birth, nor was I born, and there is none comparable to Me.") This is the end of the Tafsir of Surat Al-Ikhlas, and all praise and blessings are due to Allah.

INTRODUCTION TO CHAPTER (SURAH) 113: AL-FALAQ (THE DAYBREAK, DAWN)

Ibn Kathir's Introduction

The Position of Ibn Mas`ud concerning Al-Mu`awwidhatayn

Imam Ahmad recorded from Zirr bin Hubaysh that Ubayy bin Ka`b told him that Ibn Mas`ud did not record the Mu`awwidhatayn in his Mushaf (copy of the Qur'an). So Ubayy said, "I testify that the Messenger of Allah informed me that Jibril said to him, (Say: "I seek refuge with the Lord of Al-Falaq.")(113:1) So he said it. And Jibril said to him, (Say: "I seek refuge with the Lord of mankind.") (114:1) So he said it. Therefore, we say what the Prophet said."

The Virtues of Surahs Al-Falaq and An-Nas

In his Sahih, Muslim recorded on the authority of `Uqbah bin `Amir that the Messenger of Allah said, (Do you not see that there have been Ayat revealed to me tonight the like of which has not been seen before) They are (Say: "I seek refuge with, the Lord of Al-Falaq.")(113:1) and; (Say: "I seek refuge with the Lord of mankind.") (114:1)) This Hadith was recorded by Ahmad, At-Tirmidhi and An-Nasa'i. At-Tirmidhi said, "Hasan Sahih."

Another Narration

Imam Ahmad recorded from `Uqbah bin `Amir that he said, "While I was leading the Messenger of Allah along one of these paths he said,

«يَا عُقْبَةُ أَلَا تَرْكَبُ؟»

(O `Uqbah! Will you not ride) I was afraid that this might be considered an act of disobedience. So the Messenger of Allah got down and I rode for a while. Then he rode. Then he said,

«يَا عُقْبَةُ، أَلَا أُعَلِّمُكَ سُورَتَيْنِ مِنْ خَيْرِ سُورَتَيْنِ قَرَأَ بِهِمَا النَّاسُ؟»

(O `Uqbah! Should I not teach you two Surahs that are of the best two Surahs that the people recite) I said, `Of course, O Messenger of Allah.' So he taught me to recite (Say: "I seek refuge with the Lord of Al-Falaq.") (113:1) and (Say: "I seek refuge with the Lord of mankind.") (114:1) Then the call was given to begin the prayer and the Messenger of Allah went forward (to lead the people), and he recited them in the prayer. Afterwards he passed by me and said,

«كَيْفَ رَأَيْتَ يَا عُقَيْبُ، اقْرَأْ بِهِمَا كُلَّمَا نِمْتَ وَكُلَّمَا قُمْتَ»

(What do you think, O `Uqayb Recite these two Surahs whenever you go to sleep and whenever you get up.)" An-Nasa'i and Abu Dawud both recorded this Hadith.

Another Narration

«إِنَّ النَّاسَ لَمْ يَتَعَوَّذُوا بِمِثْلِ هَذَيْنِ:»

(Verily, the people do not seek protection with anything like these two:

(قُلْ أَعُوذُ بِرَبِّ الْفَلَقِ)

(Say: "I seek refuge with the Lord of Al-Falaq.")(113:1) and;

(قُلْ أَعُوذُ بِرَبِّ النَّاسِ)

(Say: "I seek refuge with (Allah) the Lord of mankind.")) (114:1)

Another Narration

An-Nasa'i recorded that `Uqbah bin `Amir said, "I was walking with the Messenger of Allah when he said,

«يَا عُقْبَةُ قُلْ»

(O `Uqbah! Say!) I replied, `What should I say' So he was silent and did not respond to me. Then he said,

«قُلْ»

(Say!) I replied, `What should I say, O Messenger of Allah' He said,

«(قُلْ أَعُوذُ بِرَبِّ الْفَلَقِ)»

(Say: "I seek refuge with the Lord of Al-Falaq.") So, I recited it until I reached its end. Then he said,

«قُلْ»

(Say!) I replied, `What should I say O Messenger of Allah' He said,

«﴿قُلْ أَعُوذُ بِرَبِّ النَّاسِ﴾»

(Say: "I seek refuge with the Lord of mankind.") So, I recited it until I reached its end. Then the Messenger of Allah said,

«مَا سَأَلَ سَائِلٌ بِمِثْلِهَا، وَلَا اسْتَعَاذَ مُسْتَعِيذٌ بِمِثْلِهَا»

(No person beseeches with anything like these, and no person seeks refuge with anything like these.)"

Another Hadith

An-Nasa'i recorded that Ibn `Abis Al-Juhani said that the Prophet said to him,

«يَا ابْنَ عَابِسٍ أَلَا أَدُلُّكَ أَوْ أَلَا أُخْبِرُكَ بِأَفْضَلِ مَا يَتَعَوَّذُ بِهِ الْمُتَعَوِّذُونَ؟»

(O Ibn `Abis! Shall I guide you to -- or inform you -- of the best thing that those who seek protection use for protection) He replied, "Of course, O Messenger of Allah!" The Prophet said,

«﴿قُلْ أَعُوذُ بِرَبِّ الْفَلَقِ﴾ ﴿قُلْ أَعُوذُ بِرَبِّ النَّاسِ﴾ هَاتَانِ السُّورَتَانِ»

(Say: "I seek refuge with the Lord of Al-Falaq.")(and (Say: "I seek refuge with the Lord of mankind.")(These two Surahs (are the best protection).) Imam Malik recorded from `A'ishah that whenever the Messenger of Allah was suffering from an ailment, he would recite the Mu`awwidhatayn over himself and blow (over himself). Then if his pain became severe, `A'ishah said that she would recite the Mu`awwidhatayn over him and take his hand and wipe it over himself seeking the blessing of those Surahs. Al-Bukhari, Abu Dawud, An-Nasa'i and Ibn Majah all recorded this Hadith.

It has been reported from Abu Sa`id that the Messenger of Allah used to seek protection against the evil eyes of the Jinns and mankind. But when the Mu`awwidhatayn were revea- led, he used them (for protection) and aban- doned all else besides them. At-Tirmidhi, An-Nasa'i and Ibn Majah recorded this. At-Tirmidhi said, "This Hadith is Hasan Sahih."

CHAPTER (SURAH) 113: AL-FALAQ (THE DAYBREAK, DAWN), VERSES 001-005

Surah: 113 Ayah: 1, Ayah: 2, Ayah: 3, Ayah: 4 & Ayah: 5

(بِسْمِ اللَّهِ الرَّحْمَنِ الرَّحِيمِ)

In the Name of Allah, the Most Gracious, the Most Merciful.

﴿ قُلْ أَعُوذُ بِرَبِّ ٱلْفَلَقِ ۝ ﴾

1. Say: "I seek refuge with (Allâh), the Lord of the daybreak,

﴿ مِن شَرِّ مَا خَلَقَ ۝ ﴾

2. "From the evil of what He has created,

﴿ وَمِن شَرِّ غَاسِقٍ إِذَا وَقَبَ ۝ ﴾

3. "And from the evil of the darkening (night) as it comes with its darkness; (or the moon as it sets or goes away),

﴿ وَمِن شَرِّ ٱلنَّفَّـٰثَـٰتِ فِى ٱلْعُقَدِ ۝ ﴾

4. "And from the evil of those who practice witchcraft when they blow in the knots,

﴿ وَمِن شَرِّ حَاسِدٍ إِذَا حَسَدَ ۝ ﴾

5. "And from the evil of the envier when he envies."

Transliteration

1. Qul aAAoothu birabbi alfalaqi 2. Min sharri ma khalaqa 3. Wamin sharri ghasiqin itha waqaba 4. Wamin sharri alnnaffathati fee alAAuqadi 5. Wamin sharri hasidin itha hasada

Tafsir Ibn Kathir

Ibn Abi Hatim recorded that Jabir said, "Al-Falaq is the morning." Al-`Awfi reported from Ibn `Abbas, "Al-Falaq is the morning." The same has been reported from Mujahid, Sa`id bin Jubayr, `Abdullah bin Muhammad bin `Aqil, Al-Hasan, Qatadah, Muhammad bin Ka`b Al-Qurazi and Ibn Zayd. Malik also reported a similar statement from Zayd bin Aslam. Al-Qurazi, Ibn Zayd and Ibn Jarir all said, "This is like Allah's saying,

(He is the Cleaver of the daybreak.)." (6:96) Allah said,

Chapter 113: Al-Falaq (The Daybreak, Dawn), Verses 001-005

(From the evil of what He has created,) This means from the evil of all created things. Thabit Al-Bunani and Al-Hasan Al-Basri both said, "Hell, Iblis and his progeny, from among that which He (Allah) created."

(And from the evil of the Ghasiq when Waqab,) Mujahid said, "Ghasiq is the night, and `when it Waqab' refers to the setting of the sun." Al-Bukhari mentioned this from him. Ibn Abi Najih also reported a similar narration from him (Mujahid).

The same was said by Ibn `Abbas, Muhammad bin Ka`b Al-Qurazi, Ad-Dahhak, Khusayf, Al-Hasan and Qatadah. They said, "Verily, it is the night when it advances with its darkness." Az-Zuhri said,

(And from the evil of the Ghasiq when Waqab,) "This means the sun when it sets." Abu Al-Muhazzim reported that Abu Hurayrah said,

(And from the evil of the Ghasiq when Waqab,) "This means the star." Ibn Zayd said, "The Arabs used to say, `Al-Ghasiq is the declination (of the position) of the heavenly body known as Pleiades. The number of those who were ill and stricken with plague would increase whenever it would decline, and their number would lessen whenever it rose.'"

Ibn Jarir said, "Others have said that it is the moon."

The support for the people who hold this position (that it means the moon) is a narration that Imam Ahmad recorded from Al-Harith bin Abi Salamah. He said that `A'ishah said, "The Messenger of Allah took me by my hand and showed me the moon when it rose, and he said,

《تَعَوَّذِي بِاللهِ مِنْ شَرِّ هَذَا الْغَاسِقِ إِذَا وَقَبَ》

(Seek refuge with Allah from the evil of this Ghasiq when it becomes dark.)" At-Tirmidhi and An-Nasa'i both recorded this Hadith in their Books of Tafsir in their Sunans. Allah said,

(And from the evil of the blowers in knots,) Mujahid, `Ikrimah, Al-Hasan, Qatadah and Ad-Dahhak all said, "This means the witches." Mujahid said, "When they perform their spells and blow into the knots."

In another Hadith it has been reported that Jibril came to the Prophet and said, "Are you suffering from any ailment, O Muhammad" The Prophet replied,

《نَعَمْ》

(Yes.) So Jibril said, "In the Name of Allah, I recite prayer (Ruqyah) over you, from every illness that harms you, from the evil of every envious person and evil eye. May Allah cure you."

Discussion of the Bewitchment of the Prophet

In the Book of Medicine of his Sahih, Al-Bukhari recorded that `A'ishah said, "The Messenger of Allah was bewitched until he thought that he had relations with his wives, but he had not had relations with them." Sufyan said, "This is the worst form of magic when it reaches this stage." So the Prophet said,

«يَا عَائِشَةُ، أَعَلِمْتِ أَنَّ اللهَ قَدْ أَفْتَانِي فِيمَا اسْتَفْتَيْتُهُ فِيهِ؟ أَتَانِي رَجُلَانِ فَقَعَدَ أَحَدُهُمَا عِنْدَ رَأْسِي وَالْآخَرُ عِنْدَ رِجْلَيَّ، فَقَالَ الَّذِي عِنْدَ رَأْسِي لِلْآخَرِ: مَا بَالُ الرَّجُلِ؟ قَالَ: مَطْبُوبٌ، قَالَ: وَمَنْ طَبَّهُ، قَالَ: لَبِيدُ بْنُ أَعْصَمَ: رَجُلٌ مِنْ بَنِي زُرَيْقٍ حَلِيفٌ لِيَهُودَ، كَانَ مُنَافِقًا، قَالَ: وَفِيمَ؟ قَالَ: فِي مُشْطٍ وَمُشَاطَةٍ، قَالَ: وَأَيْنَ؟ قَالَ: فِي جُفِّ طَلْعَةٍ ذَكَرٍ، تَحْتَ رَاعُوفَةٍ فِي بِئْرِ ذَرْوَانَ»

(O `A'ishah! Do you know that Allah has answered me concerning that which I asked Him Two men came to me and one of them sat by my head while the other sat by my feet. The one who was sitting by my head said to the other one, `What is wrong with this man' The other replied, `He is bewitched.' The first one said, `Who bewitched him' The other replied, `Labid bin A`sam. He is a man from the tribe of Banu Zurayq who is an ally of the Jews, and a hypocrite.' The first one asked, `With what (did he bewitch him)' The other replied, `With a comb and hair from the comb.' The first one asked, `Where (is the comb)' The other answered, `In the dried bark of a male date palm under a rock in a well called Dharwan.') `A'ishah said, "So he went to the well to remove it (the comb with the hair). Then he said,

«هَذِهِ الْبِئْرُ الَّتِي أُرِيتُهَا، وَكَأَنَّ مَاءَهَا نُقَاعَةُ الْحِنَّاءِ، وَكَأَنَّ نَخْلَهَا رُؤُوسُ الشَّيَاطِينِ»

(This is the well that I saw. It was as if its water had henna soaked in it and its palm trees were like the heads of devils.) So he removed it (of the well). Then I (`A'ishah) said, `Will you not make this public' He replied,

«أَمَّا اللهُ فَقَدْ شَفَانِي، وَأَكْرَهُ أَنْ أُثِيرَ عَلَى أَحَدٍ مِنَ النَّاسِ شَرًّا»

(Allah has cured me and I hate to spread (the news of) wickedness to any of the people.)"

INTRODUCTION TO CHAPTER (SURAH) 114: AN-NAS (MANKIND)

Ibn Kathir's Introduction

See INTRODUCTION TO CHAPTER (SURAH) 113: Al-Falaq (The Daybreak, Dawn)

CHAPTER (SURAH) 114: AN-NAS (MANKIND), VERSES 001-006

Surah: 114 Ayah: 1, Ayah: 2, Ayah: 3, Ayah: 4, Ayah: 5 & Ayah: 6

(بِسْمِ اللَّهِ الرَّحْمَـنِ الرَّحِيمِ)

In the Name of Allah, the Most Gracious, the Most Merciful.

﴿ قُلْ أَعُوذُ بِرَبِّ ٱلنَّاسِ ۝ ﴾

1. Say: "I seek refuge with (Allâh) the Lord of mankind,

﴿ مَلِكِ ٱلنَّاسِ ۝ ﴾

2. "The King of mankind -

﴿ إِلَـٰهِ ٱلنَّاسِ ۝ ﴾

3. "The Ilâh (God) of mankind,

﴿ مِن شَرِّ ٱلْوَسْوَاسِ ٱلْخَنَّاسِ ۝ ﴾

4. "From the evil of the whisperer (devil who whispers evil in the hearts of men) who withdraws (from his whispering in one's heart after one remembers Allâh).

﴿ ٱلَّذِى يُوَسْوِسُ فِى صُدُورِ ٱلنَّاسِ ۝ ﴾

5. "Who whispers in the breasts of mankind.

﴿ مِنَ ٱلْجِنَّةِ وَٱلنَّاسِ ۝ ﴾

6. "Of jinn and men."

Transliteration

1. Qul aAAoothu birabbi alnnasi 2. Maliki alnnasi 3. Ilahi alnnasi 4. Min sharri alwaswasi alkhannasi 5. Allathee yuwaswisu fee sudoori alnnasi 6. Mina aljinnati waalnnasi

Tafsir Ibn Kathir

These are three attributes from the attributes of the Lord, the Mighty and Majestic. They are lordship, sovereignty and divinity. Thus, He is the Lord of everything, the King of everything and the God of everything. All things are created by Him, owned by Him, and subservient to Him. Therefore, He commands whoever is seeking protection to seek refuge with the One Who has these attributes from the evil of the whisperer who withdraws. This (the whisperer) is the devil that is assigned to man. For verily, there is not any of the Children of Adam except that he has a companion that beautifies wicked deeds for him. This devil will go to any lengths to confuse and confound him. The only person who is safe is He Whom Allah protects.

It is confirmed in the Sahih that he (the Prophet) said,

»مَا مِنْكُمْ مِنْ أَحَدٍ إِلَّا قَدْ وُكِّلَ بِهِ قَرِينُهُ«

(There is not a single one of you except that his companion (a devil) has been assigned to him.) They (the Companions) said, "What about you, O Messenger of Allah" He replied,

»نَعَمْ، إِلَّا أَنَّ اللهَ أَعَانَنِي عَلَيْهِ فَأَسْلَمَ، فَلَا يَأْمُرُنِي إِلَّا بِخَيْرٍ«

(Yes. However, Allah has helped me against him and he has accepted Islam. Thus, he only commands me to do good.) It is also confirmed in the Two Sahihs from Anas, who reported the story of Safiyyah when she came to visit the Prophet while he was performing I`tikaf, that he went out with her during the night to walk her back to her house. So, two men from the Ansar met him (on the way). When they saw the Prophet, they began walking swiftly. So, the Messenger of Allah said,

»عَلَى رِسْلِكُمَا، إِنَّهَا صَفِيَّةُ بِنْتُ حُيَيَ«

(Slow down! This is Safiyyah bint Huyay!) They said, "Glory be to Allah, O Messenger of Allah!" He said,

»إِنَّ الشَّيْطَانَ يَجْرِي مِنِ ابْنِ آدَمَ مَجْرَى الدَّمِ، وَإِنِّي خَشِيتُ أَنْ يَقْذِفَ فِي

$$\text{«قُلُوبِكُمَا شَيْئًا، أَوْ قَالَ: شَرًّا»}$$

(Verily, Shaytan runs in the Son of Adam like the running of the blood. And verily, I feared that he might cast something into your hearts -- or he said -- evil.) Sa`id bin Jubayr reported that Ibn `Abbas said concerning Allah's statement,

(The whisperer (Al-Waswas) who withdraws.) "The devil who is squatting (perched) upon the heart of the Son of Adam. So when he becomes absentminded and heedless he whispers. Then, when he remembers Allah he withdraws." Mujahid and Qatadah also said this.

Al-Mu`tamir bin Sulayman reported that his father said, "It has been mentioned to me that Shaytan is Al-Waswas. He blows into the heart of the Son of Adam when he is sad and when he is happy. But when he (man) remembers Allah, Shaytan withdraws." Al-`Awfi reported from Ibn `Abbas;

(The whisperer.) "He is Shaytan. He whispers and then when he is obeyed, he withdraws." As for Allah's saying;

(Who whispers in the breasts of An-Nas.) Is this specific for the Children of Adam as is apparent, or is it general, including both mankind and Jinns

There are two views concerning this. This is because they (the Jinns) are also included in the usage of the word An-Nas (the people) in most cases.

Ibn Jarir said, "The phrase Rijalun min Al-Jinn (Men from the Jinns) has been used in reference to them, so it is not strange for the word An-Nas to be applied to them also." Then Allah says,

(Of Jinn and An-Nas.) Is this explanatory of Allah's statement,

(Who whispers in the breasts of An-Nas.) Then, Allah explains this by saying,

(Of Jinn and An-Nas.) This is supportive of the second view. It has also been said that Allah's saying,

(Of Jinn and An-Nas) is an explanation of who is it that whispers into the breasts of mankind from the devils of mankind and Jinns. This is similar to Allah's saying,

o(And so We have appointed for every Prophet enemies -- Shayatin among mankind and Jinn, inspiring one another with adorned speech as a delusion.) (6:112) Imam Ahmad recorded that Ibn `Abbas said, "A man came to the Prophet and said, `O Messenger of Allah! Sometimes I say things to myself that I would rather fall from the sky than say (aloud openly).' The Prophet said,

$$\text{«اللهُ أَكْبَرُ، اللهُ أَكْبَرُ الْحَمْدُ لِلهِ الَّذِي رَدَّ كَيْدَهُ إِلَى الْوَسْوَسَةِ»}$$

(Allah is Most Great! Allah is Most Great! All praise is due to Allah Who sent his (Shaytan's) plot back as only a whisper.)" Abu Dawud and An-Nasa'i also recorded this Hadith.

This is the end of the Tafsir. All praise and thanks are due to Allah, the Lord of all that exists.

(Every effort has been made to assure the accuracy of this publication. If, however, any errors are noticed by the reader, we would kindly request notification to be corrected in future editions.)

www.ingramcontent.com/pod-product-compliance
Lightning Source LLC
Chambersburg PA
CBHW081105080526
44587CB00021B/3458